FISCAL POLICY, STABILIZATION, AND GROWTH IN

DEVELOPING COUNTRIES

FISCAL POLICY, STABILIZATION, AND GROWTH IN

DEVELOPING COUNTRIES

Edited by Mario I. Blejer and Ke-young Chu

International Monetary Fund
September 1989

Library of Congress Cataloging-in-Publication Data

Fiscal policy, stabilization, and growth in developing countries / edited by Mario I. Blejer and Ke-young Chu.

    p. cm.

    Includes bibliographic references.

    ISBN 1-55775-034-3

    1. Fiscal policy—Developing countries. 2. Economic stabilization—Developing countries. I. Blejer, Mario I. II. Chu, Ke-young, 1941–
HJ1620.F57   1989
339.5'09172'4—dc20   89-15237
                                               CIP

*Both this book's cover and its interior
were designed by the IMF Graphics Section.*

The following symbols have been used throughout this book:

...   to indicate that data are not available;

—   to indicate that the figure is zero or less than half the digit shown, or that the item does not exist;

–   between years or months (e.g., 1988–89 or January–June) to indicate the years or months covered, including the beginning and ending years or months;

/   between years (e.g., 1988/89) to indicate a crop or fiscal (financial) year.

"Billion" means a thousand million.

Details may not add to totals shown because of rounding.

The term "country," as used in this book, does not in all cases refer to a territorial entity which is a state as understood by international law and practice; the term also covers some territorial entities that are not states but for which statistical data are maintained and provided internationally on a separate and independent basis.

Price: $22.50

Address orders to:
External Relations Department, Publication Services
International Monetary Fund, Washington, D.C. 20431
Telephone: (202) 623-7430

Contents

v

Foreword

Over the past two decades, the traditional concept and practice of fiscal policy have undergone fundamental changes. Some of these changes have accompanied the reassessment of Keynesian economics. Others have originated in the growing interdependence of the world's economies. Greater capital mobility and availability of information, as well as the growing share of imports and exports in the national incomes of many countries, have ensured that the effects of fiscal policy changes on a country's economic activity will be reduced, the more open its economy is. Some of the changes have followed the recognition that, in addition to the linkages across countries, there are also linkages through time. This year's fiscal actions do not affect economic variables (output, prices, employment) just this year but also in future years. This is especially true when fiscal actions result in the accumulation of public debt, in capital flight, or in distortions in the economy.

Some of the changes in attitude toward fiscal policy have come from a realization that institutions in developing countries are often different from those in industrialized countries. The institutional environment of the developing countries implies that there are stronger linkages between, say, fiscal developments in the central governments, on the one hand, and in the rest of the public sector (central bank, local governments, public enterprises, social security institutions, and so forth), on the other. There has also been growing attention paid to the micro, or structural, aspects of fiscal policy. While in traditional Keynesian economics, fiscal policy actions could be assumed to be summarized in a few numbers (the amounts of aggregate expenditure, taxes, and the fiscal deficit), in the developing countries this assumption is much less justified because of the impact of fiscal measures on the efficiency of the economy. Furthermore, it may be more difficult to come up with a generally satisfactory measure of the fiscal deficit in these countries.

The present book reflects some of these developments. It emphasizes linkages across space, through time, and among components of public sector, as well as between macro and micro aspects of fiscal policy. It brings together the work of economists who have been, so to speak, at the front lines of policy action—individuals who, with only one exception, have worked in the Fiscal Affairs Department of the International Monetary Fund and, as a consequence, have been intimately involved in the fiscal reforms and the fiscal policies of many developing countries. These authors have not been mere spectators, but rather practitioners who have learned from direct experience and have tried, in their papers, to sort out some of the general lessons they learned.

Economists who have not been intimately involved with issues of fiscal policy in developing countries will undoubtedly find many aspects of this book worthy of additional research. I hope that other economists will analyze and research some of the ideas discussed in these articles in a more relaxed way than those who wrote them could. Do more efficient fiscal measures reduce or increase the short-run need for deficit reduction in adjustment programs? Is there a role for fiscal policy in the mobilization of savings for growth? Is there a relationship among fiscal policy, public debt, and capital flight? What is the role of fiscal policy in so-called heterodox stabilization programs? What are the impacts of exogenous shocks on the fiscal accounts and on the fiscal policies of developing countries? What should be the fiscal policy reactions of those countries to these shocks? Is there a link between the fiscal policy actions of industrial countries and the performance of developing countries' economies? What is the link between the fiscal deficit and the balance of payments of developing countries? These are some, but not all, of the questions raised in this book. It is my hope that the book will convey to the reader the richness and the variety of fiscal experiences in developing countries and will stimulate other economists to do more work in these important areas. Given the seriousness of the debt crisis and the connection between that crisis and fiscal policy, such research would certainly be desirable. It is also my hope that these papers will continue helping policymakers to improve the quality of policymaking in their respective countries.

Vito Tanzi
Director
Fiscal Affairs Department

Acknowledgments

The editors wish to thank the contributing authors for consenting to release their papers for inclusion in this volume, as well as for cooperating actively in preparing the papers in the required format. Seven of the 13 papers included have been published previously and appear here with the kind permission of their respective publishers. The views expressed in all of the papers are those of their respective authors and should not be interpreted as those of the Fund.

The editors also wish to thank Paul Gleason and Sara Kane for providing valuable editorial help, and Professors Arnold Harberger and John Whalley for commenting on the manuscripts in the initial stage of their preparation for publication. Their suggestions led to a significant improvement in the organization and presentation of the papers in the volume.

Preparing a volume like this one for publication is a demanding and time-consuming task, sometimes requiring efforts going above and beyond the call of duty. The editors are particularly indebted to M. Regina Llana, who, together with Leda Montero, provided indispensable editorial and secretarial assistance.

Last, but not least, the editors wish to express their gratitude to the many staff members of the Fund's Fiscal Affairs Department who provided guidance, encouragement, and support for this project.

Part I

Introduction

Introduction

Mario I. Blejer and Ke-young Chu

I. Overview

The implications of fiscal policy in developing countries have long been a focus of interest and discussion in macroeconomic analysis. The effects of fiscal policy and fiscal deficits on aggregate demand; on absorption, with the consequent impact on domestic inflation; on the level and composition of economic activity; and on the external balance have been at the core of stabilization programs. Studies have been made of fiscal policy's role in promoting growth and in sustaining the development process by improving the quantity and quality of investment and savings. In this context, there has been growing concern that, when there were micro and macro disequilibria, stabilization programs alone would not induce satisfactory growth and development.

It has also become apparent that many countries, particularly in the developing world, face critical problems arising from the growing frequency and magnitude of external shocks. External shocks also have direct implications for the fiscal sector, particularly in countries with underdeveloped tax systems reliant on the taxation of international trade. The severity and unpredictability of external shocks, therefore, pose critical problems for formulating and executing fiscal policy in these countries, and there is increasing interest in devising analytical tools to formulate proper responses to external developments.

Fiscal policy instruments are also strongly interrelated with many other economic policy instruments. The lack of credibility of fiscal policy in some countries could trigger capital flight and a deterioration in the external balance. Such external policy instruments as exchange rates, tariffs, subsidies, and trade liberalization have fiscal impacts and important fiscal policy implications. Thus, these instruments should be used in coordination with fiscal policy and in a proper sequence.

Fiscal policy has always been a critical element of Fund-supported adjustment programs and, in this context, the issues described above have loomed large in the financial planning process. The theoretical and analytical interest in these issues, and their direct policy relevance have motivated Fund staff to undertake research on these topics, despite the con-

3

siderable work on related topics already done in the Fund. A considerable number of studies on the specific aspects of fiscal policy in developing countries have been prepared recently in the Fund's Fiscal Affairs Department, many of them in the Special Fiscal Studies Division. This volume consists of 13 such studies—some of which have been circulated largely for discussion within the Fund as working papers, while others have been published in professional journals or conference proceedings— placed within a coherent framework.

II. FISCAL POLICY FOR STABILIZATION, SAVINGS, AND GROWTH

Part II consists of four papers focusing on the policy issues relating to the crucial role of fiscal policy in attaining and sustaining stability and growth. Stability and growth are phenomena that are both conflicting and complementary. Stability is a precondition for sustained growth; if a country wishes to attain and sustain macroeconomic stability, it should reduce excess aggregate demand throughout the economy. A lasting reduction in excess demand, in turn, can be facilitated and, in some cases, achieved only by means of a sustained growth in income. However, and in spite of these obvious truths, in many countries policies intended to promote growth often end up undermining stability. Fiscal policies are often used to induce a rapid expansion of aggregate demand, and, in many cases, they become a primary source of economic imbalance and instability.

A central issue in this area is how to enhance the complementary relationship between stabilization and growth. In "Fiscal Policy, Growth, and the Design of Stabilization Programs," Vito Tanzi explores ways to improve stabilization programs in general and, more specifically, the Fund's framework for stabilization programs by strengthening their supply-oriented structural core. For example, while a number of fiscal policy instruments can reduce a budget deficit in the short run, each instrument should be assessed on the basis of its ability to increase potential output and thus bring about a more durable fiscal adjustment. This strengthening would make the stabilization program more durable not only by facilitating the current fiscal adjustment but also by reducing the required future fiscal adjustment; that is, by properly combining stabilization with structural policies, an economy could grow out of its government debt. Tanzi suggests, therefore, that the Fund should support a relaxation of fiscal adjustment if a country is prepared to improve the quality of its stabilization program.

The low level of domestic savings is a critical bottleneck in the growth process in developing countries. Savings are low for a variety of reasons: the insufficient rates of return to capital and the absence of both well-functioning capital markets and institutions to compensate for the risks that are usually involved in saving and investment activities. This tends to dampen the propensity to save and invest. The traditional tax incentives designed to induce increases in domestic saving may not only be distortionary and place additional pressure on the budget but are also likely to be ineffective because of the low interest elasticity of saving in developing countries. In "Fiscal Policy and Mobilization of Savings for Growth," Mario I. Blejer and Adrienne Cheasty discuss possible fiscal policy roles in promoting saving in such an environment. Based on theoretical and empirical studies showing the limitations of tax policy in this area, they suggest an alternative use of fiscal policy: to create a planned budgetary surplus and to arrange the efficient channeling of the surplus into investment.

In "Fiscal Rigidities, Public Debt, and Capital Flight," Alain Ize and Guillermo Ortiz present a model in which fiscal rigidities and the lack of fiscal discipline are the sources of capital flight. In an unstable economic setting where the government is perceived to have weak fiscal discipline, a large fiscal imbalance without decisive policy action to reduce it gives rise to the public's expectations that the imbalance will be financed through inflationary taxation. These expectations induce domestic bondholders to switch to foreign bonds. In such a setting, the government's attempt to finance the external imbalance through foreign borrowing could encourage capital flight unless credible fiscal discipline is restored.

High inflation not only has critical allocative and distributional implications but is also detrimental to the growth process. Disinflation is costly, however, and finding an efficient disinflation process is a challenge for policymakers. In "High Inflation, 'Heterodox' Stabilization, and Fiscal Policy," Mario I. Blejer and Adrienne Cheasty critically review the analytical aspects of the design of the recent heterodox stabilization programs in Israel and in three South American countries (Argentina, Bolivia, and Brazil). The positive side of these programs has been their apparent success in mobilizing public support for the implementation of drastic disinflation policies that have usually entailed significant costs during the period of adjustment. The paper concludes, however, that these policies would not have been able to provide long-run benefits without the use of fiscal policies to eliminate the sources of inflation, and that many elements — such as freezes, controls, and incomes policies — imply economic, political, and administrative costs and could damage the long-run growth potential of the economy.

III. FISCAL POLICY AND THE WORLD ENVIRONMENT

Many developing countries have been subjected to unusually large and unpredictable external shocks since the early 1970s. Aggregate economic activity and domestic prices in industrial countries became much more volatile in the 1970s than in the earlier decade, and the world prices of oil and non-oil commodities, the value of major currencies, and world interest rates also became highly unstable. After the abandonment of fixed exchange rates, the fluctuations in the values of key currencies made the effective exchange rates of developing countries much more unstable, depending on the major currencies to which their currencies were pegged. These external shocks had direct implications for the fiscal sector of many developing countries. They intensified the fluctuations (and thus magnified uncertainties) in government revenue and foreign grants, as well as in the availability of, and the conditions for, financing. External shocks also elicited diverse fiscal policy reactions, which had different degrees of success in neutralizing the impact of the shocks on the domestic economy. The papers in Part III focus on some of the fiscal policy implications of such external shocks and other exogenous developments.

In "Fiscal Policy Responses to Exogenous Shocks in Developing Countries," Vito Tanzi analyzes the factors associated with recent external shocks, their impact on fiscal variables, and the policy responses in developing countries. He discusses the implications of three kinds of fiscal policy responses to rising revenue resulting from external factors: a decrease in debt, an increase in public investment, and an increase in current public expenditure. Tanzi also discusses the implications of alternative policy responses (a reduction of public spending and an increase in domestic borrowing) to declining revenue. While noting the limitations of various fiscal policy instruments in developing countries and the consequent inevitability of cuts in capital spending in the face of a negative external shock, Tanzi emphasizes that the adverse impact of the shock could be mitigated through improved efficiency.

The second paper adds a more empirical dimension to the analysis by studying the fiscal policy responses of a group of developing countries to external shocks. In "External Shocks and Fiscal Adjustment in Developing Countries: Recent Experiences," Ke-young Chu presents an overview of fiscal developments in 18 developing countries from 1962 to 1982. He focuses on how aggregate government expenditure responded to both the anticipated and unanticipated components of external shocks. Chu's analysis suggests that an unexpected downturn in revenue and the lags in formulating and executing effective fiscal policy responses pose serious problems for developing countries. The study stresses the importance of a longer-term view in formulating and executing fiscal stabilization programs.

The last paper brings the analysis closer to an important source of external shocks for developing countries: economic fluctuation in industrial countries. Industrial countries are the dominant force in international capital transactions and in international trade in both manufactures and primary commodities. World trade prices and volumes, as well as lending conditions, are determined in important respects by the economic conditions in industrial countries, including their policy mixes. In "Transmission of Effects of the Fiscal Deficit in Industrial Countries to the Fiscal Deficit of Developing Countries," Ahsan H. Mansur and David J. Robinson analyze the channels through which fiscal shocks are transmitted from the industrial to the developing countries. One important channel consists of the impact of the fiscal and monetary policy mix in industrial countries on world interest rates, and the latter's impact on the debt-service burden, import capacity, growth, and fiscal balances in developing countries. Mansur and Robinson draw a number of policy implications for both groups of countries.

IV. INTERACTION OF POLICIES

The role of fiscal policy cannot be discussed meaningfully in isolation. The linkages between fiscal, monetary, and external sector policies are an important element of the analysis. The number of examples is indeed large. Bank financing of government deficits is a significant source of inflation in many countries. This channel for government financing provides a direct linkage between fiscal and monetary policies. The government's budgetary operations also affect the external balance through their impact on aggregate demand, on domestic savings and investment balance, and on individual taxes and subsidies. All four papers in Part IV deal with some of these linkages.

In "Fiscal Expansion and External Current Account Imbalances," Gloria Bartoli builds an empirical model which explains the external current account balances of a number of developing countries on the basis of their domestic savings-investment gap. The model focuses on the fiscal sector's contribution to this gap. The results suggest that not only the changes in the fiscal balance but also how these changes are achieved have important implications for the external balance.

In "Lags in Tax Collection and the Case for Inflationary Finance: Theory with Simulations," Vito Tanzi examines methods of financing budget deficits in developing countries by expanding the conventional analysis of inflationary financing to analyze its impact on the tax system. In analyzing how inflation could affect real tax revenue, Tanzi focuses on the role of four critical parameters: (1) the price elasticity of the tax system, (2) the ratio of tax revenue to national income, (3) the ratio of the money supply to national income, and (4) the elasticity of the demand for real balances with respect to national income. The analysis suggests that based on realistic assumptions using these parameters, the existence of lags in tax collection implies that the government's gains from inflationary financing are likely to be lower than is commmonly assumed.

In "Government Spending, the Real Interest Rate, and Liquidity-Constrained Consumers' Behavior in Developing Countries," Nicola Rossi develops a dynamic optimization model to test empirically the interest rate's impact on savings in developing countries where consumers face binding liquidity constraints. The results suggest the dominance of the liquidity constraints, relative to interest rates, in the determination of savings. Rossi argues that the dominance of the liquidity constraints, which is more pronounced in low-income countries than in other developing countries, may help to explain the low interest elasticity of savings in the former group. The results indicate that while domestic saving is responsive to the real interest rate, large changes in the rate of interest would be required to induce significant increases in domestic saving.

The final paper in Part IV deals with the conflict between, and complementarity of, fiscal and external policy instruments. In "Fiscal Dimensions of Trade Policy," Ziba Farhadian-Lorie and Menachem Katz review the literature and focus on two important aspects of this policy interaction. The first aspect is the efficiency of trade taxation. Although the presence of the cost of tax collection and other tax policy objectives (such as revenue, protection, and market failure) dilutes the strength of the conclusion, the authors argue that the share of trade taxes in the optimal tax basket is still lower than the actual shares in many developing countries (as shown in the empirical section of the paper). The second aspect is the static and dynamic role of fiscal policy in the external adjustment; here, Farhadian-Lorie and Katz focus on the impact of fiscal policy instruments on the external balance under fixed and flexible exchange regimes.

V. Fiscal Policy Issues in Selected Countries

Part V, the final part of this volume, consists of two studies dealing with recent fiscal policy experiences in the Philippines and Israel, respectively. These studies shed light on some of the issues dealt with earlier in the volume in the context of actual experiences in specific countries.

In "Effects of the Budget Deficit on the Current Account Balance: The Case of the Philippines," Ahsan H. Mansur estimates the budgetary impact on the external balance of the economy by building a small econometric model. In this model, the budget affects import demand through both the impact of expenditure on domestic absorption and the impact of bank financing of the deficit, through its impact on the money supply and domestic prices. The budget, in turn, is affected by imports through their impact on tariffs, a major component of tax revenue. Mansur concludes that the budgetary impact on the external balance was significant for the Philippines.

In "The Inflationary Process in Israel, Fiscal Policy, and the Economic Stabilization Plan of July 1985," Eliahu S. Kreis analyzes Israel's recent stabilization program. From 1973 through the mid-1980s, Israel experienced extremely high and volatile inflation which originated largely in the country's fiscal imbalance. Unlike earlier programs, which had addressed either inflation or the external imbalance, the July 1985 program focused on improving, concurrently, both price stability and the external balance. Kreis concludes that the program has been successful in achieving these objectives without incurring significant real costs.

VI. Concluding Remarks

The papers in this volume analyze the roles of fiscal policy in promoting and sustaining stabilization and growth in developing countries. In examining these crucial roles, the papers stress the importance of considering, in the analysis, the close interdependence between fiscal, monetary, and external sector policies.

The experiences of the 1970s and the 1980s have highlighted the fact that stabilization and adjustment are, indeed, necessary conditions for growth. At the same time, these experiences have indicated that efficient structural measures are of crucial importance in mobilizing domestic and foreign savings to attain a sustained rate of growth. The 1970s and 80s have also provided additional evidence regarding the implications of the volatile external environment for the fiscal sector in developing countries, as well as the impact of fiscal policy on the external sector.

The papers in this volume have certainly not exhausted the stock of fiscal policy issues that deserve researchers' attention. Among the issues that need to be investigated further, an important one relates to the budgetary implications of structural measures, both in the fiscal and nonfiscal areas. For example, it would be useful to study the short-run and long-run impacts on the fiscal balance of structural reforms in goods, labor, money, and capital markets, as well as the impact of trade liberalization. Other issues include the effects of uncertainty on the performance of the fiscal sector and on fiscal discipline. For example, it would be useful to study how the level of public expenditure is planned in the face of uncertainty about the magnitude of public revenue and how these plans are subsequently revised. It would also be of great interest to study how the fiscal authorities in developing countries reach a political consensus on the fiscal policy stance. The roles of both public enterprises and public financial institutions are also very important topics. An additional issue, which has implications for the design and implementation of specific fiscal adjustment policies, concerns the methodology used to measure and assess the impact of a country's fiscal stance; although a number of studies have been done on this topic,[1] it remains underresearched.

---

[1] See, for example, the studies in a recent Fund publication, *The Measurement of Fiscal Impact: Methodological Issues*, IMF Occasional Papers, No. 59 (Washington: International Monetary Fund, 1988).

Part II
Fiscal Policy, Stabilization, and Growth

1

Fiscal Policy, Growth, and the Design of Stabilization Programs

Vito Tanzi*

I. INTRODUCTION

The objectives of Fund-supported stabilization programs include a balance of payments that is viable over the medium run, the promotion of growth in a stable economic environment, price stability, and the prevention of excessive growth in external debt. These objectives do not have the same weight, but each is important in stabilization programs. A narrow interpretation of the Fund's role would emphasize the balance of payments objective and de-emphasize the others.

This paper deals with the role of fiscal policy in stabilization programs, emphasizing the structural aspects of fiscal policies, since, over the years, these aspects have attracted less attention than has demand management. The Baker initiative of October 1985 called attention to the importance of these structural aspects. The paper does not discuss other elements of program design, such as incentive measures implemented through the exchange rate, import liberalization, financial deregulation, or pricing policy, even though these structural elements are obviously important. In countries in which institutions necessary for the *effective* use of other policies are not adequately developed, fiscal policy may be the main avenue to economic development and stability, although, unfortu-

*An earlier version of this paper was presented in Spanish at a seminar that was organized jointly by the Fund and by the Instituto Torcuato di Tella and held near Buenos Aires on October 13-16, 1986. In 1987, the two institutions jointly published the seminar papers, in English as *External Debt, Savings, and Growth in Latin America* (Washington) and in Spanish as *Deuda externa, ahorro y crecimiento en América Latina* (Buenos Aires). The views expressed in this paper are strictly personal ones. They are being aired in the hope that they will stimulate a discussion of an issue of considerable importance to both the Fund and its member countries. I have benefited from valuable comments on previous drafts by many colleagues.

nately, political pressures, external shocks, and administrative shortcomings have frequently weakened government control over this instrument. Tax evasion, inflation, and the proliferation of exonerations have reduced the government's control of tax revenues, while political pressures, fragmentation of the public sector, and inadequate monitoring systems have undermined its ability to keep public expenditure in check. Far from being the stabilizing force in the economy that it should be, fiscal policy has, itself, in too many instances, become a major destabilizing force contributing to disequilibrium in the external sector.[1]

In recent years the connection between fiscal developments and external sector developments has been increasingly recognized. Some have gone so far as to suggest a "fiscal approach to the balance of payments" that considers fiscal disequilibrium as the main cause of external imbalances.[2]

Although growth was always a primary objective of economic policy, the sustained rates of growth experienced by most countries until the mid-1970s (except for occasional and transitory periods of balance of payments difficulties) made it possible for the Fund, in negotiating stabilization programs, to concentrate on the objective of stabilization, concerning which it had more expertise and an accepted mandate. The increase in the oil price during the 1970s, and especially the more recent debt crisis accompanied by the sharp fall in commodity prices, brought about a new environment in which external sector disequilibrium could not be easily financed. This forced many countries to pursue (over longer periods than they had earlier) stabilization policies aimed at reducing external imbalances or the rate of inflation — policies that some critics considered inimical to growth.

In the face of external shocks, some countries (for example, the Republic of Korea) succeeded in stabilizing their economies and in advancing once again along the road of economic development. Others were less successful. When the need to pursue stabilization policies extended over several years, the short-run political costs of these policies began to loom larger than the longer-run economic benefits; political fatigue set in, and some countries became restive under the harness of traditional stabiliza-

---

[1] In this paper, the impact of fiscal developments on the balance of payments is emphasized. Of course, this relationship is not unidirectional. In some cases, fiscal disequilibrium may initially be created by developments in the balance of payments (say, a fall in export prices), and the important question is whether the government should finance the shortfall or should immediately or progressively lower domestic spending to reflect the lower real income of the country. See, on this, Tanzi (1986), Tabellini (1985), and Chu (1986).

[2] For the connection between the fiscal deficit and the balance of payments, see Kelly (1982) and Tanzi and Blejer (1984).

tion programs. Critics cried more loudly that stabilization policies were inhibiting growth. They attracted a larger following and advised policymakers to abandon stabilization policies recommended by the Fund, concentrating instead on growth, regardless of the consequences for the balance of payments and the rate of inflation. They espoused the position that inflation is a lesser evil than stagnation and that the external sector can be kept in equilibrium by means of quantitative restrictions and export subsidies, or by repudiating external debt obligations.

As already mentioned, stabilization and growth have always been legitimate policy objectives. Although in the past it was thought that, at any given moment, a country could focus on policies aimed specifically at only one of these objectives, the view that it is unwise to separate these objectives currently predominates. Stabilization programs must pay attention to growth to ensure that stability is not won at the price of stagnation.[3] Growth policy must pay attention to stability to ensure that the pursuit of growth is not aborted by excessive inflation or by pressures on the external sector, as has happened in several cases in recent years. Achieving growth without stability may be technically impossible over the longer run; achieving stability without growth may be politically impossible, except in the short run. This paper attempts to reformulate the fiscal design of stabilization programs in order to emphasize the growth objective.

If stabilization were the only objective of economic policy, stabilization programs could rely mostly on traditional demand-management policies.[4] Achieving stabilization *with* growth, however, requires demand-management policies to be complemented by policies aimed at increasing potential output. Misguided structural policies have reduced potential output by misallocating resources and by reducing the growth rates of the factors of production. They have thus been the main cause of stagnation and a contributor to economic instability. The design of adjustment programs should integrate stabilization with growth, or demand-management policies with structural, supply-side policies.

II. Fiscal Policy and the Design of Fund Programs

Stabilization programs can, in theory, emphasize either specific or general fiscal policies. For example, the member country and the Fund could

---

[3]This is particularly important in order to reduce, over time, the burden of the countries' foreign debt.

[4]Of course, changes in the exchange rate, which have often been part of traditional stabilization programs, have incentive effects in addition to their demand-management effects.

agree on a whole range of specific fiscal measures, such as changes in various taxes and tax rates, and changes in specific public expenditures, subsidies, and public utility rates. These measures, however, would have to add up to the required adjustment in aggregate demand *and* supply. They would have to reduce the balance of payments disequilibrium and the rate of inflation to the desired levels by reducing aggregate demand *and by increasing aggregate supply.* For the purpose of identification, I shall call this the "microeconomic approach to stabilization programs," an approach that explicitly recognizes both the demand-management and the supply-management aspects of fiscal policy. It recognizes that fiscal policy changes usually affect not only aggregate demand but also aggregate supply.[5]

Alternatively, the country and the Fund could limit their agreement on a program to general, macroeconomic variables. In the extreme version of this alternative, the Fund and the country might not even discuss specific fiscal policies, but would limit not only their agreement but also their discussions to the size of the fiscal deficit and to the expansion of bank credit associated with that deficit. If specific policies were discussed, it would be to assess their immediate impact on the size of the fiscal deficit and on aggregate *demand.*

In this approach, supply-side aspects of fiscal policy (what I have called the supply-management aspects) would be largely ignored. I shall call this the "macroeconomic approach to stabilization policy." This approach implies that once the size of the deficit has been determined, the balance of payments consequences of that deficit have also been determined, regardless of the specific measures that the country may employ to achieve the stipulated level of fiscal deficit.[6] Whether the deficit is reduced by raising

---

[5]Over the years, what I have called the supply-management aspect of fiscal policy has received far less attention than the more traditional demand-management aspect. To put it differently, price (or micro) theory has rarely been integrated with income (or macro) theory. Fiscal policy based on a Keynesian framework has normally concentrated on the effects of changes in tax levels and public spending levels on aggregate demand. Supply management is a relative newcomer to economic policy, even though it was clearly recognized by Joseph Schumpeter in his classic book, *The Theory of Economic Development,* first published some seventy years ago. Supply management emphasizes that the way factors of production are used may be more important than their amounts. It emphasizes that growth requires not only that the factors of production keep growing at a desirable pace but also that they be allocated as efficiently as possible. If, for example, investment grows but it is progressively channeled into less productive projects, the country's output may not grow.

[6]Most of the formal models that link the fiscal deficit to the balance of payments follow this approach. In these models, it is the size of the macroeconomic variables (the saving rate, the investment rate, the fiscal deficit, etc.) that plays the leading role. These variables are rarely disaggregated, so the possibilities connected with better resource allocation are not explored.

taxes or by cutting spending, and regardless of the specific tax and spending measures used to achieve such a reduction, the balance of payments consequences are assumed to be the same.[7]

Although these alternative designs of stabilization programs have probably never been pursued in their pure forms, over the years the formulation of stabilization programs has been much closer to the macroeconomic, than to the microeconomic, alternative,[8] in conformity with the common interpretation of the guidelines on conditionality.[9] *Until recent years*, stabilization programs established fiscal ceilings on the basis of an implicit model that connected monetary expansion associated with the fiscal deficit to developments in the balance of payments. The countries themselves would then choose the specific ways in which the fiscal ceilings would be observed. It was left to the authorities to determine which tax rates should be changed, which new revenue measures should be adopted, and which expenditures should be reduced (or expanded), although Fund missions did provide some advice based, where possible, on technical assistance reports. As Sir Joseph Gold puts it, ". . . performance criteria . . . must be confined to macroeconomic variables . . . . The concept of 'macroeconomic' variables involves the idea of aggregation . . . . [and] includes the broadest possible aggregate in an economic category." Gold goes on to state that ". . . the Fund should not become involved in the detailed decisions by which general policies are put into operation . . ." He concludes that "[s]pecific prices of commodities or services, specific taxes, or other detailed measures to increase revenues or to reduce expenditures would not be considered macroeconomic variables."[10]

Specific measures (such as the elimination of subsidies) were on rare occasions made performance criteria in Fund programs, but the main reason for doing so was often deficit reduction and thus demand management.[11] Fiscal changes without direct and immediate bearing on the size of the fiscal deficit (say, revenue-neutral tax reforms) did not receive explicit attention in formal agreements, even though they might have a bearing on the efficiency of the economy. Changes that would increase the fiscal deficit in the short run but would have desirable supply-side effects on the economy in the medium run were not encouraged. The observance

---

[7]It must be understood that even this macroeconomic approach will have to depend on specific measures to raise revenue or reduce spending.

[8]The theoretical design of Fund programs as generally interpreted has been much closer to what I have called the macroeconomic approach.

[9]See, for example, Gold (1979), especially pp. 30-34.

[10]Ibid., pp. 32-33.

[11]In the case of subsidies, one additional reason was their direct effect on the current account of the balance of payments when the subsidies encouraged the consumption of imported commodities.

of the fiscal ceilings was the most essential fiscal element of a stabilization program.

If the country wanted advice on its tax structure, on the structure of its public spending, or on their respective administration, it could request technical assistance from the Fund. No conditionality was attached to the provision or the use of this advice, although Fund missions have occasionally used technical assistance reports to provide advice to the countries, especially on how to raise revenue.[12] Technical assistance has been the major channel through which the Fund has directly influenced the structure of tax systems and their administration and, to a lesser extent, the structure of public spending.

With important qualifications, this macroeconomic approach to stabilization programs predominated until a few years ago. Starting with extended Fund facility programs, however, Fund missions began paying more attention to structural aspects in general, and specific fiscal aspects in particular,[13] and today much more attention is paid to structural (supply-side) elements in stabilization programs. The transition from the macroeconomic to the microeconomic approach is, however, far from complete. The approach followed in negotiating stabilization programs begins with an estimation of the required reduction in a country's fiscal deficit, given its balance of payments position and the foreign financing presumed to be available, and proceeds, separately and often ex post, to a discussion of specific policies.[14] The connection that is likely to exist, especially over the medium run, between the "required" deficit reduction and the specific measures adopted to make that reduction possible is not accounted for in setting program ceilings. For example, the removal of growth-retarding taxes is not encouraged if alternative revenue sources are not immediately available, since such a removal will immediately increase the fiscal deficit and, given the underlying model used, will presumably lead to a deterioration in the country's external position. Thus, the approach still goes from the macroeconomic to the microeconomic, and much attention is focused on the size of the deficit and on its financing.

Nevertheless, recent Fund programs have increasingly recognized that the specific measures through which fiscal deficits are reduced may determine, especially over the medium and long runs, whether a stabilization program will have durable, beneficial effects on the balance of payments

---

[12]Technical assistance is provided by the Fund only at the request of a member country's authorities.

[13]The extended Fund facility was established in September 1974 to provide financial assistance in support of medium-term programs of up to three years to overcome structural balance of payments maladjustments. The first request for an extended arrangement, which was made by Kenya, was approved by the Fund in July 1975.

[14]In actual negotiations, the sequence may not be exactly as described.

and on growth, or whether these effects will vanish as soon as the program is over. An adequate macroeconomic framework (consistent with a viable balance of payments and with price stability in the short run) is a necessary, but not a sufficient, condition for growth and for stability over the longer run. In addition, stability requires efficient structural policies.

Should the Fund and the authorities focus mainly on macroeconomic fiscal variables, as they traditionally have? Or should they make specific fiscal policies equally important in designing a program? Putting it more starkly, should the Fund be prepared to walk away from an arrangement with a country in which resources have been badly misallocated, thus reducing its growth potential, if an acceptable core of structural policies is missing, even though the traditional *macroeconomic* framework appears adequate? Should Fund missions start the analysis of a program by identifying such a "structural core of required policies" — that is, a set of specific supply-side measures — that *must* be implemented over the course of the program before the macroeconomic ceilings are set?[15] The answers to these questions are not as obvious as they might at first appear, since convincing arguments can be presented on both sides.

A first argument in favor of continuing with the traditional macroeconomic approach is that, *at least in theory*, this approach is objective. Whether or not performance criteria are satisfied is an issue subject, in most cases, to quantification and verification and is thus beyond dispute.[16] As such, this approach reduces the uncertainty faced by authorities. They know that if the country satisfies the performance criteria, it will obtain the agreed financial support from the Fund. And, once again, those performance criteria normally relate to macroeconomic variables.

A second, and perhaps more important, argument is that performance criteria based on ceilings imply less political interference by the Fund in the internal affairs of countries than do criteria related to specific measures. Authorities are likely to object to having to agree to modify a tax in a given way or to modify the level or pattern of public spending.[17] Critics

---

[15]This might require a change in the conditionality guidelines approved by the Fund's Executive Board. Of course, whenever there was no presumption that resources had been badly misallocated, Fund programs would continue to focus on a macroeconomic framework.

[16]"Performance criteria are always objective in order that a member will not be taken by surprise by a decision of the Fund to impede transactions under a stand-by arrangement. The member has maximum assurance, therefore, about the circumstances in which it can engage in transactions with the Fund." — Gold (1979), p. 32.

[17]A few programs have made the *total* level of public expenditure a performance clause. This can be considered a departure from the traditional narrow interpretation of conditionality guidelines. Generally, the formal agreements have focused on the difference between public expenditure and revenue (i.e., on the deficit).

who find present Fund conditionality too rigid are likely to object even more to what might be seen as an extension of that conditionality. Examples of this reaction exist in connection with Fund recommendations to eliminate or reduce subsidies. Many observers feel that these are political decisions that should be left to the authorities and that the Fund should, at most, offer only an opinion on them.

A third argument in favor of the traditional approach is that discussions of fiscal ceilings, as well as the review of the outcome of these discussions at Fund headquarters, require fewer and less specialized staff resources than do discussions of specific measures. For an institution concerned about its own budget, this is an important consideration. The design of a program can be based on a relatively straightforward view of the relationship between fiscal deficits and the balance of payments. Once some assumptions are made, it is far easier to decide what the size of a fiscal ceiling should be than to decide the details of specific policy changes and how these changes would influence program objectives.

A fourth argument, closely related to the preceding one, is that, *at least in the fiscal area*, it is far easier to write a letter of intent in which a country's formal commitments are couched in the form of general ceilings than to write documents that spell out formal commitments in terms of many specific policy changes. It is always difficult, for example, to specify the precise requirements of a tax reform.

There are, however, arguments that caution against *exclusive* or *excessive* emphasis on traditional performance criteria that emphasize fiscal ceilings. They favor paying close attention to the microeconomic aspects of fiscal policy, such as the structure of individual taxes, the structure of expenditure, the allocation of investment, the prices charged by public utilities, and public employment. To avoid any misunderstanding on this issue, I should emphasize here that the questions raised below about fiscal ceilings should not be interpreted as supporting Fund critics of conditionality. They simply call attention to the arguments (a) that a good stabilization program must not rely exclusively on demand management, and (b) that the ceilings used to serve demand management should not be set independently from the structural changes that the country is willing to make. The main justification for this change of emphasis is that, provided the supply response is not insignificant and occurs fairly rapidly, the more far reaching the structural reform agreed to by the country, the greater will be that supply response (in terms of output, exports, capital repatriation, and the like). Such a supply response may imply that a less stringent demand-management policy is necessary.

Problems have at times been encountered when ceilings have been imposed on macroeconomic variables. These problems are mentioned to indicate that a program that relies exclusively on performance criteria related to macroeconomic variables may not provide the hoped-for results. First, the longer ceilings on macroeconomic variables are in use, the more ways countries learn to get around them. Ceilings are most useful when a country complies not just with the letter of an agreement but also with its spirit. Unfortunately, there have been instances in which countries have complied with the letter, and defied the spirit, of agreements. They have engaged in operations aimed at circumventing the ceilings in order to draw resources from the Fund without making genuine adjustments. To deal with this problem, the Fund has been compelled, in some programs, to increase the number of performance clauses related to the fiscal deficit. This has created a perception of excessive conditionality.

Second, the usual formulation of a stabilization program may give the impression that the relationship between fiscal deficits and program objectives, and especially their relationship with the balance of payments, is clear cut and unambiguous. It may give the impression of a single-valued functional relationship — that is, so much fiscal deficit implies so much deficit in the current account of the balance of payments. Unfortunately, our knowledge about important economic relationships (such as (1) that between changes in the money supply and changes in prices, and (2) that between changes in prices, changes in nominal exchange rates, and their effects on the balance of payments) is too limited to inspire excessive confidence about the precise level of the fiscal deficit required to achieve a given change in the current account of the balance of payments or in other economic objectives. The truth is that a given fiscal deficit may be associated with a *range* of balance of payments outcomes.[18]

Third, the ceilings may, in some cases, divert attention from the basic objectives of economic policy. Meeting the ceilings within the program period may come to be seen as an end in itself. During this period, programs may be judged successful or not depending on whether ceilings are being met rather than on whether the ultimate objectives of the program (durable improvement in the balance of payments, growth, price stability, and so forth) are being achieved.

Finally, and most important, excessive reliance on macroeconomic ceilings may divert attention away from the *quality*, as well as the *durability*, of the specific measures used by a country to comply with its performance clauses. Let me give some examples, starting with the question of the durability of the fiscal measure. The question to be raised is the following: will a fiscal measure have a permanent impact on the fiscal deficit? Will, for example, a revenue increase or an expenditure cut affect the deficit for

---

[18]Programs recognize this problem by including (a) reviews to ensure that additional measures are taken to stay on track and (b) a commitment to take additional measures as needed.

years to come, or will it have a once-for-all effect? This is an important question if the program's objective is, as it should be, a permanent improvement in the economy.

In some cases, tax payments by enterprises have been paid in advance at the request of the government,[19] or public expenditures have been postponed (through the building up of arrears or the postponement of inevitable expenditures),[20] so that the country can meet the fiscal ceilings and, thus, make the next drawing. In other cases, temporary sources of revenue (once-for-all taxes, temporary surtaxes, tax amnesties, sales of public assets, and so forth) have allowed the country to stay within the agreed ceiling without doing anything to reduce its underlying or core fiscal deficit.[21] At times, governments have used up so much of their political capital in introducing these temporary measures that they no longer have had the stamina necessary to make the permanent and growth-promoting policy changes required to achieve durable adjustment with growth.

In addition to the question of the durability of the fiscal measures (of whether their effects will survive the program), there is the important question of the quality (or, if one wishes, the economic efficiency) of those measures. As far as short-term demand-management policy is concerned, whether a country reduces the fiscal deficit by raising revenue or by cutting expenditure is inconsequential.[22] It is also inconsequential whether it does it through the use of measures that have disincentive effects, or of measures that do not have such effects. The stabilization program will fail if the ceiling is not observed; it will not fail if it is observed through the use of growth-retarding measures.

The above discussion should not be interpreted as arguing that stabilization programs should no longer rely on demand management based on a macroeconomic framework that sets ceilings on relevant macroeconomic variables. In my view, the need for such a framework is too obvious to require justification. The discussion simply argues that this framework

---

[19]A few years ago, the government of a given country pressured a large foreign enterprise to advance tax payments for the next three years so as to allow the country to comply with the fiscal ceiling.

[20]This is commonly the case with real wages for public employees, which are at times reduced to unsustainable levels during the program but bounce back to a more normal level when the program is over. Permanent adjustment would more likely result from a reduction of the permanent public sector work force than from what is often a temporary reduction in real wages. On the issue of arrears in the payments of goods and services by the government, see Diamond and Schiller (1987).

[21]For a definition of the concept of core fiscal deficit, see Tanzi and Blejer (1984), p. 119.

[22]This is true regardless of the present level of taxation in the country.

needs to be supplemented by measures aimed at ensuring that stabilization programs are, first, durable and, second, as growth promoting as possible. According to the present guidelines on conditionality, under which the Fund staff operates, the change advocated in this paper might not be possible. A decision taken by the Executive Board of the Fund on March 2, 1979 states that "Performance criteria will normally be confined to (i) *macroeconomic variables,* and (ii) those necessary to implement specific provisions of the Articles [of Agreement] or policies adopted under them. Performance criteria may relate to other variables only in exceptional cases . . ." (italics added).

III. STABILIZATION POLICY AND ECONOMIC GROWTH

Growth-promoting stabilization policy requires that the reduction in the fiscal deficit be carried out through fiscal measures that are (a) durable in their effects, and (b) efficient in their impact. In other words, the policies chosen must not self-destruct once the program is over and must achieve their deficit-reducing objective with the least possible inhibition of economic growth.

The efficiency of fiscal instruments is important for growth, as much recent work on this issue has demonstrated. Work effort, exports, productive investment, saving, capital flight, foreign investment, and so on can be affected by the choice of specific fiscal instruments.[23] These choices may play a large role in determining the amount of foreign resources a country will have available during and after the program period. Thus, the relationship between changes in the size of fiscal deficits and changes in the ultimate objectives of economic policy, such as growth and stability, is inevitably influenced by the fiscal policy measures utilized. It can make a substantial difference to the growth prospects of a country if the fiscal deficit is reduced by eliminating a totally unproductive expenditure or by raising a tax that has strong disincentive effects, even though in terms of traditional stabilization policy (in terms of short-run fiscal deficit reduction) the result would appear to be the same. The more efficient the measures used to achieve a *given* deficit reduction, the greater will be the rate of growth, and, assuming an unchanged monetary policy, the lower will be the rate of inflation.

---

[23]The Fiscal Affairs Department of the Fund has produced a series of papers on this issue in the past few years. Some of these papers were published in Gandhi and others (1987). For specific studies of the relationship between export taxes and exports, see Tanzi (1976), Okonkwo (1978), and Sanchez-Ugarte and Modi (1987).

The implication of the above conclusion for stabilization programs is obvious: provided that a country is willing to implement considerable structural measures early enough in a program so that the positive effects of these measures can be felt relatively soon, the Fund should be prepared to require less reduction in the overall fiscal deficit (i.e., to require less austerity) than it would if the structural package were less far reaching or if the country delayed its introduction. Thus, the Fund should explicitly recognize, at the time it enters into an agreement with a country, a trade-off between quantity and quality of fiscal adjustment—one that would also be influenced by the timing of the introduction of the structural measures. This trade-off should be recognized and, possibly, formalized in program design and negotiations.[24]

This is not the place to discuss in detail the quality of the fiscal measures that could form the structural core of a stabilization program, but a few examples may help convey the importance of this issue. Suppose that an agricultural commodity of wide consumption (say, wheat, corn, or rice) has been subject to an export tax in a country negotiating a Fund program. The elimination of this tax would reduce tax revenue and thus raise the fiscal deficit. This, in turn, would have monetary and, consequently, balance of payments implications, which the *macroeconomic* framework used for Fund programs would assess. But let us consider whether there are countervailing supply-side effects. The removal of the tax would raise the domestic price of the commodity and lead to a reduction in domestic consumption, thus making an additional supply available for exports.[25] In addition, the removal of the export tax would encourage producers to produce more of that product. When this additional production became available, exports would increase further. Since the availability of foreign ex-

---

[24]The potential output of a country is likely to grow if (a) the rate of investment grows while its average productivity and the average productivity of the other factors of production (labor, land, and so on) do not change, or if (b) the average productivity of the factors of production increases owing to the removal of distortions, or to technological change, even though the supply of the production factors does not change. If the distortions have, as has often been the case, reduced the country's ability to earn foreign exchange or have led to the misuse of the foreign exchange available, their removal will, over time, increase the flow of foreign exchange available to the country. In other words, the removal of the distortions would have the same effect as an increase in foreign lending to the country. It would thus reduce the need to constrain demand, since this need, in a typical Fund program, is often a function of the scarcity of foreign exchange.

[25]It should be recalled that an export tax on a commodity X can be decomposed into a production tax on X and a consumption subsidy on X. Thus, the removal of the export tax removes the subsidy to domestic consumption and removes the tax on production. Domestic consumption falls while production and, presumably, exports rise.

change is always a key factor in a stabilization program, focusing only on the demand effect (through the increase in the fiscal deficit) that the elimination of the tax will have, and ignoring the supply effect (through the incentive to produce and export more), is likely to introduce a bias against the elimination of that tax. It may thus lead to programs that require greater demand reduction than was necessary.[26]

Or suppose that some additional spending is carried out by the government to repair a road that facilitates the shipping of agricultural products out of the country. Here again, the short-run negative effect on the balance of payments associated with the larger fiscal deficit is partly or fully neutralized by the positive effect associated with larger exports. These examples may be extreme, but they are far from rare. It would be easy to provide additional illustrations of the link between quantity and quality of fiscal adjustment.

A perusal of stabilization programs indicates that despite an increasing awareness of these issues, political difficulties, guidelines on conditionality, and timing concerns have prevented their being taken formally into account in Fund programs.

In negotiating programs, the Fund has attempted, with increasing frequency, to ensure that cutbacks in government expenditure are focused on less productive activities. The World Bank's guidance is sought in this connection. Nevertheless, obvious political sensitivities have limited the degree of Fund involvement in decisions on expenditure policy. As a result, the expenditure policies pursued have, in several instances, not been as supportive of the growth objective as they could have been.[27]

An examination of actual cutbacks in capital expenditure in various countries indicates that they have, at times, been borne by some of the more productive projects. To reduce the budget deficit, cutbacks have in some cases affected productive, externally financed projects despite the fact that loans for part of the total cost of the projects were highly concessionary. In other cases, cutbacks have focused on productive, domestically financed, small-scale projects, while externally financed, highly visible, but less productive projects backed by important donors have been protected. Even where a core investment program has been agreed between the country and the World Bank, higher implementation rates for lower-priority projects have often occurred.

---

[26]Of course, if the authorities propose to reduce the fiscal deficit through an increase in export taxes, then the negative supply-side effects of this policy would require even greater demand management than when these effects were ignored.

[27]At this point it may be useful to state the obvious: that government decisions are often influenced more by political considerations than by considerations of economic efficiency.

A common feature of such policies has been the disproportionate cutback in expenditure on materials, supplies, and maintenance, relative to other types of expenditures. As a result, the condition of roads, bridges, public buildings, irrigation projects, airports, and other public sector infrastructure has deteriorated by more than would have been required notwithstanding the inevitability of certain adjustments necessitated by the debt crisis.[28] Inadequate maintenance eventually requires expensive projects for reconstruction of deteriorated plants and equipment.[29] In agricultural regions, impassable roads have drastically limited the impact of market-oriented policies aimed at encouraging increased agricultural production. Shortages of materials and supplies have also dramatically limited the productivity of public sector employees, whether in education, medical care, agricultural extension, or tax administration. Across-the-board cutbacks in expenditure have been common. Such an approach fails to address the enormous waste of expenditure in many politically sensitive but unproductive sectors, including defense spending. Significant cutbacks in public sector employment remain the exception. As a result, efforts to cut the public sector wage bill have typically resulted in a deterioration in real wages, which are often greatest among the higher-paid civil servants. The factors encouraging corruption, low productivity, and multiple jobs of civil servants have therefore been intensified.

Tax increases have, in some instances, included measures that can be expected to have detrimental effects on growth. This has, at times, occurred in countries that already had very high tax ratios. For example, on many occasions the rates of export duty have been raised (or an export duty has been imposed) following devaluation, on grounds that the exporters would enjoy some sort of "windfall" profits. However, devaluations often simply offset past cost increases. Import surcharges have been levied, or the rates of import duties have been raised, for balance of payments and revenue reasons. As these surcharges have been imposed on products already highly taxed, they have, by increasing the differences between taxed and untaxed imports, increased distortions and reduced growth prospects.[30] Surcharges on the income taxes of individuals and

---

[28]These expenditures are generally classified as "current" rather than "capital" expenditures. Therefore, the common view that stabilization programs must protect "investment" may not necessarily lead to the best policy. In some cases, the most productive expenditures are "current" ones.

[29]There is now a growing concern among some experts that the present reductions in fiscal deficits associated with these lower expenditures for maintenance of roads and other infrastructure will necessitate much higher expenditures (and thus higher deficits) in future years, as the lack of maintenance will require expensive rebuilding. This is, again, an example of the shifting of the fiscal deficit from the present to the future.

[30]Imports subjected to import duties are often less than 50 percent of total imports, so that substantial rate increases on the taxed imports are needed to generate significant tax revenue. Of course, as the rates increase, so does smuggling.

corporations have often been used. Sometimes countries have raised payroll taxes or taxes on interest incomes with undesirable repercussions on employment, saving, and capital flight. In a few cases, countries have levied taxes on expatriate employment raised the rates of mining taxes, or levied taxes on foreign exchange transactions, thus discouraging foreign participation in economic development.

The main point of this discussion is worth repeating. The impact of changes in fiscal deficits on economic objectives depends to a considerable extent on the quality of the specific measures employed. A change in the quality of those measures will change the relationship between the fiscal deficit and the balance of payments, especially over the medium and long runs. The required reduction in the fiscal deficit (that is, the required austerity) needed to achieve a given effect on the basic objectives of economic policy will be more severe as less efficient measures are chosen. For this reason, stabilization programs should systematically deal with microeconomic issues of public finance in addition to other structural policies. Programs must include needed structural changes and must integrate them with the macroeconomic framework.

Several problems arise in connection with the implementation of the approach suggested in this paper. They relate to (a) our knowledge of incentive effects, (b) timing considerations, and (c) political implications.

As to the first point, one could argue that not enough is known about the incentive effects of particular policies to place precise quantitative values on them. The validity of this argument is apparent, but irrelevant. Stabilization programs often rely on exchange rate devaluation, even though precise estimates of these responses are not available. They also rely on changes in real interest rates, even though, again, the size of the response of financial (and real) saving to changes in real rates cannot be known with precision. The important point is to have a sense of the direction of the effects and some "feel" for their size. If one waited for precise and objective quantifications of these effects, no formal agreement on a stabilization program would ever be included.

As to the timing issue, one could agree that the choice of better policies would *in time* bring about a more efficient economy and higher rates of growth. But what about the present? Would not, for example, the elimination or the reduction of an efficient tax, or an increase in a highly productive government expenditure, raise the deficit in the short run, thus necessitating more external or inflationary financing? A simple answer is that important structural changes often bring with them immediate changes in expectations that can influence individuals and corporations to make further changes reinforcing their initial effects.[31] For example,

---

[31]This is particularly true when the attitude of the government indicates that these changes are not likely to be reversed soon.

changes that create an environment more favorable to the private sector may encourage individuals to repatriate capital, encourage foreign enterprises to invest in that country, and facilitate foreign borrowing. More foreign money is likely to be made available to countries pursuing structural reforms.[32] Still, part of the answer is that, as shown in the example of the export tax, some real effects will often occur early. If structural changes are made early in a program, or even before its formal approval by the Fund, their supply-side effects would probably also occur within the program's duration, so that the initial negative effect on the size of the fiscal deficit could be balanced by a positive effect in the latter phase of the program. Reluctance to allow some initial expansion in the deficit through, say, the removal of inefficient taxes may contribute to the postponement of essential structural adjustment.[33] Finally, this timing question is not limited to these policies. For example, the existence of J-curves indicates that the same problem exists with the effect of exchange rate devaluation. Also, so-called ratchet effects may postpone the time when the impact of demand-management policies is felt on effective demand.

The proposed departure is not without political implications. The conditionality guidelines may have to be amended to make it possible for the Fund to include, in a stabilization program, formal understandings about tax or expenditure reforms in the countries that approach the Fund for programs and where there are significant structural distortions.[34] In some ways, this would be a change of form more than substance, because the Fund has already, in recent programs, gotten involved in structural aspects and has tried to persuade some countries to implement particular policy changes. Countries' authorities may object to the proposed changes, especially if they perceive them it as additional conditionality without receiving anything in return. Nevertheless, if they became aware that, at the time a program was negotiated, there might be some trade-off between the size of the required *macroeconomic* adjustment, on the one hand (the required austerity), and structural changes, on the other, their objections to the proposed change might, in some cases, be less serious than one would assume a priori.

---

[32]It should be recalled that the Baker initiative is postulated on this assumption.

[33]Many structural changes can be made revenue neutral by removing some taxes (adding some expenditure) while adding some other taxes (reducing some other expenditure).

[34]That is, some of the documents that reflect the formal understandings between the Fund and the country must spell out the details of the agreement between the two parties as to the tax modifications, changes in public expenditures, and so forth.

IV. CONCLUDING REMARKS

The above discussion indicates that if at all possible, a more inductive approach to determining the particulars of the fiscal policy required in stabilization programs would be desirable. According to this approach, in addition to identifying the range of adjustment needed at the macroeconomic level, the Fund, in cooperation with the member country's experts, would make an inventory of the various changes in both the level and structure of taxes and of public expenditure that would be required to promote the country's growth objective.[35] In this search, the Fund would have to take into account the importance the country's authorities attached to such objectives as equity and the provision of basic needs. The task would then be to determine whether the proposed changes added up to a macroeconomic adjustment package that was consistent with the balance of payments objective. The structural adjustment would be made up of a basic structural core of fiscal measures constituting a sine qua non for a program. If this structural core did not add up to the macroeconomic adjustment assumed to be needed, the Fund and the local experts would look for progressively less efficient ways to add to revenues or to reduce expenditures. If the country's economic difficulties were assumed to originate exclusively in excess demand (that is, if no major structural problems were identified), the negotiations would proceed along more traditional lines.

The country's authorities would be aware that there was a trade-off between the size of the needed demand constraint and the extent of the structural changes. They would know that the more daring and timely they were in introducing structural changes, the more flexibility they would have in demand management. In essence, the program would be made up of three elements, possibly all of major importance: (a) the traditional macroeconomic framework with ceilings and targets; (b) the structural core; and (c) the investment core, which presumably would indicate, on the basis of World Bank recommendations, the minimum investment, as well as the allocation of that investment, consistent with both growth and balance of payments objectives.

One should not underestimate the difficulties, both technical and political, that a formal pursuit of this alternative would present; and one should recognize that this alternative would be considerably more labor intensive for both the Fund and the countries' experts and policymakers. It is an alternative that would require further thought before it could be fully

---

[35]Obviously, other structural aspects would also be considered.

implemented.[36] Initial experimentation in well-chosen and willing countries would be indispensable to a full assessment of its general feasibility
and to an outline of the procedural steps to be followed.

In this year [1987] when the Nobel Prize in economics has been given to
James Buchanan for his contributions to public choice theory, it may be
appropriate to conclude this paper with a few highly personal thoughts on
the political implications of the suggestions it contains.

While aggregate demand may grow independent of structural policies,
so that a traditional stabilization program will be sufficient in itself to
bring about the needed reduction in that demand and, thus, the needed
adjustment to the economy, it is more often the case that excess demand
exists not (or not only) because demand has grown more than it should
have but (or but also) because supply (including that of foreign exchange)
has been constrained by misguided structural policies. For example, financial savings may have been reduced by constraints on nominal interest
rates or by excessive taxation of interest income; this reduction may have
constricted the supply of domestic financial savings available to finance
the deficit and private investment in non-inflationary ways, and because
of capital flight, it may have reduced the availability of foreign exchange.[37] Agricultural output may have been reduced by low producer
prices that necessitated the import of food. Agricultural exports may
have been limited by excessive export taxes, by overvalued exchange
rates, and by low prices paid to producers. Food supplies may have been
limited by the deterioration of transportation systems brought about by
misallocation of public expenditures. In all these examples, the *supply* has
been reduced, thus creating imbalances that, in time, have manifested
themselves as excessive demand. In these cases, demand-management
policies alone would have reduced the symptoms of these imbalances but
would not have eliminated the causes. Thus, stabilization programs might
succeed stabilization programs without bringing about a durable adjustment unless the basic causes of imbalances were addressed.

One major difficulty in dealing with these basic issues is that the policies that I have called "misguided" may be misguided only in an economic,
and not in a political, sense. Public choice theorists would emphasize the
fact that these policies may be quite rational, at least in the short run, if
they were assessed from a purely political viewpoint.[38] They would argue

---

[36]The full and formal introduction of structural changes into the theoretical design of
Fund programs should be considered one of the main challenges to our future research
effort.

[37]For an analysis of the ways in which deficits get financed in developing countries
and of the limits to those sources of financing, see Tanzi (1985).

[38]All the literature on rent-seeking, which represents an important chapter of the
economics of public choice, would support this view. See, especially, Buchanan, Tollison, and Tullock, eds. (1980); and Tollison (1982).

that structural problems do not necessarily exist because policymakers have made technical mistakes in their policymaking, perhaps because of poor economic understanding. Rather, public choice theorists would argue that through these policies, policymakers have tried to promote their own political objectives. Furthermore, the time horizons of policymakers are generally so short that they do not take full account of the long-run implications of their policies on the economy. These policies create "rents" for groups whose support the government needs in order to stay in power, even though such policies may, in time, reduce the incomes of the majority of citizens.[39]

If this public choice interpretation of economic policy is at least partly valid—and I do not know to what extent it is—it implies that policies aimed at structural reform will often be resisted more than macroeconomic stabilization policies. They would be resisted because they would remove these rents from precisely those whose support the government needed and would thus reduce the leverage that the policymakers had over consituencies whose support they needed to stay in power. In part, structural reforms would weaken the government in power's *raison d'être*. As a consequence, it would seem to follow from these theories that major structural reforms have the best chance of being carried out when there is a major political change—that is, when a government that has long been in power is replaced by a totally different one—so that the political interests of the new policymakers are not tied to existing structural policies. This public choice-inspired hypothesis should be amenable to testing. It seems to have some plausibility, but only a careful analysis of actual situations will permit one to accurately assess its validity as a tool in explaining changes that occur in economic policy.

REFERENCES

Buchanan, James M., Robert D. Tollison, and Gordon Tullock, eds., *Toward a Theory of the Rent-Seeking Society*, Texas A&M University Economic Series, No. 4 (College Station: Texas A&M University Press, 1980).

Chu, Ke-young, "External Shocks and the Process of Fiscal Adjustment in a Small Open Developing Economy" (unpublished, International Monetary Fund, March 2, 1987).

---

[39]For example, if agricultural prices are kept low in order to subsidize the real wages of urban dwellers, the government may acquire the support of the latter, but the cost may be a low rate of growth and increasing economic difficulties in the long run. See, for example, some of the studies in Harberger, ed. (1984).

Diamond, Jack, and Christian Schiller, "Government Arrears in Fiscal Adjustment Programs" in *Measurement of Fiscal Impact: Methodological Issues*, ed. by Mario I. Blejer and Ke-young Chu, IMF Occasional Papers, No. 59 (Washington: International Monetary Fund, 1988), pp. 32-47.

Gandhi, Ved P., and others, *Supply-Side Tax Policy: Its Relevance to Developing Countries* (Washington: International Monetary Fund, 1987).

Gold, Joseph, *Conditionality*, IMF Pamphlet Series, No. 31 (Washington: International Monetary Fund, 1979).

Harberger, Arnold C., ed., *World Economic Growth* (San Francisco: Institute for Contemporary Studies, ICS Press, 1984).

Kelly, Margaret R., "Fiscal Adjustment and Fund-Supported Programs, 1971-80," *Staff Papers*, International Monetary Fund (Washington), Vol. 29 (December 1982), pp. 561-602.

Okonkwo, Ubadigbo, "Export Taxes on Primary Products in Developing Countries: The Taxation of Cocoa Exports in West Africa" (unpublished, International Monetary Fund, November 29, 1978).

Sanchez-Ugarte, Fernando, and Jitendra R. Modi, "Are Export Duties Optimal in Developing Countries? Some Supply-Side Considerations," in Ved P. Gandhi and others, *Supply-Side Tax Policy: Its Relevance to Developing Countries* (Washington: International Monetary Fund, 1987), pp. 279-320.

Tabellini, Guido, "Fiscal Policy Response to the External Shocks of 1979 in Selected Developing Countries: Theory and Facts" (unpublished, International Monetary Fund, December 26, 1985).

Tanzi, Vito, "Export Taxation in Developing Countries: Taxation of Coffee in Haiti," *Social and Economic Studies* (Kingston, Jamaica), Vol. 25 (March 1976), pp. 66-76.

_____ , "Is There a Limit to the Size of Fiscal Deficits in Developing Countries?" in *Public Finance and Public Debt: Proceedings of the 40th Congress of the International Institute of Public Finance*, Innsbruck, 1984, ed. by Bernard P. Herber (Detroit, Michigan: Wayne State University Press, 1986), pp. 139-52.

_____ , "Fiscal Policy Responses to Exogenous Shocks in Developing Countries," *American Economic Review: Papers and Proceedings of the Ninety-Eighth Annual Meeting of the American Economic Association* (Nashville, Tennessee), Vol. 76 (May 1986), pp. 88-91.

_____ , and Mario I. Blejer, "Fiscal Deficits and Balance of Payments Disequilibrium in IMF Adjustment Programs," in *Adjustment, Conditionality, and International Financing*, ed. by Joaquín Muns (Washington: International Monetary Fund, 1984), pp. 117-36.

Tollison, Robert D., "Rent Seeking: A Survey," *Kyklos* (Basel), Vol. 35 (Fasc. 4, 1982), pp. 575-601.

2

Fiscal Policy and Mobilization of Savings for Growth

Mario I. Blejer and Adrienne Cheasty*

I. INTRODUCTION

The mobilization of domestic financial resources may be analyzed on two levels: first, one needs to determine the total volume of savings and how these may be channeled into the financial system in order to make them available for investment; and second, once resources are being absorbed into the financial market, one needs to determine how the system may function most efficiently in directing these resources to where they are most needed in the economy. Thus, the government may attempt to mobilize resources by affecting the supply side (savings) or the demand side (domestic investment) of the economy. On the savings side, the government may be concerned, first, with increasing total savings, and then with ensuring that a significant portion of savings is directed toward the financial system. Given this level of "loanable funds savings,"[1] the government may wish (i) to overcome imperfections (distortions) in the capital market, which prevent investors from using these funds to finance projects which yield the highest social rates of return; and (ii) to raise the potential rates of return attainable by savers by itself engaging in capital expenditures (mainly on infrastructure and public goods) which generate no immediate pecuniary profit but which increase the effectiveness of private projects and thus the demand for loanable funds to finance them. These last two roles of government may be characterized as entailing the removal of negative externalities, which distort the social return to

*This paper was first published in *The Role of the Public Sector in the Mobilization of Domestic Financial Resources in Developing Countries* (New York: United Nations, 1986).

[1]This phrase has been borrowed from Howrey and Hymans (1978).

capital, and as enhancing positive externalities, which increase the social return to capital.

Underlying this description of the role of government is the assumption that private capital markets are not perfect. If they were, there would be no distortion in the supply of, or the demand for, loanable funds. On the supply side, the socially optimal level of savings and its allocation between markets would already exist, and, therefore, attempts by the government to change either aggregate savings or its composition would lower long-run economic welfare. On the demand side, rates of return to capital would provide the correct signals to investors, and market arbitrage (as described by Coase (1960)) would internalize the external benefits or costs to investment. While the extent and gravity of imperfections in capital markets continue to be a matter of debate, there are several reasons why existing imperfections are exacerbated in developing countries. In consequence, if the government can play any role in mobilizing domestic financial resources, that role will be more crucial in developing countries, where the private sector is less able to generate and allocate loanable funds productively.

This paper will discuss the mobilization of domestic financial resources in three sections. Section II will examine the characteristics of developing countries which hinder the performance of their capital markets. Section III will discuss the traditional tax policies governments have used to try to compensate for poorly developed financial systems. Because there are evident problems (both microeconomic and macroeconomic) associated with such policies, Section IV will discuss an alternative solution open to a government which wishes to generate loanable funds savings. The government itself may become a net saver by generating a budgetary surplus and thus freeing financial resources for use by the private sector. Governments can be compensated for the fiscal discipline this strategy requires by sizable benefits at the macroeconomic level.

II. Characteristics of Developing Country Financial Markets

Several characteristics of developing country capital markets make it likely that savings will be low and that they will include a large share of nonloanable funds—that is, resources not available for the purchase or creation of new capital. Wealth holders in developing countries frequently make intertemporal transfers of wealth by holding consumer durables, such as jewelry, works of art, or livestock, which are not defined as savings; by buying land or housing, forms of saving/investment which only indirectly generate output; or by holding financial assets outside the financial system, in informal ("curb") markets, which cannot be measured as savings or offered openly to investors. This non-optimal level and allocation of savings may arise for the following reasons:

(1) *The capital market is undiversified and fragmented.* The size of the capital market in developing countries is small, and the scope for diversification of financial institutions and financial instruments or assets is limited. Typically, the banking system is confined to one central city, supplemented perhaps by a few peripatetic administrators of development bank credit. The equity market in such countries is rarely well developed, which means that investments in physical capital tend to be few and large relative to the total size of the financial capital market, with consequent wide differentials in the rates of interest offered on different loans. These differentials are exacerbated by poor communications, which prevent the flow of information and advertising of the quantities and prices of funds available. Thus, it is difficult to pool funds and to arbitrage rates. (The largest information distortion, of course, is the dissimulation of all transactions which take place in informal markets, where the government, for example, cannot bid for funds.) Furthermore, the government may often have very clearly defined sectoral priorities which it expresses through a conscious policy of making different quantities of funds available, at different interest rates, to different demanders. The result of these shortcomings is the market's inability to generate a single clearing rate of return to financial capital. Wedges driven between borrowing and lending rates may lead to such anomalies as an individual saver finding, on the one hand, that banking his savings is not worthwhile, but, on the other hand, that borrowing to support a planned enterprise is too expensive. This leads to increased use of retained earnings for investment in developing countries, compared with the countries where financial intermediation is more developed, reducing both the pool of loanable funds and the likelihood that the rate of return to financial saving will equal the cost of capital.

(2) *Financial returns to savings and/or investments are insufficient.* The discrepancies between borrowing and lending rates described above may make returns in the financial system unattractive. Returns may be inadequate for two other reasons. First, controls and intervention are widespread in many developing countries. Fixed interest rate policies quickly lead to financial repression as foreign interest rates change, exchange rates move, or the inflation rate rises. In this case, even if the capital market were characterized by complete information and open access, savings would fall short of investment and loanable funds would have to be rationed, since their price would be prevented from functioning as an effective allocative mechanism. Second, in less urbanized areas of

some developing countries, nonfinancial assets (such as housing, jewelry, or livestock) may serve as currency substitutes, and this may raise their liquidity premium above what bankers would perceive it to be. The rate of return to nonfinancial assets might also perhaps be higher outside cities if these assets were valued for nonpecuniary benefits attributed to them. (An example would be the accumulation of unprofitable land to consolidate an estate.) In such cases, it becomes difficult for the financial sector to measure the opportunity cost of alternative assets, and thus to offer a competitive rate of return. In a large capital market, equilibrium prices which take into account all available alternatives may emerge quickly, but in the markets of developing countries, the number of transactions that take place may be insufficient to permit the market to clear and thus provide equilibrium valuations of nonpecuniary benefits.

(3) *Financial assets bear uncompensated risks.* The distortions in returns described above would occur even in a riskless economy. In fact, however, potential savers may perceive risks to entering the financial system which they do not consider are compensated for by an adequate risk premium on the rate of return because of the various rigidities in the market which prevent the emergence of a clearing rate. The liquidity of financial savings may not be guaranteed in many developing countries, where frequent changes of government policy (or, indeed, of government regime) close banks, change interest rates, retire bonds, or alter the purchasing power of the currency, often with little or no advance notice. These abrupt changes in policy are often the result of unavoidable exogenous shocks, and even if such shocks do not affect the stability of the financial system or the political system, they may cause the costs of imports and exports to fluctuate widely, making financial assets denominated in domestic currency a bad risk unless interest rates are free to vary with the expected rate of exchange rate depreciation.[2]

Savers may perceive a further risk in the danger that financial assets will sooner or later be taxed. Typically, the tax base in developing countries is narrow, and governments are constantly searching for ways to widen it. Income and wealth already denominated in financial terms are by far the easiest to tax, so that, while a government may be aware of all the caveats attached to the taxation of savings, it may find the revenue-raising potential of a wealth tax or a capital-gains tax, on financial assets, impossible to resist. Nonfinancial assets, which are intrinsically harder to value and which are much further removed from the notice of the taxing

---

[2]The relevant exchange rate here may be the relative price of a particular commodity, rather than the value of the currency, in an economy where asset markets are fragmented because, in such a case, for example, the only funds available to a potential importer may come from his own previous export trade.

authorities, may be seen by investors as yielding a far more certain stream of future returns.

III. TRADITIONAL ROLE OF GOVERNMENT IN DEVELOPING COUNTRIES' DOMESTIC FINANCIAL MARKETS

In theory, all of the distortions described could be removed by adjusting the incentives to holding financial assets appropriately, either through taxes or credit policy. As is evident from the description of these distortions, however, the most intransigent problem may be one of information. The government may not have complete information on the rate of return that would compensate people for the costs of storing savings in a faraway city, for forgone nonpecuniary benefits, and for perceived risks. In a larger capital market, sufficient numbers of transactions would take place for the clearing rate of return to manifest itself, but in developing countries the whole problem reduces to the fact that, because the capital market is so small, if the government wants incentives to be appropriate, it has to set the level of these incentives itself without receiving signals from the market. In a second-best world, although the government was unable to locate the market-clearing price precisely, it might at least try to encourage savings and investment by increasing returns through tax policy (providing either broad-based or selective incentives) or by favoring certain projects through credit policy.

Tax policies to mobilize saving are intended to work by increasing the return to future consumption—either to savings in general or to savings held in a specific form. Under most tax systems, savings are taxed twice, first when total income is taxed, whether it is consumed or saved, and then again when savings generate interest. It has been argued[3] that if this discrimination were to be lifted or lessened, total savings would rise. The scope for increasing saving in this way extends as far as the extreme case where only expenditure is taxed.[4] Likewise, if the penalty for saving were lighter on some forms of assets than others, people would tend to shift into those assets.

The policy recommendations which follow from this argument range from broad-based proposals to convert present income taxes into personal taxes on consumption expenditure or into a value-added tax on the basis

---

[3]For example, as discussed in McLure (1980).

[4]Since it is possible to subsidize investment through making the cost of capital negative, it might also be possible for the government to subsidize saving through a direct subsidy on interest income. However, discussion of the use of tax policy to encourage saving usually envisages a movement to a pure consumption tax but not beyond it.

of consumption, to highly specific tax incentives, such as altering the tax treatment of social security contributions.[5] On the one hand, it is notable that broad-based incentives have not been widely used: of 96 countries surveyed for the 1983 edition of Coopers and Lybrand's *International Tax Summaries*, only Vanuatu, the Turks and Caicos Islands, and The Bahamas had well-developed sales taxes in lieu of income taxes. The fact that no country employing a value-added tax used it to replace an income tax suggests that revenue-raising characteristics (and perhaps distributional characteristics) are deemed to be far more important than any gains in aggregate savings.

On the other hand, many countries exempt interest income derived from certain assets or institutions; some countries exempt all dividend income or certain types of dividend income; and some countries' tax policies favor retained earnings. For instance, interest on various types of bank deposits is exempt from taxation in Argentina, Guatemala, Iran, the Republic of Korea, Malta, Panama, and Paraguay; and financial company and/or investment company income is tax exempt in Argentina, Cyprus, the Dominican Republic, the Netherlands Antilles, and Panama. Housing is favored by the exemption of building society income (in Dominica, South Africa, Swaziland, and Venezuela) and mortgage bank income (in the Dominican Republic). Saving in illiquid, low-risk, low-return forms is encouraged by exemptions or deductions on life insurance or provident fund contributions (in India and Malaysia), the income of insurance companies (in the Netherlands Antilles), and income from pension funds (in the Federal Republic of Germany and Nigeria). Dividends are favored in different ways (which entail different distortions): by exempting from tax the dividends of new companies in France, intercorporational dividends in India, dividends paid to foreigners in the Republic of Korea, and new equity derived from retained earnings in Indonesia. Governments may also try to increase nonbank government financing by exempting interest and gains from government securities (as in Argentina, Panama, South Africa, Swaziland, and Venezuela). Other specific savings incentives are more unusual: for example, Brazil requires employers to put 8 percent of employees' salaries (above social security contributions) into untaxed bank accounts in the names of the employees. In Brazil also (as in the Netherlands Antilles, Norway, Portugal, and Sweden), certain companies' reserves (usually designated formally for future purchases of capital) are not taxed. Brazil further exempts the income of corporations (up to 25 percent of the corporations' total tax liability) if it is invested in the Fundo de Investimentos da Amazônia (FINAM)—the financial organization responsible for developing the Amazon region. More generally, if people are assumed to

---

[5]The effect of this policy has been simulated by Becker and Fullerton (1980).

derive utility from making bequests, it might also be argued that countries which do not levy an inheritance tax are favoring saving compared with countries which impose such taxes.

1. Microeconomic Consequences of Tax Incentives

a. Income and Substitution Effects

The reluctance to apply broad-based savings incentives perhaps stems from the recognition that "even if a change in tax policy would increase welfare by reducing discrimination against capital accumulation, it does not follow that its adoption would result in more saving."[6] This is so because a reduction in the return to saving through a capital income tax has both an income effect and a substitution effect. The increase in the relative cost of saving makes individuals prefer present consumption to saving (and, therefore, to future consumption). However, the tax-induced drop in the rate of return is equivalent to a drop in the lifetime income the individual can realize. If the individual desires to spread his consumption evenly over his lifetime, he will have to maintain a higher level of saving, in light of the increased cost of saving, than he would otherwise have chosen; indeed, he may find he has to save more than he did before, in order to maintain a stable (though reduced) consumption pattern. Summers (1981) notes a further effect arising from the imposition of a tax if it reduces the rate of interest. As the rate of interest falls, the present value of future earnings rises (because it becomes more costly to substitute savings out of present income for future income in order to sustain future consumption). Thus, lifetime income—that is, present and future earnings—rises somewhat to offset the reduction caused by the income effect.

Given these effects, a reduction in the distortion caused by the tax will have an ambiguous result. Since we cannot, a priori, tell whether capital income taxes will decrease or increase saving, we cannot predict whether the removal of that distortion will move people into saving because it becomes relatively more profitable, or out of saving because, given the higher return to saving, they need to save less than before to maintain the level of consumption they had planned for the rest of their lives.[7]

b. Interest Elasticity of Saving

From the discussion above, it is apparent that there is no strong theoretical reason why savings incentives should increase aggregate savings.

---

[6] McLure (1980), p. 311.

[7] This argument has abstracted from business saving, which is, of course, a large part of total saving. However, life-cycle utility-maximizing individuals will buy and sell equity in firms in order to maintain their desired consumption patterns. Thus, the ability and desire of the firm to save will ultimately be determined by the same income and substitution effects which dictate individual saving responses.

The question becomes an empirical one — whether, in reality, the savings-increasing relative price change (the substitution effect) is bigger than the savings-decreasing income change. This combined effect is measured by the uncompensated interest elasticity of saving. There exists a sizable literature in which attempts are made to estimate this elasticity. Unfortunately, most of these estimates have been made for industrial countries. It may be argued, however, that the better-functioning capital markets in these countries would allow a more responsive flow of funds following an interest rate change, compared with countries where the capital market suffers from the defects described earlier. Thus, interest elasticity estimates for industrial countries could serve as upper-bound indicators of interest elasticity estimates in developing countries. Boadway ((1984), p. 313) cites several studies which found saving to be more or less insensitive to changes in interest rates. This finding is borne out by repeated time-series results on the proportionality of the long-run consumption function. Boskin (1978) calculated an interest elasticity of saving of 0.4 for the United States, but this estimate has been considered a higher limit and subsequent studies have strongly questioned his calculations. For instance, Howrey and Hymans (1978) found that no definition of saving (loanable funds, flow of funds, or national income accounts) showed a significant interest rate effect. While their results have, in turn, been criticized, subsequent studies for specific middle- and low-income countries continued to show either an insignificant relationship between the interest rate and saving or a very small positive elasticity.[8]

It must also be remembered that, even if there is a positive interest elasticity of saving, it will not be of significance for policy if the change in the interest rate necessary to effect significant changes in saving, welfare, and output is too large. The small size of the estimated interest elasticities suggests that the required interest rate changes would be costly. Even Boskin's estimate of a 0.4 elasticity would imply that a 2.5 percent increase in interest rates would be necessary to engender a 1 percent increase in total savings. In low- and middle-income countries (including China, India, and oil exporters) an optimistic estimate of the ratio of gross domestic savings to gross domestic product (GDP) in 1982 (according to the World Bank's *World Development Report, 1984*) would be 20 percent. Thus, to raise S/GDP by 1 percentage point, it would be necessary to change the real after-tax interest rate by $(1/0.2) \cdot (1/0.4)$ percent — that is, by 12.5 percent. This strong result is indirectly supported by the results of Mackenzie's (1982) simulation model, which was calibrated for U.S. data. It estimated the changes in output that could be expected after various combined wage and saving tax changes under different labor supply elas-

---

[8]See International Monetary Fund (1983) for a discussion.

ticities and interest elasticity of saving scenarios. Mackenzie found that if the tax rate on saving were reduced by 50 percent at the same time labor income taxes were reduced by 20 percent, then, in an economy with an interest elasticity of saving of 0.4 and a unitary labor supply elasticity, output would increase by only an average of 0.12 percent per annum during the first ten years after the policy change. If the labor income tax had not been reduced, then presumably the effect on output of a change in interest income tax would have been weaker.

In sum, given the small and uncertain magnitude of interest rate effects on savings and output (as indicated in economic theory, because income and substitution effects at least partially offset each other, and as indicated in empirical work by the lack of evidence of a strong interest elasticity of savings), the other potential uses of interest rates as policy instruments, and the international constraints imposed on interest rate determination in open economies, it is not surprising that governments have not often attempted to influence aggregate savings directly through changes in the rate of interest.

Studies for industrial countries suggest, however, that the composition of savings can be affected significantly when incentives to hold wealth in various assets differ.[9] Unfortunately, these studies are not applicable to developing countries, where the desired change in assets is not between different financial assets but between financial assets as a whole, on the one hand, and "nonloanable funds" assets, on the other. As described in the previous section, the premiums placed on nonfinancial assets because of their liquidity value or their nonpecuniary benefits may not be eliminated by marginal changes in the returns to financial assets. Thus, there exists little statistical evidence of success in overcoming these seemingly qualitative differences between financial and nonfinancial assets in developing countries.

Hence, while the specialized incentives listed above, which are undertaken in a sizable number of countries, may succeed in changing the form of the financial assets in which savings are held, they do not properly address the problem of attracting a larger supply of loanable funds from nonfinancial stores of wealth.

c. Distortions Created by Tax Incentives

Even if tax incentives to save did generate a large response in the quantity of savings, it would not necessarily follow that the government should use them as policy instruments to increase aggregate financial savings, because the distortions inherent in them might not be less detrimental to economic welfare than heavier taxes; this would be true whether or not

---

[9]See, for example, Hills (1984) and Saunders and Klau (1985), pp. 177ff.

savings were affected. Any tax on savings distorts the choice between present and future consumption. As discussed, for example, in Becker and Fullerton (1980), the distortions are worsened when different types of savings are taxed at different rates, because if after-tax rates of return are equalized across different types of savings, then, given non-uniform tax rates, the pretax return to each type of asset must be different. This distorts the flow of funds into each type of asset. This is why incentives to change the *composition* of savings are effective, but if the government wishes only to alter the level of savings, a system of specific tax incentives, implying many different tax rates, may lower welfare more than a heavier, but uniform tax system. The problem is exacerbated in developing countries, where misperceptions and lack of information about the real rates of return to various assets (owing, for example, to their nonpecuniary benefits) make it very difficult to set tax incentives to achieve desired directions and magnitudes of portfolio adjustment.

Some specific examples of distorting tax incentives would be the removal of interest receipts from the personal tax base—which would encourage firms to use debt financing and distort the debt-equity choice unless dividend income were also exempted—and vice versa. The exclusion of capital gains from taxation creates an economic distortion, in that it mainly raises the rate of return to corporate income and thus may change the institutional structure of an economy. Besides, the administrative costs involved in a highly differentiated tax structure are much higher than when the tax rate is uniform and exemptions minimal.

A further distortionary effect is present even in broad-based incentives to save: incentives lead to a less progressive tax structure if the rich have a greater propensity to save than the poor.

One argument often made in favor of tax incentives is that they alleviate some of the distortionary effects of inflation on the tax system. Becker and Fullerton (1980) show that, in inflationary circumstances, effective tax rates will be much higher than statutory rates; and, the lower the tax rate, the smaller the differential between the two rates. Thus, McLure (1980) is able to demonstrate that the greatest welfare gains from saving incentives come through offsetting the inflation-induced boost in effective tax rates. However, this argument ignores two common characteristics of developing countries which would vitiate the effects of saving incentives. First, inflation, particularly at the high rates often observed in developing countries, is difficult to predict. As Sanchez-Ugarte ((1985), p.16) concludes (in a discussion primarily directed at investment incentives, but with wider applicability), "Tax incentives have to be announced in advance, which gives a large margin for error favoring either investors or the government. Correcting the income tax for inflation, rather than using tax incentives, results in less distortion and is less costly."

Second, financial repression is very common in developing countries,[10] so that their real interest rates may be very low or negative and loanable funds may consequently be in such short supply that investment is constrained by a rationing of finance.[11] Because interest rates are not free to rise with inflation, the effective tax rate is not boosted by inflation, as it would be in a free-market economy, and, therefore, there is no increased distortion from the effect of the inflation component of the interest rate that a reduction in tax rates on the nominal interest rate could offset. Thus, the "inflation" argument in favor of tax incentives for saving is not valid in a financially repressed economy. Indeed, Ebrill ((1984), p. 13) makes the point that "the distortion to savings decisions implied by the existence of financial repression may be far larger than that associated with the fact that interest income is subject to income tax." Given an interest rate ceiling, financial repression increases as inflation increases. Therefore, a more appropriate goal for a government which wishes to increase saving would be to use tax policy to prevent inflation, instead of trying to offset inflation indirectly by using incentives which have the effect of (very imprecisely) indexing some selected returns to inflation.

To summarize, neither the theory of savings behavior nor the empirical evidence on the response of saving to changes in its rate of return supports the use of tax incentives as an instrument to increase financial saving. Besides, tax incentives create economic distortions which may leave the economy worse off than it would be under the distortions of a uniform tax system.

2. Macroeconomic Consequences of Tax Incentives

In order to obtain a comprehensive evaluation of the results of using incentive policies to promote aggregate savings and investment, it is not enough to assess the direct effects the specific tax incentives may have, and the distortions they may impose, on particular sectors of the economy; it is also crucial to take into consideration their macroeconomic consequences. Tax incentives involve, in most cases, the loss of actual and/or potential fiscal revenues and, therefore, they are bound to have direct budgetary implications. Such a loss of revenue will require either an increase in some other source of income or a commensurate cut in government expenditures. Without either action, a budgetary gap, which would require additional financing resources, will remain. In other words, the implementation of a policy based on the granting of tax incentives may result in either the need to increase other taxes and/or reduce government expenditures, or in a budget deficit.

---

[10]See, for example, International Monetary Fund (1983).

[11]This is the McKinnon-Shaw hypothesis, as described by Ebrill ((1984), p. 10), and tested by Molho ((1985), especially p. 22).

It is thus very difficult, and to some extent misleading, to assess the outcome of tax incentives when they are considered in isolation. It is necessary to have information on the additional measures the government will adopt in order to carry out the incentive policy. If existing taxes are increased or new taxes are imposed, it is necessary to evaluate their impact on the overall economy, and their consequences for savings and investment, before a complete picture of the tax incentives' effects can be obtained. The same applies to cuts in expenditures. If, on the one hand, in order to enable the government to establish a tax-incentive system, it becomes necessary to cut government expenditures which have been complementary to private sector investment, the overall positive effect of the tax incentives may be extremely small. If, on the other hand, the expenditure cuts are in areas related mainly to government consumption, the effectiveness of tax incentives may actually be enhanced.[12]

When, however, no measures are actually taken to compensate for the loss of revenue, a program of tax incentives will definitely result in budget imbalances, the effects of which can only be assessed if information about the financing of such imbalances can be obtained. In general, it is possible to say that fiscal deficits tend to put pressure on aggregate demand, which, in turn, may result in higher inflation, balance of payments disequilibrium, and—if deficits are debt financed—in higher real interest rates and the crowding out of the private sector. It is evident that all these results will have detrimental effects on the investment and saving process.

If tax incentives ultimately lead to an acceleration in the inflationary process, this outcome may cancel, to a large extent, the benefits to the private sector which are intended to arise from the tax-incentive program. There are a number of channels through which high and accelerating inflation may discourage saving and investment. In the first place, inflationary situations tend to involve higher perceived risk and uncertainty. Such an environment is generally not conducive to dynamic and sustained investment and saving.

High rates of inflation are often accompanied by falls in economic activity or, at least, in the growth rate, and these tend to reduce the incentive to invest.[13] High rates of inflation also tend to be accompanied by a progressive overvaluation of the exchange rate. This eventually leads to a scarcity of foreign exchange which subsequently reduces imports of basic commodities. Imports are initially encouraged by the overvaluation of the exchange rate but are subsequently discouraged by the reduced availability of foreign exchange, which inevitably brings about import controls.

---

[12]See Section IV on this issue.
[13]For a discussion, see Tanzi and Blejer (1985).

Sooner or later, domestic firms find that they cannot function at the previous level because of a lack of basic materials which they used to import. This leads to unemployment, falling profits, and, consequently, lower investment.

In addition, a high rate of inflation is always accompanied by an increase in the variance of relative prices. As the rate of inflation becomes progressively higher, the variance of relative prices increases. This increases uncertainty about sectoral allocation and discourages investment or, at least, leads it into less efficient channels. It is widely held that inflation leads to the predominance of financial decisions over technological or cost-reducing ones, which results in a reduction in savings available for productive capital formation.

Another effect of inflation is the attempt by the government to suppress it by controlling the growth of some prices, particularly exchange and interest rates. Intentional overvaluation of the exchange rate tends to depress the availability of savings for domestic uses, since individuals come to expect large devaluations at some future dates and will thus be attracted by the alternative of holding foreign securities and foreign exchange. This is so-called currency substitution, or the substitution, in people's portfolios, of foreign-issued liabilities for domestically denominated ones, thus diverting domestic resources from financing domestic investments. With respect to interest rate controls, in many cases they lead to the emergence of negative real rates, depressing savings and worsening the currency-substitution problem.

IV. An Alternative Strategy: The Government as Saver

1. Generation of a Surplus

In view of the microeconomic and macroeconomic costs of tax incentives, it seems reasonable to search instead for savings-mobilization policies which do not lead to fiscal imbalances. As has been discussed in the first section, the most serious barrier to the attainment of an appropriate savings level in developing countries seems to be rooted in the lack of a properly working capital market including well-developed financial intermediaries. As an alternative to specific tax incentives, the government can alleviate some of the shortcomings associated with developing country capital markets by constructing some sort of proxy for the financial market. This would provide an argument for a planned *budgetary surplus*. In other words, the government should aim to set its total tax revenues and its total expenditures (both current and capital) at levels that would yield an overall surplus, which could then be made available, on a competitive and nonconcessionary basis, to the private sector as well as to public enterprises. This would provide the government with a powerful and flexible tool that would facilitate, to a considerable extent, the efficient allocation of private investment. That such an approach may succeed is shown by the Japanese experiences in the decade after the Meiji Restoration (1868) and in the period following World War II. Under such an approach, the availability of credit financed by surpluses in the government budget is seen as an integral part of fiscal policy. But, unlike incentives and controls, it puts in the hands of the government an instrument that is exceedingly flexible, through which resources can be directed toward productive investments carried out by foreign and domestic private entrepreneurs and toward investments with high social significance. In this way, the government, in addition to increasing savings, would stimulate entrepreneurship, attract foreign resources, and thus affect not just the quantity but also the quality of investment. The generation of a government surplus, because of the level of governmental economic commitment and discipline it demonstrates, tends to enhance the confidence of the private sector. This confidence, in turn, stabilizes or boosts aggregate demand and thus maintains the size of the tax base and legitimizes the tax collection that caused the surplus in the first place. A tax system which is uniform and predictable, and which is associated with prudent macroeconomic management, may make higher rates more acceptable than they would be in a tax system with many exemptions that is associated with a fiscal position perceived to be unsustainable in the longer run.

Several surveys carried out in many developing countries have shown beyond any doubt that lack of foreign investment and the inability of many enterprises and individuals to obtain credit are serious obstacles to development. It is therefore probable that *credit* incentives would be extremely useful, especially for the creation of new enterprises. Although *tax* incentives may also play a role, they are likely to be less effective in the overall economy. On the one hand, tax incentives, by increasing the liquidity of established enterprises, may facilitate their development, but they normally do not provide very much help to start-up enterprises which do not have access to funds needed for an initial fixed investment. Credit incentives, on the other hand, have an impact in both areas.

As stressed by Tanzi (1976), credit incentives financed by surpluses in the government budget should be a crucial component of fiscal policy in developing economies—a component which has not received the attention it deserves. Moreover, such a course of action puts in the hands of the government an instrument to promote savings and investments which does not suffer from the main shortcomings of tax incentives.

2. Role of Government Investment

The recommendation that the government run an overall surplus and place the funds generated by this surplus in the private capital market does not mean that the government itself should cease to act as an investor. The level of aggregate savings and their channeling into productive uses will tend to be positively related to the expected rate of return on the available investments. Given this, it is possible to postulate that the government could increase domestic savings by undertaking actions which increase the perceived rate of return on private sector investments. One way of doing this would be to invest directly in projects which would result in positive externalities to the private sector.

It is a well-accepted proposition that in developing countries private and public investment are related, although there is considerable uncertainty about whether, on balance, public sector investment raises or lowers private investment. In broad terms, public sector investment can cause crowding out if it utilizes scarce physical and financial resources that would otherwise be available to the private sector, or if it produces marketable output that competes with private output. Yet public investment that is related to infrastructure and the provision of public goods can also clearly be complementary to private investment. Public investment of this type can enhance the possibilities for increasing the expected rate of return on private investment by raising the productivity of capital, increasing the demand for private output by increasing demand for inputs and ancillary services, and augmenting overall resource availability by expanding aggregate output and savings.

The overall effect of public investment on private investment will, therefore, depend on the relative strength of these various effects, and there is no a priori reason to believe that they are necessarily substitutes or complements. In a recent study,[14] a private investment function was derived which took into account the effects of government policies, particularly on financial credit and government capital formation. The study attempted to make an empirical distinction between public investment related to the development of infrastructure and other types of public investment which may, in fact, substitute for private capital formation. Empirical results indicate that (i) if the flow of domestic credit available to the private sector were reduced for whatever reason, including greater absorption of credit by the public sector to finance budget deficits, then private investment, and consequently economic growth prospects, would tend to decline; and (ii) an increase in the infrastructural component of government direct investment would raise private investment (probably by increasing its potential profitability), but similar increases in other

---

[14]See Blejer and Khan (1984).

types of public investment (e.g., in sectors producing marketable output) would appear to crowd out, and therefore reduce, private sector investment.

Therefore, saying that the government should run an overall surplus is not equivalent to precluding a role for the government as investor. However, its investment should be undertaken primarily to mobilize further domestic resources through the more effective use of existing resources.

V. Conclusion

The limitations which characterize developing country capital markets make traditional government policies, and tax incentives in particular, unsuitable for mobilizing domestic savings. Not only does their efficacy remain unproven—at the theoretical, as well as the empirical, level—but they also create distortions and budgetary and other macroeconomic problems which may leave the economy worse off than it would be under a uniform and stable tax system with higher rates. Prudent macroeconomic management and the maintenance of a public sector surplus will not only avoid these distortions but also provide a pool of loanable-funds savings to private sector investors; this will compensate for limitations in the capital market which the private sector could not overcome on its own. Thus, the generation of public sector savings is a fitting role for government in a developing country.

References

Becker, C., and D. Fullerton, "Income Tax Incentives to Promote Saving," *National Tax Journal* (Columbus, Ohio), Vol. 33 (September 1980), pp. 331-51.

Blejer, Mario I., and Mohsin S. Khan, "Government Policy and Private Investment in Developing Countries," *Staff Papers*, International Monetary Fund (Washington), Vol. 31 (June 1984), pp. 379-403.

Boadway, R.W., and D.E. Wildasin, *Public Sector Economics*, 2nd ed. (Boston: Little, Brown, 1984).

Boskin, M.J., "Taxation, Saving, and the Rate of Interest," *Journal of Political Economy* (Chicago), Vol. 86 (April 1978), pp. S3-S27.

Coase, R., "The Problem of Social Cost," *Journal of Law and Economics* (Chicago), Vol. 3 (October 1960), pp. 1-44.

Coopers and Lybrand, *International Tax Summaries, 1983* (New York: John Wiley and Sons, 1983).

Ebrill, Liam P., "The Effects of Taxation on Labor Supply, Savings, and Investment in Developing Countries: A Survey of the Empirical Literature" (unpublished, International Monetary Fund, April 3, 1984).

Hills, J., *Savings and Fiscal Privilege* (London: Institute for Fiscal Studies, 1984).

Howrey, E.P., and S.H. Hymans, "The Measurement and Determination of Loanable Funds Saving," *Brookings Papers on Economic Activity: 3* (1978), The Brookings Institution (Washington), pp. 655-705.

International Bank for Reconstruction and Development, *World Development Report, 1984* (New York: Oxford University Press, 1984).

International Monetary Fund, *Interest Rate Policies in Developing Countries: A Study by the Research Department of the International Monetary Fund,* IMF Occasional Papers, No. 22 (Washington, 1983).

Mackenzie, George A., "The Macroeconomic Supply Effects of Tax Rate Changes" (unpublished, International Monetary Fund, December 30, 1982).

McLure, Charles E., Jr., "Taxes, Saving and Welfare: Theory and Evidence," *National Tax Journal* (Columbus, Ohio), Vol. 33 (September 1980), pp. 311-20.

Molho, Lazaros E., "Interest Rates, Saving and Investment in Developing Countries: A Re-examination of the McKinnon-Shaw Hypotheses" (unpublished, International Monetary Fund, October 7, 1985).

Sanchez-Ugarte, Fernando, "A Supply-Side Look at Tax Incentives: Definition, Design, and Selection Criteria of Efficient Tax Incentives" (unpublished, International Monetary Fund, June 5, 1985).

Saunders, P., and F. Klau, "The Role of the Public Sector: Causes and Consequences of the Growth of Government," *OECD Economic Studies,* No. 4 (Spring 1985).

Summers, L.H., "Capital Taxation and Accumulation in a Life Cycle Growth Model," *American Economic Review* (Nashville, Tennessee), Vol. 71 (September 1981), pp. 533-44.

Tanzi, Vito, "Fiscal Policy, Keynesian Economics and the Mobilization of Savings in Developing Countries," *World Development* (Oxford, England), Vol. 4 (October-November 1976), pp. 907-17.

_____, and Mario I. Blejer, "Fiscal Policy in an Economy with High Inflation and High Debt," *Anales de la Asociación Argentina de Economía Política: XX Reunión Anual* (Buenos Aires), Vol. 4 (1985), pp. 1423-51.

3

Fiscal Rigidities, Public Debt, and Capital Flight

Alain Ize and Guillermo Ortiz*

I. INTRODUCTION

One of the salient features of the recent debt crisis in several Latin American countries has been the coexistence of inverse capital flows. In particular, while the proceeds of public external borrowing were flowing in, private capital was flowing out, as domestic investors made massive switches from domestic financial assets into foreign assets.[1] Since domestic public debt was generally quite substantial, a large proportion of these domestic assets were government obligations. Thus, while domestic creditors were reducing their exposure to public debt, foreign creditors were increasing theirs.

One explanation for this portfolio substitution is the asymmetrical information available to economic agents: domestic creditors predicted a crisis well before foreign bankers. Although this argument is probably not completely devoid of empirical relevance, it hinges on the existence of substantial long-run irrationality, as this phenomenon occurred over several years and on a scale that should have eventually attracted the attention of the international banking community and led it to revise its lending operations much earlier.

There exists, however, a fully rational way to justify these seemingly contradictory capital flows. It involves asymmetric risk, rather than

*This paper was first published in the June 1987 issue of International Monetary Fund *Staff Papers*. Useful comments by Mario I. Blejer and Masahiro Kawai are gratefully acknowledged.

[1]This phenomenon has puzzled many observers of the Latin American scene. See, in particular, Díaz Alejandro (1984) and Sachs (1984 a). Another type of asymmetry in capital flows, private capital flowing out at the same time the proceeds of private external borrowing were flowing in, is analyzed in Khan and Ul Haque (1985).

asymmetric information. The debt crisis corresponded, in many cases, to a fiscal crisis in which governments were faced with the prospect of not being able to keep servicing their debts, domestic or foreign, as fiscal rigidities prevented a sufficiently rapid adjustment of the budget deficit, following, in particular, the occurrence of large external shocks and fast-rising external debts. In this situation, perceived risks of default on government obligations grew rapidly. However, while a declared default on foreign obligations is a major step which entails large potential costs to the borrowing country,[2] it is much easier to default in all but name on domestic debt: all this requires is a discrete devaluation which, by raising the price level, erodes the real value of domestic debt. Faced with an asymmetry of exposure between domestic and foreign debt, domestic wealth holders are likely to be the first to pull the trigger on the debt crisis because they perceive themselves as "junior" creditors.[3] Furthermore, if domestic assets can be taxed, private capital flight can be encouraged by public foreign borrowing, because the government may be perceived as counting on revenue from domestic asset taxation to service its higher foreign debt in the future. Paradoxically, a country committed to servicing its external obligations can thus be more prone to capital flight, as domestic creditors suspect that the government may be able to maintain external debt servicing only by taxing domestic assets.

The notion that investors shift away from domestic assets to avoid inflation taxes brought about by fiscal disequilibrium underlies the whole literature on speculative attacks.[4] However, the origins and implications of the weak fiscal stance of the government have seldom been explored, since the analysis has been generally limited to the consideration of an "excessive" rate of credit creation, with money the only asset explicitly considered. From the existing literature it is particularly difficult to understand why governments do not implement timely corrective measures to prevent a balance of payments crisis. Nor, in spite of the arguments given above, is it clear why the public does not acquire domestic bonds,

[2]See Sachs (1984 b) and Eaton, Gersovitz, and Stiglitz (1986).

[3]Empirical support for that hypothesis can be found in Dooley (1986). This study finds, on the basis of a cross-section sample of eight countries, that capital flight is inversely related to the risk premium on external debt and, therefore, to the differential risk faced by residents and nonresidents.

[4]See the seminal contributions in Salant and Henderson (1978) and Krugman (1979). More recent contributions include Flood and Garber (1984); Obstfeld (1984 a and b); Connolly and Taylor (1984); and, in the case of Mexico, Blanco and Garber (1986). Sweder van Wijnbergen (1986) independently developed a model, which is somewhat similar to ours, relating fiscal rigidities to asset taxes and capital flows, while Dooley and Isard (1986) present a general conceptual framework that derives asset demands under risk of asset taxation and analyzes their macroeconomic impact in a two-country framework.

which could be as good an inflation hedge as foreign bonds and may be closer substitutes for domestic money. Ex ante, exchange risk is not a satisfactory explanation, since the interest premium on domestic bonds could fully adjust to discount expected movements in the exchange rate. Moreover, in some countries, domestic banks have been offering dollar-denominated deposits.

To justify capital flight and the preference for foreign over domestic instruments, it seems more appropriate, then, to generalize the risk factor associated with the overall financial solvency of the public sector to all domestic public debt—not only to money. The government's weak fiscal stance, which may force it to impose an inflation tax, could also induce it to reduce domestic debt servicing on bonds.

If prices are not perfectly flexible, a country may also experience the exchange rate overshooting that is often the product of balance of payments crises, such as the one experienced by Mexico in 1982. With price inertia, domestic debt servicing cannot be instantaneously reduced through a devaluation-induced jump in the price level. It can, however, be reduced through a fall in the domestic real interest rate, which is possible, even with interest rate parity, if, following an initial depreciation, the real exchange rate gradually appreciates over time, reducing the return on foreign bonds in terms of domestic currency. An expectational equilibrium is thus generated, as the public's fear of lower returns on domestic assets leads it to shift into foreign instruments, provoking an overshooting that enables the authorities to lower domestic interest rates without violating interest rate parity.

In this paper, we develop simple models to clarify these issues, using the recent experience of Mexico as an illustration. Section II relates the occurrence of speculative attacks to the solvency of the public sector in an economy with interest-bearing debt and perfect price flexibility but imperfect asset substitution. In a departure from the usual speculative-attacks literature, endogenous lending ceilings are derived which are fully consistent with the behavior of both domestic and foreign creditors. Section III explores exchange rate dynamics and overshooting phenomena in the opposite case of price inertia and perfect asset substitution. Section IV illustrates the results of the analysis using Mexico's recent experience, and the final section offers concluding comments.

II. Public Debt and Capital Flight

Consider an economy in which prices are perfectly flexible and purchasing power parity (PPP) holds continuously, so that the real exchange rate equals one. The government finances its deficit through domestic and foreign debt. For greater simplicity, real domestic debt is taken as a single composite of money and bonds, b^h, with an average real interest cost r^h. Since b^h is an aggregate and r^h is the real average interest rate, r^h can be negative, even when the real rate on the bond component is positive, if the inflation tax on money balances outweighs the real interest rate paid on bonds.[5] With the domestic price index as a deflator, except for the real foreign debt, b^w, and the real interest rate, r^f, which are expressed in terms of foreign prices—the real budget restriction of the public sector can be written as

$$g + r^h b^h + r^f b^w = t + \dot{b}^h + \dot{b}^w \tag{1}$$

where dotted variables are time derivatives and g and t—real expenditures and taxes, respectively—are assumed to be fixed, reflecting fiscal weaknesses. Residents hold both domestic and foreign assets, but foreigners do not hold domestic assets. Consider the portfolio equilibrium condition

$$b^h = \lambda b^f \exp \sigma[r^h - r^f] \tag{2}$$

where b^f represents privately held foreign bonds and σ the semielasticity of substitution between home and foreign assets. Define

$$W = b^h + b^f \tag{3}$$

as real private financial wealth. Using equations (2) and (3), we can express the total interest bill on public sector debt for a given level of private wealth as[6]

$$R = r^f b^w + \left[r^f + \frac{1}{\sigma} \log \frac{b^h}{\lambda(W - b^h)} \right] b^h \tag{4}$$

---

[5]Conversely, r^h could become negative, even with no inflation, if domestic bonds were sufficiently imperfect substitutes for foreign bonds. In practice, however, the margin for imposing a pure interest tax on bonds without additional inflation is likely to be limited, first, because nominal rates must be positive and this constraint rapidly becomes binding unless the initial inflation rate is already high and, second, because the degree of substitutability between foreign and domestic bonds may be high. Hence, higher inflation can be expected to be the main vehicle of asset taxation, both because it directly erodes money balances and because it allows for negative real interest rates on bonds.

[6]Real wealth is assumed to be constant. Although a discrete devaluation does, in fact, reduce wealth, nothing of substance would be changed by incorporating changes in wealth into the analysis.

Equation (4) may be rewritten as

$$R = r^f(b^w + b^h) - \phi(b^h, \sigma)$$

(5)

where

$$\phi = \frac{-b^h}{\sigma} \log \frac{b^h}{\lambda(W - b^h)}$$

(6)

As shown on the right-hand side of equation (5), the interest bill can be decomposed into two elements: $r^f(b^w + b^h)$ corresponds to the cost of servicing total public debt at the real world interest rate; the second term, $-\phi$, can be positive or negative depending on portfolio composition. On the one hand, when $b^h > \lambda b^f$, the government must pay a premium on domestic debt and ϕ is negative. On the other hand, when $b^h < \lambda b^f$, ϕ is positive and the government can extract a "tax revenue" on domestic assets.

The ϕ contours shown in Figure 1 have the usual inflation tax shape. Tax revenue from private holdings of domestic debt first rise and then fall as the proportion of these holdings in total private wealth rises. Initially, $\phi(0, \sigma) = 0$; ϕ then rises with b^h, reaches a maximum when $b^h = \bar{b}^h$, and then falls gradually toward $-\infty$ as b^h approaches W. As σ rises, the maximum obtainable tax revenue falls, and ϕ becomes null when σ approaches $+\infty$ (the perfect-asset-substitution case).

The shape of the iso-interest contours, $R(\sigma)$, can then be diagrammed as in Figure 2. For $b^h = 0$, all contours corresponding to the same R intersect the vertical axis at the same point, independently of σ. For a given σ, the contours rise as b^h becomes positive; reach a maximum where $b^h = \hat{b}^h$, the point at which $r^h b^h$ is minimized;[7] then start falling, with their slopes reaching minus one where $b^h = \bar{b}^h$, and toward $-\infty$ as b^h reaches toward W. As σ rises, their curvature decreases; when σ approaches $+\infty$, they become straight lines with slopes of minus one, shown as R^*s in Figure 2.

The government can intervene by borrowing abroad and reducing domestic debt. In Figure 2, this operation moves the economy leftward on a line with a slope of minus one. If assets are perfect substitutes, the total interest bill remains invariant, and the economy moves on the same R^* contour. When σ is finite and assets are imperfect substitutes, a marginal intervention leaves the interest bill unchanged when $b^h > \bar{b}^h$, since the

---

[7]To see this, note that $dR = r^f db^w + d(r^h b^h) = 0$ on an iso-interest contour. The slope is zero when $db^w = 0$, which corresponds to the point where $d(r^h b^h) = 0$, where the asset tax is maximized.

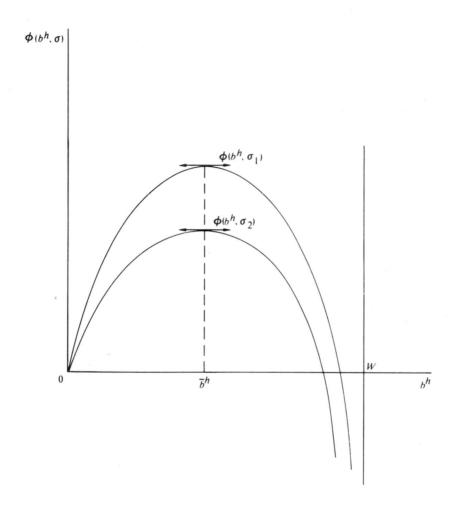

Figure 1. Asset Tax Revenue

slope to the R contour at that point equals minus one. Elsewhere, a change in debt composition alters R. When $b^h > \bar{b}^h$, the asset tax revenue rises when the composition of public debt shifts toward foreign obligations. When $b^h < \bar{b}^h$, the opposite situation occurs.

Consider now the following experiment: Suppose that a permanent negative fiscal shock, $\Delta(t - g) < 0$, hits the economy, while the budget is initially in equilibrium with $\dot{b}^h = \dot{b}^w = 0$. If assets are perfect substitutes,

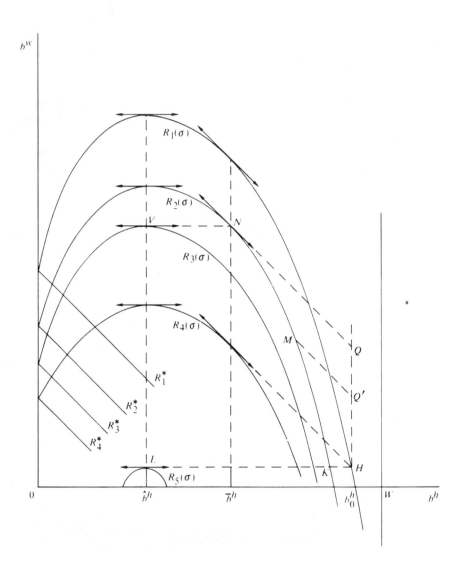

Figure 2. Iso-Interest Contours

an immediate default will be unavoidable, since the total interest bill cannot be altered by intervention. A reduction of the domestic debt burden is more likely to occur than a default on foreign debt, because the former is much simpler to achieve. With perfect price flexibility, all it takes is a discrete devaluation, which, by instantaneously raising the domestic price level, reduces b^h and moves the economy horizontally to the left in Figure 2, until an R^* contour is reached that is low enough to close the fiscal gap.[8]

However, if assets are imperfect substitutes, the imposition of capital losses for domestic wealth owners can be avoided if a change in debt composition can, by itself, reduce R sufficiently. Suppose that the economy is initially on the $R_1(\sigma)$ contour at a point such as H in Figure 2, where $b^h = b_0^h > \bar{b}^h$. At that point, the total interest bill is above its minimum attainable level. A discrete devaluation could reduce the interest bill to R_5, where $R_5(\sigma)$ is the iso-interest contour whose tangent at the point of maximum asset tax revenue (L in Figure 2) passes through H. Alternatively, a debt swap could reduce it to the level R_4, where $R_5 < R_4 < R_1$, and $R_4(\sigma)$ is the lowest interest contour that could be reached by intervention from H. Thus, through devaluation or intervention, the government maintains at that point a margin of solvency. However, asset taxation is unpopular and detrimental to the economy because of its distortionary impact. Since a devaluation-induced capital loss is clearly even less popular, it is easy to understand why a government may prefer to postpone any type of adjustment, particularly a devaluation, for as long as possible. We assume this is the case, which is equivalent to the government having a commitment to a fixed exchange rate rule.

Consider then what happens when a negative fiscal shock hits the budget. If $\Delta(g - t) < (R_1 - R_4)$, the government remains fully solvent and rational creditors, whether domestic or external, should be fully willing to finance the emerging fiscal gap by acquiring new debt. The authorities could then, for example, increase foreign borrowing along a vertical trajectory, from H up to Q, the point from which the minimum iso-interest contour that can be reached is $R_2(\sigma)$, such that $\Delta(g - t) = R_1 - R_2$. To the extent that the government would rather devalue than default on its foreign obligations, and since the R_2 contour could no longer be reached beyond Q through intervention, foreign borrowing beyond Q would eventually require a discrete devaluation to maintain foreign debt servicing. To avoid a certain capital loss, domestic creditors should, at that point, shift from domestic into foreign assets, forcing the government to intervene. Capital flight, financed by a large burst of foreign borrowing, will occur as a result, moving the economy from Q to N.[9]

---

[8]Although it does not have the same legal implications, a discrete unexpected devaluation can be perceived by the public as a partial default on domestic debt, since it amounts to unilaterally changing the terms of an implicit debt contract between the government and private agents.

[9]Similar dynamics would result if the deficit had initially been financed by internal borrowing. In that case, domestic borrowing first rises, and then collapses, as the economy moves back to N following a burst of capital flight.

The new steady-state equilibrium is at N, and the fixed exchange rate rule should be abandoned at that point. To see this, let $R_3(\sigma)$ be the iso-interest contour whose tangent to the point of maximum domestic asset taxation, V in Figure 2, goes through N. Since $R_2 - R_3 > 0$, a margin is still available to service additional borrowing, and foreign lending can, in principle, continue. However, if the government is committed to honoring its foreign obligations, any further external borrowing will require a default on domestic obligations, since the total interest bill can no longer be reduced by reshuffling debt through intervention. Even if there is a one-to-one conversion of new foreign borrowing into capital flight, the total interest bill rises and a jump devaluation remains unavoidable. Thus, any additional external borrowing should give rise to a larger increase in the private demand for foreign assets, as domestic creditors try to protect themselves from a certain capital loss. Since no net additional financing can therefore be obtained,[10] a rational government should, at that point, abandon the fixed exchange rate rule and finance the deficit by means of a higher tax on domestic assets, which would be made possible by the switch in private portfolio composition and the higher rate of depreciation, as documented in the usual speculative-attacks literature. Here, however, the timing of the attack is determined within the model, instead of by an exogenous stock of foreign reserves.

Point N will only be reached by a government that is willing to postpone an exchange rate adjustment, and to keep servicing its foreign debt, whatever the final cost of taxing its domestic obligations. The associated level of inflation or of financial repression can be so high, however, that it forces the government to abandon its exchange rate policy earlier, or to contemplate a partial default on its foreign obligations as a less costly way of closing its financing gap. If this is anticipated by investors, capital flight will occur earlier on the HQ segment, say at Q', when all the desired portfolio substitution from domestic into foreign assets can be carried out before intervention ceases or foreign lending is cut off. The new endpoint on the R_2 contour, M, is associated with a lower level of asset taxation. Depending, therefore, upon the perceived comparative willingness of the government to accept earlier exchange rate adjustment or higher eventual asset taxes, the economy may end up at any point of the KN segment. If the government's intentions are not known, capital flight should gradually accelerate as foreign borrowing increases, since the rising level of asset taxation that will eventually be needed makes a collapse of a pegged exchange rate more and more likely over time, either because the govern-

---

[10]Countries with already-heavy asset taxation may be reluctant to engage in further international borrowing, since the additional foreign debt may be immediately exchanged for domestic debt and converted into deposits abroad.

ment may stop intervening or because foreign creditors may decide on
their own to stop lending.[11] Furthermore, since, in the context of uncertainty, the collapse of the exchange rate regime cannot be perfectly anticipated, a jump devaluation will necessarily occur at the time of the collapse, as documented in the speculative-attacks literature.[12]

III. PRICE INERTIA AND OVERSHOOTING

In the previous model, an immediate adjustment in the debt-servicing
burden following a devaluation could be obtained as a result of an instan-
taneous adjustment of the price level which reduced the real value of domestic debt. However, if prices are not perfectly flexible, adjustment can
only be achieved by reducing the real interest rate. In this section, it will
be shown that real interest rates can be substantially reduced even when
a large share of domestic debt is composed of interest-bearing instruments that are close substitutes for foreign bonds, so that interest rate
parity holds. Real interest rates will fall if a large overshooting of the real
exchange rate is engineered when the nominal exchange rate collapses.

Let P^{h*} be the equilibrium domestic price level obtained when PPP
holds. Setting the foreign price equal to one, $P^{h*} = E$, where E is the
nominal exchange rate. Suppose that P^h adjusts, with some inertia, toward its PPP equilibrium level[13]

$$\frac{\dot{P}^h}{P^h} = \frac{\dot{P}^{h*}}{P^{h*}} + \nu\frac{(P^{h*} - P^h)}{P^h} \tag{7}$$

With P^h as a deflator, equation (7) may be expressed in real terms as

$$\frac{\dot{e}}{e} = \nu(1 - e) \tag{8}$$

where e is the real exchange rate. Since e can differ from 1, the budget

---

[11]The default risk on foreign loans implied here could be assimilated in the sovereign
risk analyzed in the debt repudiation literature. (See Sachs (1984 b).) The benefits from
defaulting that are emphasized here—less inflation and financial repression—are not
usually considered in the literature.

[12]See, in particular, Lizondo (1983) and Flood and Garber (1984).

[13]A more usual adjustment equation would be of the type $\dot{P}^h = \dot{P}^{h*} + \nu(P^{h*} - P^h)$.
However, when converted into real terms, the inflation rate becomes a determinant of
the speed of adjustment. Although this would not alter the analysis in any significant
way, a simpler formulation in real terms was chosen.

restriction needs to be rewritten as

$$g + r^h b^h + r^f e b^w = t + \dot{b}^h + e\dot{b}^w \tag{9}$$

Suppose, finally, that interest rate parity is verified, so that

$$r^h = r^f + \dot{e}/e \tag{10}$$

Then, if we replace r^h from equation (10) and $\dot{e}/e$ from equation (8) with their equivalents, and transpose terms, equation (9) becomes

$$\dot{b}^h = [r^f + \nu(1 - e)]b^h + (r^f b^w - \dot{b}^w)e + g - t \tag{11}$$

Equations (8) and (11) form a differential system in e and b.

Assume that price adjustment is fast enough so that the impact of additional external borrowing on the stock of foreign debt can be ignored. On the one hand, in the phase diagram of Figure 3, equation (8) is simply an inertial adjustment that gives rise to a horizontal equilibrium schedule, ee. On the other hand, the bond equilibrium schedule corresponding to equation (11), bb, is positively sloped around the equilibrium exchange rate if the following condition is satisfied:

$$\nu b^h + (\dot{b}^w - r^f b^w) > 0 \tag{12}$$

In this case, a higher b^h requires a compensating increase in e to maintain the budget in equilibrium. This is because a higher b^h implies greater domestic debt servicing, which can be neutralized in one of two ways: by increasing the value of net public capital inflows caused by a devaluation when $\dot{b}^w - r^f b^w$ is positive; or, by reducing r^h, which is only possible, with interest rate parity, if the exchange rate gradually appreciates after an initial devaluation. The latter effect is validated through price adjustment and applies to the value of domestic debt; this accounts for the first term appearing in condition (12). Suppose then that condition (12) is verified, in particular because price inertia is not too strong, so that the first term in condition (12) outweighs the second when there are net public capital outflows. It can be seen from Figure 3 that the dynamics of adjustment have the saddle-path property.

Suppose now that an unanticipated negative public finance shock—for example, a reduction in the flow of external lending—hits the budget. The bb schedule shifts leftward (Figure 4) and the real exchange rate overshoots before returning slowly to equilibrium. The interpretation is straightforward: The shock reduces the ability of the government to service its domestic debt. The public then shifts toward foreign bonds and the

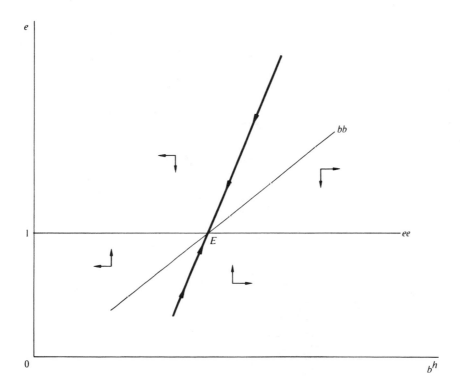

Figure 3. Dynamics of Adjustment in the Price-Inertia Case

nominal exchange rate depreciates, in turn inducing a depreciation of the real exchange rate, since the price level does not jump owing to inertia. The ensuing gradual appreciation of the exchange rate toward equilibrium reduces the return of foreign bonds in domestic-currency terms and — through interest rate parity — the interest rate on domestic bonds, thus allowing for the collection of an interest tax and the adjustment of public finances. As the price level starts rising, real domestic bond balances fall and the domestic interest rate recovers gradually, until bond balances have been reduced to a level that can be serviced at the world interest rate.

Several remarks can be made. First, the overshooting mechanism depicted in Figure 4 is the same as the one in Dornbusch's well-known 1976 paper. However, while in Dornbusch's model interest rate movements are essentially monetary phenomena arising from the monetary equilibrium

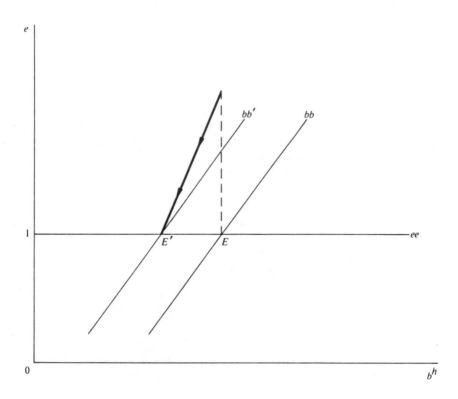

Figure 4. Dynamics of Overshooting

condition, in our model they are purely fiscal manifestations produced by the need to equilibrate the budget restriction of the government. Second, there is a direct relationship between the magnitude of the overshooting and the amount of foreign public debt. As the burden of foreign debt servicing net of new foreign loans increases, the bb schedule becomes steeper and the size of the real exchange rate jump needed to accommodate a fiscal shock increases. When foreign debt is large enough to reverse the sign of condition (12), adjustment through overshooting is no longer feasible with a single exchange rate regime.[14] Third, the adjustment of domestic bond balances to the level that can be serviced by the government at the world interest rate provides a simple theory of private

[14]Overshooting would still work, however, with a dual exchange system, since in that case the burden of foreign debt servicing would not increase when there was a devaluation.

bond portfolio composition if it is extended to a longer-term horizon that includes current account adjustments. In particular, if a certain level of real financial wealth is desired, the public will have to acquire abroad those bonds that cannot be serviced internally. Fiscally weaker countries can thus be expected to have higher shares of foreign bonds in private portfolios. Finally, given that short-term fiscal adjustment requires real exchange rate overshooting if prices are not fully flexible, and given that the more "dollarized" an economy, the smaller will be its taxable base, it is clear that the existence of dollar-denominated domestic bonds tends to be destabilizing because it increases the size of the overshooting. Since the government may elect to default on its domestic dollar debt in order to avoid an excessive jump in the real exchange rate, investors may eventually lose confidence in this type of bond if its share in total domestic debt becomes substantial. This can explain why foreign dollar bonds may be preferred to their domestic counterparts.

IV. THE MEXICAN EXPERIENCE

In order to illustrate the correspondence between the recent Mexican experience and the models outlined above, Table 1[15] gives data on the real public sector deficit for 1978-84 and on the corresponding sources of funds.

The first obvious observation is that public deficit grew steadily from 1978 to 1982, the combined result of runaway public spending and lagging non-oil revenues, with the latter mostly stemming from falling real prices of goods and services produced by state enterprises. Up to 1981, the deficit was financed by rapidly growing oil revenues derived from expanding exports and favorable world prices; by a steady increase in domestic credit, made possible by rapid economic growth; and by a significant tax on both money and bond balances, with the latter facilitated by negative or low foreign real interest rates and by the continuous real appreciation of the peso. From 1978 to 1980, foreign lending to the public sector was largely used to cover interest payments and did not, therefore, constitute a significant financing source.

In 1980, signs of a lack of confidence in the path followed by the Government began to appear. Devaluation expectations, induced by a rapidly appreciating exchange rate, led to a growing dollarization of the economy, as was reflected in the expansion of dollar-denominated domestic debt, which became the main source of domestic finance in 1981. Together with

---

[15]Details on the elaboration of this table can be found in the Appendix.

Table 1. Real Budget Restriction of the Mexican Public Sector, 1978–84

(*In billions of 1978 pesos*)

	1978	1979	1980	1981	1982	1983	1984
Use of funds							
Pre-oil deficit	109	142	236	416	429	83	78
Domestic debt interest	2	−2	14	23	37	30	22
Foreign debt interest	46	56	61	70	158	143	141
Source of funds							
Oil income	27	38	110	122	150	190	171
Inflation tax	17	24	36	36	95	64	42
Interest tax	13	11	47	16	222	65	52
Changes in real money balances	8	18	1	2	−15	−33	−5
Changes in real peso bond balances	18	36	38	51	105	−60	−30
Changes in real dollar bond balances[1]	—	8	20	73	−45	−31	−62
External borrowing	58	65	64	229	132	83	44
Statistical discrepancy	16	−3	−5	−20	−20	−22	29
Memorandum items:							
Capital flight[2]	14	21	68	160	179	105	48
Real exchange rate	22.8	19.3	15.4	12.8	24.0	24.4	18.5
Nominal exchange rate	22.8	22.8	23.2	26.2	148.5	161.3	190.0

Source: Banco de México, *Indicadores Económicos*, various issues. Also see the Appendix of this paper.

[1]Mexdollar balances. For an explanation of how the Mexdollar system worked, see Ortiz (1983).

[2]Computed as errors and omissions plus variation in short-term assets held abroad by residents.

dollarization, capital flight accelerated sharply from 1980 on, reflecting growing doubts about the public sector's ability to honor its domestic debt commitments, both in pesos and in dollars.

The year 1981 marked the turning point in the development of the crisis. The pre-oil primary budget deficit (primary deficit, net of petroleum revenue) continued to explode while oil revenues reached a plateau, mainly because of falling oil prices and the continued appreciation of the peso. Despite substantial growth in domestic credit in real terms, owing to the Mexdollar system, a huge financing gap had to be covered by foreign borrowing, which, in that single year, rose in dollar terms by as much as it had in the previous five years. Simultaneously, capital outflows, as measured by the sum of errors and omissions plus variations in short-term assets held abroad by residents,[16] reached more than $10 billion,

---

[16]There has been a wide debate on the issue of measuring capital flight. See, for example, Dooley (1986). While the definition used here has clear shortcomings, it has the advantage of simplicity.

most of which occurred in the second half of 1981, when the lack of fiscal adjustment, in the face of adverse external shocks, became quite evident.[17]

In 1982, the peak of the crisis, the budget deficit grew even larger, providing another clear indication of fiscal rigidities.[18] The other dominant events were, of course, the interruption of foreign borrowing following a last burst of intense borrowing undertaken to sustain the peso in the face of the large capital outflows observed from March to August; and the final collapse of the Mexdollar system, after a massive loss of investor confidence in Mexdollar bonds. In August, Mexdollars were converted by the Government into pesos at 70 pesos per dollar, while the free exchange rate shot up to 130 pesos at the end of the month. This clearly amounted to a partial default by the state on its domestic dollar obligations.

The ongoing fiscal deficit and the foreign debt crisis created an enormous financial gap, which could not be financed by an increase in real domestic credit, given the exhaustion of the Mexdollar system and the massive capital outflows.[19] A portion of the deficit was financed by higher oil revenues associated with the depreciation of the peso. But even after accounting for oil income, there was still a shortfall of 317 billion pesos in 1982 which had to come, in effect, from taxes on domestic assets. As seen in Table 1, 30 percent of this shortfall was covered by an inflation tax, the rest by a huge interest tax.

---

[17]See Ortiz (1985) for an account of the economic events of this period. Apart from the lack of control over the deficit, another costly mistake of the López Portillo administration was maintaining the nominal value of the peso. In the context of our model, devaluing earlier would have been greatly desirable, because it would have increased the peso revenues obtained from foreign borrowing and oil earnings. For example, a real 50 percent devaluation implemented at the end of 1980 would have raised oil income in 1981 by 61 billion (1978) pesos and reduced the need for foreign debt by more than two thirds in that year, even though the burden of servicing that debt would have increased as a result of the higher exchange rate. By improving government finance, the reduction in foreign indebtedness would, in turn, have helped stabilize the exchange market, as was pointed out earlier in our discussion of the model.

[18]Public spending grew, although the Government had already announced spending cuts on at least three occasions, in July 1981 and in February and April 1982. Its credibility was understandably damaged by those repeated failed attempts. Besides the downward rigidity of expenditures, two other factors help to explain the increase in the deficit: (1) a fall in non-oil tax income owing to the recession, and (2) exchange losses suffered when the Government converted Mexdollar deposits into pesos at a rate of 70 pesos per dollar. The loss was compounded by the Government's nationalization of the banking system, which had been forced to convert dollar loans at 50 pesos per dollar.

[19]Although real peso bond balances grew twice as much in 1982 as they had in the previous year, this was essentially the result of the forced conversion of dollar bonds into pesos. Altogether, money and domestic bonds grew by only 45 billion 1978 pesos, versus 126 billion in 1981.

The years 1983 and 1984 marked the aftermath of the crisis. The Government finally reduced its pre-oil primary deficit from its peak of 429 billion pesos in 1982 to around 80 billion pesos — quite an impressive achievement. But despite the higher oil revenues associated with devaluation, this deficit reduction failed to compensate for the continued deterioration of net foreign capital inflows[20] (−60 billion pesos in 1983 and −97 billion pesos in 1984, down from −26 billion pesos in 1982 and 159 billion pesos in 1981) and for the fall in real domestic credit associated with higher inflation, negative or low growth, and the portfolio reallocation resulting from the public's preference for foreign bonds. Thus, high inflation and interest taxes were still needed; 106 billion pesos were obtained from money, and 117 billion pesos from bonds, during 1983-84.

In order to provide readers with a better appreciation of how these tax revenues were collected, the dynamics of the free exchange rate are shown in Chart 1, which uses the monthly closing date of the peso spot

---

[20]Foreign borrowing less interest on foreign debt.

Chart 1. Real Exchange Rates, 1982–84

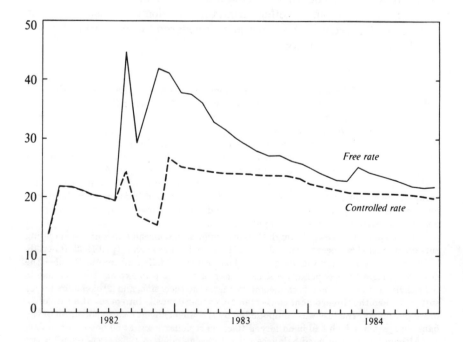

Source: Banco de México, *Indicadores Económicos.* Real exchange rates were obtained by deflating nominal exchange rates with the ratio of Mexican to U.S. consumer price indices.

Chart 2. Real Domestic and Foreign Returns, 1978–84

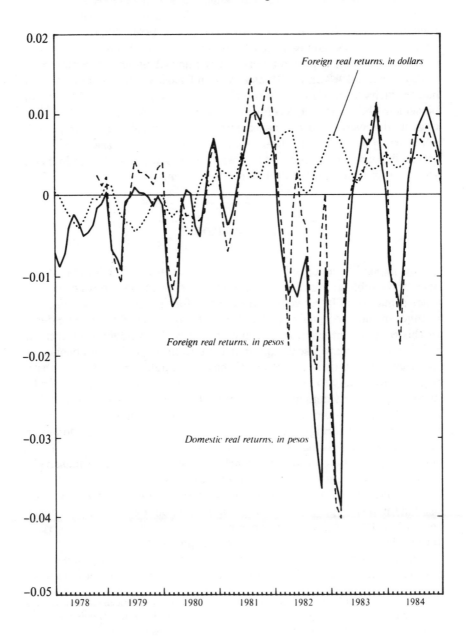

price on the New York foreign exchange market. The chart shows that overshooting reached its peak in August 1982. The free exchange rate then appreciated fairly smoothly until the end of 1984.[21] This gradual appreciation allowed domestic real interest rates to fall below the world rate, to significant negative levels (below minus 1 percent per month) in 1982 and early 1983 and 1984, as shown in Chart 2, which compares real bond returns in Mexico and in the United States during 1978-84. As can be seen in the chart, the foreign real return in dollars was much higher than its domestic peso counterpart in 1982, early 1983, and early 1984, while owing to the expected real appreciation of the peso, the foreign real return in pesos, computed on the basis of the forward exchange market, was broadly comparable to the domestic return.

V. Conclusions

This paper has analyzed the linkages between fiscal rigidities, public debt, and exchange market adjustments. It is based on the concept that asset demands shift between domestic and foreign bonds in response to changes in the perceived ability of the state to service its domestic debt. In this context, internal or external shocks with an adverse impact on public finance create fiscal gaps that have to be filled, in the absence of fiscal adjustment, by taxing domestic holders of public debt. Asset substitution is then likely to give rise to capital flight or to sharp exchange rate movements. It was demonstrated that with imperfect asset substitutability, capital flight could be financed by foreign borrowing. This was a rational outcome if foreign creditors expected the state to tax its domestic creditors in order to maintain foreign debt servicing. In turn, it was rational for domestic creditors to attack the local currency and massively convert their domestic assets into foreign bonds so as to avoid a devaluation-induced default on domestic assets. In contrast to methods used in the usual speculative-attacks literature, debt ceilings fully consistent with rational behavior on the part of both domestic and foreign creditors of the public sector were derived endogenously.

We also showed that exchange rate overshootings are likely to occur in response to unanticipated public finance shocks if prices are not fully flexi-

---

[21]September and October 1982 are out of line owing to an expectational error caused by setting the controlled exchange rate during those months at an unrealistically low level, given the rates of inflation that had prevailed since the previous January. On the other hand, in mid-1984 a small speculative bubble was created by a combination of "bad news" concerning the inertia of inflation and the behavior of oil prices and external interest rates.

ble. Price inflexibility implies that the real value of domestic debt cannot fall instantaneously, so that domestic debt servicing must be reduced through a fall in domestic real interest rates. In turn, with interest rate parity, this reduction can only result from an expected real exchange rate appreciation following an initial discrete devaluation.

We recognize that claims of rational behavior based on underlying fundamentals clearly should not be pushed too far. Nonetheless, our models suggest ways of interpreting the recent Mexican experience that do not rely on sheer speculation and disequilibrium dynamics, and that seem to be reasonably well supported by available evidence from the recent Mexican crisis.

This approach can be extended in a number of directions. Among them, two lines of analysis in particular merit investigation: (1) the introduction of a fully stochastic framework, such as that recently used by Penati and Pennachi (1986) for the monetary model; and (2) the analysis of fiscal rigidities and asset substitution in a richer intertemporal framework, which could integrate issues of credibility and temporal inconsistencies.[22]

APPENDIX

Notes on Table 1: Budget Restriction of the Mexican Public Sector

The data for Table 1 were obtained from various issues of the Bank of Mexico's *Indicadores Económicos.* The public sector deficit figures correspond to the concept of "financial deficit," *less* oil tax income and interest payments. Domestic public debt was obtained as the sum of total domestic credit given by the financial sector to the public sector, *plus* bonds sold directly to the public. Foreign credit was obtained from balance of payments data.[23] Finally, the figure for domestic dollar credit was computed as the flow of dollar credit granted by the financial sector, *less* foreign credit obtained by development banks, since this portion is already accounted for as external credit. From the comparison of the nominal figures, a statistical-discrepancy term was obtained for each year. A further

---

[22]The concept of fiscal weaknesses or fiscal rigidities could perhaps be endogenized. In Ize and Ortiz (1984) and Ize (1985), spending rigidities are related to the set of political pressures the government faces.

[23]Average yearly controlled rates were used to convert balance of payments figures, since it was at those rates that the state sold its foreign currency surplus to the private sector.

separation between money and bonds was obtained by dividing domestic peso credit from banks to the public sector into interest-bearing and non-interest-bearing assets, according to the proportion of M1 into peso liabilities of the financial system.

Figures were then deflated by the yearly average consumer price index. Real interest payments on domestic debt were computed by applying the U.S. real interest rate, obtained by deflating the treasury bill rate using the consumer price index, to the stock of domestic bonds. To permit greater clarity of interpretation, interest payments on foreign debt were kept in nominal terms and taken directly from the balance of payments. In the case of peso credit flows, real increases were obtained by deflating end-of-period nominal balances by the end-of-period price index. The inflation tax on money balances was computed to be consistent with this deflation procedure, and the peso bonds tax was obtained as a residual.

REFERENCES

Blanco, Herminio, and Peter Garber, "Recurrent Devaluation and Speculative Attacks on the Mexican Peso," *Journal of Political Economy* (Chicago), Vol. 94 (February 1986), pp. 148-66.

Connolly, Michael, and Dean Taylor, "The Exact Timing of the Collapse of an Exchange Rate Regime and Its Impact on the Relative Price of Traded Goods," *Journal of Money, Credit and Banking* (Columbus, Ohio), Vol. 16 (May 1984), pp. 194-207.

Díaz Alejandro, Carlos, "Latin American Debt: I Don't Think We Are in Kansas Anymore," *Brookings Papers on Economic Activity: 2* (1984), The Brookings Institution (Washington), pp. 335-403.

Dooley, Michael P., "Country-Specific Risk Premiums, Capital Flight and Net Investment Income Payments in Selected Developing Countries" (unpublished, International Monetary Fund, March 11, 1986).

_____, and Peter Isard, "Tax Avoidance and Exchange Rate Determination" (unpublished, International Monetary Fund, January 2, 1986).

Dornbusch, Rudiger, "Expectations and Exchange Rate Dynamics," *Journal of Political Economy* (Chicago), Vol. 84 (December 1976), pp. 1161-76.

Eaton, Jonathan, Mark Gersovitz, and Joseph Stiglitz, "The Pure Theory of Country Risk," NBER Working Paper No. 1984 (Cambridge, Massachussetts: National Bureau of Economic Research, April 1986).

Flood, Robert, and Peter Garber, "Collapsing Exchange Rate Regimes: Some Linear Examples," *Journal of International Economics* (Amsterdam), Vol. 17 (August 1984), pp. 1-13.

Ize, Alain, "Investment, Capital Flight and Political Risk: The Case of Mexico" (unpublished, Mexico City: El Colegio de México, January 1985).

_____, and Guillermo Ortiz, "Political Risk, Asset Substitution and Exchange Rate Dynamics: The Mexican Financial Crisis of 1982," Documentos de Trabajo No. 5 (Mexico City: El Colegio de México, October 1984).

Khan, Mohsin S., and Nadeem Ul Haque, "Foreign Borrowing and Capital Flight: A Formal Analysis," Staff Papers, International Monetary Fund (Washington), Vol. 32 (December 1985), pp. 606-28.

Krugman, Paul, "A Model of Balance of Payments Crisis," Journal of Money, Credit and Banking (Columbus, Ohio), Vol. 11 (August 1979), pp. 311-25.

Lizondo, Saúl, "Foreign Exchange Futures Prices Under Fixed Exchange Rates," Journal of International Economics (Amsterdam), Vol. 14 (February 1983), pp. 69-84.

Obstfeld, Maurice (1984 a), "Speculative Attack and the External Constraint in a Maximizing Model of the Balance of Payments," NBER Working Paper No. 1437 (Cambridge, Massachussetts: National Bureau of Economic Research, August 1984).

_____ (1984 b), "Rational and Self-Fulfilling Balance of Payments Crisis," NBER Working Paper No. 1486 (Cambridge, Massachussetts: National Bureau of Economic Research, November 1984).

Ortiz, Guillermo, "Currency Substitution in Mexico: The Dollarization Problem," Journal of Money, Credit and Banking (Columbus, Ohio), Vol. 15 (May 1983), pp. 174-85.

_____, "Economic Expansion, Crisis and Adjustment in Mexico (1977-1983)," in The Economics of the Caribbean Basin, ed. by Michael Connolly and John McDermott (New York: Praeger, 1985), pp. 68-98.

Penati, Alessandro, and George Pennachi, "Optimal Portfolio Choice and the Collapse of a Fixed Exchange Rate Regime" (unpublished, Philadelphia: University of Pennsylvania, August 1986).

Sachs, Jeffrey (1984 a), "Latin American Debt: I Don't Think We Are in Kansas Anymore — Comment," Brookings Papers on Economic Activity: 2 (1984), The Brookings Institution (Washington), pp. 405-407.

_____ (1984 b), "Theoretical Issues in International Borrowing," NBER Working Paper No. 1189 (Cambridge, Massachusetts: National Bureau of Economic Research, August 1983).

Salant, Stephen, and Dale Henderson, "Market Anticipation of Government Policies and the Price of Gold," Journal of Political Economy (Chicago), Vol. 86 (August 1978), pp. 627-48.

van Wijnbergen, Sweder, "Fiscal Deficits, Exchange Rate Crises and Inflation" (unpublished, Washington: International Bank for Reconstruction and Development, February 1986).

4

High Inflation, "Heterodox" Stabilization, and Fiscal Policy

Mario I. Blejer and Adrienne Cheasty*

I. INTRODUCTION

The role of fiscal policy differs, depending on the economic circumstances in which it is undertaken, on the additional policy instruments used, and on the specific objectives it is designed to achieve. This paper examines the stabilization programs introduced by Argentina, Bolivia, Brazil, and Israel between July 1985 and March 1986, when hyperinflation was an imminent threat to each of these economies, so that a primary policy aim had to be the attainment of a quick and drastic reduction in inflation.

These stabilization programs are interesting from a fiscal point of view, not only because the behavior of fiscal variables under very high inflation differs from fiscal responses under a regime of stable prices but also because the packages contained some innovative elements, which, themselves, affected the role that fiscal policy was called upon to play.

The programs were considered innovative for two reasons. First, they created major discontinuities in the trends of the main macroeconomic variables, rather than following the gradual adjustment paths of traditional stabilization packages. For this reason, they have usually been referred to as "shock" programs. Second, in most cases, they included a number of incomes-policy elements, such as wage and price freezes, together with exchange rate pegging and deindexation measures. These components have been characterized as "heterodox," as compared with the "orthodox" emphasis on demand management through fiscal and monetary instruments. However, in practice, traditional "fundamental" policies, mainly in the monetary and fiscal areas, formed the bulk of each program. In fact, the designers of the shock programs considered the

*This paper was first published in the August 1988 issue (Vol. 16, No. 8) of *World Development* (Oxford, England: Pergamon Journals, Ltd.).

combination of heterodox and fundamental (demand-management) policies crucial to the success of the programs.

The objective of this paper is to make the analytical aspects of the design of these programs explicit, so that the relationship between their traditional and innovative elements is highlighted, with particular emphasis on the role of fiscal policy.

The paper contains three main sections. The first substantive section (Section II) discusses briefly the economic rationale for the policy measures in a representative shock program by putting them in the perspective of recent theories of inflation determination. Section III provides a taxonomic description of the aims and measures of the shock programs, and, in particular, the specific contribution of the heterodox elements. Section IV describes in detail the role played by fiscal policy, the interactions between inflation and budgetary policies, and the feedbacks between the heterodox and the fiscal elements of the programs, in order to throw light on the appropriate role of fiscal instruments in stemming hyperinflationary pressures.[1]

II. Analytical Underpinnings of the Shock Programs

1. Inertia, Credibility, and Money Supply

Although the designers of the shock programs each started with different aims, policy constraints, and country characteristics, their approaches to the inflation problem were similar. The general view was that, once inflation reaches a very high rate, two different kinds of variables become important in its generation and perpetuation. First, as recognized in traditional adjustment programs, demand pressures on domestic prices arising from excess absorption are a crucial determinant of inflation. This implies that fundamental variables must be restricted; demand-management policies, therefore, have a central role to play in the shock programs. Second, and less traditionally, inflation is also considered to be strongly influenced by inertial forces, which are determined mainly by expectational variables. Inflationary expectations (either informal or institutionalized into indexation schemes) tend to be self-fulfilling, since individuals' behavior is consistent with their predictions about inflation. Given a history of high inflation, and the expectation that the inflation pattern will be difficult to break, inertia will affect the response to an ac-

---

[1] In many cases, available data were not specific enough to quantify the issues discussed in this paper. The issues are included, however, because of both their conceptual importance and the large body of qualitative evidence that indicates their significance in the context of the shock programs.

tual change in policy regime — greatly reducing the flexibility of economic policy, slowing the speed of reaction to policy change, and so increasing the costs of adjustment. The heterodox elements of the shock programs were an attempt to break free of inertia by severing the link between yesterday's and today's inflation.

The relationship between inertial forces and demand-management policies operates in two directions. On the one hand, it must be recognized that inertial forces cannot be translated into effective price increases unless monetary policy is accommodating. In traditional models of inflation, the money supply is a truly discretionary policy variable and, therefore, inertial inflation cannot play a permanent role. If a government decides to stop increasing the money supply, incipient inflation, arising from expectations or from higher demand, will not be realized, because people will not have the liquidity to bid up the general price level (though relative prices may change as demand shifts).

On the other hand, it is obvious from the many failed attempts at stabilization in Argentina, Bolivia, Brazil, and Israel that, in reality, the process of money creation may be subject to many pressures and be propelled by the inflationary process itself. The impetus to increase the money supply may come, therefore, from outside the realm of the monetary authorities. In particular, monetary policy is rarely completely independent of fiscal policy. In most cases, then, a restrictive monetary policy will be difficult to implement, unless the fiscal forces or other outside influences which affect money creation are controlled. Furthermore, if the monetary authorities attempt to cut the money supply (or reduce its rate of growth) without arranging for complementary decisions to be taken in other sectors of the economy, the adjustment of these other sectors to decreased liquidity may be haphazard and painful.

While, on the one hand, monetary control can vitiate the potential influence of inertia on the price level, on the other hand, the prior existence of inertia may reduce the effectiveness of traditional demand-management policies. The argument is as follows: One thesis of the rational-expectations school[2] says that inflation can be stopped abruptly, with low transition costs, if the government implements drastic fiscal and monetary policies which are consistent with price stability. However, in order to be effective, these policies must be *credible* — the public must be convinced that fiscal and monetary restraint will be maintained for a long time. Unfortunately, there is no simple way in which the government can convince the public that its policies will be sustained. If, for example, the public does not believe that the government can persist in the enforcement of tight policies because it fears high unemployment, then inflation-

---

[2]See, for example, Sargent (1982).

ary expectations will remain entrenched. Faced with this situation, the government will not be inclined to adopt tight policies at all, and, since high inflation will persist, the public's expectations will have proved to be self-justifying or "rational."

In countries with a long history of inflation and failures of disinflationary policies, the public may not accept the government's announced long-term disinflationary targets because of deep-rooted pessimism about the government's ability to control inflation. This causes considerable downward rigidity in basic, longer-term inflationary expectations. These basic inflationary expectations are, in addition to institutional mechanisms, the forces behind the concept of "expectational inflationary inertia" and make use of a monetary and fiscal squeeze as the basic disinflationary instrument very costly. To avoid the high costs, in terms of employment and output, that arise from the combination of monetary restraint and inflationary inertia, the "heterodox" stabilization packages augmented demand management with temporary incomes policies, including initial price freezes.

The question is, of course, what ensures that the expectational inertia will be overcome by the package of wage-price-exchange rate freezes. Certainly, there is no guarantee that incomes policy will reduce basic inflationary expectations, but there are two indications that it could. First, provided that the proper adjustments in the fundamentals (such as the current account of the balance of payments and the budget deficit) have been made, the imposition of a price (and an exchange rate) freeze can help the government demonstrate that the economy can function effectively without inflation and without any stresses in strategic areas — such as the current account or the debt-income ratio. As a result of this demonstration effect, individual agents may become convinced that low inflation is a realistic possibility.

Second, as long as the government combines incomes policy with a fixed exchange rate, there is an explicit or implicit commitment not to resort to inflation to achieve other objectives (by, for instance, allowing real wages to erode, in order to make the economy more competitive). When the fundamentals are consistent, this commitment may be credible and may carry over to the period after controls are lifted.

To summarize, program designers augmented traditional demand-management theories by considering that the money supply is usually accommodating and that it might be forced to accommodate not only demand pressures created by an elevated level of absorption but also demand pressures created by individuals who behaved "as if" absorption was high, even when it was not. Given the added cost that these "inertial" demand pressures implied for traditional stabilization programs (a cost which some felt explained the failure of traditional stabilization programs in the past), it was important to add "transitional" policies which would change expectational and indexation-induced inflation without a prolonged lagged adjustment period.

2. Inflation-Tax Financing of Fiscal Deficit

Although there are many plausible mechanisms through which monetary expansion is generated by the inflation process itself,[3] one central variable behind money supply growth is the fiscal deficit.[4] One way of describing, somewhat simplistically, the relationship between inflation, the deficit, and the money supply is in terms of the so-called inflation-tax model.

When the desired deficit cannot be financed by debt issue, the government will generally finance it by money creation. The real deficit is thus financed by changes in the real value of the debt and inflation-tax revenue on holdings of real money balances. However, the demand for real money balances falls as inflation rises. In other words, the base of the inflation tax is eroded as the tax rate rises. Hence, if the government wishes to maintain a given real deficit regardless of the inflation rate, it will have to "levy" the inflation tax necessary to finance that deficit by increasing the nominal money stock at higher and higher rates as the inflation rate rises. This model of inflation has the implication that countries may face a maximum sustainable fiscal deficit (indicated by D^* in Figure 1), given their private sectors' willingness to hold other types of government debt. In brief, if the government tries to finance a deficit higher than this maximum, the money supply will always exceed the demand for money, so that the necessary inflation-tax revenue will not be forthcoming. If the government persists in printing money, inflation will get higher and higher with-

---

[3]Monetary policy is quite likely to be accommodating when there is high inflation because (i) there may be no formal policy of restricting credit to the private sector, even though the authorities have decided to impose *fiscal* restraint; or (ii) even if the monetary authorities desire to reduce private sector credit pari passu with public sector credit, they will face strong resistance. Pressures will come, for example, from firms that have granted wage increases consistent with high inflation and will face difficulties and, ultimately, bankruptcy if they do not get the credit they need to pay these increases.

[4]There are clearly many other sources of monetary growth that do not originate in fiscal deficits. A detailed examination of the working of monetary policy instruments and the evolution of monetary and reserve aggregates is needed to complete a theory of monetary hyperinflation. This, however, goes beyond the scope of this paper. On this subject, see, for example, Calvo and Fernandez (1983). They analyze the possibility of affecting the steady-state level of inflation, at a *given* budget deficit, by means of monetary management, mainly through changes in the reserve ratio of commercial banks.

Figure 1. Limitations on Inflation-Tax Revenue

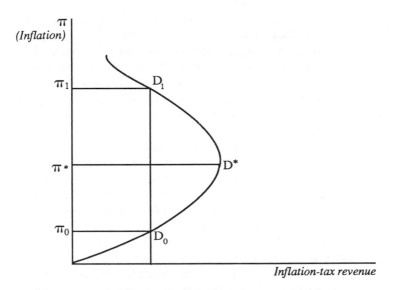

Note: D_0 denotes an "efficiently financed" deficit, D_1 the same
deficit "inefficiently financed," and D* the maximum sustainable
deficit.

out increasing the government's control of real resources. In these circumstances, hyperinflation will be a strong possibility.[5]

According to this hypothesis, then, there is an absolute limit to government's deficit financing. This limit is determined by the attainment of a "threshold" inflation rate. If this inflation rate is exceeded, then adjusting the money supply would not allow the government to maintain its real deficit.[6]

---

[5]In perfect-foresight models, a sufficient condition for the emergence of hyperinflation would be an exogenous, nonmarginal shock to push the inflation rate past the threshold at which the deficit becomes unsustainable. In models which include any element of inertia, either caused by expectations or any other structural rigidity, hyperinflation can be induced without an exogenous shock.

[6]This is strictly correct in the steady state. Calvo (1978) and Barro and Gordon (1983) have developed models in which the government can continue to extract resources even at very high rates of inflation. Their models demonstrate that when inflationary expectations, formed rationally in the light of the government's revenue objectives, are given at a particular date, the government can generate more revenue if it selects a rate of monetary expan-

A second implication of this hypothesis is that, for the more plausible shapes of the money-demand schedule, the same deficit could be observed at a high inflation rate as at a low inflation rate.[7] (In Figure 1, the deficit is the same at $\pi_0(D_0)$ and $\pi_1(D_1)$.) At the high inflation rate, π_1, the deficit would be financed "inefficiently." Hence, in economies experiencing very high levels of inflation, an effective policy of increasing the demand for money might allow the government to maintain the deficit at its current level while reducing inflation. Given the dependence of money demand on inflationary expectations and general confidence in the economy, the policy problem is to find the combination of expectation-changing policies sufficient to permit the economy to jump from the "high-inflation trap," where real money demand is low, to the "efficiently" financed deficit, where desired money holdings are higher. If it were, indeed, possible for the government to maintain its deficit, and hence its real level of absorption, and still bring down the inflation rate through expectational policies, a more general question would then become relevant: Might it not be possible to reduce the inflation rate without cutting real output? In the shock-program countries, the search for ways to cut inflation while minimizing output loss became very important and gave a rationale for the implementation of policies, such as price freezes and exchange rate fixing, which were considered necessary to ensure a transition from one equilibrium level of inflation to another.[8]

III. Terms of the Shock Programs

Despite substantial differences in specific policies from country to country, the twin concepts of the importance of government credibility and the limits to inflationary financing of the fiscal deficit described in Section II

---

sion greater than is expected by the public. When the public eventually begins to anticipate the greater expansion and revises its expectations, the government can choose an even higher rate of monetary growth, and so on. Such a process could theoretically result in infinite rates of monetary expansion and inflation, and in such a situation there would be no equilibrium.

[7]This exposition does not take into account the inverse relationship between normal taxes and inflation-tax financing which has been pointed out by Tanzi (1977). This relationship and its implications will be discussed in Section IV.

[8]Bruno and Fischer (1985) commented that "The existence of a high inflation trap suggests that it may be possible to reduce the inflation rate in a high inflation economy by policies typically regarded as unsound, such as fixing the exchange rate, or freezing nominal wages or prices, in an attempt to make the transition from a high to a low inflation steady-state."

may be seen as the pillars upon which the shock programs were built. The rationale for the general features which were common to the various programs is based on these concepts, which also provide the basis for a consistent classification of the different categories of measures adopted as part of the disinflation strategy.

1. General Features

The first common feature of the programs was the authorities' aim of bringing down inflation *drastically* and *immediately*. This must be seen in the context of the historical record: the failure of the authorities' previous attempts to slow inflation gradually and the resulting skepticism concerning stabilization schemes.

A second common feature was their *comprehensiveness:* the programs encompassed policies directed at most of the more important macroeconomic variables. A comprehensive plan was considered necessary because the objective was to bring down inflation immediately. A partial approach could have resulted in serious distortions which might have endangered the entire plan in the short term and damaged the country's growth potential over the medium term; for example, if wage policy had been excluded from the plan, a rise in real wages (in terms of tradable goods) would have led to a balance of payments crisis. However, a comprehensive plan was also necessitated by the authorities' understanding of how inflation was determined. On the one hand, if inflation was generated by both excess absorption and inertial forces, a successful plan could not confine itself to the adjustment of the key macroeconomic variables, such as the current account or public debt ratios, but should include nominal policies which address expectations. On the other hand, a successful program could not deal only with inflationary inertia when the fiscal stance and other fundamental variables were incompatible with low inflation levels and with sustainable growth.

The third common feature of the programs was the attempted *synchronization* of the heterodox policies, especially that of the exchange rate and wage policies with the price freeze. When inflation was to be abruptly halted, such precise alignment in the timing of all of the policy measures was viewed as essential if serious distortions in relative prices were to be avoided in the initial stages of the program.

2. Classification of Shock-Program Measures

The elements of a broadly defined or "representative" shock program can be grouped into three different types: (1) preparatory reforms; (2) expectation-adjusting policies; and (3) demand-management policies. A short description of the measures in each category is provided here.

a. Preparatory Reforms

These were implemented prior to the formal launching of the plan and included equilibrating adjustments in key relative prices (goods prices, wages, exchange rate, interest rate, etc.) and, in some cases, structural reforms in fiscal, monetary, and other key policy areas.

The need to resort to some pre-equilibration mechanisms arose from the perception that the creation of large discontinuities in inflation through the administrative control of nominal variables, including wage and price freezes, might exacerbate existing disequilibria in one or more markets. If markets were in disequilibrium at the time their prices were frozen, then pressures to equilibrate would be manifested through quantity adjustments, as well as continued price pressures. Hence, a logical precursor of the freezes contained in the shock programs would be attempts to equilibrate goods, factor, and asset markets, so that legislation would merely validate and publicize the underlying economic realities, rather than trying to force an unrealistic alignment of markets.

A clear trade-off between equilibrating and non-equilibrating prices was perceived prior to the program. On the one hand, upward price adjustments made at the beginning of the program would, indeed, have hampered the decline of inflation and, thus, eroded the credibility of the program. On the other hand, if prior equilibration had not taken place, price freezes would soon have come under strain when pressures to correct the disequilibrium prices emerged. In addition, freezing prices when they were out of equilibrium could tend to perpetuate any distortions that might follow disinflation. Moreover, if the disequilibrium price freeze were maintained for a significant period, these distortions would seriously damage the country's ability to grow by responding to economic incentives.

b. Expectation-Adjusting Policies

Expectation-adjusting policies were "impact" measures, whose effects were expected to be felt immediately after the policy announcement was made. Their objective was to attack directly the inertial component of inflation by creating a hiatus between past and present inflation and, in this manner, dampening expectations of future inflation. Two types of measures in this category could be distinguished: (1) temporary "shock" measures, and (2) impact measures on fundamental variables.

Temporary "Shock" Measures. Some "shock" measures were designed to be transitional. They were to lead a frontal attack on inertia designed to bring about abrupt changes in expectations. Measures of this sort included freezes of key prices and were designed to create large discontinuities with the previous policy regimes and to affect basically all relative prices: (1) domestic prices, (2) the exchange rate, (3) wages, (4) returns to forward contracts, and (5) returns to financial assets. In cases where indexation mechanisms had institutionalized the inflation link, these types of policies could include a direct (e.g., legislated) break in the indexation system. Furthermore, in all of the shock programs, the announcement of the program was, itself, considered important in affecting expectations. Thus, in each country, the policy package was announced formally and *en bloc* by the authorities.

Impact Measures on Fundamental Variables. Other shock measures were designed to overcome inertia by adopting policies which would generate a confident and sustained conviction that future government actions would be consistent with lower inflation rates. Since expectations are usually rooted in the actual behavior of fundamental variables, the shock measures included the following: (1) very large immediate (in some cases, one-time or temporary) adjustments in fiscal variables;[9] and (2) announcements of future radical changes in these variables.

Impact measures differed from traditional demand-management policies in that they had one or more of the following characteristics: (1) they were expected to have an immediate impact on the fiscal deficit, domestic credit, the trade balance, etc.; (2) the immediate adjustments they implied were large in size relative to traditional measures taken via more permanent, sustainable demand-management policies; and (3) given their once-and-for-all nature, or the detrimental effects that they could have had in the long run, they were expected to be temporary.

Announcements of future reforms were intended to affect fundamental variables in the longer run; their immediate impact was to lend credibility to the government's declared intention to sustain the changed policy regime.

c. Traditional Demand-Management Policies

In tandem with the impact measures, more conventional policies were used to alleviate demand pressures. They included mainly deficit reduction and credit restraint, and were expected to have the traditional gradual impact on the economy.

3. Some Remarks on Heterodox Elements of Programs

Of the various categories of policies incorporated in the shock programs, the highly visible impact, or expectation-adjusting, policies have

---

[9]The main impact measures on fundamental variables were the introduction of forced-saving schemes, which substituted for other tax revenue in the short run. In the public mind, these forced-saving schemes became strongly identified with the shock programs.

given rise to the most debate. Some of these are fiscal in nature and will be discussed in the next section. Others, including direct controls and various deindexation mechanisms, were intended to change recalcitrant inflationary expectations without having a major effect on traditional fiscal and other demand-management variables. As will be discussed later, even when impact policies are intended to alter expectations rather than the "fundamentals," they are normally associated with budgetary costs and reductions in activity, and, therefore, it would be misleading to claim that such policies can reduce inflation without adversely affecting the real side of the economy. In addition to asking questions about the indirect cost of impact policies, one may also ask what specific role these policies have played. Without understanding their mechanisms, one cannot assess the extent to which the shock programs actually departed from traditional stabilization packages.

The assumptions underlying the inclusion of policies to overcome inertia in most of the stabilization programs were as follows: (1) that inflationary expectations take time to adjust and may prolong inflation beyond the point where underlying fundamental variables warrant price increases; and (2) that inflationary expectations can only be affected in the short term by impact policies, including price and wage controls. However, even if (1) is a correct description of reality, expectations could change rapidly in response to drastic and credible changes in fiscal and monetary variables, without the government having to resort to additional impact measures, as assumed in (2). Moreover, even when impact policies are deemed an essential component of the stabilization package, it is important to consider their costs and the complications involved in their implementation.

a. Price Controls

Price controls have been among the more prominent impact policies used. While there is little disagreement with the notion that without fundamental adjustments, price controls cannot alter the underlying inflationary pressures in the economy, it has also become apparent that the implementation of price and wage controls *at disequilibrium levels* makes them untenable, increases their distortionary effects, and thus hinders economic growth. Moreover, if the controls are not expected to be sustained, people will move out of money and nominal assets and into goods at an accelerated rate, thus exacerbating the inflationary pressure on the price level and making expectations of inflation and the rupture of price controls self-fulfilling.

In addition, wage and price controls may be associated with extra output losses arising from the large discontinuities, the administrative complications, and the uncertainties that wage and price freezes create in the economy. In other words, a program with price controls could conceivably imply a larger output loss than would be expected at the outset of a program without incomes policies.

The types of costs that arise from price controls may well have a direct fiscal component. Even if prices are, and remain, in equilibrium, the administrative (and, in some cases, political) costs to government of controlling prices directly are significant. If prices start in a disequilibrium position, either the government or the private sector will have to bear the cost of the discrepancy between the quantities supplied and demanded. When the government bears the cost—through increasing producer subsidies, for example—the price of the good has only been controlled in a very narrow sense and the operation has a clear fiscal cost.

It should be noted that no matter how carefully prices are aligned in equilibrium at the beginning of a program, only rarely will that equilibrium remain relevant once the program goes into effect. Setting equilibrium prices in one regime; initiating a program whose main aim is a drastic, sudden, and complete change in that regime; and expecting prices to be invariant to the change makes sense only in a world where not only inflation but also any reduction in the government deficit and any changes in exchange and interest rates, as well as labor and financial markets, are all completely neutral with respect to the structure of relative commodity prices. More generally, only technologically neutral growth would be compatible with such a policy regime (a condition more restrictive than most theoretical assumptions about growth and one very unlikely to be achievable in practice).

A specific problem associated with freezing prices when they are out of equilibrium relates to public sector tariffs. If they are fixed at a disequilibrium level at the outset of the program, this implies the emergence of a subsidy on public services. Maintaining the price freeze will not only ensure the perpetuation of this subsidy but may also lead to the gradual substitution of government services for high-priced goods. Insofar as this takes place, it will increase the total amount of government subsidy payments.

In general, any subsidy element in prices which remains during a freeze will tend to worsen the budget deficit and/or the financial situation of public enterprises. This, in turn, constitutes an expansionary fiscal policy, increasing both demand pressures and expected inflation.[10] If, however, the subsidy is not recognized in the government budget but, instead, must be borne by private sector producers, shortages will occur which will worsen inflationary expectations and diminish the credibility of the government's policy stance. Hence, use of a disequilibrium set of prices lowers the prob-

---

[10]Chu and Feltenstein (1978) show that this happened in Argentina during the 1970s.

ability that a price freeze can be sustained, in addition to substantially raising its cost and its impact on the budget.

When the economy is at full employment, the ability of price controls to suppress inflation may be diminished further. Controls may be more costly and less effective than under conditions of excess capacity, because supply constraints become apparent almost immediately and, consequently, all the extra pressure created by increased subsidies and transfers has to be repressed through the price freeze at a high and increasing cost. A relatively slack economy, therefore, makes a price freeze less likely to be involuntarily removed and less costly to administer.

The contribution of sectoral excess supplies was apparent in the seemingly well-managed price freezes in both Israel and Argentina, where excess supplies (1) permitted the price freeze to work, and (2) reduced the costs associated with its removal.[11] However, it is possible that the creation of excess supplies can be achieved only at the expense of the program goals of minimum output loss and reactivation of long-term growth. For instance, it has been suggested that the maintenance of a very high interest rate immediately after the introduction of a shock program will encourage the running down of inventories and, thus, alleviate prior supply constraints.[12] The corollary to a policy of maintaining very high interest rates, however, is that investment will be depressed, perhaps to such an extent that total production falls, creating sizable output losses.

In practice, high ex post real interest rates appeared in most of the shock-program countries, but these arose either because financial risks and inflationary expectations did not diminish or as a consequence of the restrictions on financing the public sector through credit creation, coupled with the impact of the increase in the demand for money that was created when inflation fell. In other words, given the fact that its other policies affected the interest rate, the government had very limited scope for an independent interest rate policy as a means of controlling the amount of slack in goods markets and, thus, phasing out the price freeze.

b. Deindexation Schemes

Another issue to which the shock programs attached great importance was the removal of formal indexation. According to the theory of inertial inflation, one of the main culprits in prolonging inflation, after underlying real causes of price pressure are removed, is widespread indexation of the economy. The indexation mechanisms have two components: (1) a mechanical link between past inflation and present price increases and (2) an ex-

---

[11]See Blejer and Liviatan (1987).
[12]Ibid.

pectational component, whereby indexation schemes minimize the variance of expected future incomes in such a way that individuals do not anticipate large discontinuities in either their permanent incomes or in the consumption power that those incomes provide. Therefore, if a deindexation scheme were to be successful, it would have to, on the one hand, create an abrupt discontinuity between past and present price increases and, on the other, generate changes in expected permanent income significant enough to make individuals alter their consumption patterns.

The effort to deindex the economy in the context of the shock programs may be analyzed by looking separately at labor and capital markets. It can fairly be said, in both cases, that the amount of deindexation which actually took place was minimal, despite the prominence accorded to it in the programs.

Regarding wages, the so-called "deindexation schemes" did not result in any long-run changes in the expectations of individuals about the level of their permanent incomes which might have changed their consumption and savings patterns, nor did they bring about any structural change in the system, and in the mechanics, of wage formation. Although wages were frozen in all the countries considered except Bolivia, the public was, in general, given to understand that the freeze was a short-term measure and that former levels of real wages could be restored, if not by legislation, then through the bargaining process. In fact, in some cases, there was refinement of the protection with which the indexation mechanisms offset the effect of inflation on incomes.[13] In theory, the price freeze itself would have accomplished the same end as the deindexation schemes. If the freeze had succeeded in abruptly cutting inflation, from then on the relevant inflation rate to be taken into account in the indexation equations would have been correspondingly less important. This is, in fact, what happened. The price freeze dampened the inflationary spiral. However, if inflation should increase again, for any exogenous reason, the same inflation growth as before could occur in each country, given that the wage-indexation mechanisms, although slightly changed in some cases, remain essentially in place.

Analogously, there was very little deindexation of financial assets. In Argentina, there were no formal deindexation announcements concerning financial assets, although the application of the conversion scale to financial contracts was regarded as a deindexation measure, sufficient in itself to accomplish deindexation. In Israel, the indexation of long-term

---

[13]In Israel, for example, since October 1985 formal indexation of wages has been restored, and it has even been enhanced: cost of living adjustments of 80 percent will henceforth be paid after the cumulative increase in the consumer price index reaches 4 percent, or every three months.

financial assets was not disrupted. The only substantive change was the prohibition of foreign exchange-linked deposits with maturities of less than one year. Likewise, in Brazil, the only deindexation that was enforced was on financial instruments of less than one year's maturity. While a year's standstill was imposed on the indexation of longer-term assets, this pause was costless to asset holders (unless they tried prematurely to liquidate their assets), because long-term assets could be indexed to a new government bond, which would, by design, be fully adjusted for inflation.

As was true for wages, the most important program element in the treatment of financial assets was the breaking of the link between past inflation and present returns. This was done in Argentina and Brazil by applying a conversion table to financial contracts in an effort to eliminate the expected (but, because of the price freeze, unrealized) inflation component of the contracts. This prevented potentially large real transfers of income from debtors to creditors, thus avoiding creation of dissatisfaction which could have undermined the price freeze in the same way that dissatisfaction created by forcing firms to fulfill past wage contracts at the expense of profits could have. Again, as was true for wages, the disruption was a purely temporary, though politically important, phenomenon, and the crucial characteristic of an indexation scheme—the ability to index wealth to inflation—remained substantively unchanged.

In summary, wage and asset-return freezes and conversion tables cannot be seen as true deindexation schemes. They did not create any durable change in the ability of the economy to prevent the re-emergence of inflation. In that respect, the importance accorded them by the designers of the shock programs (relative to fiscal and monetary policy) may have been excessive. Given the use of the other "impact" measures, however, a necessary role did emerge for them in legitimizing the use of incomes policies and price freezes in order to validate the legislated disruptions in wage and price trends and, thus, to overcome inertia.

IV. FISCAL POLICY AND HIGH INFLATION

In the shock programs, fiscal policy was used to achieve by far the greater part of the adjustment of fundamental variables. Performance under the stabilization programs highlighted the fact that high inflation and the implementation of shock measures have some particular implications for fiscal policy, which are analyzed in this section.

The traditional conclusion that cutting the fiscal deficit leads to reductions in inflation is supported by the inflationary-financing model: since deficits are assumed to be financed by the inflation tax, a smaller deficit will "require" less inflation. However, the optimal fiscal policy for bringing down very high inflation may be different from the optimal fiscal policy in an economy with a stable price level, because the former will be complicated by the interrelationships between fiscal policy and inflation, as well as by the possible existence of inertial inflation, in which the fiscal policy stance plays a less direct role.

A number of these issues are discussed here, with particular focus on the following five aspects: (1) the size of the deficit may itself be a function of the inflation rate; (2) different fiscal policies may affect inflation in different ways, so that success in reducing inflation through cutting the deficit will depend on the specific type of policy used to reduce excess government absorption; (3) different fiscal policies have different effects on aggregate demand and on output, so that the optimal fiscal package should attain the necessary reduction in absorption while minimizing output losses; (4) the composition of economic activity, and specifically of the financial system, is not invariant to inflation, which suggests that tax bases may not be inflation-neutral; and (5) even if inflation is not reduced, attempts to reduce it through impact policies may affect the budget.

1. Effects of Inflation on the Budget

While the size of the fiscal deficit affects inflation because of inflation-tax requirements, the other methods of financing the deficit are not invariant to inflation. This weakens the neat, hypothesized dichotomy between inertial and demand-driven inflation, because if it is the case that the higher is inflationary financing, and the lower are traditional revenues, then reducing the inflation rate may allow a higher level of public spending to be sustained (financed by a recovery in traditional revenues), even if all fiscal policies remain unchanged. As Tanzi (1978) has shown, the *net* gain from inflation-tax revenue, in terms of ability to finance a fiscal deficit, is much smaller when the loss in traditional revenues is taken into account than when the inflation tax is calculated in isolation. In the long run, the economy's growth potential without inflation (as compared with its potential in an inflationary environment) may be much greater than is usually recognized.

The calculation of the low-inflation budget corresponding to a given set of policies in a country suffering from high inflation is complicated by the fact that while almost every element of the budget is affected by inflation, these elements have different elasticities. If the elasticity of government expenditure with respect to increases in nominal income is greater than the nominal income elasticity of government revenue, then the real deficit will rise with inflation, faster than the simple real-money-balances model would predict.[14] Likewise, reductions in inflation may generate unexpected gains or losses in revenues and expenditures.

On the expenditure side, the inclusion of nominal government interest payments in the deficit greatly magnifies the percentage increase in interest payments, relative to the percentage increases in other expenditure and in revenue, as the inflation rate rises. This effect is particularly marked when most of the debt is not indexed and nominal interest rates are flexible.[15]

On the revenue side, it can be shown that the real value of tax collections falls when inflation is high, because of the inevitable lag between the date the tax legally falls due and its date of collection (and because of other elements of the tax system).[16] Bracket creep in progressive-income-tax schedules offsets some of the collection lag-induced decline, but countries with high inflation quickly develop indexed tax systems, which protect taxpayers against inflation-induced increases in their real tax obligations.[17]

In order to minimize the negative impact of inflation on the budget, revenue buoyancy should be maximized and administrative lags minimized. If taxes and other instruments are to grow in line with nominal income, regressive schedules should be avoided, as should specific tax rates. Negotiated values applied to imports or domestic goods subject to excises can also lead to large losses of buoyancy as inflation increases. The same is true of public sector tariffs, which are often the most difficult prices in the economy to index fully. Furthermore, it should be noted that utility bills are often paid far less frequently than other obligations. Subsidies also tend to emerge on central bank interest rates, and these, too, contribute to the public sector deficit, whether or not the subsidy is made explicit in public sector accounts.

Lags in revenue collection are usually not balanced by lags in expenditure. It has often been said that the government is more efficient in indexing its obligations than its assets. For instance, attempts to lag payment of the public sector wage bill may cut this month's inflation, but this will

---

[14]This is one explanation of why countries tend to find themselves in the high-equilibrium inflation trap, rather than at an inflation level corresponding to an efficiently financed deficit. The presence of inflation-endogenous elements in the budget makes the deficit likely to overshoot the low-level equilibrium.

[15]It could be argued, however, that because the inflation component of interest is not income but rather amortization, the impact on demand of interest payments that reflect inflation is much smaller than the impact of other expenditure components. (See Tanzi, Blejer, and Teijeiro (1987).)

[16]See Tanzi (1977).

[17]Besides, income taxes have tended to be less important in the shock-program countries than in industrial countries.

probably make deindexation much less acceptable to public servants should the government later decide to implement an adjustment program.

On the one hand, in the initial phases of the programs, the "passive" reductions in the deficit as inflation fell were very striking. In Brazil, the drop in inflation reduced the public sector borrowing requirement from 27 percent of gross domestic product (GDP) in 1985 to an estimated 10 percent in 1986,[18] with nearly 18 percentage points of this reduction arising from the reduction in indexed debt service. The Argentine deficit also fell significantly, and while this drop also partly reflected a fall in monetary correction payments, the impact of the automatic effect on revenue recovery associated with the slowdown of inflation was particularly striking.[19]

On the other hand, it is ironic to note that the revenue gain associated with the slowing down of inflation is smaller, the more perfectly the fiscal system has adapted to inflation prior to a stabilization program (by minimizing collection lags, etc.). The Brazilian tax reform of December 1985 provided a good example of the possible post-inflation costs of having succeeded in adapting to inflation. The tax reform included a reduction in withholding to facilitate the indexing of tax liabilities, which, in turn, was designed to improve real revenues. However, the reduction in withholding implied that lags in collecting revenue were lengthened. Under high inflation, because of the impact of indexing tax liabilities, the gains from the reduction in withholding apparently had exceeded the losses; under low inflation, only the losses from the longer collection lag remained. Moreover, when inflation is high, it may pay the government to introduce complex administrative systems, with much policing and high penalties, in order to minimize losses from lagged payments. Once inflation falls to reasonable levels, however, these systems may be inappropriate and cost more than they earn for the government, given that the cost of any delay has dropped.[20]

---

[18]Before further fiscal reforms were implemented in November 1986.

[19]The characterization of this increase in revenue as "automatic" does not imply that it should not be counted when evaluating the fiscal effort undertaken as part of the program. The increased real revenue represented a cost to the private sector and, in that sense, is not qualitatively different from an increase in revenue generated by higher tax rates.

[20]The tendency of high inflation to generate complex administrative and regulatory structures will damage a country's ability to return to growth after the shock program unless there is a concomitant liberalization of the system. The need for such liberalization was ignored in shock programs other than the one in Bolivia (except for the structural fiscal measures, which are discussed in the next section), despite its possible importance for sustaining the programs' success in the long term.

2. Tax Rate Increases Versus Cuts in Government Activity

In practice, cutting deficits tends very often to affect the level of prices. Hence, in situations where price stability is a central goal, restrictive fiscal measures must be chosen with special care. In inertial systems where inflationary spirals are fueled by formal and informal indexation, deficit cutting through relative price realignments (such as increasing indirect tax rates, reducing government subsidies, or raising public sector fees and tariffs) may impart an upward push to inflation which more than offsets any gradual alleviation of price pressures brought about through budget contraction. If the government wants to cut the deficit through revenue measures, it will thus be important to remove or relax indexation mechanisms beforehand. While inflation persists, however, individuals will be wary of permitting the government to remove these "insurance systems" which prevent their wealth from being eroded. Hence, *simultaneous* implementation of tax changes and indexation-removal schemes may be crucial to the success of both policies. This is an additional reason why, in the shock programs, the "synchronization" of policies (discussed in the previous section) played an important role.

If indexation schemes cannot be canceled, it is likely that reducing the deficit through reductions in real government activity — for example, by cutting expenditures on wages or goods and services — will be more successful in inducing a quick fall in inflation than will tax, tariff, or subsidy adjustments. It is also probable that cuts in transfers will affect inflation only with a lag if transfer recipients have slowly adapting expectations or if they perceive the transfer cut as temporary: their demand will not fall immediately by the full amount of the cut in their current income.

However, cuts in government activity may be regarded as undesirable, since they may create political difficulties by placing the full burden of adjustment on a few people (civil servants and government suppliers). In addition, governments may not be convinced that their levels of absorption are too high or unsustainable.[21] If inflation is inertial (in the sense that it could be reduced without reducing the sustainable deficit), then cuts in government activity could be inappropriate. (This issue is discussed in detail in the next subsection.)

In the recent shock programs, the major instruments used to reduce the fiscal deficit were rate increases and subsidy cuts, rather than reductions in government activity. The importance of fiscal contraction in bringing down prices, through whatever method, was viewed as outweighing any negative impact of the rate increases on the price level. Moreover, it

---

[21] None of the countries discussed was considered to be at full employment and, thus, government demand was viewed as a crucial component of effective aggregate demand.

was also claimed that severe rate increases at the outset of a program could actually mitigate inflationary expectations, since they would reduce the government's need to implement further price shocks in the future, as well as pre-empting relative price distortions, as discussed above.

The experience of the shock programs suggests that large rate changes may be undertaken with relatively small effects on the price index.[22] This suggests that, empirically, governments need not be overly concerned with using price-related instruments to cut the fiscal deficit, despite the arguments outlined above.[23]

3. Fiscal Policy Implications of Minimizing Output Losses

One of the most consuming concerns in implementing the shock programs was the desire to avoid recession during the period of adjustment. As discussed earlier, it was believed that output losses could be avoided, inasmuch as inflation was inertial—that is, it could be reduced without cuts in aggregate demand. Ideally, expectations would be changed without changing the government deficit. In reality, however, *temporary* deficit cuts were seen as efficacious ways of changing people's expectations, raising their confidence in economic management, and increasing their demand for money — even if inflation was purely inertial.[24] Implicit in this belief was the idea that the improvement in private sector expectations would lead to a surge in activity which would offset the decline in government absorption. In general, tax- and price-changing policies have a smaller multiplier effect on aggregate demand than government direct expenditure; this would suggest that deficit cuts implemented with the objective of changing expectations, rather than purely to cut total absorption, should be effected by changes in prices rather than in government

---

[22]In Brazil, for example, compulsory levies of 25–30 percent on cars, gasoline, and alcohol were introduced in July 1986. Following the introduction of these measures, the authorities modified the index used to measure official inflation in order to purge the impact of the levies from the index. For July and August, inflation was 5.3 percent in the unpurged version, and 2.9 percent in the purged version, of the index. Likewise, in Bolivia, where, at the outset of the program, the price of gasoline rose by 750 percent, and domestic prices of other publicly provided goods and services were raised to reflect the 93 percent devaluation, the inflation rate in the month following the start of the program was 56 percent — 10 percentage points lower than the 66 percent rate of the month before implementation of the program. (All the figures represent monthly averages.)

[23]This conclusion is probably valid, even though part of the explanation for the insignificant impact on prices could be problems with the way the price indices were constructed.

[24]Many economists have suggested that the long-run sustainable deficit would probably have to be overshot during a shock program, not only in order to convince people of the government's determination to switch to conservative fiscal management but also to generate excess supplies in the economy which would allow price freezes to be maintained. (See Blejer and Liviatan (1987), and Dornbusch and Fischer (1986).)

activity. It is also possible that policies which affect prices are more easily reversible than those which involve reductions in staff and in maintenance, so that rate changes are more suited to temporary deficit cuts. These characteristics of price-realigning fiscal policies, together with evidence from the shock programs that the price adjustments provoke relatively little inflation, suggest that as a general rule, price-realigning fiscal policies are probably a more efficient means of achieving deficit reduction than cuts in activity. However, though increases in taxes and prices may have a smaller impact on present growth than decreases in government activity, it has been argued, with respect to minimizing output losses over the longer run, that pricing measures will depress long-term future growth by damaging incentives in the economy.[25] If high marginal tax rates are inimical to growth, the tax base may deteriorate (relative to GDP if the high rates lead to shifts out of taxed activities, or in line with the fall in GDP if growth prospects are damaged). In other words, closing the short-run deficit may be done at the cost of increasing pressures on the long-run deficit. If the public perceives an inconsistency, the government's fiscal policy will not be credible, and inflationary expectations will not be reduced by the imposition of short-run fiscal restrictions.

The extensive use of *temporary fiscal measures* in the recent shock programs has constituted a striking difference between them and more traditional adjustment programs. An explanation for this is that the emphasis in the shock programs on announcement effects and quick results meant that if deficit cuts were to be used to reduce inertial inflation, they would have to be large and to generate a very rapid inflow of real resources to the government. The need for a large collection of revenue up front is, by definition, almost too extreme to be sustained without large output losses, and the usual presumption is that extreme measures will be replaced later by gradual policies on either the revenue or the expenditure side. In other words, the reduction in permanent income is expected to be much smaller than the immediate reduction in current income. This presumption itself, however, ensures that the public will accept much larger temporary deficit cuts than permanent ones and therefore allows expectations to be affected more quickly.

Temporary overshooting of fiscal adjustment may also give the government room to implement long-run, growth- (and possibly revenue-) enhancing structural changes which are costly in the short run. An example of this, in the context of the shock programs, was provided by the cuts in government employment, which reduced long-run labor costs but necessitated immediate provision of funds for relocation and redundancy payments.

---

[25]Liviatan (1986).

The largest temporary measures in the programs were the forced-saving schemes. In conception, these were designed to have no effect whatsoever on permanent incomes. It should be noted in this context that the impact of forced-saving schemes on the government's long-run financing gap is more or less invariant to whether or not the government pays back the forced loan. On the one hand, if the loan is repaid, government expenditure will rise by that amount in the year the repayment takes place. On the other hand, repayment creates credibility in the loan as an asset and permits the government to refinance the loan. If the loan is not repaid, present government expenditure will be lower, but the government will find it more difficult to raise revenue through such a scheme again. In both cases, the net impact on the financing gap could be the same.

While temporary fiscal measures have immediate effects which cannot be sustained, *structural fiscal measures* which improve future fiscal management will sustain the long-run fiscal balance but may have no immediate revenue impact. Such measures (such as the announcement of tax reforms in Argentina and Bolivia, and of civil service reform in Israel) are included in shock programs because of the support they supposedly give government credibility — in other words, they have a pure, though tempo rary, announcement effect. Their value depends on how plausible they are ex ante (so that their announcement will have some impact), and on how soon they actually begin to be carried out. If the policies are not implemented, government credibility will be eroded; there will be a "reverse announcement effect" in the sense that, because the policy was introduced with much publicity, government failure to implement it will be more noticeable than if it had never been publicized, and future promises to use such policy measures will be received with less confidence.

A related reason to include announcements of future fiscal policies in a shock program is that they minimize the loss of future output by providing guidelines for long-range private sector decisions. In particular, private investment may depend on future, as well as present, rates of interest, so that government's projected credit use over the life of a planned investment may affect that investment decision.

4. Growth of the Financial System Under Inflation and Its Tax Implications

A feature of tax systems in many high-inflation countries is their relatively strong reliance on financial transactions as a tax base. This occurs for two reasons. First, the financial system's share of GDP tends to grow as the country adapts successfully to inflation. The financial structure gets larger and more sophisticated, since, in order to preserve the national currency as the unit of account, more complicated financial transactions are developed which incorporate indexation mechanisms to capture changes in nominal values more completely. Hence, the share of income and profits taxes, etc. from the financial sector may grow more rapidly than the rate of inflation.[26] Second, as inflation rises, the government's traditional inflation tax base, money, shrinks. The logical alternative tax bases are the money substitutes which have become attractive as inflation hedges.

If the volume of financial transactions is, indeed, affected by the inflationary process, it could also be expected that a fall in the rate of inflation will reduce the relative size of the financial sector. In particular, the demand for money substitutes tends to fall drastically as inflation disappears, since they become less valuable as inflation hedges. It is therefore likely that, following rapid disinflation, financial tax bases will shrink, both on asset transactions and on incomes.[27] Revenue losses on income taxes will be exacerbated if banks may offset losses they may incur against their tax obligations.

This effect was observed in practice. In the countries which introduced shock programs, the financial sector fell into difficulties as inflation dropped. In Brazil, for example, the private banking system shed 140,000 workers in the first weeks of the program. Brazil also suffered revenue losses as a consequence of the tax reform implemented just before the Cruzado Plan. Financial system taxes were adjusted in the reform, with relatively higher rates being placed on inflation-hedging assets and transactions (such as stock exchange trading) which helped maintain real wealth, and relatively lower rates on assets whose returns were not so elastic with respect to inflation. These reforms meant that when inflation fell, the private sector's shift into the latter type of assets created a permanent revenue loss.

The public financial sector, in particular, may be expected to be vulnerable to the large inflation cut observed during the initial phase of a successful shock program. Public sector banks will be worse off than their private sector counterparts if they are not free to shed labor. Also, public bank portfolios (particularly in development banks) tend to be in longer-term and less tradable assets, so that portfolios can react to large changes in inflation only with long lags. In the interim, the profitability, and indeed the viability, of the public financial sector may be endangered.

---

[26]The growth of the financial sector with the increase in the rate of inflation is likely to reach a limit. If hyperinflation develops, a shift away from use of the national currency as the unit of account and an extreme shortening in the length of contracts will be observed. The process is generally accompanied by extensive financial disintermediation.

[27]The validity of this argument hinges on the type of interest rate policy followed, since changes in relative interest rates could affect the relative sizes of the various segments of the financial system, thus differentially affecting the asset income tax base.

While inflation may affect the financial sector, government management and regulation of asset markets may affect the rate of inflation. Given an excess money supply, pressures on domestic goods prices will be higher, the fewer the domestic and foreign assets that individuals are permitted to hold. Limitations on the types of assets and on the available composition of private portfolios may arise because capital markets are relatively unsophisticated. However, government regulations, such as exchange restrictions and institutionally set interest rates, also shrink portfolio options and may thereby exacerbate inflation.

5. The Interrelationship of Fiscal and Impact Policies in Shock Programs

Regardless of the degree of success of impact policies in reducing inflation, they themselves may be expensive for the budget. For instance, the cost of implementing a price freeze may be substantial. If public utility prices are frozen at low rates, the budget will suffer. If prices are frozen with an element of government subsidy in them, the subsidy will be perpetuated; and if they happen to be frozen at low disequilibrium rates relative to prices of other goods, the aggregate subsidy will increase as individuals substitute the relatively cheaper subsidized goods for competing ones.

Other labor policies of the government may also be expensive. For example, redundancy payments and pension, social security, or health scheme payoffs make the costs of laying off public servants quite high in terms of a single year's deficit.

If successful adjustment generates a sudden improvement in the balance of payments, which leads to a drop in revenue from trade taxes, this loss must also be factored into post-program revenue projections. In Argentina, for example, the shortfall in 1985 revenue owing to external restraint was estimated at half a percentage point of GDP.

V. CONCLUSIONS

The experiences of Argentina, Bolivia, Brazil, and Israel under the recent shock programs offer insights concerning, first, the innovative elements of the packages and, second, fiscal policy in the presence of high inflation and unorthodox strategies for curbing it. It is certainly true that these programs, and in particular their so-called heterodox components, have succeeded in catching public attention and mobilizing public support, at least in the short run, for the implementation of policies that usually involve significant costs during the period of adjustment. Public confidence in the government and in its policies is such a crucial element in restoring stability and in attaining a successful level of economic management, recovery, and growth that these programs' innovations cannot be dismissed lightly.

However, it is difficult to make stronger claims about the virtues of shock programs based on the recent evidence. Although direct controls and freezes can attain a very dramatic and immediate fall in the rate of inflation, it has not proven possible to reduce inflation for more than a short period by means of impact policies alone. In fact, there are strong indications that the size and quality of adjustment of fundamental variables was the most compelling catalyst in achieving inflation cuts, possibly through their impact on expectations, as well as their direct impact on excess absorption. Likewise, it is becoming increasingly clear that pure expectational policies cannot play a decisive and independent role in actually changing deep-rooted public perceptions and bringing down inflation without imposing real losses on the economy.

Furthermore, freezes, controls, and incomes policies are not costless. They entail administrative and political costs, as well as economic costs in terms of shortages, bottlenecks, losses of efficiency, and, possibly, damage to long-run growth potential, particularly when prices are frozen out of equilibrium. Moreover, they may also have a fiscal cost by causing the budget to deteriorate, thus eroding the authorities' ability to adjust the fundamental variables successfully. When evaluating the benefits of these policies, it is important to consider these implicit and explicit costs.

The assumptions on which the use of impact policies has been based may be difficult to define in operational terms, particularly the concept of inertial inflation as an independent source of price pressures. It is, in fact, possible that the inertial component of inflation is not separable from the "real" component, so that, though price freezes are actually working to overcome some inertia in inflation, their influence cannot be perceived unless a fundamental adjustment is taking place at the same time. More generally, given their direct and indirect dependence on the reduction of excess absorption, as well as the danger they entail of compromising a country's long-run growth potential, the shock programs have not revealed any practical or painless way of cutting inflation.

We are, however, not left with the result that traditional demand-management policies function exactly as economists had always believed in adjusting the price level. In particular, the conduct and effects of fiscal policy in high-inflation countries, by themselves or in the context of shock programs, may differ from what is described in conventional analyses. Fiscal management becomes more difficult, in that policymakers must take into account additional complications arising from the persistence of the inflationary process and from the transition from high to lower levels of inflation. Of these, we have discussed the facts that a high-inflation deficit is not the same as a low-inflation deficit; that a tax base which is optimal under high inflation may disappear as inflation drops; and that administrative mechanisms which are cost-effective under high inflation may appear too cumbersome under lower inflation.

On the one hand, some of the general intuitions embodied in the shock programs may also provide important lessons for fiscal policy. Large, temporary fiscal measures may play a valuable role in adjustment, as may announcements of future changes in fiscal regime. On the other hand, some accepted beliefs about fiscal policy do not seem to have been supported in practice. For example, deficit reduction through tax and rate increases was not shown to generate significantly higher inflation than deficit adjustment through cuts in activity.

In sum, from the evidence at hand at this point, it could be said that while shock programs have heightened our awareness that the manipulation of expectations may significantly affect the outcome of an adjustment program, expectation-changing policies are not a substitute for fundamental adjustment achieved by adopting an appropriate fiscal and monetary stance, and may be successful only when implemented in conjunction with traditional demand-management policies. The implementation of the latter policies is not, unfortunately, as straightforward in the presence of expectation-changing policies as in the traditional case; and the success of the policies, when they are called upon to ward off hyperinflation, is more difficult to ensure than when inflation is not an important determinant of the behavior of fiscal variables.

REFERENCES

Barro, Robert J., and David B. Gordon, "Rules, Discretion and Reputation in a Model of Monetary Policy," *Journal of Monetary Economics* (Amsterdam), Vol. 12 (July 1983), pp. 101-21.

Blejer, Mario I., and Nissan Liviatan, "Fighting Hyperinflation: Stabilization Strategies in Argentina and Israel, 1985-86," *Staff Papers*, International Monetary Fund (Washington), Vol. 34 (September 1987), pp. 409-38.

Bruno, Michael, and Stanley Fischer, "Expectations and the High Inflation Trap" (unpublished, September 1985).

Calvo, Guillermo A., "Optimal Seigniorage from Money Creation: An Analysis in Terms of the Optimum Balance of Payments Deficit Problem," *Journal of Monetary Economics* (Amsterdam), Vol. 4 (August 1978), pp. 503-17.

———, and Roque B. Fernandez, "Competitive Banks and the Inflation Tax," *Economic Letters* (Lausanne), Vol. 12 (Nos. 3-4, 1983), pp. 313-17.

Chu, Ke-young, and Andrew Feltenstein, "Relative Price Distortions and Inflation: The Case of Argentina, 1963-76," *Staff Papers*, International Monetary Fund (Washington), Vol. 25 (September 1978), pp. 453-93.

Dornbusch, Rudiger, and Stanley Fischer, "Stopping Hyperinflations Past and Present," *Weltwirtschaftliches Archiv* (Tuebingen), Vol. 122 (No. 1, 1986), pp. 1-14.

Liviatan, Nissan, "Inflation and Stabilization in Israel: Conceptual Issues and Interpretation of Developments" (unpublished, International Monetary Fund, November 4, 1986).

Sargent, Thomas J., "The Ends of Four Big Inflations," in *Inflation: Causes and Effects*, ed. by Robert E. Hall (University of Chicago Press, 1982), pp. 41-97.

Tanzi, Vito, "Inflation, Lags in Collection, and the Real Value of Tax Revenue," *Staff Papers*, International Monetary Fund (Washington), Vol. 24 (March 1977), pp. 154-67.

_____ , "Inflation, Real Tax Revenue, and the Case for Inflationary Finance: Theory with an Application to Argentina," *Staff Papers*, International Monetary Fund (Washington), Vol. 25 (September 1978), pp. 417-51.

_____ , Mario I. Blejer, and Mario O. Teijeiro, "Inflation and the Measurement of Fiscal Deficits" (unpublished, International Monetary Fund, March 13, 1987).

Part III

Fiscal Policy, Stabilization, and the World Environment

5

Fiscal Policy Responses to Exogenous Shocks in Developing Countries

Vito Tanzi*

During the past decade, the developing countries have been subjected to various exogenous shocks that have made the pursuit of sound economic policy, and particularly sound fiscal policy, very difficult. In this paper, I discuss the factors associated with these exogenous shocks; the impact of these shocks on fiscal variables; and some of the policy responses by countries. "Exogenous shocks" are defined as uncontrollable external events that have substantial effects on a country's income level.

I. Factors Associated with Exogenous Shocks

The most important exogenous shocks have been the following:

1. Changes in Export Earnings

Many developing countries rely heavily on the export of one or a few commodities (oil, coffee, copper, etc.) for their foreign exchange earnings. Shocks may originate in unexpected changes in their prices arising from changes in supply conditions or in the demand for these commodities. A frost in Brazil that raises the international price of coffee also raises the foreign exchange earnings of other coffee exporters. An oil embargo by the major Middle Eastern oil exporting countries had the same effect on

*This paper was first published in the May 1986 issue of *American Economic Review*. The assistance I have received from Ke-young Chu and Bassirou A. Sarr is greatly appreciated.

the earnings of other oil exporting countries. Major world booms and re-cessions, by affecting commodity demand, have generated positive or neg-ative shocks for developing country exports.

2. Changes in Major Import Prices

The most obvious example is provided by oil price movements since 1973. In view of the great importance of oil in many countries' imports, when oil prices rose sharply in the 1970s, the real incomes of many oil importing countries were significantly reduced.

3. Change in Cost of Foreign Borrowing

As many developing countries are heavy borrowers, an increase in the interest rate in international capital markets can be an important exoge-nous shock. The cost of international borrowing to a given country can also go up because of a changed perception of the risk associated with lending to that country. Although the effects on borrowing costs may be the same, the latter is not a truly "exogenous" shock. When the cost of borrowing rises, it affects the cost of new funds as well as the cost of ser-vicing the existing stock of foreign debt. If the debt is large and its matu-rity is short, the rise in interest expenditure can be substantial. If the foreign debt is mostly public, budgetary expenditures are directly affected.

4. Changes in Availability of Foreign Credit

This type of shock is not the same as the previous one. Around 1982, the world witnessed a dramatic reduction in the willingness of commer-cial banks to lend to many developing countries. Mexico, for example, saw its foreign borrowing fall from $18 billion in 1981 to $5 billion in 1983. The debt crisis made new loans unavailable to many countries, thus reducing their ability to continue using this source to finance their current expendi-ture levels.

5. Changes in Level of Foreign Grants

In many countries, and especially in the smaller ones, an important ex-ogenous shock may come in the form of sudden changes in the availability of foreign grants or of concessionary loans. Countries that have relied on these sources for their domestic expenditure will be forced to reduce their spending when those grants are no longer available. Examples of these shocks abound, especially in Africa.

6. Changes in Other Factors

Shocks may at times also be associated with such factors as changes in foreign workers' remittances, in direct foreign investment, in capital outflows carried out by nationals, and so on. In many cases, these changes can be traced to the countries' own policies; therefore, they are not genuinely exogenous.

II. Effects of Exogenous Shocks on Fiscal Variables

The factors mentioned above affect not just the incomes of countries but also their fiscal variables. They may improve or worsen the fiscal situation and, by so doing, may bring about policy responses. The automatic impact of external shocks on the fiscal variables is likely to be much more important in developing countries than in industrial countries. At the same time, the ability of developing countries to neutralize these effects, if they wish to do so, is much more limited.

In industrial countries the external shocks affect incomes and economic activity much more than the fiscal variables themselves, since the fiscal sector is closely linked to the external sector. Therefore, the observed changes in the fiscal variables can be attributed to policy responses. For example, when the oil price increase in 1974 reduced the real incomes of industrial countries, their governments responded by increasing public spending in the form of transfers to families. This increase in public spending was not automatic but reflected a conscious, discretionary governmental reaction. Apart from the cyclical impact that affected tax revenues, the increases in fiscal deficits in the Organization for Economic Cooperation and Development (OECD) countries in 1975 were policy induced.

In the developing countries, the impact of external shocks on the fiscal variables is much more direct or automatic. Therefore, the observed change in the fiscal variable should not be attributed mainly to policy changes. For this reason, it is very difficult, when dealing with developing countries, to isolate the changes in fiscal variables that reflect genuine policy responses from those that reflect automatic effects. Thus, studies that attempt to estimate from observed fiscal changes the fiscal policy response to exogenous shocks are likely to reach misleading conclusions.

The reason for the above conclusion is the close link that exists in developing countries between the budget and the foreign sector. This link depends on (a) the high proportion of foreign trade taxes in total revenue, (b) the high proportion of domestic sales taxes collected from imports, (c) the heavy reliance of corporate income taxes on exports of mineral products, (d) the public sector's reliance on foreign borrowing or foreign grants, (e) the high proportion of foreign debt that is public, (f) the widespread attempts in these countries to insulate some domestic prices from movements in world prices, and so on.

Foreign trade taxes (import duties plus export duties) account for more than one third of developing countries' total tax revenue. This estimated share, however, does not convey the full importance of the external sector in public revenue, since corporate income taxes, which are mostly collected from mineral exports, account for another 18 percent and "domestic" taxes on goods and services are often levied largely on imported goods. More than 50 percent of the tax revenue of developing countries may be directly related to the foreign sector. Furthermore, in many of these countries some of the important export sectors (petroleum, phosphates, bauxite, etc.) are government owned. (See Tanzi (1987).) When the prices of those commodities change, the effect on public revenue can be direct and immediate. Much of the developing countries' foreign borrowing is done by the public sector. When the availability or the cost of foreign loans changes, government resources are, again, immediately and directly affected.

To some extent, the same close link between the fiscal sector and the foreign sector exists on the expenditure side. Some government expenditures are financed by earmarked taxes. When tax revenue declines because of external shocks, the resources available for these expenditures also decline. The sizes of many subsidies depend on the differences between the international prices and the domestic prices of some imported products. When the international price increases or the exchange rate appreciates, the amount of the subsidy, and thus the budget deficit, also increases. Some external shocks have an immediate impact on the financing of investment expenditure, since concessionary loans or grants are often tied to specific projects; thus, when the availability of these loans or grants changes, the amount of resources available for investments also changes.

In conclusion, while shocks affect real incomes in both industrial and developing countries, they have far more pronounced and direct effects on the fiscal sectors of the latter.

III. POLICY RESPONSE

Some literature is relevant for those assessing what the "optimal" fiscal reaction of developing countries to exogenous shocks should be. (See Tabellini (1985).) However, much of this literature is highly theoretical and assumes that over the short run, policymakers can control the policy instruments; it also assumes that they have sufficient interest and knowledge to pursue optimal policies. Unfortunately, the real world is much more complex. Some obstacles that exist in *all* countries are far more important in developing countries than elsewhere.

First, there are the contrasting views on how developing countries' economies operate and how they respond to various policy tools. Under the best of circumstances, policymakers would receive conflicting advice. The ongoing controversy about Fund programs is an indication of this phenomenon. Second, some of the civil servants entrusted with implementing the policies decided upon by the policymakers may not respond in the required fashion. For example, it is easy to change a tax law; it is much more difficult to make the tax administrators fully implement the change. Third, statistics that are essential for good policymaking are often not available or are available with considerable delays or with sizable errors. Fourth, changes in policy instruments are often neutralized by the reaction of forces outside the control of the policymakers or even of the the civil servants. For example, an increase in import duties or in income tax rates may have little effect on revenue if smuggling is easy and tax evasion is rampant. Fifth, the authorities often find unacceptable, for various reasons, policies that may be seen as desirable by economists. Considering all these reasons, one should expect different fiscal responses to exogenous shocks in developing countries than in industrial countries. There is also the complication that exogenous shocks generate not just fiscal imbalances but also external imbalances, which may not be easily financeable. The policymakers often find themselves in situations where they have to coordinate conflicting objectives concerning internal and external imbalances.

The countries that, in the 1970s, were faced with rising public revenues owing to higher export prices generally reacted in three different ways. The first, and very small, group considered the increase as a temporary windfall which would affect only marginally the permanent income of the country and of the government. These countries used the additional revenue to pay off foreign debt or to accumulate foreign assets (foreign exchange or real assets). They thus were in a position to liquidate these assets in future years when foreign earnings declined, in order to maintain domestic spending on some trend which they hoped would be permanent. This behavior is an application of the permanent-income hypothesis of consumption to the government.

The second, and larger, group engaged in capital accumulation at home by expanding public investment. Provided that the investment had as high a rate of return as the country could have received on foreign assets, that the "additional" investment spending had been limited to the windfall income, and that this spending could have been phased out when the windfall income began to disappear, this policy response could have been

considered a good one. However, experience indicates that these requirements often were not met. Investment was often not as productive as it
could have been, since it was distorted by poor management and by political considerations, was often too large, and was too rigid to be phased out
when conditions made such action appropriate. These countries faced difficulties when the windfall disappeared and foreign financing dried up.
These changes called for a quick reduction of investment expenditure.

The third, and largest, group increased public spending by increasing
public employment, the amount of transfers, investment, and so on. In this
particular situation, when the decline in foreign earnings inevitably came,
the countries were tied to patterns and levels of spending that were difficult to change. As long as foreign loans were available, the countries used
these to maintain spending at levels that could no longer be sustained
with ordinary revenue. This reaction prolonged the problem and, in many
cases, made it worse by leaving the countries with huge foreign debts.
When the crisis came, and the countries found that they had to adjust,
since financing was no longer available, the consequences were very
serious.

Shocks that reduce public sector revenue are even more difficult to
deal with. In this case, countries are often unable to make up the revenue
losses in the short run. The loss of foreign trade taxes could, in theory, be
compensated for by increasing income taxes or taxing domestically produced products. But income taxes take a very long time to introduce and
collect, and their scope is limited in developing countries. For this reason,
countries have often been forced to rely on inferior revenue sources, such
as inflationary finance, regressive excises, or the building up of arrears.

IV. Conclusions

Unlike the situation in industrial countries—where the government
has much greater control over revenue sources, revenues are rarely tied
to the foreign sector, and there is always the option of selling bonds domestically to generate additional domestic revenue for the public sector in
a non-inflationary way—in the developing countries the degree of freedom in the policy area is much more limited, for some of the reasons already indicated. Another reason is that the potential for generation of
domestic non-inflationary and non-tax sources of revenues is extremely
limited. Therefore, in the absence of foreign borrowing, and once the possibility of financing spending through the building up of arrears has been
exhausted, there is a limit to the amount of public spending (expressed in
real terms or as a share of gross national product). This is not a rigid limit,

but it exists all the same. (See Tanzi (1985).) Attempting to exceed that limit will bring about inflation, since the government will have to finance the additional spending through money creation. This channel itself has a limit, and inflationary finance may reduce the real value of tax revenue. (See Tanzi (1978).) That absolute limit on real government spending falls when an exogenous shock reduces tax revenue; it falls even more when foreign borrowing is constrained by the unwillingness of commercial banks to lend to the country. Of course, within the budget itself, to the extent that the servicing of foreign public debt increases, other expenditures have to be reduced even more.

Thus, often the only realistic alternative that these countries have is to reduce public spending. As it is often politically difficult to reduce current spending in the short run, the adjustment pressure is often shifted to capital spending. This is normally seen as an undesirable type of adjustment, although if unproductive investment projects are eliminated, it may not be as undesirable as is often believed.

REFERENCES

Tabellini, Guido, "Fiscal Policy Response to the External Shocks of 1979 in Selected Developing Countries: Theory and Facts" (unpublished, International Monetary Fund, December 26, 1985).

Tanzi, Vito, "Inflation, Real Tax Revenue, and the Case for Inflationary Finance: Theory with an Application to Argentina," *Staff Papers*, International Monetary Fund (Washington), Vol. 25 (September 1978), pp. 417-51.

_____, "Is There a Limit to the Size of Fiscal Deficits in Developing Countries?" in *Public Finance and Public Debt: Proceedings of the 40th Congress of the International Institute of Public Finance*, Innsbruck, 1984, ed. by Bernard P. Herber (Detroit, Michigan: Wayne State University Press, 1986), pp. 139-52.

_____, "Quantitative Characteristics of the Tax Systems of Developing Countries," in *The Theory of Taxation for Developing Countries*, ed. by David M. G. Newbery and Nicholas II. Stern (New York: Oxford University Press, 1987), pp. 205-41.

6

External Shocks and Fiscal Adjustment in Developing Countries: Recent Experiences

Ke-young Chu

I. Introduction

In many developing countries, a major feature of the fiscal sector is the importance of government revenue deriving directly or indirectly from external trade. This results from both the dominance of trade in their economies and their weak administrative capability, which makes them rely heavily on the taxation of external trade because it can be easily administered.[1]

Therefore, in highly open developing countries, the fluctuations in external trade can be transmitted directly to the fiscal sector. The large fluctuations in trade and the uncertainty surrounding them pose serious problems for the formulation and execution of fiscal policy.

The international economic environment for developing countries has changed substantially since the early 1970s. The cyclical fluctuations of industrial economies have become more pronounced than they were in the 1960s, and the prices of internationally traded goods–particularly primary commodities–have become more volatile. Against this background, the overall fiscal deficits of developing countries, on average, were higher, and fluctuated more sharply, during 1972-82 than during 1962-71.

The fiscal and external sectors could interact through a number of channels. A greater fluctuation in the target for government expenditure could result in a greater fluctuation in actual expenditure. A greater fluc-

---

[1]Trade is not the only external factor (though it is a major one) with important fiscal implications. Other factors include the availabilities of foreign credit, grants, and investments. See Tanzi (1986).

tuation in the target for government expenditure could originate in a greater fluctuation in external trade if the targets were based on anticipated revenue, which, in turn, would depend on anticipated future trade.

Increased fluctuation in the fiscal balance may be a direct consequence of increased fluctuation in external trade, an important revenue base. Another important source of fiscal instability is fluctuation in the availability of foreign financing, which also is related to world economic conditions. Furthermore, errors in anticipation, other constraints on policy instruments, lags, and possible asymmetry of government responses could not only aggravate fiscal instability but also contribute to both the greater persistence, and the worsening, of fiscal imbalances.

This paper analyzes fiscal developments in a group of 18 developing countries during 1962-82 and examines empirically several aspects of fiscal adjustment processes. It asks such questions as the following: How did fiscal balances behave during different phases of recent world trade cycles? How did revenue and expenditure contribute to fluctuations in the deficit during these cycles? Were increases in fiscal deficits and the consequent fiscal crises following the two recent world recessions attributable to a reduction in revenue or to an expansion of expenditure? Given the institutional dependence of revenue on external developments, how did government expenditure behave during the trade and fiscal cycles? How did expenditure respond to anticipated and unanticipated external shocks? How did fiscal discipline affect the long-run performance of individual countries in the group? Was the long-run deterioration in the fiscal balance related in any way to the amplitude of the fluctuation of the fiscal balance–that is, was the long-run fiscal deterioration partly a consequence of the fiscal fluctuation? What were the policy implications of the greater fiscal fluctuation?

The organization of this paper is as follows. Section II describes fiscal developments in the 18 sample developing countries during 1962-82. Section III analyzes sources of fiscal fluctuation in the sample countries, with particular emphasis placed on the relationship between trade cycles and fiscal cycles. Section IV analyzes fiscal policy responses to external shocks and the consequent fiscal imbalances. Section V draws conclusions from this analysis.

II. Overview of Fiscal Developments in Eighteen Developing Countries

The 18 sample countries are the developing countries for which consistent fiscal and external trade data are readily available from 1962 through

1982. During this period, world trade fluctuated markedly, particularly around the times of the two world recessions in 1975 and 1981-82. The sample consists of 4 countries in Africa, 7 in Asia, 1 in the Middle East, and 6 in the Western Hemisphere. (See Table 1.) Most are highly open, non-oil primary commodity exporters that rely heavily on the taxation of international transactions for their central government revenues.[2] In 1980, such taxation accounted, on average, for 20 percent of total government revenue and 25 percent of tax revenue; for several countries, it accounted for more than 30 percent of total government revenue, suggesting the importance of the external sector as a source of government revenue. (See Table 2.) The importance of the external sector is much greater than is suggested by these statistics, because these countries also rely indirectly on the external sector for revenue—particularly on revenue from the taxation of incomes or transactions deriving from international transactions.[3]

Table 1. Eighteen Developing Countries: Location, Openness, and Major Exports, 1980[1]

	Openness	Major Exports[2]		
Location	Share of trade value in GDP	Total	Primary commodities	Services	Manu- factures
	percent	*number of countries*			
All sample countries	75.1	18	12	4	2
Africa	60.6	4	4	0	0
Asia	96.5	7	3	2	2
Middle East	90.6	1	0	1	0
Western Hemisphere	57.2	6	5	1	0

[1] Based on data from International Monetary Fund, *International Financial Statistics* (Washington), various issues.

[2] Based on the classification used for the Fund's World Economic Outlook exercises. The sample countries were the following: Africa: Kenya, Malawi, South Africa, and Zambia; Asia: India, Malaysia, Nepal, Pakistan, Singapore, Sri Lanka, and Thailand; Middle East: Jordan; and Western Hemisphere: Brazil, El Salvador, Honduras, Jamaica, Nicaragua, and Panama.

[2] The term "openness," as used in this paper, refers to an economy's dependence on external trade. Consequently, describing an economy as open does not necessarily indicate that it has a liberal trade regime.

[3] For an analysis of the tax systems in a broader sample of developing countries, see Tanzi (1982). That paper shows that the importance of the taxation of international transactions is a fairly general characteristic of tax systems in developing countries.

Table 2. Eighteen Developing Countries: Importance of Taxation on International Transactions, 1980[1]

	Average Share of Tax Revenue from International Transactions in:	
	Total revenue	Total tax revenue
	percent[2]	
All sample countries	19.9	25.2
	number of countries	
All sample countries	18	18
Shares (in percent)		
40 or more	1	3
30–40	4	4
20–30	4	4
10–20	3	1
0–10	6	6

[1]Based on data in International Monetary Fund, *Government Finance Statistics Yearbook* (Washington), Vol. 9 (1985).

[2]Simple average.

1. Long-Term Trend

One of the notable changes seen in the fiscal balances of the sample countries over the years is the deterioration in overall deficits. Deficits, on average, more than doubled, increasing from 2.8 percent of gross domestic product (GDP) during 1962-71 to 5.9 percent of GDP during 1972-82. (See Table 3, Part A.) This increase in deficits resulted entirely from sharp increases in expenditures as a percentage of GDP, as they, on average, exceeded increases in revenues.[4]

Between the two periods, the external balances of the sample countries also deteriorated sharply as a result of increases in imports. The average trade balance deficit almost doubled, from 5.8 percent to 10.5 percent of GDP; the average current account deficit also deteriorated.

2. Fluctuation

The deterioration in fiscal balances of the 18 developing countries between 1962-71 and 1972-82 was accompanied by increased fluctuation of

---

[4]Data cover only the central government. In some sample countries, the fiscal performance of the public sector could diverge substantially from that of the central government owing to the fiscal activities of the local government and public enterprises. All the time-series data used in this study are based on calendar years; exceptions are fiscal data for India, Kenya, and Pakistan.

Table 3. Eighteen Developing Countries: Developments in Fiscal
Balances and External Trade, 1962–82[1]

(*Percentage of GDP*)

	1962–71	1972–82
	A. Average Over Time[2]	
Fiscal balance		
Deficit	2.8	5.9
Foreign financing of deficit	1.4	1.6
Revenue[3]	16.0	18.9
Expenditure	18.8	24.8
External trade		
Total trade	53.6	63.5
Exports	23.9	26.5
Imports	29.7	37.0
Trade balance deficit	5.8	10.5
Current account deficit	2.6	5.5
	B. Fluctuation Over Time[2,4]	
Fiscal balance		
Deficit	1.4	2.5
Foreign financing of deficit	0.7	1.2
Revenue	1.3	1.8
Expenditure	1.8	3.0
External trade[5]		
Total trade	3.9	6.8
Exports	1.7	3.5
Imports	2.8	4.7

[1]Based on data from International Monetary Fund, *International Financial Statistics* (Washington), various issues.

[2]Simple average.

[3]In this study, revenue includes foreign grants whenever data are available in *International Financial Statistics.*

[4]Measured by the standard error of the regression of the series on time trend—that is, the standard deviation of the residuals of the regression. Based on data taken from *International Financial Statistics,* various issues.

[5]Excluding Zambia.

fiscal balances around their trends. The indices of fluctuation of overall deficits almost doubled, on average, from 1.4 to 2.5; similar indices for both revenues and expenditures also increased between the two periods. (See Table 3, Part B.) This increased fluctuation of fiscal balances was accompanied by similarly increased fluctuations in revenue, foreign financing, and external trade. The indices of fluctuation in trade values increased, on average, from 3.9 to 6.8 as a result of greater instability of both exports and imports.

The large fluctuation in fiscal balances of the sample countries was particularly notable during the two recent world trade cycles of 1971-76 and 1977-82. (See Section III for details.)

The increases in the fluctuations of fiscal balances and trade values did not exceed the increases in their averages. Similarly, there is no evidence that the dispersions of the fluctuations become more pronounced if they are normalized by their averages.

This overview suggests that the increase in the fluctuation of fiscal balances was restrained, in the sense that it did not exceed the increase in deficits. This proportionality itself raises a serious question, however, about the proper relationship between deficits and their fluctuation, because a simple extrapolation of this proportionality implies that the fiscal balance should not fluctuate when fiscal equilibrium is maintained over a number of years. This implication is obviously unrealistic, because it should not be unusual for the fiscal balance to fluctuate even if the balance averages zero over a period of years. It is, therefore, realistic to expect the increase in the fluctuation of fiscal deficits to be less than proportional to the increase in their levels. From this perspective, the increasing fluctuation in fiscal deficits and the cyclical appearance of fiscal crises are disturbing.

III. External Shocks, Fiscal Policy Responses, and Fiscal Fluctuations

1. Sources of Fluctuation in Deficits

In Section II, it was shown that for the 18 sample countries, expenditures fluctuated more than revenues during the sample period. This result suggests that the fluctuation in expenditures, rather than that in revenues, was the immediate cause of the unstable deficits. To test this hypothesis, the fluctuation of the deficit is regressed on the fluctuations of revenue and expenditure, all as percentages of GDP, separately for each sample country as follows:

$$ed_{it} = -\alpha_{ri} er_{it} + \epsilon_{it} \tag{1}$$

$$ed_{it} = \alpha_{gi} eg_{it} + \eta_{it} \tag{2}$$

where ed_{it}, er_{it}, and eg_{it} denote deviations of the deficit (d_{it}), revenue (r_{it}), and expenditure (g_{it}) as percentages of GDP for country i from their respective trends, which are derived by regressing d_{it}, r_{it}, and g_{it} on the time trend. The estimated equations (1) and (2) would indicate not only whether revenue or expenditure was a dominant factor underlying the fluctuation of the deficit but also the extent of the correlation between the fluctuations of revenue and those of expenditure. The relative dominance of revenue would yield a higher coefficient of determination for equation (1) than for equation (2); a positive correlation between revenue and expenditure fluctuations would yield estimates $\hat{\alpha}_{ri}$ and $\hat{\alpha}_{gi}$ smaller than 1.[5]

The estimation results are summarized in Table 4. The results suggest expenditure fluctuations as the dominant cause of the instability in the fiscal balances. The adjusted coefficients of determination average 0.13 for equation (1) and 0.60 for equation (2). The estimates of the coefficients $\alpha._i$ are statistically significant in only 7 out of the 18 cases for equation (1), but 17 cases out of 18 for equation (2), at the 5 percent level. The results also suggest a strong positive correlation between the fluctuations of revenue and those of expenditure; the coefficients $\hat{\alpha}._i$ average larger for expenditure (0.65) than for revenue (0.05), but are substantially less than 1 in both equations (1) and (2). The correlations between deficits and revenues are estimated to be weak.

These results, however, do not necessarily refute the importance of the external circumstances as an *ultimate* cause of fiscal instability. Whereas the fluctuations of expenditures may have originated in unstable fiscal targets not necessarily related to the external circumstances, it is not inconceivable that external circumstances were responsible for the fluctuations in expenditure, either by affecting the target expenditure or by affecting the part of expenditure that was an instrument for fiscal adjustment. Moreover, in many countries, a substantial part of govern-

---

[5]The estimate of α_{ri} is

$$\hat{\alpha}_{ri} = -\left(\Sigma\, er_{it} ed_{it}\right)\Big/\Sigma\, er_{it}$$

The deviations ed_{it}, er_{it}, and eg_{it} are related by the identity

$$ed_{it} = -er_{it} + eg_{it}$$

Therefore

$$\hat{\alpha}_{ri} = 1 - \left(\Sigma\, er_{it} eg_{it}\Big/\Sigma\, er_i\right)$$

The expected value of $\hat{\alpha}_{ri}$ will be 1 if er_{it} and eg_{it} are not correlated; it will be less than 1 if they are positively correlated, greater than 1 if they are negatively correlated. A similar proof can also be shown for $\hat{\alpha}_{gi}$.

Table 4. Eighteen Developing Countries: Relative Importance of Fluctuation of Revenue and Expenditure in Fluctuation of Deficits, 1962–82

	Regression of Deficit on[1]	
	Revenue	Expenditure
Average statistics[2]		
Adjusted R	0.13	0.60
Coefficient ($\hat{\alpha}_{.1}$)	0.05	0.65
Statistical significance of coefficient ($\hat{\alpha}_{.1}$)	*number of countries*	
Significant at:		
1 percent	4	14
5 percent	7	17
10 percent	7	17
20 percent	10	17
Not significant at		
20 percent	8	1

[1]The regressions are conducted on the deviations of deficits, revenue, and expenditure, as percentages of GDP, from their respective trends for individual countries. The trends are estimated by regressing the deficits, revenue, and expenditure, as percentages of GDP, on time trends. Based on data from International Monetary Fund, *International Financial Statistics* (Washington), various issues.

[2]Simple averages for all the 18 sample countries.

ment capital outlays is directly linked to foreign financing, which became much more volatile during 1972-82 than it had been earlier.

2. Trade Cycles, Policy Responses, and Fiscal Cycles

At this stage of analysis, it is instructive to survey the developments in the fiscal and external sectors of the 18 sample countries over the two recent world trade cycles during 1971-82 (Table 5). Since the fluctuation of fiscal balances is, in an important way, the product of the interactions between external developments and fiscal policy, a brief discussion of the policy responses to external shocks would provide a useful background for the subsequent description of external and fiscal developments.

During a period of large increases in export earnings and aggregate demand, the government may use fiscal policy to dampen aggregate demand by increasing tax rates or by restraining the growth of expenditure. If it adopts this cautious fiscal approach, the resulting improvement in the fiscal balance will lead to a reduction in bank financing and a slowdown in the growth of government debt. It could also lead to an accumulation of domestic or foreign assets for use during the subsequent declining phase of the trade cycle and the ensuing increase in fiscal imbalance. But al-

Table 5. Eighteen Developing Countries: Fluctuations of Fiscal and External Balances During the Two Recent World Trade Cycles, 1971–82[1]

(Percentage of GDP)[2]

| | 1971–76 | | | | | | 1977–82 | | | | | |
| | Expansion | | | | Contraction | | Expansion | | | | | Contraction |
	1971	1972	1973	1974	1975	1976	1977	1978	1979	1980	1981	1982
Fiscal balance												
Deficit	5.1	4.3	4.8	3.5	5.9	7.0	5.5	6.8	7.4	8.6	8.3	9.5
Revenue	18.0	18.1	18.1	19.4	19.9	18.6	19.7	20.2	21.2	21.5	22.0	21.7
Expenditure	23.1	22.4	22.9	22.9	25.8	25.6	25.2	27.0	28.6	30.1	30.3	31.2
External balance												
Trade deficit	9.0	7.5	6.4	11.9	13.9	8.5	8.1	9.7	9.0	14.5	16.3	15.2
Exports	21.1	21.8	24.3	27.4	24.9	27.3	28.5	29.1	32.7	32.5	29.4	26.1
Imports	30.1	29.3	30.7	39.3	38.8	35.8	36.6	38.8	41.7	47.0	45.7	41.3
Total trade	51.2	51.1	55.0	66.7	63.7	63.1	65.1	67.9	74.4	79.5	75.1	67.4

[1]Based on data from International Monetary Fund, *International Financial Statistics* (Washington), various issues.
[2]Simple average across the sample countries.

though this cautious approach is desirable from the standpoint of macro-economic stability, its adoption depends on the government's ability to re-sist political and social pressures to greatly expand government services in a period of rising revenue. These pressures are understandably intense because of, among other reasons, the growing population in many developing countries and the accompanying increase in the demand for services. The pressures will be particularly intense if the increase in export earnings is perceived by the public to be long lasting.

Policy options are more limited during the recessionary phase of trade cycles. A negative external shock, such as a decline in prices, can increase imbalances in both the external and fiscal sectors. The government can draw down financial assets accumulated during a revenue boom. In the absence of accumulated assets, the mix and the speed of policy responses depend on a variety of factors.

No imbalance, whether external or fiscal, arising from a lasting negative shock can be financed indefinitely. The government can restrain expenditures and rely on nominal and real devaluation to improve its external balance. Devaluation will increase revenue if ad valorem export and other related taxes are a dominant part of revenue. If import duties and other taxes on imported goods are dominant, and particularly if these taxes are specific, much of the positive impact of the devaluation will be offset by a decline in imports and import-related taxes. The devaluation will also increase the nominal value of expenditure on government imports and foreign interest payments. Indirectly, it would also raise government spending on goods and services, including wage payments. The net impact of a devaluation on the fiscal balance depends on many factors, including the share of trade taxes in revenue, the shares of imported goods and interest payments in expenditures, the character of the tax system, the extent of domestic inflation generated by the devaluation, and the extent to which public sector wages and salaries are indexed to inflation.

The government can also attempt to increase tax revenue by raising tax rates. Experience suggests, however, that such a policy is often difficult to implement effectively as a short-run fiscal adjustment measure. First, the weakness in tax administration in most developing countries precludes the effective implementation of higher tax rates; an increase in export tax rates can lead to increased tax evasion, rather than increased tax revenue, particularly when the export industry is suffering from an adverse external shock. Second, high tax rates, even if successfully administered, weaken the external competitiveness of the economy, either directly, when export taxes are imposed, or indirectly, when import duties are levied on imported inputs for export industries.

The fluctuations of both fiscal and external balances followed cyclical patterns during these periods. In the trade cycles, a lag of about one year between the peaks in exports and imports is noted.[6] During the 1971-76 cycle, a downturn in exports took place in 1975, whereas a significant downturn in imports took place in 1976. During the 1977-82 cycle, a significant downturn in exports took place during 1981-82, and a major downturn in imports in 1982, although this observation is tentative because the 1977-82 cycle should really be extended beyond 1982.

Fiscal cycles lagged trade cycles by about a year; revenue cycles lagged export cycles, possibly as a result of the usual lags in collection of taxes; and expenditure cycles tended to lag the revenue cycles. Thus, during the 1971-76 cycle, revenues continued to expand in 1975 and experienced a significant downturn only in 1976, whereas exports declined in 1975. Expenditure expanded at an accelerated pace in 1975 and declined only slightly in 1976. During the 1977-82 cycle, a downturn in revenue took place in 1982, whereas exports began to decline in 1981. Expenditure continued to expand in that year. Reflecting these cyclical movements of revenues and expenditure, fiscal deficits peaked in 1976 and again in 1982. During the 1971-76 fiscal cycle, the increase in deficits in 1975 was the result of a decrease in revenue not sufficiently offset by a small downward adjustment in expenditure. During the 1977-82 cycle, the increase in deficits in 1982 was the result of a decline in revenue reinforced by a continued increase in expenditure. During both the 1971-76 and the 1977-82 fiscal cycles, the adjustment of expenditure was slow and limited compared with the decline in revenue.

A more pronounced cyclical picture of fiscal balances is obtained by normalizing the timing of the cycles — that is, by averaging the fiscal balances across the sample countries after adjusting for the slight difference in the timing of the cycles among the sample countries. As shown in Table 6, the fluctuation becomes more pronounced, but the same broad conclusions emerge. Revenue cycles lagged export cycles for a number of reasons, including administrative lags in tax collection. The movements of revenue and deficits indicate that the adjustments in expenditure following the downturns in revenue were not sufficient to contain deteriorations in fiscal balances.

One notable phenomenon observed during the 1972-76 cycle is the sharply larger dispersion of changes in revenue, deficits, and exports across the countries in the recession phase of the fiscal and trade cycles than in the expansion phase. Apparently the extent of the declines in ex-

---

[6]See Rangarajan and Sundararajan (1976); Hemphill (1974); and Chu, Hwa, and Krishnamurty (1983) for the role of exports in the determination of imports in developing countries where the level of imports is constrained by the availability of foreign exchange.

Table 6. Eighteen Developing Countries: Fiscal Developments During the World Recessions of 1975 and 1981–82

(Percentage of GDP)

	1975 Recession		1981–82 Recession	
	Years preceding expansion	Recession	Years preceding expansion	Recession
	1972–74	1975	1978–80	1981–82
Revenues[1]				
Average	1.7	− 2.1	2.8	− 0.7
Standard deviation	1.6	3.9	3.6	1.3
Deficits[1]				
Average	− 0.3	2.2	0.6	—
Standard deviation	2.6	4.4	4.6	2.6
Export developments				
Exports				
Average	2.1	− 2.6	1.2	− 3.9
Standard deviation	2.5	5.3	2.8	5.0

[1]Changes during the expansionary and the contractionary phases, which were not necessarily identical in terms of their timing and duration, are aggregated. The fiscal cycles lagged the trade cycles by about a year.

ports and revenues was more heterogeneous than the increase among the countries. This phenomenon is not observed during the 1978-82 cycle, but then the data do not cover the complete phases of that cycle, which was extended beyond 1982.

IV. ANTICIPATION, FISCAL DISCIPLINE, AND FISCAL FLUCTUATION

1. Government Revenue and Fiscal Cycles

The fairly well-synchronized cycles of fiscal balances and trade in most of the sample countries originate in the institutional setting in which the government relies heavily on the external sector for its revenue. The external factors often encompass not only exports but also the availability of credit, the cost of credit, the availability of foreign grants, and import prices.[7] The following tests are based only on merchandise trade. For the time-series test summarized in Table 7, revenues are regressed on current

[7]This institutional setting is emphasized in Tanzi (1982, 1986) for developing countries in general, particularly Tanzi ((1986), p.89), and in Morgan (1979) for oil exporting countries in particular.

Table 7. Eighteen Developing Countries: Time-Series Results for External Trade and Government Revenue, 1964–82

		Regression of Revenue on[1]		
	Results for Total Sample	Exports	Total trade	Cases with time trend included
Adjusted R^2	0.44	0.50	0.32	
Coefficients				
Average of estimates		0.24	0.24	0.07[2]
Number of countries	18	6	12	5
Statistically significant at:				
1 percent	7	3	4	4
5 percent	14	5	9	5
10 percent	14	5	9	5
20 percent	15	5	10	5
Not significant at				
20 percent	3	1	2	0

[1]Revenue, exports, and total trade values are all expressed as percentages of GDP. Revenues are regressed on either exports or total trade values (current or lagged by one year) with or without a time trend as an additional variable for individual countries.

[2]Average for the 18 sample countries, with the coefficients of the time trend assumed to be zero for the countries for which such trend is not included in the regression.

or lagged exports and total trade values, with or without a time trend. The estimated coefficients are statistically significant at the 5 percent level for 14 of 18 sample countries, and at the 20 percent level for 15 of 18 countries. For the cross-section test summarized in Table 8, the index of fluctuation of revenue is regressed on the index of fluctuation of trade value. The result indicates a positive correlation between the fluctuations of revenue and trade across the sample countries. Against the institutional setting described above, together with the time-series evidence, this correlation should be interpreted as an indication of the impact of trade instability on revenue instability. In the regression for the period 1962-82, the coefficient of the variable representing the fluctuation of trade value is statistically significant at the 5 percent level; for the subperiod 1972-82, when the fluctuation of trade values became more volatile, the coefficient becomes even more significant.

Is it possible that the trade cycles were a consequence, rather than a cause, of the fiscal cycles? It is conceivable that expansionary fiscal policies caused a deterioration in external competitiveness, erosion of the revenue basis, and ultimately fiscal crisis. Alternatively, expansionary fiscal policy, itself, might have originated in the trade cycles. For example, the world recession might have necessitated increases in government expen-

Table 8. Eighteen Developing Countries: Cross-Section Results for External Trade and Government Revenue, 1962–82[1]

	Regression of Fluctuation of Revenue on Fluctuation of Trade Values				
	Coefficients				
Sample Periods	Constant	Fluctuation of trade value	Dummy[2]	SEE[3]	Adjusted R
1962–82	0.61 (1.02)	0.18* (2.67)	−7.02* (−2.43)	1.37	0.23
1962–71	0.90 (1.90)	0.09 (1.52)	−1.46 (−7.99)	1.58	0.02
1972–82	−0.22 (−0.35)	0.37** (3.69)	−7.42 (−3.13)	1.18	0.41

[1]A single asterisk (*) indicates significance at the 5 percent level, while a double asterisk (**) indicates significance at the 1 percent level. Figures in parentheses below the coefficients are t-statistics.

[2]Representing Singapore, which has a relationship between revenue and trade fluctuations that is radically different from those of the other sample countries.

[3]Standard error of estimate.

diture for the alleviation of the adverse impacts of the recession on the economy, in general, and on the poor segment of the population, in particular. These two channels are plausible, but obviously different from the channel—running from external developments, through changes in revenue, to the fiscal fluctuation focused on in this paper. It should be noted, however, that even in the first of these alternative channels, the role of the government's anticipation of external developments in the formulation of fiscal policy cannot be overemphasized. Furthermore, the synchronization of the fiscal cycles among the sample countries in relation to the world trade cycles indicates the importance of external developments in fiscal cycles and fiscal crises. For the second of the two possible channels, which was mentioned above as plausible, the correlation between the fluctuations of revenue and expenditure should be negative, since a world recession induces a revenue shortfall (resulting from a smaller tax base) and an excess in expenditure (resulting from anticyclical fiscal policy). The positive correlation between revenue and expenditure for most sample countries suggests that expenditure has been, to a certain extent, an important policy instrument for fiscal adjustment rather than for anticyclical economic stabilization.

2. Fiscal and External Imbalances and Government Expenditure

In this section, the process according to which government expenditure was determined in the 18 sample countries is examined. Ideally, the key hypotheses underlying the model should be tested by designing more country-specific structural models. This section focuses on analyzing the fluctuation of fiscal balances in a fairly large number of sample countries. Therefore, the analytical framework is made simple and uniform for all the sample countries. This simple relationship may be written as

$$\Delta g_t = \theta_0 + \theta_1 t + \theta_2 fb_t^e + \theta_3 eb_t^e + \theta_4 ds_t \tag{3}$$

where

Δg_t = change in *total* government expenditure
fb_t^e = anticipated fiscal imbalance, defined as the difference between the anticipated fiscal balance and the target balance
eb_t^e = anticipated external imbalance, defined analogously as in the fiscal imbalance
ds_t = unanticipated component of an external shock

and

t = time

Total expenditure includes the target component: in equation (3), the change in this target component is captured by the constant, θ_0, and any acceleration or deceleration is captured by the time trend with a constant coefficient, θ_1. It should also be recalled that the anticipated imbalances, fb_t^e and eb_t^e, are assessed at the optimal levels of the policy instruments based on the anticipated external shock.[8]

Equation (3) postulates that government expenditure is determined partly as a result of a systematic drift in its target component and partly as a result of the optimization process. The first two terms reflect the change in the target component, the next two terms the fiscal response to the anticipated shock, and the last term a fiscal response to the unanticipated shock.

In testing the model empirically, a number of further simplifying assumptions have to be made.

First, the government is assumed to regard a certain level of fiscal and external (current account) deficits as sustainable and to regard any deviations of fiscal and external balances from these sustainable deficits as imbalances. The anticipated imbalances are the deviations of anticipated fiscal and external balances from these sustainable levels. The unanticipated shock is defined as the deviation of revenue from anticipated revenue.

---

[8]A positive imbalance indicates either a surplus or a deficit smaller than the target deficit; a negative imbalance indicates a deficit larger than the target deficit.

Therefore, the fiscal and the external imbalances and the unanticipated shock in equation (3) may be written as

$$fb_t^e = b_t^e - \bar{b}_t \tag{4}$$

$$eb_t^e = cab_t^e - \overline{cab}_t \tag{5}$$

$$s_t = r_t - r_t^e \tag{6}$$

where b_t, cab_t, and r_t denote, respectively, the fiscal balance, external balance, and revenue as percentages of GDP, with superscript e indicating an anticipated value and the bar $(-)$ over a variable indicating a sustainable level.

Second, the government is assumed to form anticipations by looking backward. Specifically, the government is assumed to anticipate the fiscal and the external current account balances and revenue on the basis of the following autoregressive equations:

$$b_t^e = \phi_{11} b_{t-1} + \phi_{12} b_{t-2} + \phi_{13} b_{t-3} \tag{7}$$

$$cab_t^e = \phi_{21} cab_{t-1} + \phi_{22} cab_{t-2} + \phi_{23} cab_{t-3} \tag{8}$$

$$r_t^e = \phi_{31} r_{t-1} + \phi_{32} r_{t-2} + \phi_{33} r_{t-3} \tag{9}$$

Therefore, equation (3) may be rewritten as

$$\Delta g_t = \theta_0 - \theta_2 \bar{b}_t - \theta_3 \overline{cab}_t + \theta_1 t + \theta_2 b_t^e + \theta_3 cab_t^e + \theta_4 s_t \tag{10}$$

On the assumption that the targets for fiscal and external deficits are constant, the model may be estimated by regressing the change in expenditure on time, anticipated fiscal and external balances, and unanticipated revenue shock. In addition, possible asymmetric responses of expenditure may be tested by introducing dummy variables into equation (3). For example, possible asymmetric responses of expenditure to either an improvement or a deterioration in the anticipated fiscal balance may be tested by replacing $\theta_2 b_t^e$ by $\theta_2 b_t^e + \theta_2' b_t^e d_{1t}$ where d_{1t} takes the value 1 for the period of an anticipated fiscal improvement and -1 for the period of a deterioration. Similarly, possible asymmetric responses to the unanticipated revenue shock may be tested by replacing $\theta_4 s_t$ by $(\theta_4 s_t + \theta_4' s_t d_{2t})$, where d_{2t} takes the value 1 for the period of a revenue excess and -1 for the period of a revenue shortfall.

The constant term and the coefficient of the time trend in equation (3) cannot be straightforwardly interpreted, because they reflect not only the trend component of expenditure but also the target levels of fiscal and external deficits. The coefficients θ_2 and θ_3 of b_t^e and cab_t^e in equation (10) would reflect the responses of expenditure to the anticipated fiscal and external imbalances.

Note that, in estimating equation (3) for each of the 18 sample countries, not all of the coefficients are necessarily expected to be statistically significant for all of the sample countries. On the basis of several key assumptions maintained in the specification of the model, statistical significance of the coefficients θ_2 and θ_4 would suggest the presence of fiscal discipline in the particular sample country. Given the statistically significant coefficients θ_2 and θ_4, the magnitude of the coefficients would suggest the extent of fiscal adjustment necessary in view of a given magnitude of fiscal imbalance. The explanatory power of the equation may not necessarily be high for all countries, since many variables other than those considered in the framework of the optimization may also be important determinants of government expenditure. The regression would indicate correctly the extent to which government expenditure was determined by the variables included in the equation, as long as the omitted variables were not correlated with the variables included in the equation.

Table 9 summarizes the results of the tests conducted on the basis of the data for the sample countries. The results for equation (3), without the external-imbalance term or the asymmetry dummies, are summarized in Part A. The adjusted coefficients of determination average 0.35 for the sample countries, suggesting that a substantial, although not overwhelming, part of the fluctuation of expenditure is accounted for by the variables included in the equation.[9] It is not surprising that large variations in government expenditure are left unexplained. Fiscal responses to external shocks were diverse, as suggested by the large dispersion of fiscal deficits and expenditures across the sample countries that was discussed in Section III.[10]

At the 20 percent level, the coefficient of the time trend is significant for 6 of the sample countries. The coefficient of the anticipated fiscal imbalance is also significant for 7 countries, and that of the unanticipated revenue shock is significant for 11 countries. At the 5 percent level, the number of countries for which the coefficients of the time trend, anticipated fiscal imbalance, and unanticipated revenue shock are reduced, respectively, to 3, 3, and 10.

---

[9]The adjusted coefficients of determination average 0.41 for 12 countries for which the anticipated fiscal imbalance or the unanticipated revenue shock is found to be significant at the 20 percent level.

[10]See Tanzi (1986) for discussion of the patterns of fiscal responses to external shocks in developing countries.

Table 9. Seventeen Developing Countries[1]: Factors Underlying
Changes in Expenditure, 1967–82

	Test of Statistical Significance At Level of (*in percent*)				Estimated[2] Coefficient
	20	10	5	1	
	A. Symmetric Responses Assumed				
Systematic drift					
Time trend	6	5	3	2	0.14
Responses to shock					
Anticipated fiscal imbalance	7	5	3	1	0.26
Unanticipated revenue shock	11	10	10	7	0.92
Adjusted R^2					0.35
D-W					2.09
	B. Symmetric Responses Tested				
Systematic drift					
Time trend	8	6	3	2	0.22
Responses to shock					
Anticipated fiscal imbalance	8	7	4	2	0.53
Of which: countries for which the asymmetry dummy is significant	3	3	1	0	
Asymmetry dummy	4	4	2	0	– 0.04
Unanticipated revenue shock	10	10	10	6	0.88
Adjusted R^2					0.40
D-W					2.07

[1]Excluding Zambia. D-W denotes Durbin-Watson statistic; in one of the regressions, the D-W statistic is in an inconclusive region, whereas in the rest of them, the D-W statistics suggest the absence of serial correlations.

[2]Simple average of the estimated coefficients for all the sample countries.

The estimated coefficients of the anticipated fiscal imbalance and the unanticipated revenue shock average, respectively, 0.26 and 0.92. These estimates suggest that, on average, the adjustments of government expenditure were only 26 percent of the anticipated fiscal imbalances and 92 percent of the unexpected revenue excesses or shortfalls.[11]

Possible asymmetric responses of government expenditure are tested as follows. First, equation (3) is re-estimated with an asymmetry dummy variable for the unanticipated revenue shock variable. The results do not support the hypothesis that expenditure responded asymmetrically to

---

[11]The estimation results of the same equation without the coefficient θ_3 of the external-imbalance term constrained to be equal to zero are available; the anticipated external-imbalance term is not statistically significant for a large number of countries, and the other results are broadly the same as in Part A of Table 9.

the unexpected revenue shock. Second, the asymmetry dummy variable is replaced by an asymmetry dummy variable for the anticipated fiscal imbalance. Part B of Table 9 summarizes the results of this test. The results confirm the dominant role of the unanticipated revenue shock in the fluctuation of expenditure. The evidence is weak on the role of anticipated fiscal imbalances in the fluctuation of expenditure and possible asymmetric responses of expenditure to changes in such imbalances.

Thus, at the 20 percent level, the coefficient of the anticipated fiscal imbalance is statistically significant for 8 of the 18 sample countries; for 4 of these 8 countries, the asymmetry dummy variable is significant; the coefficient of the unanticipated revenue shock is significant for 10 countries. At the 5 percent level, the coefficient of the anticipated fiscal imbalance is statistically significant for 4 countries, and the coefficient of the unanticipated revenue shock is significant for 10 countries. The coefficients of the anticipated fiscal imbalance average substantially less than one (0.53), whereas those of the unanticipated revenue shock average closer to, but still less than, one (0.88).

For a large proportion of the sample countries, government expenditure is found to have increased in a systematic fashion as a function of time. In the regression reported in Table 8, the coefficient for the time trend is statistically significant for 6 countries at the 20 percent level and for 3 countries at the 5 percent level. The coefficients average 0.14, indicating a significant tendency of upward drift in government expenditure not accounted for by the imbalance variables or the unanticipated revenue shock.

3. Policy Rule and Fiscal Performance

The extent to which the fiscal imbalance affects the formulation and execution of fiscal policy is an important determinant of the fiscal performance. Table 10 compares the long-run fiscal performances of the sample countries with the results obtained in the preceding subsection on the policy rule. For the 12 countries for which the coefficient of the anticipated fiscal imbalance or the unanticipated revenue shock is fairly significant (for example, at the 10 percent level), the deficits increased, on average, by 2.1 percent of GDP between 1962–71 and 1972–82. For the rest of the sample countries, for which the coefficient is not significant, the deficits increased on average by 4.9 percent of GDP. Thus, the countries that could be described as having been more fiscally disciplined are found to have experienced, on average, a smaller deterioration in the fiscal balance than the rest of the sample countries.

A similar result is also obtained for the increase in expenditure. Thus, government expenditure for the first group of countries increased by 5.5 percent of GDP, that for the second group by 6.8 percent of GDP.

Table 10. Eighteen Developing Countries: Policy Rule and Fiscal Performance

Policy Rules	Number of Countries	Fiscal Performance Between 1962–71 and 1972–86	
		Increase in	
		Deficit	Expenditure
		percentage points of GDP	
Countries whose government expenditure responded significantly to anticipated fiscal deficit or unanticipated revenue shock	12	2.1	5.5
Countries whose government expenditure did not respond to anticipated fiscal deficit or unanticipated revenue shock	6	4.9	6.8

V. SUMMARY AND CONCLUSIONS

This paper has explored ways of explaining growing fiscal deficits in developing countries and their increased fluctuations. The paper surveyed fiscal developments in 18 sample countries during 1962-82 and analyzed possible factors underlying the fiscal developments and their relative importance.

The importance of direct and indirect taxation of international trade in many developing countries makes it inevitable that external shocks will affect the fiscal sector directly and immediately. Trade instability directly affects revenue instability. In this institutional setting, fiscal policy is viewed as a result of an optimization process in which not only fiscal policy objectives and fiscal discipline but also a number of constraints may play critical roles. The constraints originate in the government's imperfect foresight, technical features of public investment projects, and difficulties encountered in reaching political consensus. With weak fiscal discipline, incorrect anticipations concerning revenue developments may have important implications for both the long-term developments in fiscal imbalances and the fluctuation of fiscal balances.

In this paper, data for the 18 sample countries indicated a substantial deterioration in fiscal balances and their increased fluctuation during 1962-82. They also showed that the fiscal cycles closely followed the trade cycles, particularly around the times of the two recent world recessions

(1975 and 1981-82). Thus, in each of the two fiscal cycles studied that included world recessions, an increase in revenue followed an expansion in trade, while a decrease followed a contraction. It was shown that an increase in expenditure followed the increase in revenue; downward adjustment in expenditure following the contraction of revenue was too slow and small to prevent major deterioration in the fiscal balance.

Empirical tests indicated that a substantial, though not overwhelming, part of changes in government expenditure can be explained by variables intended to reflect the government's efforts to balance the need to contain the size of the fiscal imbalance against the need to maintain expenditure at a certain level. The results indicated that in a fairly large number of countries, expenditure responded to anticipated fiscal imbalances and unanticipated revenue shocks in a manner that contained the fiscal imbalance. The evidence of such responses was stronger for the unanticipated revenue shock than for the anticipated fiscal imbalance. The use of expenditure as an instrument to contain external imbalance was not evident. The test did not support the hypothesis that expenditure responses to fiscal imbalances could be asymmetric.

The negative results on the asymmetry hypothesis contradict the observations of the time series on aggregate trade, revenue, and fiscal deficit. These time series suggest that during the recent two major world trade cycles, downward adjustments in expenditure were slow and small compared with upward movements during periods of increasing trade and revenue; this observation of aggregate time series suggests that the downward rigidity of expenditure contributed to the persistent fiscal imbalances and fiscal crises. Therefore, in contrast to the results obtained from regressions, the behavior of the aggregate time series suggests that the long-run deterioration of fiscal balances may not be unrelated to the fluctuation of revenues and imbalances.

The larger fluctuation of expenditure than of revenue and the dominance of expenditure fluctuation as the cause of deficit fluctuation are noteworthy. The empirical analysis, however, indicated that the ultimate cause of deficit fluctuation and recurrent fiscal crises in developing countries was, in no small part, the unstable external environment.

On the basis of the particular anticipation scheme assumed in this paper, anticipated fiscal imbalances triggered less strong fiscal adjustment than did unanticipated revenue shocks for a large number of countries. This phenomenon indicates that the adjustment was short term and perhaps unduly costly. Although the results should be viewed as highly tentative, it may not be a coincidence that the long-run deterioration in the fiscal balance was significantly larger for those sample countries that did not respond to shocks than for those countries that did.

BIBLIOGRAPHY

Artus, Jacques R., "The Behavior of Export Prices for Manufactures," *Staff Papers*, International Monetary Fund (Washington), Vol. 21 (November 1974), pp. 583-604.

Chow, Gregory C., *Analysis and Control of Dynamic Economic Systems* (New York: John Wiley and Sons, 1975).

Chu, Ke-young, E.C. Hwa, and K. Krishnamurty, "Export Instability and Adjustments of Imports, Capital Inflows, and External Reserves: A Short-Run Dynamic Model," in *Exchange Rate and Trade Instability: Causes, Consequences, and Remedies*, ed. by David Bigman and Teizo Taya (Cambridge, Massachusetts: Ballinger, 1983), pp. 195-214.

Crockett, Andrew D., "Stabilization Policies in Developing Countries: Some Policy Considerations," *Staff Papers*, International Monetary Fund (Washington), Vol. 28 (March 1981), pp. 54-79.

Davis, Jeffrey M., "The Economic Effects of Windfall Gains in Export Earnings 1975-78" (unpublished, International Monetary Fund, February 29, 1980).

Fleming, J. Marcus, "Domestic Financial Policies Under Fixed and Under Floating Exchange Rates," *Staff Papers*, International Monetary Fund (Washington), Vol. 9 (November 1962), pp. 369-80.

_____, "Targets and Instruments," *Staff Papers*, International Monetary Fund (Washington), Vol. 15 (November 1968), pp. 387-402.

Heller, Peter S., "A Model of Public Fiscal Behavior in Developing Countries: Aid, Investment, and Taxation," *American Economic Review*, Vol. 65 (June 1975), pp. 429-45.

Hemphill, William L., "The Effect of Foreign Exchange Receipts on Imports of Less Developed Countries," *Staff Papers*, International Monetary Fund (Washington), Vol. 21 (November 1974), pp. 637-77.

Holmes, Malcolm R.G., "Control of Government Expenditure: Some Institutional Considerations" (unpublished, International Monetary Fund, June 28, 1982).

International Monetary Fund, *World Economic Outlook, April 1985: A Survey by the Staff of the International Monetary Fund* (Washington, 1985).

Mansfield, Charles Y., "A Norm for a Stabilizing Budget Policy in Less Developed Export Economies," *Journal of Development Studies*, Vol. 16 (July 1980), pp. 401-11.

Mantel, Rolf, and Ana M. Martirena-Mantel, "Exchange Rate Policies in a Small Economy: The Active Crawling Peg," *Journal of International Economics* (Amsterdam), Vol. 13 (November 1982), pp. 301-20.

Morgan, David R., "Fiscal Policy in Oil Exporting Countries, 1972-78," *Staff Papers*, International Monetary Fund (Washington), Vol. 26 (March 1979), pp. 55-86.

Morrison, Thomas K., "Structural Determinants of Government Budget Deficits in Developing Countries," *World Development* (Oxford, England), Vol. 10 (June 1982), pp. 467-73.

Rangarajan, C., and V. Sundararajan, "Impact of Export Fluctuations on Income–A Cross-Country Analysis," *Review of Economics and Statistics* (Cambridge, Massachusetts), Vol. 58 (August 1976), pp. 368-75.

Rodriguez, Carlos A., "A Stylized Model of the Devaluation-Inflation Spiral," *Staff Papers*, International Monetary Fund (Washington), Vol. 25 (March 1978), pp. 76-89.

Smith, Warren L., and Ronald L. Teigen, eds., *Readings in Money, National Income, and Stabilization Policy* (Homewood, Illinois: Richard D. Irwin, 1965).

Tabellini, Guido, "Fiscal Policy Response to the External Shocks of 1979 in Selected Developing Countries: Theory and Facts" (unpublished, International Monetary Fund, December 26, 1985).

Tanzi, Vito, "Fiscal Disequilibrium in Developing Countries," *World Development* (Oxford, England), Vol. 10 (November 1982), pp. 1069-82.

_____ , "Fiscal Policy Responses to Exogenous Shocks in Developing Countries," *American Economic Review, Papers and Proceedings of the Ninety-Eighth Annual Meeting of the American Economic Association* (Nashville, Tennesee), Vol. 76 (May 1986), pp. 88-91.

_____ , "Quantitative Characteristics of the Tax Systems of Developing Countries," in *The Theory of Taxation for Developing Countries*, ed. by David M. G. Newbery and Nicholas H. Stern (New York: Oxford University Press, 1987), pp. 205-41.

Zaidi, Iqbal M., "Saving, Investment, Budget Deficits, and the External Indebtedness of Developing Countries" (unpublished, International Monetary Fund, January 13, 1984).

7

Transmission of Effects of the Fiscal Deficit in Industrial Countries to the Fiscal Deficit of Developing Countries

Ahsan H. Mansur and David J. Robinson

I. INTRODUCTION

In recent years the aggregate fiscal deficits of both industrial and developing countries have increased markedly and have also tended to move in concert. Although this parallel movement may be partly coincidental, there are a number of reasons to believe that the fiscal outturn in developing countries (during the first half of the 1980s) was, at least partly, adversely affected by the deterioration in the aggregate fiscal deficit of industrial countries. Burdened with external debt obligations and subjected to external financing constraints, developing countries were vulnerable to external shocks in the form of higher interest rates and/or economic recession.[1]

Conventional analysis suggests that an increase in the fiscal deficit of industrial countries leads to an increase in their imports from developing countries and to an improvement in the latter's terms of trade. However, for developing countries burdened with external debt and facing an external financing constraint, an expansionary fiscal policy in the industrial countries leading to an increase in the global interest rate may cause an increase in their interest payments, which could offset the favorable ef-

---

[1]Large external borrowings to finance public sector development programs during the second half of the 1970s, and to pursue countercyclical fiscal policies in the early 1980s, led to a rapid accumulation of external debt by the developing countries. Total outstanding debt of the non-oil developing countries (excluding debt owed to the Fund) increased from less than $100 billion at the beginning of 1974 to more than $700 billion by the end of 1982, and during the same period, long-term debt in relation to gross domestic product (GDP), and to exports of goods and services, was doubled.

fects noted above, and worsen their balance of payments, lower their economic growth, and increase their fiscal deficits. This paper presents a theoretical discussion of the main transmission mechanisms involved, followed by a number of simulation exercises showing the short- and medium-term effects of fiscal expansion in industrial countries on the economic growth and fiscal deficit of developing countries facing an external financing constraint.

The key finding of the paper is that an increase in the aggregate fiscal deficit of industrial countries that is not matched by increased private sector savings is likely to worsen the fiscal balance of developing countries. This observation differs somewhat from the standard analysis because in analyzing the transmitted effects of a higher fiscal deficit from industrial to developing countries, both the analytical and simulation models presented here highlight the role of the interest rate, the level of external debt, and the current account constraint, in addition to the conventionally emphasized transmission of the output effect.

The size of the transmitted effect depends on the size of external debt and policy reactions in developing countries. A fiscal expansion in industrial countries may have some initial positive effects on the exports of developing countries, their terms of trade, and output and, consequently, on their fiscal balance, but these are likely to be more than offset in the aggregate by the effect of higher interest rates. Given a current account constraint, higher debt-service payments lead to import compression and to a reduction in output growth. Compression of imports may be induced through quantitative restrictions and unchanged domestic product prices; but if domestic prices in developing countries are allowed to adjust without recourse to quantitative restrictions, either the relative prices of their products or their terms of trade will deteriorate to keep imports in line with the current account constraint. On the fiscal side, these developments imply lower revenues, increased government expenditure on interest payments, and larger fiscal imbalances. If developing countries allow the exchange rate to adjust in line with external developments, the medium-term costs (in the form of lower growth and higher fiscal deficit) could be significantly reduced. The simulations also indicate that if the industrial countries, as a group, had maintained their composite fiscal deficit at its 1977-79 level, the global interest rate would have been lower and the developing countries would have enjoyed slightly higher growth and lower fiscal imbalances both in the short and medium term. The simulations are also broadly consistent with the stylized facts that characterized economic developments during much of the first half of the 1980s.

The plan of the paper is as follows. In Section II we develop a simple two-country analytical model to illustrate the linkages through which the key endogenous variables (e.g., interest rate, output, terms of trade, and

determinants of the current account balance) are affected by an exogenous shift in industrial countries' fiscal deficit. The model, under certain
assumptions, can explain the stylized facts characterizing financial developments in industrial and developing countries in the early 1980s. Section III briefly sets out the specifications of key behavioral relationships
and the working of the complete simulation model, which allows for extensions, including the accumulation of capital and public sector debt (external and domestic) and the effects of these accumulations on the interest
rate, exchange rate, output growth, and fiscal outturns in both the short
and medium term. Section IV describes a number of simulation experiments designed to analyze the quantitative effects of shifts in the fiscal
deficit in industrial countries and the sensitivity of these effects to
changes in key parameters. Some concluding remarks are presented in
Section V.

II. A Simple Model of the International Transmission of Fiscal Policies of Industrial Countries

This section sets out a simple macroeconomic model that emphasizes
the effects of fiscal policy in industrial countries on the fiscal balance in
developing countries. The model starts from the proposition that an autonomous increase in the fiscal deficit in industrial countries will boost
their output in the short run, notwithstanding an increase in the real interest rate.

These developments affect the fiscal outturn of developing countries in
a number of ways. On the expenditure side, interest payments increase on
both external and domestic public sector debt, owing to the higher global
interest rate; the foreign component of development expenditure also increases if the binding current account constraint leads to an exchange
rate adjustment. On the revenue side, in the short run, revenue will increase if exports, imports, and domestic economic activities in developing
countries are favorably affected by the shift in aggregate demand in industrial countries. However, the adverse effects of the higher interest
rate may reverse the initial favorable effects of fiscal expansion in the
industrial countries, and output and trade expansion may decline globally
in both the short term and the medium term, with negative effects on the
fiscal outturns for the developing countries.

The interrelationship between the fiscal situation in developing countries and fiscal policy in the industrial world may be highlighted by the
specification of a simple fiscal deficit relationship for developing countries
(D^*), along with a simultaneous system of equations determining the in-

terest and exchange rates and output of industrial and developing countries in terms of a two-country model.[2]

To highlight the linkages and qualitative effects on the endogenous variables, we start with a simple two-country model with four equations, determining interest rate, relative price, and output levels. The price of the industrial countries' product is assumed to be fixed and used as the numeraire, and the relative price movement or the terms of trade effect arises from variations in the price of the developing countries' product. The relative price is determined, inter alia, by the level of imports consistent with the current account constraint; if the relative price is maintained at a fixed level in the face of external shocks (for example, higher interest rates), the level of imports into the developing countries is determined quantitatively. For expositional clarity, we make a number of restrictive assumptions, some of which are relaxed in the empirical analysis presented in Section III.

We assume that the credit market is fully integrated among industrial countries and that a single rate of interest applies to all industrial countries. Ex ante, investment in industrial countries is assumed to depend on the real interest rate (R):

$$I = I(R)$$

Private sector savings (S) in industrial countries depend on the real interest rate (R) and income (Y). In line with the consensus that changes in the public sector deficit (D) are likely to be offset, at least partly, by alterations in private savings behavior (the Barro-Ricardo effect), we define the measured private savings as

$$S = S(Y, R) + \theta \cdot D$$

where θ = the Barro-Ricardo coefficient reflecting the private sector's induced response to public sector dissaving.[3]

The expression $S(Y, R)$ is the component of private savings that corresponds to net wealth accumulation and $\theta \cdot D$ is the Barro-Ricardo component reflecting the private sector's induced response to public sector dissaving.

---

[2]Throughout this paper, the variables without asterisks refer to industrial countries, and those with asterisks refer to developing countries.

[3]Based on a simple model of aggregate consumption behavior with expected taxes and interest rates assumed to remain constant in the future, Blanchard (1985) and Masson and Knight (1986) have shown that θ should equal unity minus the ratio of the government's discount rate to that of the private sector.

Domestic output in industrial countries is assumed to be demand-determined, depending on domestic absorption (A), which is a function of income, the real interest rate, and the government deficit. This is a flexible output model with a fixed price for the output of industrial countries. Developments in developing countries have no effect on this output.

$$Y = F[A(Y, R, D)]$$

Macroeconomic equilibrium in industrial countries can be expressed in terms of a simple two-equation model of income and interest rate determination:

$$S(R, Y) - I(R) - (1 - \theta) \cdot D + SER^*(R) - CA' = 0 \tag{1}$$

$$Y - F[A(Y, R, D)] = 0 \tag{2}$$

where $SER^*(R)$ is the service sector deficit of developing countries and CA' is the external sector current account balance excluding the service sector; the current account constraint $(\overline{CA})$ implies that

$$CA' - SER^*(R) = \overline{CA}$$

$$S_Y, F_A, A_Y, A_D, SER_R^* > 0; \quad \text{and} \quad (S_R - I_R) > 0 \,[4]$$

$$A_R < 0; \quad 1 \geq \theta \geq 0$$

For developing countries, the current account constraint is assumed to be fixed and equal to the financing available from industrial countries.[5] If the interest rate increases, the service account balance would deteriorate, implying a reduction in imports, if it is not offset by a favorable growth in exports. The reduction in imports could be induced either through a decline in the relative price (p) of developing countries' product (in terms of industrial countries' product) or by the imposition of quantitative restrictions (to avoid a deterioration of developing countries' terms of trade).

---

[4]The assumption that $(S_R - I_R) > 0$ is weaker than the assumptions $S_R > 0$ and $I_R < 0$. A higher real interest rate reduces consumption, given the rate of time preference and expected future wage income; however, since current income is increased for households holding positive net claims, the sign of S_R may be ambiguous. Here, the weaker restriction implies that, if intended savings decline with higher interest rates, such savings fall by less than the intended investment.

[5]In line with the stylized facts of the early 1980s, this assumption reflects the severely limited availability of external financing from industrial countries.

Quantitative restrictions, however, do not benefit exports, whereas a reduction in the relative price does and thus helps ease import compression. Depending on the exchange regime under consideration, the current account constraint may be specified as fixed price with quantitative control:

$$X^*(Y, \bar{p}) - M^*(Y, R, \bar{p}) - SER^*(R) = -CA' \qquad (3)$$

or as flexible price without quantitative control:

$$X^*(Y, p) - M^*(Y, R, p) - SER^*(R) = -CA' \qquad (3')$$

where

$$X_Y^*, M_p^*, M_Y^*, SER_R^* > 0; \qquad X_p^*, M_R^* < 0, \qquad \text{and}$$

p is the relative price of developing countries' output in terms of industrial countries' output.

Output in developing countries is assumed to be constrained by the availability of imports (equation (4)). A relaxation of the current account constraint and/or lower interest payments and higher exports would allow higher imports and, thus, higher growth:

$$Y^* = F^*(Y, R, M^*); \qquad F_Y^*, F_M^* > 0, \qquad \text{and} \quad F_R^* < 0 \qquad (4)$$

The fiscal deficit for developing countries may be specified as

$$D^* = RY^*(Y^*, t_Y) + RIMP^*(M^*, t_m) + REX^*(X^*, t_x)$$

$$- G^*(R, p) \qquad (5)$$

where

$$RY_{Y^*}^*, RY_{t_Y}^*, RIMP_{m^*}^*, RIMP_{t_m}^*, REX_x^*, REX_{t_x}^*, \qquad \text{and}$$

$$G_R > 0; \qquad \text{and} \quad G_p^* < 0$$

where RY^* = domestic-based revenue; $RIMP^*$ = revenue from import duty; REX^* = revenue from export duty; G^* = government expenditure and net lending; and t_x, t_m, and t_Y are, respectively, the tax parameters for export (X^*), import (M^*), and domestic-based taxes. Equation (5) indicates that the fiscal policies of industrial countries influence the fiscal outturns of developing countries through their impact on the latter's interest rate, output, exchange rate, imports, and exports.

Equations (1)-(5) determine five endogenous variables: the output levels of industrial and developing countries (Y and Y^*, respectively), industrial countries' real interest rate (R), relative price (p), and the budget deficit of developing countries (D^*). The exogenous variables are limited to the fiscal deficit in industrial countries (D), the current account constraint, the external debt of developing countries, and the factors (not specified) that may influence the five endogenous variables noted above. In its present form, the model is partly recursive. Given the constrained level of the current account balance and the outstanding external debt of developing countries, Y and R are determined simultaneously by equations (1) and (2); the relative price or the levels of imports and output in developing countries can be obtained by substitution in equations (3) or (3') and (4), respectively. Finally, the fiscal balance of developing countries (D^*) can be derived through substitution of these four endogenous variables in equation (5).

In this simple system the effect of a higher fiscal deficit on the output of industrial countries depends on the expansionary effects of the higher fiscal deficit, the service sector surplus, and the improvements in the terms of trade relative to the contractionary effect of a higher interest rate. If the private sector treats a portion of domestic government bonds as a component of its net worth, implying that full Barro-Ricardo equivalence does not hold,[6] an increase in the fiscal deficit of industrial countries would create an imbalance between global savings and investment, and might lead to a rise in the interest rate to restore equilibrium.[7] If the elasticity of investment with respect to interest is low, the crowding-out of private investment would be so small that an increase in fiscal expansion would have a positive effect on domestic absorption and output in industrial countries. (See Appendix I for details.) The conditions under which an expansionary fiscal policy leads only to a smaller increase in the interest rate also imply a greater expansionary effect on output.

Given the current account constraint as specified in equation (3) or (3'), an expansionary fiscal policy would worsen (improve) the terms of trade of developing countries if the favorable output effect from higher exports is less (more) than the increased external debt servicing owing to higher interest rates, resulting in a decline (increase) in developing countries' im-

---

[6] Empirical observations generally suggest that neither complete debt neutrality nor the full inclusion of government bonds in private net wealth is supported on the basis of the data; for more on empirical observations, see Kochin (1974), Tanner (1979), Buiter and Tobin (1979), and Masson and Knight (1986).

[7] The relationship between the fiscal deficit and interest rates was found to be significant for the United States by Muller and Price (1984), de Leeuw and Holloway (1985), and Bovenberg (1988).

ports and a reduction (increase) in their growth rate. Thus, on the one hand, developing countries whose external debt-servicing obligations are not tied to market interest rates may benefit from fiscal expansion in the industrial countries in the short run. On the other hand, for heavily indebted developing countries with a large proportion of debt contracted at floating market rates, a higher interest rate may lead to severe import compression, lower output growth, and a deterioration in the budget deficit in the absence of additional adjustment measures.

This simple model does not, of course, fully capture the long-run impact of fiscal policy changes. Although a higher real interest rate may be expected to continue, the effects on output, the exchange rate, and the current account may be altered or reversed substantially over time as the process of capital formation is adversely affected by higher interest rates and as the process of asset and wealth accumulation influences saving and investment behavior and balance of payments flows. These longer-term aspects of the effects of fiscal policy changes are examined through simulation experiments in Section IV.

The model presented in this section is broadly consistent with the stylized facts of the period 1979-85. The average real interest rate increased by more than 4 percentage points during 1979-85, when the composite fiscal balance of the major industrial countries increased by more than 2 percentage points in relation to gross national product (GNP). (See Table 1.) In line with the higher interest rate, debt-service payments of developing countries increased by 70 percent during 1979-85 in terms of U.S. dollars and, in relation to exports of goods and services, they increased rapidly from 14 percent in 1979 to 20.5 percent in 1985. The payment obligations of the heavily indebted countries increased at a much faster rate, from around 30 percent of exports of goods and services in 1980 to about 50 percent by 1982.[8] Furthermore, a deterioration in the terms of trade and a decline in gross capital formation also contributed to a marked slowdown in economic growth in developing countries. Both reduced imports and slower economic growth contributed to a slower growth in revenue, and, together with an increase in expenditure through higher interest payments, they led to a doubling of the fiscal deficit to around 5 percent of gross domestic product (GDP).

Notwithstanding the qualitative inferences that may be made from these preliminary observations, a number of empirical questions remain unresolved. First, how significant, in quantitative terms, is the effect of a

---

[8]In the following years the debt-service ratio for the heavily indebted countries declined to around 40 percent, owing to rescheduling agreements with the creditors and to increases in exports resulting from the world economic recovery.

Table 1. Selected Variables for the Industrial and Developing Countries, 1979–85

	1979	1980	1981	1982	1983	1984	1985
Fiscal balance (central government)[1]							
Industrial countries							
Unadjusted fiscal balance	−2.8	−3.3	−3.6	−4.6	−5.4	−5.0	−4.9
Cyclically adjusted balance	−3.0	−2.9	−2.7	−2.7	−3.5	−3.7	−3.7
Developing countries	−2.4	−1.5	−3.6	−5.4	−5.6	−4.7	−4.6
Interest rate (nominal)[2]	9.9	12.7	14.2	11.7	9.2	9.7	8.5
Interest rate (real)[3]	0.8	1.0	4.3	4.7	4.3	5.1	4.4
Central government interest expenditure (in percent of total expenditure and net lending)							
Industrial countries	7.0	7.5	7.6	8.3	8.8	9.7	10.5
Developing countries	6.9	6.3	7.2	8.7	11.0	13.1	14.4
Of which: non-oil developing countries	(7.6)	(6.9)	(8.2)	(9.8)	(12.4)	(14.8)	(16.3)
Real GDP/GNP							
Industrial countries[4]	3.4	1.3	1.4	−0.4	2.7	4.7	3.0
Developing countries[5]	4.2	3.5	2.1	1.6	1.4	4.1	3.2
Of which: 15 heavily indebted countries	(6.1)	(5.0)	(0.5)	(−0.4)	(−3.4)	(2.2)	(3.1)
Debt-service payments of developing countries (percentage of exports of goods and services)	14.1	12.9	16.2	19.5	18.9	20.1	20.5
Of which: 15 heavily indebted countries	(34.7)	(29.6)	(39.0)	(49.4)	(42.5)	(41.1)	(38.7)
(billion U.S. dollars)	82.6	100.5	127.4	138.1	127.6	142.1	140.3
Terms of trade for primary product exporters[6]	0.3	−7.4	−10.3	−5.9	1.5	3.9	−3.7
Gross capital formation (in percent of GDP)							
Developing countries	25.9	25.9	25.5	24.3	23.3	22.9	22.4
Of which: 15 heavily indebted countries	(24.9)	(24.7)	(24.5)	(22.3)	(18.2)	(17.4)	(16.5)

Sources: International Monetary Fund, World Economic Outlook, April 1987: A Survey by the Staff of the International Monetary Fund; Government Finance Statistics Yearbook, various issues.

[1] As a percentage of GNP/GDP; industrial country data cover the seven major industrial countries.
[2] Weighted averages of short-term nominal interest rates of the seven major industrial countries.
[3] The composite consumer price increase of the industrial countries has been used as the price deflator.
[4] Annual percentage change in the composite real gross national product (GNP).
[5] Annual percentage change in the composite real GDP.
[6] Annual percentage change.

change in the fiscal deficit in industrial countries on the fiscal outturn for developing countries? Second, what are the long-run effects on the key endogenous variables when the dynamic processes described above are taken into account? We need a dynamic empirical model to answer these questions, even in a very simplified way, and such a model is considered in the next section.

III. THE SIMULATION MODEL

The simulations were carried out on a medium-sized model incorporating 12 behavioral equations and 30 definitional equations or identities. In essence, the structure of the model is very similar to the one in Section II. However, in order to take into account the longer-term effects of a fiscal expansion, the model has been expanded here to include important stock-flow constraints, and the role played by relative prices has also been expanded. For example, as shown in Section III.1 below, real interest rates and national income are still determined by the interaction of savings and investment decisions with the current account in a fashion similar to equations (1) and (2) above.[9] To bring in dynamic factors, real GDP is made a function of potential output, which, in turn, depends on capital stock and investment; and consumption depends on consumers' wealth, which reflects the size of previous government deficits, current account surpluses, and investment. The forms of the import and export equations in the empirical model are also similar to those embodied in equation (5) in Section II. The main difference here is that we explicitly allow for the effects of import compression on exports, as described in Section III.2 below. As was done for the analytical model, we consider both fixed- and flexible-price specifications for developing countries. We allow for some interaction among the financing of the fiscal deficit, money supply, and domestic price determination in developing countries.

The behavioral equations and estimates of their parameters are based on a survey of the existing empirical literature. In cases where the estimated parameter values tend to vary among countries, we generally used a value in the midrange. The data used are largely taken from various issues of the following Fund publications: *International Financial Statistics*, *Government Finance Statistics Yearbook*, and *World Economic Out-*

---

[9]Except that the empirical model has an equation for consumption rather than savings, since consumption functions have been more commonly estimated in econometric work.

look. Stock variables, which are endogenous to the model in a dynamic context (for example, private sector wealth, public sector debt, and capital stock), are estimated by an accumulation of the relevant flows. The baseline values of some key economic variables used in the simulations are set out in Table 2.

This section provides only a brief description of the structure of the model and its key equations; a full description of the simulation model and a discussion of the associated parameters are provided in Appendices II and III, respectively. The model can be broadly divided into three parts: the real sector in industrial countries, in which the real interest rate is determined; the trade sector, through which the effects of external shocks are transmitted to developing countries; and the real and fiscal sectors in developing countries, which describe how changes in the external environment affect these countries.

1. The Real Sector in Industrial Countries

The real sector in industrial countries is composed of three basic relationships determining output, consumption, and investment. Capacity output is derived from a simple Cobb-Douglas function containing the capital stock and labor, with the capital stock endogenously determined from the investment function described below and labor supply taken as exogenous. The output function essentially describes changes in output from the baseline level, with higher real capacity output (YCR) leading to higher real output over a period. Output growth can also be temporarily disturbed by changes in real government expenditure:

$$\Delta \ln Y = \alpha_1 \ln (YCR/Y)_{-1} + \beta_1 \cdot \theta \cdot \Delta \ln (G/P); \qquad \alpha_1, \beta_1 > 0$$

Based on empirical estimates for the United Kingdom made by Laidler and O'Shea (1980), a 1 percent increase in real government expenditure (G/P) is assumed to give rise to a 0.15 percent increase in real GDP, when θ, the Ricardian constant, is 0.5.

The consumption function is based on the formulation of Blinder and Deaton (1985):

$$(CP/P) = (W/P)^{\alpha_2} \cdot (YDIS/P)^{\beta_2} \cdot e^{\gamma_2 NR + \delta_2 EINF}$$

$$\alpha_2, \beta_2 > 0; \qquad \gamma_2, \delta_2 < 0$$

Real private consumption (CP/P) is positively dependent on real wealth (W/P) and real disposable income ($YDIS/P$), and negatively dependent on

Table 2. Baseline Values of Main Economic Variables Used in the Simulations, 1977-84

	1977	1978	1979	1980	1981	1982	1983	1984
Industrial countries				Percentage of GDP				
Fiscal deficit	-3.3	-3.4	-3.0	-3.5	-3.9	-4.4	-5.7	-5.0
Non-oil developing countries				Million U.S. dollars				
Exports[1]	124.0	139.8	178.3	212.3	206.0	200.2	205.6	235.4
Imports[1]	135.6	166.0	203.7	247.0	251.4	225.2	212.8	227.0
Interest payments	14.3	22.0	32.2	49.2	66.9	78.1	71.0	79.2
Current account deficit	-21.7	-31.6	-48.5	-75.2	-94.5	-72.1	-36.5	-21.9
External debt	359.0	390.6	439.1	524.9	621.1	708.0	748.5	793.4
				Percentage of GDP				
Revenue[2]	19.4	19.6	19.6	19.9	20.1	20.4	20.4	19.9
Import taxes	3.3	3.3	3.3	3.5	3.3	3.4	3.1	2.9
Other	16.1	16.2	16.3	16.3	16.8	16.9	17.3	17.0
Expenditure	23.7	23.7	23.7	24.2	25.8	27.2	26.6	25.8
Interest	1.6	1.8	1.8	1.7	2.2	2.8	3.4	3.9
Other	22.1	21.9	21.8	22.5	23.6	24.4	23.2	21.9
Fiscal deficit	-3.6	-3.5	-3.2	-3.7	-5.0	-6.2	-5.6	-5.2

[1] Exports to, and imports from, industrial countries.
[2] Excluding grants.

nominal interest rates (NR) and expected inflation $(EINF)$.[10] Disposable income is defined to exclude the portion of savings that takes place to offset changes in the real government deficit (the Barro-Ricardo effect).

Since the interest elasticity of consumption, γ_2, is a key parameter in the simulations, a brief discussion of its value may be helpful. On purely technical grounds, γ_2 is expected to be negative in sign, as an increase in interest rates encourages saving.[11] Blinder and Deaton, like other researchers, encountered significant difficulties in finding a stable and well-determined estimate. Their estimates (for the United States) vary from -2.3 to -0.8, with the former being slightly better in econometric terms than the latter. In our baseline simulation we assume $\gamma_2 = -0.8$, which appears intuitively reasonable and closer to other results (for example, Masson and Knight (1986)). The sensitivity of the results to the value of this parameter is examined in Section IV below.

The investment function is based on Masson and Knight's formulation:

$$\frac{I}{YC} = \alpha_3 \frac{Y}{YC} + \beta_3 \frac{K(-1)}{YC(-1)} + \gamma_3 R; \qquad \alpha_3 > 0; \qquad \beta_3, \gamma_3 < 0$$

Investment is positively related to the gap between actual output and capacity output, and negatively related to the real interest rate (R) and to the capital stock (K) in the previous period. This equation implies that real private investment adjusts, with a lag, to an optimal capital stock, dependent on both real interest rates and expected output (proxied by actual output).[12]

Finally, the identity

$$CA = Y - C - I - G$$

closes the system. With the current account also determined by export and import equations, as described below, this relationship can essentially be seen as the equation determining the real interest rate, bringing domestic absorption into line with the current account.

---

[10]See Blinder and Deaton (1985) for a discussion of why the nominal, rather than the real, interest rate appears to matter. In our model, the two are effectively the same. Other variables that Blinder and Deaton find significant (for example, the relative price of consumer durables) have been omitted.

[11]Note that the income effect of higher interest rates on wealth holders is taken into account in the definition of disposable income, $YDIS$.

[12]See Masson and Knight (1986) for a detailed derivation of this formulation.

2. Trade Flows

Developing countries are assumed to face a rigid current account constraint in nominal terms, equal to the actual current account deficit in each year. With interest payments determined by interest rates and the outstanding debt, this determines the trade balance.

The price and volume of exports for developing countries are determined separately, following Khan and Knight (1981). Export volume is supply-determined, and export price reacts to equate the supply to world demand, with a lag. Export supply itself is a function of three factors — capital stock in the export sector (proxied by real GDP), relative prices, and the supply of imported inputs (proxied by import volume). Three points should be noted here. First, growth in industrial countries has an immediate impact on export price, rather than on export supply (although supply is subsequently affected by the corresponding improvement in relative prices). Second, import compression reduces export volume. Thus, if developing countries are forced to reduce imports, this, in turn, reduces exports, creating a vicious circle. Third, export prices for developing countries can and do differ from the domestic prices in both industrial and developing countries, allowing relative prices to play a role in the model.

When the nominal exchange rate is held constant, imports are determined simply as a residual, given the current account balance, available exports, and debt-servicing obligations. In the longer term, of course, such exchange rate rigidity is unrealistic. Therefore, in alternative simulations, a simple import demand equation dependent on real income and relative prices is added, with the exchange rate adjusting to achieve the required trade balance.

3. The Fiscal and Real Sectors in Developing Countries

The specification of the fiscal sector in developing countries is relatively straightforward. Tax revenues are directly dependent on import value (in domestic currency) and GDP. Interest payments on government foreign debt are related both to the exchange rate and to a weighted average of market and concessional interest rates. Interest payments on domestic debt are related to domestic interest rates, which are initially assumed to be fixed in nominal terms.[13] Other government expenditures are assumed to be fixed in real terms. Changes in the government deficit

---

[13]The capital market in developing countries is assumed to be completely insulated from that of industrial countries, so developing countries' interest rates are independent of those in industrial countries. In the alternative simulation, however, the domestic interest rate is assumed to change in line with domestic inflation.

in developing countries, induced by external shocks or otherwise, can be financed either by recourse to the sale of domestic debt[14] or by borrowing from the domestic banking system. In the latter case, the increase in money stock adds to inflation through a simple price equation similar to that of Khan and Knight (1981). Real GDP in developing countries (Y^*) is specified as a function of import volume (MV^*).

$$\ln(Y^*) = \alpha_4 \ln(MV^*); \qquad \alpha_4 > 0$$

This formulation ignores many important factors, but it is sufficient to allow us to focus on the effects of import compression on developing country growth. The coefficient α_4 is set equal to 0.3. (See the survey by Goldsborough and Zaidi (1986).)

Overall, the model works in broadly the same way as the theoretical model described in Section II. However, in the longer term, the temporary boost to industrial countries' GDP caused by the fiscal expansion wears off, and — reflecting reduced investment and thus lower capacity output — real GDP falls below the baseline level, lowering developing country exports. In addition, a sustained higher government deficit adds significantly to private sector wealth, and the higher interest payments boost disposable income. If the Ricardian constant is less than 1, both these factors tend to increase consumption, creating an upward pressure on interest rates and adding to the import compression faced by developing countries.

IV. SIMULATION RESULTS

Before we turn to the simulation results themselves, some brief introductory comments may be helpful. First, the simulation model was calibrated to produce the actual outturn over the period 1976-84 with the given policy stance. The results of changes in policies are therefore all expressed in terms of divergences from this baseline. Second, as noted above, the effects of a fiscal policy change depend critically on policy responses to the change in other areas in both industrial and developing countries. We assume that monetary policy in industrial countries is adjusted to maintain prices at the baseline level,[15] whereas in developing

---

[14]Not, however, by borrowing abroad, since we assume that foreign borrowing by developing countries is fixed.

[15]This implies that changes in nominal and real interest rates in industrial countries are identical.

countries it adjusts only to take into account any changes resulting from the monetary financing of the government deficit. In the first round of simulations, the exchange rate and the domestic interest rate in developing countries are assumed to be fixed at the baseline levels. In later simulations, we examine the effects of allowing interest and exchange rates in developing countries to adjust, in line with some simple policy rules described below.

1. A Sustained Increase in Expenditure in Industrial Countries

The model was first used to examine the effects of a sustained debt-financed increase in government expenditure, sufficient to increase the fiscal deficit by about 1 percent of GDP in the first year, and maintained in real terms thereafter.[16]

a. Macroeconomic Effects

The macroeconomic impact of the fiscal expansion can be divided into two stages. In the first year, the fiscal stimulus raises real GDP in industrial countries by about 0.5 percent, and the real interest rate by about 1.4 percentage points (Table 3 and Chart 1). The boost in industrial countries' demand results in some increase in developing countries' export prices, but this is more than offset by the effect of higher interest rates on their debt-service payments. Consequently, in the short run, import volume falls — which further weakens exports — and results in a 0.4 percentage point fall in real GDP.

In the medium term, the effects of the initial fiscal stimulus on industrial countries' income die away, as economic activity moves back in line with underlying supply conditions. Government debt and government interest payments in industrial countries continue to mount and exert a significant effect on consumption, reducing the level of savings available to finance the deficit at current interest rates. At the same time, the reduction in capacity output caused by the reduced investment results in a fall in real GDP. Both these factors increase the global real interest rate (2.6 percentage points from the baseline) and weaken the demand for imports from developing countries. Consequent further compression of imports in developing countries reinforces the weakness of exports and significantly reduces the growth of real GDP (by 1.3 percent).

---

[16]The actual increase in expenditure applied was about 0.8 percent of GDP. However, the ensuing rise in interest rates increased the ratio of interest payments to GDP, accounting for the remaining 0.2 percent.

Table 3. Effects of a Sustained Increase in Government Expenditure[1]

	Years After Initial Expansion			
	0	1	2	7
	(*Deviations from baseline values; in percent*)			
	Percentage Difference			
Industrial countries				
Real GDP	0.5	0.2	−0.1	−0.2
Real consumption	−0.5	−0.8	−1.1	−0.9
Real interest rate	1.4	1.4	1.7	2.1
	Percentage of GDP			
Fiscal deficit	1.0	1.1	2.0	2.6
Government interest payments	0.2	0.3	1.1	1.7
	Percentage Difference			
Developing countries[2]				
Real GDP	−0.4	−0.4	−0.5	−1.3
Real GNP	−0.7	−0.6	−0.8	−1.8
Consumer price index	0.2	0.5	1.4	2.7
Import volume	−2.0	−2.0	−3.1	−7.7
Export volume	−0.3	−0.5	−1.3	−3.3
Export prices	0.7	0.7	0.4	0.6
	Percentage of GDP			
Government expenditure	0.2	0.2	0.2	0.4
Interest payments	0.1	0.1	0.1	0.1
Other	0.1	0.1	0.1	0.3
Government revenue	—	—	−0.1	−0.1
Trade taxes	—	—	−0.1	−0.2
Other	—	—	—	—
Fiscal deficit	0.2	0.2	0.3	0.6

[1]Assumes a sustained debt-financed increase in government expenditure in industrial countries sufficient to increase the fiscal deficit by 1 percent of GDP in the first year.

[2]Fiscal deficit is assumed to be money-financed.

b. Effects on Fiscal Deficit of Developing Countries

In the medium term, the overall deficit of developing countries deteriorates by 0.6-0.8 percent of GDP. Although the ultimate effect on the fiscal balance is broadly similar whether the deficits are financed by additional bank credit or by debt financing, the channels are somewhat different. In the money-financed case, real GDP falls by a large amount; the bulk of the increase in the deficit is due to an increase in expenditure in relation to GDP (as expenditure is assumed to be maintained in real terms). The in-

Chart 1. A Sustained Increase in Government Expenditure
(Divergences from baseline)

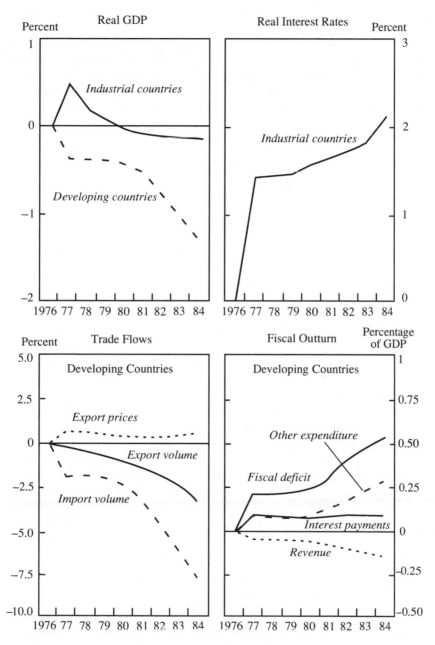

crease in interest payments and the decrease in revenue contribute moderately toward fiscal deterioration in relation to GDP.

In the case of debt financing, lower recourse to monetary financing results in lower price inflation and increasing export profitability. Given the current account constraint and the assumption of a fixed nominal exchange rate, this implies somewhat higher imports and real GDP and, therefore, higher tax revenues. However, these favorable developments are more than offset by the growth in government debt, which results in rapid growth in interest payments; thus, the medium-term fiscal outturn of a debt-financed deficit is broadly similar to that of a money-financed deficit.

c. Sensitivity to Changes in the Values of Key Parameters

Sensitivity analyses based on changes in six important parameters, and expressed in terms of the divergences from the baseline scenario, show that changes in the values of three key parameters — the interest elasticity of consumption, the Ricardian constant, and the interest elasticity of investment — can have significant quantitative effects on the results (Table 4). The impact of changes in the first two of these parameters increases over time, as the effect of the fiscal expansion on wealth and disposable income increases. If the interest elasticity of consumption is zero, the entire burden of adjustment has to be borne by investment, requiring a very large increase in the interest rate. Changes in the interest elasticity of investment, however, have diminishing effects over time, since neither wealth nor disposable income directly influences investment in the model.

Relaxing the current account constraint would, of course, significantly enhance growth in the short term; in the longer term, however, the favorable effect would be substantially reduced as a result of increased interest payments on the higher level of foreign debt if accommodating finance is not available. Finally, the greater the outstanding foreign debt of developing countries, the larger the reduction in growth caused by fiscal expansion in industrial countries. The impact of higher interest payments on real interest rates is negligible.

Overall, the results are qualitatively, if not always quantitatively, robust with respect to changes in parameter values within empirically plausible ranges.

2. Transmission of Fiscal Shocks with Exchange and Interest Rate "Flexibility" in Developing Countries

A flexible domestic interest rate policy is one that allows for interest rates to be ajusted upward or downward from the baseline level in response to changes in inflation, effectively maintaining the real interest

Table 4. Sensitivity Analyses of Changes in Key Parameters
for Developing Countries

Action	Short-Term Effect[1]			Medium-Term Effect[2]		
	Real interest rate	Developing countries		Real interest rate	Developing countries	
		GDP	Deficit		GDP	Deficit
Baseline	1.4	− 0.4	0.2	2.1	− 1.3	0.6
Change long-term interest elasticity of consumption from						
− 0.8 to 0	3.2	− 1.1	0.6	15.4	− 11.2	4.5
− 0.8 to − 0.5	1.8	− 0.5	0.3	3.2	− 2.0	0.8
− 0.8 to − 2.5	− 0.7	− 0.1	0.1	0.7	− 0.4	0.2
Change interest elasticity of investment from						
− 0.8 to − 0.4	1.8	− 0.5	0.3	2.4	− 1.5	0.6
Reduce Ricardian constant from 0.5 to 0.25	1.3	− 0.3	0.2	2.9	− 1.8	0.8
Eliminate import constraint on developing country exports	1.4	− 0.3	0.2	2.1	− 1.0	0.5
Relax current account constraint by 2 percent of imports	1.8	0.7	− 0.1	2.3	− 1.3	0.6
Increase original debt stock by 25 percent	1.4	− 0.5	0.3	2.1	− 1.5	0.6

[1]In the first year.
[2]By the eighth year.

rate in each period. Similarly, a flexible exchange rate policy implies adjustments in the exchange rate to bring about the required strengthening of the trade balance in the face of higher interest payments, given the current account constraint.

Devaluation of the exchange rate in developing countries boosts exports, reduces the degree of import compression, and reduces the fall in real GDP by approximately one half (Chart 2). The effects of flexible interest and exchange rates on the fiscal deficit of developing countries are, however, not completely clear.[17] Increases in the deficit in the initial years

---

[17]The quantitative results of the following simulations are subject to considerable margins of error, owing to a lack of information on the structure of government debt in developing countries. In the simulations, it is assumed that 50 percent of domestic government debt would be subject to the flexible interest rate policy.

Chart 2. A Sustained Increase in Government Expenditure with Flexible
Exchange and Interest Rates in Developing Countries
(Divergences from baseline)

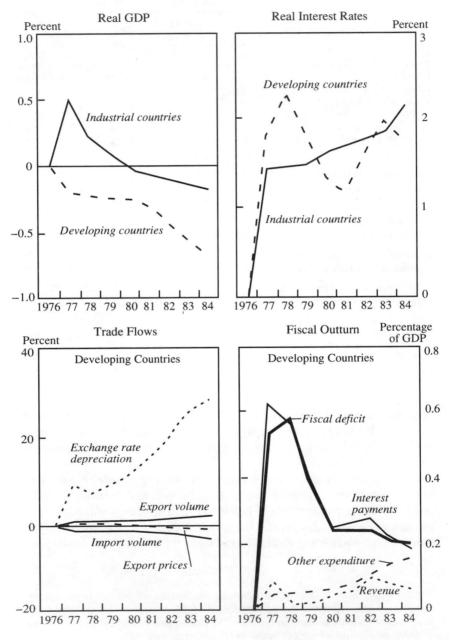

are due to sharply higher interest payments on foreign and domestic public debt resulting from the exchange rate depreciation and a higher nominal interest rate. In the medium term, in either the money-financed or debt-financed case, the overall fiscal deficit increases marginally less than in the fixed-price scenarios described earlier. Deficit financing through domestic bank borrowing increases inflation and requires a much larger nominal devaluation to achieve the necessary real depreciation of the exchange rate. In the bond-financing case, inflation is lower and, consequently, the domestic interest rates and the fiscal deficit are initially lower. In the medium term, however, government debt and interest payments increase rapidly in relation to GDP, with consequent adverse effects on the fiscal deficit.

A policy of maintaining the domestic interest rate unchanged in nominal terms may improve the fiscal deficit in the short term. However, in the medium term, this policy would reduce the attractiveness of government bonds to the private sector and would eventually imply a financing of the deficit through inflationary means, with all the disadvantages that would entail.

3. Effect of Maintaining Industrial Countries' Fiscal Deficit at the 1977 Level

Finally, we consider the outcome of maintaining the industrial countries' fiscal deficit at its 1977 level (approximately 3 percent of GDP), assuming policies in developing countries remain fixed as defined in Subsection IV.1.[18] In the first few years, the effect would have been minimal, since the deficit of industrial countries remained stable in relation to GDP (Chart 3). From 1980 onward, however, containment of the fiscal deficit in industrial countries would have significantly lowered the global interest rate as well as the fiscal deficit of developing countries.

The simulations suggest that real GDP in the industrial countries would have fallen by an average of about 1/3 of 1 percent during 1980-83; real interest rates would have been 1 percentage point lower in 1981, and nearly 3 percentage points lower in 1983 (when the actual deficit peaked). Developing country interest payments would have fallen sharply, allowing imports to increase by 4 percent in real terms by 1984, and real GDP could have been about 0.8 percent higher than in the baseline.

The fiscal situation of developing countries also would have improved

---

[18] A reduction in industrial countries' fiscal deficit would, under flexible policies, imply an appreciation of the exchange rate and lower domestic interest rates in developing countries. Since the exchange rate is likely to have been overvalued, and domestic interest rates too low, in developing countries, this would seem a perverse reaction, and the assumption of fixed policies seems more reasonable.

Chart 3. Maintaining Industrial Countries' Fiscal Deficit
as a Percentage of GDP at Its 1977 Level
(Divergences from baseline)

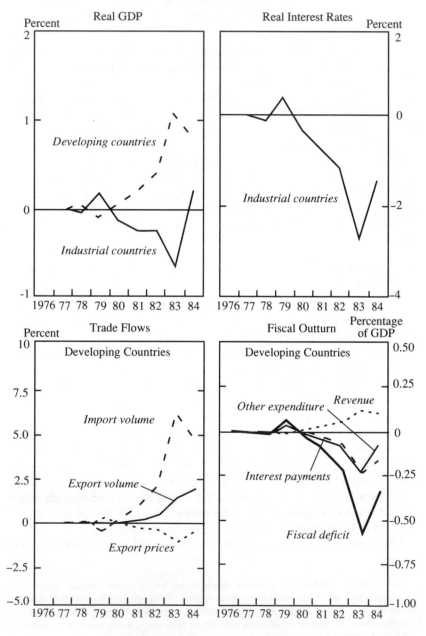

by about 0.4 percent of GDP by the end of the period. In all, about one fifth of the increase in the overall fiscal deficit of developing countries between 1977 and 1984 could be ascribed to the fiscal expansion in industrial countries.

V. CONCLUSIONS

Both the analytical and empirical analyses presented in this paper suggest that, for plausible values of key parameters, an increase in the fiscal deficit of industrial countries causes higher real interest rates, leading to an increase in external debt-service payments for developing countries. Where developing countries face a current account constraint, these higher debt-service payments generally more than offset the boost to exports caused by high demand in industrial countries, and result in import compression and slower growth. The fiscal deficit of developing countries also tends to increase, owing to lower revenue (from import duties and domestic-based taxes) and higher outlays (in relation to GDP).

The quantitative effects, of course, vary considerably among different economies, depending, inter alia, on the size of their external debt, the dependence of their outputs on imports, and the share of taxes coming from international trade. In the short run, the heavily indebted countries are likely to be far more adversely affected than those countries whose commercial borrowing from external sources is limited and whose external financing comes mostly from official or multilateral sources. In the aggregate, however, our simulations suggest that if industrial countries had held their fiscal deficits at the level of 1977, the fiscal deficit in developing countries would have been almost ½ of 1 percent of GDP lower by 1983-84. The simulations also indicate that if the exchange rate is allowed to adjust in response to external developments, the adverse effects on both output and the budget deficit would be sharply lower in the medium term, compared with the fixed-price scenario.

However, it should be emphasized that the higher fiscal deficit in industrial countries can explain only about one fifth of the fiscal deterioration in developing countries in recent years. In many developing countries, the increase in public spending was due to investments in inappropriate or unsuccessful projects, the continued operation of inefficient projects and enterprises originating from past investments, or a general increase in public sector operations with social progress without a commensurate increase in the revenue base. Other external shocks—such as terms of trade deterioration (apart from the fiscal deficit-induced terms of trade effect discussed in this paper), economic recession in the industrial countries, and trade restrictions — also led to slower growth and a higher fiscal deficit during the same period. Inadequate adjustments to external shocks or antirecessionary policies in many developing countries might have contributed further to the higher fiscal deficit.

A number of policy recommendations follow from our analysis. First, reductions in the fiscal deficits of industrial countries are likely to improve the growth prospects and fiscal position of developing countries, because lower global interest rates will ease the availability of imports. This conclusion differs somewhat from the standard analysis, which suggests that higher fiscal deficits in industrial countries stimulate growth in developing countries; although the standard open-economy models emphasize the transmission of output effect, this paper also highlights the role of the interest rate, the burden of external debt, and the current account constraint. We are aware that this paper does not exhaustively cover all the channels through which international transmission may take place; however, we have focused our analysis on the important ones based on stylized facts.

Second, when developing countries face a rigid current account constraint, as we have assumed in this paper, increases in interest rates are particularly important in transmitting shocks from industrial to developing countries. The latter would benefit substantially from policies aimed at lowering the global interest rate and from measures to increase capital flows to them. Third, the impact of higher fiscal deficits in industrial countries on developing countries is partly mitigated if the latter follow a flexible exchange rate policy.

APPENDICES

I. AN ANALYTICAL EXPOSITION OF THE MODEL

The total differential of a simplified version of the system of equations (1)-(4) can be expressed in matrix form as

$$
\begin{bmatrix}
S_Y & (S_R - I_R) & 0 & 0 \\
(1 - F_A \cdot A_Y) & (-F_A \cdot A_R) & 0 & 0 \\
X_Y^* & -SER_R^* & -M_p^* & 0 \\
-F_{M^*}^* \cdot M_Y^* & -F_{M^*}^* \cdot M_R^* & -F_X^* \cdot X_p & 1
\end{bmatrix}
*
\begin{bmatrix}
dR \\
dY \\
dp \\
dY^*
\end{bmatrix}
=
\begin{bmatrix}
(1 - \theta) \\
F_A \cdot A_D \\
0 \\
0
\end{bmatrix}
* dD
$$

where a subscript (i) to a function (F) denotes differentiation of that function with respect to that variable (i.e., $F_i = \partial F/\delta i$).

Given the simplified structure of the model, the first two equations determining output and interest rate in industrial countries are simultaneous. Once these two equations are solved, the equilibrium values for Y and R can be substituted in equations (3) and (4), along with the current account constraint, to solve for the relative price and output level in developing countries.

The total differential of the subsystem represented by equations (1) and (2) is

$$
\begin{bmatrix}
(1 - F_A \cdot A_Y) & (-F_A \cdot A_R) \\
& \\
S_Y & (S_R - I_R)
\end{bmatrix}
*
\begin{bmatrix}
dY \\
\\
dR
\end{bmatrix}
=
\begin{bmatrix}
F_A \cdot A_D \\
\\
(1 - \theta)
\end{bmatrix}
* dD
$$

The determinant of the coefficient matrix, Δ, is

$$
\Delta = (1 - F_A \cdot A_y)(S_R - I_R) + S_Y(F_A \cdot A_R)
$$

which, given the normal assumptions about partial derivatives, is of an indeterminate sign. If the sensitivity of absorption with respect to interest is small, Δ would be positive. A change in the fiscal deficit of the industrial countries has the following effects on the interest rate and output in the industrial countries:

$$
\frac{dY}{dD} = \frac{(F_A \cdot A_D) \cdot (S_R - I_R) + (1 - \theta)F_A \cdot A_R}{\Delta}
$$

$$
\frac{dR}{dD} = \frac{(1 - \theta) \cdot (1 - F_A \cdot A_Y) - (F_A \cdot A_D) \cdot S_Y}{\Delta}
$$

As expected, both the interest rate and output effects of an increase in the fiscal deficit are ambiguous, even if we assume $\Delta > 0$. However, output in industrial countries would expand if the sensitivity of absorption with respect to fiscal deficit is high and the interest sensitivity of domestic absorption is relatively small. Moreover, the output effect would be larger, the greater the Barro-Ricardo effect, which would tend to dampen the effect on the interest rate. If $dR/dD > 0$, the effect of fiscal expansion on the interest rate would be higher, the smaller is θ and the less the sensitivity of absorption to fiscal deficit. Thus, the conditions under which an expansionary fiscal policy leads to a smaller increase in the interest rate would also lead to a greater expansionary effect on output.

The effect of a change in the fiscal deficit on the relative price (of developing countries' output in terms of industrial countries' output) may be observed by taking the total differential of equation (3)

$$
\frac{dp}{dD} = \frac{X_Y^*}{M_p^*} \cdot \frac{dY}{dD} - \frac{SER_R^*}{M_p^*} \cdot \frac{dR}{dD}
$$

If we assume that dY/dD and dR/dD are both positive, then the relative price would decrease or increase, depending on the relative strength of the negative effect from the interest rate increase and the positive effect from output expansion in industrial countries. On the one hand, an increase in the interest rate would cause higher interest payments for developing countries, and lead to a compression of imports through a reduction in the relative price of their output in terms of industrial countries' output. On the other hand, an increase in output in industrial countries would allow for more exports from developing countries, leading to an easing of import availability through an increase in the relative price, given the current account constraint. If the interest rate effect dominates, $dp/dD < 0$ — that is, the relative price or the terms of trade would deteriorate for developing countries; the reverse would happen if the output effect dominates.

The effect of a change in the fiscal deficit on output in developing countries can similarly be expressed as

$$
\frac{dY^*}{dD} = F_M^* \cdot M_Y \cdot \frac{dY}{dD} + F_{M^*}^* \cdot M_R^* \cdot \frac{dR}{dD} + F_{M^*}^* \cdot M_p^* \cdot \frac{dp}{dD}
$$

Once again, the direction of change in output in developing countries is ambiguous, and would remain so even if we assumed (as is likely) that both dY/dD and $dR/dD > 0$, and $dp/dD < 0$. An expansion of output in industrial countries resulting from a higher fiscal deficit would increase the exports of developing countries and, through the current account constraint, also increase their imports and output. An increase in the interest rate and a deterioration in the terms of trade would both reduce the imports of developing countries and contribute to a reduction in their output. Thus, an expansion in the fiscal deficit may easily contribute to a reduction in output in developing countries through a higher interest rate.

The effects of an increase in industrial countries' fiscal deficit on the global real interest rate, on relative price, and on the levels of economic activity in the two groups of countries may be illustrated in terms of a four-quadrant diagram (Figure 1). In quadrant I (the upper right-hand

Figure 1. Effects of a Change in Fiscal Deficit on Output,
Interest Rate, and Exchange Rate

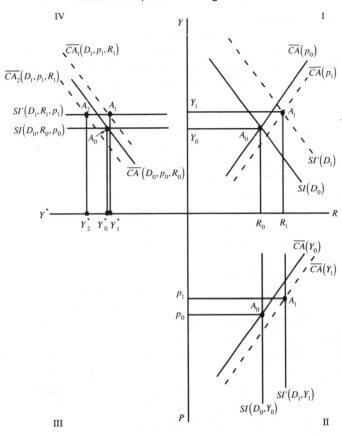

panel), we show the locus of combinations of real interest rates and output of the industrial countries (*SI*), which, for a given public sector fiscal position (*D*), equate the ex ante private savings-investment balance with the ex ante current account balance for industrial countries. The *SI* locus slopes downward because of our assumption that a rise in the interest rate causes the desired investment to fall relative to intended savings, leading to an improvement in the current account balance in real terms; given the constraint on the current account, output must decline to ensure equality in the new desired pattern of savings and investment.

The locus of the constrained current account balance, for a given level of the relative price, $\overline{CA}(p_0)$, slopes upward in (Y, R) space. The *SI* locus for industrial countries and the locus of current account constraint for developing countries, given the initial fiscal balance (D_0), interest rate (R_0), and relative price (p_0), are shown in (Y, Y^*) space in quadrant IV. Analogously, the saving-investment locus for a given budget deficit and output in industrial countries and the constrained current account balance for developing countries (given industrial countries' output level) are shown in quadrant II (the lower right-hand panel). The initial equilibrium interest rate (R_0), the relative price (p_0), and the output levels in the two groups of countries $(Y_0$ and $Y_0^*)$ are characterized by the intersection of the two loci in each quadrant (at points shown as A_0) for a given level of the fiscal deficit in industrial countries.

This diagrammatic presentation, notwithstanding the underlying simplifications, enables us to capture simultaneously the effects of a change in fiscal deficit or of shifts in other exogenous variables in industrial countries on the real interest rate, relative price, and output levels. Suppose that the industrial countries experience an expansionary fiscal policy or an autonomous increase in private sector investment, or some combination of the two. The effects of this increase are illustrated by shifts in the SI and $\overline{CA}$ curves in all three quadrants. Although the shift in each quadrant could be described in several stages, we show only the short-run final positions to reveal the analytical conclusions.

Starting from the first quadrant, the expansionary fiscal policy shifts the $SI(D_0)$ locus to $SI'(D_1)$, showing an increase in real interest rates to R_1 and an expansion of output of industrial countries to Y_1 from R_0 and Y_0, respectively. In the fourth quadrant, the $SI(D_0, Y_0)$ locus would correspondingly shift to $SI'(D_1, Y_1)$, and the locus of the current account constraint would shift to $\overline{CA}(Y_1)$; the equilibrium relative price corresponding to the interest rate R_1 would decline to p_1. The new equilibrium levels of income would be determined in quadrant IV at A_1 or A_2, the intersection of $SI'(D_1, p_1, R_1)$ with $\overline{CA}_1(D_1, p_1, R_1)$, or with $\overline{CA}_2(D_1, p_1, R_1)$. Thus, under this scenario, the new short-run equilibrium would involve a higher world interest rate, a deterioration of developing countries' terms of trade, and an expansion of output in industrial countries. The new short-run equilibrium, however, would not necessarily imply an increase in output for developing countries. If the strength of the output expansion in industrial countries is offset by a higher interest rate, the secondary effects of the output expansion on the developing countries would easily be outweighed by the negative effects of the higher interest rate; the $\overline{CA}(D_0, p_0, R_0)$ curve in quadrant IV may shift rightward to, say, $\overline{CA}_1(D_1, p_1, R_1)$. For heavily indebted developing countries, such an adverse shift is certainly possible, and would result in a decline in their output, as shown at the intersection of $\overline{CA}_1(D_1, p_1, R_1)$ and $SI'(D_1, p_1, R_1)$ in quadrant IV.

II. THE SIMULATION MODEL

The basic model consists of the following equations:[19]

Industrial Countries

Fiscal Policy

$$GDEBT = GDEBT(-1) + GEXPO + GINT - GREV$$

$$- MONFIN \tag{6}$$

$$GINT = GDEBT(-1) \cdot RN \tag{7}$$

$$GDEFR = [GDEBT/P - GDEBT(-1)/P(-1)] \cdot P \tag{8}$$

$$\ln GREV = \ln GREV(-1) + A_1 \ln[Y/Y(-1)] \tag{9}$$
$$(1.0)$$

Real Sector

$$\ln YCR = A_2 \cdot \ln[K(-1)/P(-1)] \tag{10}$$
$$(0.333)$$

$$YC = YCR \cdot P \tag{11}$$

$$\ln[Y/Y(-1)] = A_3 \ln[YCR(-1)/Y(-1)] + A_4 \cdot \theta \cdot \Delta \ln(GEXPOR) \tag{12}$$
$$(0.5) \qquad\qquad\qquad (0.296)\ (0.5)$$

$$YGNP = Y \cdot P - UT + RN \cdot FA(-1) \cdot (1 - F)$$

$$+ RF \cdot FA(-1) \cdot F \tag{13}$$

$$I/YC = A_6 \cdot R + A_7 \cdot YN/YC + A_8 * K(-1)/YC(-1) \tag{14}$$
$$(0.17) \qquad (0.34) \qquad\quad (-0.13)$$

$$\ln(CP/P) = A_9 \cdot A_{10} \ln(YDIS/P) + A_{11} \ln(W/P) + A_{12}NR$$
$$(0.5)(0.53) \qquad\qquad (0.25) \qquad\quad (-0.14)$$

$$+ A_{13} \ln[P/P(-1)] + (1 - A_9)\ln[CP(-1)/P(-1)] \tag{15}$$
$$(-1.5) \qquad\qquad\qquad (0.5)$$

---

[19]The figures directly below the coefficients (within parentheses) indicate the values of the parameters used in the simulation exercises in the baseline scenario.

$$YDIS = YGNP - GREV + GINT - (1 - \theta) \cdot D \tag{16}$$
$$(0.5)$$

$$K = K(-1) \cdot (1 - \theta_2) \cdot P/P(-1) + I \tag{17}$$
$$(0.1)$$

$$YN = Y \cdot P \tag{18}$$

Financial Sector

$$W = (1 - \theta) \cdot GDEBT(-1) + FA(-1) + K(-1) \tag{19}$$
$$(0.5)$$

$$R = RN - \ln P + \ln P(-1) \tag{20}$$

Real-External Identity

$$CA = YN - CP - I - GEXPO \tag{21}$$

External Sector

$$CA = X - M - UT + RN \cdot FA(-1) \cdot (1 - F)$$
$$+ RF \cdot FA(-1) \cdot F \tag{22}$$
$$(0.333)$$

$$M = MP \cdot MV \tag{23}$$

$$\ln MP = A_{15} \cdot \ln YN + (A_{16} - A_{15}) \cdot \ln P + A_{17} \cdot \ln MV(-1)$$
$$(1.188) \qquad (-0.469) \qquad (-0.263)$$
$$+ A_{18} * \ln MP(-1) \tag{24}$$
$$(0.369)$$

$$\ln MV = A_{19} \cdot \ln(X/P) + A_{20} \cdot \ln(MP/P*) + A_{22} \cdot \ln MV(-1) \tag{25}$$
$$(0.157) \qquad (0.122) \qquad (0.695)$$

$$CA + CA* + CAOTR = 0 \tag{26}$$

$$FA = FA(-1) + CA \tag{27}$$

Developing Countries

Real Sector and Prices

$$\ln Y^* = A_{25} \cdot \ln(X/P) \tag{28}$$
$$(0.3)$$

$$P^* = PL^*/E \tag{29}$$

$$YN^* = Y^* \cdot P^* \tag{30}$$

Fiscal Policy

$$GREV^* = GREVT^* + GREVO^* \tag{31}$$

$$\ln GREVT^* = A_{30} \cdot \ln MP^* \tag{32}$$
$$(0.98)$$

$$\ln GREVO^* = A_{31} \cdot \ln Y^* \tag{33}$$
$$(1.12)$$

$$IMP^* = X + XOTR \tag{34}$$

$$D^* = G^* - GGRANT^* - GREV^* \tag{35}$$

$$GINT^* = RN \cdot (1 - \theta_1) \cdot GDEBTF^*(-1)$$
$$(0.333)$$

$$+ RNC \cdot \theta_1 \cdot GDEBTF^*(-1)$$

$$+ RN^* \cdot GDEBTDL^*(-1) \cdot E \tag{36}$$

$$G^* = GINT^* + GEXPOR^* \cdot PD^* \tag{37}$$

$$GDEBTL^* = GDEBTL^*(-1) + E \cdot (D^* - MONFIN^*) \tag{38}$$

Monetary Policy

$$MONL^* = MONL^*(-1) + MONFIN^* \cdot E \tag{39}$$

$$\ln MONDR^* = A_{32} \cdot \ln Y^* - A_{33} \cdot \ln[P(-1)/P(-2)] \tag{40}$$
$$(1.21) \qquad\qquad (1.21)$$

$$\Delta\ln PL^* = A_{34}[\ln MON^*(-1)/PL^*(-1) - \ln MONDR^*]$$
$$(0.33)$$

$$+ A_{35}\,\Delta\ln(PE)$$
$$(0.2)$$

$$+ A_{36}\,\ln[P(-1)\cdot E(-1)/PL^*(-1)] \tag{41}$$
$$(0.27)$$

External Sector

$$FA^* = FA^*(-1) + CA^* \tag{42}$$

$$FINT^* = RN\cdot FA^*(-1)\cdot(1 - F) + RF\cdot FA^*(-1)\cdot F \tag{43}$$
$$(0.333)$$

$$UT^* = UTOTR + UT \tag{44}$$

$$YGNP^* = Y^* + UT^* - FINT^* \tag{45}$$

In addition, the following equation for developing country import demand was used in the simulations in which the exchange rate was allowed to float:

$$\ln(MV^*) = A_{40}\cdot\ln[IMP^*(-1)/P(-1)]$$
$$(0.627)$$

$$+ A_{41}\cdot\ln YR\cdot A_{42}\ln(P/P^*) \tag{46}$$
$$(0.327)\qquad(0.145)$$

Rest of the World

External Sector

$$FAOTR = -FA^* - FA \tag{47}$$

$$CAOTR = RN\cdot FAOTR(-1)\cdot(1 - F) + RF\cdot FAOTR(-1)\cdot F \tag{48}$$
$$(0.333)$$

A variable coefficient was added into each equation to ensure that it replicated the baseline data.

Definition of Variables and Coefficients

The following key defines the variables used in the model. Unless otherwise indicated, the variables with asterisks refer to developing countries; the suffix R indicates that the variable is in real terms; the suffix L indicates that the variable is in the currency of the developing country; and the suffix OTR indicates that the variable refers to the rest of the world.

CA = current account deficit

$CAOTR$ = current account deficit of the rest of the world (including the global discrepancy)

CP = private consumption

D = government deficit

E = exchange rate: units of developing countries' currency per unit of industrial countries' currency

F = proportion of foreign debt at fixed interest rates

FA = foreign assets

$FINT$ = foreign interest payments

G = government expenditure and net lending

$GDEBT$ = government debt

$GDEBTD$ = government domestic debt

$GDEBTF$ = government foreign debt

$GDEFR$ = real government deficit (increase in real government debt)

$GEXPO$ = government expenditure on goods and services (excluding interest payments)

$GGRANT$ = government grants

$GINT$ = government interest payments

$GREV$ = government revenue

$GREVO$ = government revenue from nontrade taxes

$GREVT$ = government revenue from trade taxes

I = investment

IMP = imports

IMP^* = total exports to developing countries

K = capital stock

M = imports of industrial countries from developing countries

MON = broad money stock

$MOND$ = money demand

$MONFIN$ = financing of the deficit through bank borrowing

MP = import prices

MV = import volume

P = consumer price index

R = real interest rate, defined as nominal rate less actual inflation

RF = average interest rate on fixed-rate foreign debt

RN = nominal interest rate

RNC = concessional interest rate on developing country borrowing

UT = unrequited transfers

W = wealth

X = exports of industrial countries to developing countries

Y = gross domestic product (real)

YC = capacity output (nominal)

$YDIS$ = disposable income (nominal)

$YGNP$ = gross national product

YN = gross domestic product (nominal)

θ = Ricardian coefficient

θ_1 = proportion of foreign debt held on concessional terms

θ_2 = rate of depreciation

III. Values of Parameters Used in Simulations and Data Sources

The behavioral equations and estimates for their parameters are derived from various sources, sometimes with minor adjustments. The parameters in equations (9)-(10), (14), and (32)-(33) are estimated directly from the data based on Masson and Knight (1986). The parameters in equation (14) are approximate averages of those derived in the paper for the United States, the Federal Republic of Germany, and Japan.

The relationship determining output in the industrial countries (equation (12)), as noted in the text, has essentially been improvised by the authors. It assumes that half of the difference between real and capacity output is eliminated within a year, but the speed of adjustment can be affected by changes in real government expenditure. (See Laidler and O'Shea (1980) for a similar fiscal specification; the value of A_4 was taken from their estimates.)

Private sector consumption behavior (equation (15)), is based on the "no surprise" consumption function estimated for the United States by Blinder and Deaton (1985). Variables that are not relevant for the analysis in this paper were omitted.

The behavioral relationships determining developing countries' export price (equation (24)), export volume (equation (25)), and imports (equation (46)) are based on Khan and Knight (1981).

The equation determining real output in developing countries (equation (28)) is based on Goldsborough and Zaidi (1986); their survey of the literature concludes that the value of the parameter A_{25} was between 0.14 and 0.28 for countries subject to foreign exchange rationing. The demand-for-money function (equation (40)) and the equation determining the price level (equation (41)) in developing countries are taken from Khan and Knight (1981).

The data used were largely taken from the following Fund publications: *International Financial Statistics* (various issues), *Government Finance Statistics Yearbook* (various issues), and *World Economic Outlook* (April 1987). Some stock figures were estimated by accumulating the relevant flows. The exchange rate E was derived as the ratio of an aggregate GDP deflator for developing countries and an estimated deflator in U.S. dollars (GDP in U.S. dollars divided by real GDP).

REFERENCES

Blanchard, Olivier J., "Debt, Deficits, and Finite Horizons," *Journal of Political Economy* (Chicago), Vol. 93 (April 1985), pp. 223-47.

Blinder, Alan S., and Angus Deaton, "The Time Series Consumption Function Revisited," *Brookings Papers on Economic Activity: 2* (1985), The Brookings Institution (Washington), pp. 465-521.

Bovenberg, A. Lans, "Long-Term Interest Rates in the United States: An Empirical Analysis," *Staff Papers*, International Monetary Fund (Washington), Vol. 35 (June 1988), pp. 382-90.

Buiter, Willem H., and James Tobin, "Debt Neutrality: A Brief Review of Doctrine and Evidence," in *Social Security versus Private Savings*, ed. by George M. von Furstenberg (Cambridge, Massachussetts: Ballinger, 1979), pp. 39-63.

de Leeuw, Frank, and Thomas M. Holloway, "The Measurement and Significance of the Cyclically Adjusted Federal Budget and Debt," *Journal of Money, Credit and Banking* (Columbus, Ohio), Vol. 17 (May 1985), pp. 232-42.

Goldsborough, David, and Iqbal Zaidi, "Transmission of Economic Influences from Industrial to Developing Countries," in International Monetary Fund, *Staff Studies for the World Economic Outlook* (Washington, 1986), pp. 150-95.

Khan, Mohsin S., and Malcolm D. Knight, "Stabilization Programs in Developing Countries: A Formal Framework," *Staff Papers*, International Monetary Fund (Washington), Vol. 28 (March 1981), pp. 1-53.

Kochin, Lewis A., "Are Future Taxes Anticipated by Consumers? Comment," *Journal of Money, Credit and Banking* (Columbus, Ohio), Vol. 6 (August 1974), pp. 385-94.

Laidler, David, and Patrick O'Shea, "An Empirical Macro-model of an Open Economy under Fixed Exchange Rates: The United Kingdom, 1954-70," *Economica* (London), Vol. 47 (May 1980), pp. 141-58.

Masson, Paul R., and Malcolm Knight, "International Transmission of Fiscal Policies in Major Industrial Countries," *Staff Papers*, International Monetary Fund (Washington), Vol. 33 (September 1986), pp. 387-438.

Muller, Patrice, and Robert Price, "Public Sector Indebtedness and Long-Term Interest Rates," paper presented at the World Bank-Brookings Workshop (unpublished; Washington, September 1984).

Tanner, J. Ernest, "An Empirical Investigation of Tax Discounting: A Comment," *Journal of Money, Credit and Banking* (Columbus, Ohio), Vol. 11 (May 1979), pp. 214-18.

Part IV

Interaction of Policies

8

Fiscal Expansion and External Current Account Imbalances

Gloria Bartoli*

I. Introduction

This paper analyzes, in a general equilibrium framework, how fiscal policy transmits its effects to the current account of the balance of payments. Some empirical evidence is also presented, based on data from ten Latin American countries.

The main findings of this paper are as follows. (1) The inflation tax — that is, the way in which the government deficit is financed — exerts a large negative effect on private savings and, hence, on the current account. (2) The equivalence of debt and tax financing of government expenditure (the so-called Barro neutrality hypothesis) cannot be sustained by the data. This implies a critical role for fiscal policy in the determination of external balances, since a change in the taxation-borrowing mix appears to have a major influence on the current account through its effect on saving. (3) Government capital expenditure "crowds in" private investment, possibly because it increases productivity (when it provides infrastructure and services) and/or because it provides financial resources to the private sector; government capital expenditure seems to exert a major influence on private investment that is largely independent of foreign and domestic interest rates.

There are various competing approaches to explaining the determination of the external balance, including the monetary, the absorption, and

*The author is indebted to Mario I. Blejer, Lans Bovenberg, James Boughton, Willem Buiter, Marcus Miller, and Nicola Rossi for discussions and comments that contributed substantially to the development of this paper.

the fiscal, as well as the traditional elasticities, approach. Stabilization programs designed by the International Monetary Fund have been characterized as relying for their theoretical background on a mixture of the monetary and the absorption approaches.[1] However, some aspects of the two approaches are difficult to reconcile, and neither approach can explain why the fiscal variables — and not only the financing of the deficit — are a crucial component of the Fund's stabilization programs. The fiscal approach has also been identified as the theoretical support of the fiscal component of Fund programs,[2] but, although it can be represented as the real counterpart of the monetary approach,[3] its reduced form is, in fact, an identity between the fiscal balance and the current account of the balance of payments, and, hence, the approach fails to endogenize the current account.

In recent years, a more comprehensive general equilibrium approach based on intertemporal optimization has been developed. Several models based on this approach concentrate on the role played by private agents in saving and investment decisions and analyze whether present generations expand their budget constraint by taxing future generations via government budget deficits, which, in turn, create deficits in the current account.[4] The model presented here is based on a similar theoretical framework, but it focuses on the behavior of private, as well as public, agents. The saving behavior of households is determined according to the intertemporal optimizing model of Yaari (1965) and Blanchard (1985), and investment by firms is determined by a stock-adjustment model. Government current revenue is determined by a "tax smoothing" approach, and government current expenditure is also explicitly modeled. Output is taken as given and can be formalized as supply-determined output with the quantity of factors given in the short to medium term. Only one good is considered; consequently, terms of trade changes are ruled out from the present model specification.

The intertemporal optimization models usually lack consistent empirical estimates; at the econometric level the general equilibrium approaches become very "partial" and/or the estimates are not well founded on the behavior of agents. This paper tries to fill the gap: its focus is on the empirical application of the model — namely, (1) an investigation of the forces

---

[1]International Monetary Fund, *Theoretical Aspects of the Design of Fund-Supported Adjustment Programs: A Study by the Research Department of the International Monetary Fund*, IMF Occasional Papers, No. 55 (Washington, 1987).

[2]See Beveridge and Kelly (1980), and Kelly (1982).

[3]See Chrystal (1979) and McCallum and Vines (1981).

[4]Sachs (1981), Sachs and Wyplosz (1984), Svensson and Razin (1983), Buiter (1986), Frenkel and Razin (1986), van Wijnbergen (1986), and Bovenberg (1987).

that account for current account imbalances at a microeconomic level; (2) the direct and indirect roles played by different kinds of fiscal policies in determining current account imbalances; and (3) the application of this kind of model to Fund-supported stabilization programs.

The empirical model estimated here is a five-equation system of government current expenditure, government current revenue, total investment, private saving, and the current account. These equations form a recursive model that clearly spells out both the direct effect of private behavior and of fiscal policy on the current account and the indirect effect of fiscal policy through changes induced in private sector behavior.[5]

Section II contrasts the fiscal and monetary approaches to the balance of payments at the analytical level. It describes the assumptions upon which the two approaches rest and presents the structure of the two models. It concludes by showing how the two models can be reconciled in a more general framework. Section III presents the empirical estimates of the five-equation model based on the general framework and shows the effect of specific changes in the explanatory variables on the current account. Section IV draws some conclusions regarding the policy issues raised by the empirical estimates of the model. Appendix II presents an integrated system of financial, external, and government accounts. This accounting framework, which starts with the current account of the balance of payments identity that the fiscal approach is based on, is transformed in order to provide the basis for the absorption approach and, with further elaboration, for the monetary approach.

II. Comparison Between Monetary and Fiscal Approaches to the Balance of Payments

This section analyzes the basic characteristics of the monetary and fiscal approaches to the balance of payments in a context of a fixed and a flexible exchange rate system in the short and long runs. It also compares the two models to more recent portfolio balance models of exchange rate determination.

1. Monetary Approach

The monetary approach to the balance of payments, as developed by the Fund and the University of Chicago at the end of the 1950s, stresses

---

[5]The estimations are based on a sample of ten Latin American countries: Argentina, Bolivia, Brazil, Chile, Colombia, Ecuador, Paraguay, Peru, Uruguay, and Venezuela.

the essentially monetary nature of balance of payment imbalances: "Its essence is to put at the forefront of analysis the monetary rather than the relative price aspects of international adjustment."[6]

> Accordingly, surpluses in the trade account and the capital account respectively represent excess flow supplies of goods and of securities, and a surplus in the money account reflects an excess domestic flow demand for money. Consequently, in analysing the money account, or more familiarly the rate of increase or decrease in the country's international reserves, the monetary approach focuses on the determinants of the excess domestic flow demand for or supply of money.[7]

In the original formulation, the theory is framed in a long-run perspective with the crucial assumption that the monetary authorities cannot sterilize balance of payments surpluses or deficits,[8] and that they will therefore be channeled into the money supply.[9]

The fundamental behavioral equation of the model is the money demand function:

$$M_d = pf(Y,i) \tag{1}$$

where money demand, M_d, is equal to the domestic price level, p, multiplied by a function of real income Y and nominal interest rate i. The money demand function is assumed to be stable, and the incremental demand for money is a function of the growth of nominal income. If the economy considered is a small, open economy, it would face prices and interest rates determined at the world level. Perfect international capital mobility and perfect substitutability between domestic and foreign bonds are also usually assumed. Perfect international capital mobility implies that the interest rate on domestic bonds is equal to the interest rate on foreign bonds plus the forward premium on the exchange rate — that is, covered interest parity; it should be noted that perfect capital mobility is based on

---

[6]Johnson (1975), p. 229.

[7]Frenkel and Johnson (1976), p. 21.

[8]However, the experience of the Federal Republic of Germany in the 1970s has shown that the authorities can sterilize balance of payments surpluses for long periods. (See Dornbusch (1976a) and Obstfeld (1982 and 1983).)

[9]In the case of a devaluation, the central bank experiences an increase in the value of its foreign assets, which will be balanced by the creation of an equivalent government deposit; the government can sterilize this capital gain (for example, by redeeming government bonds held by the central bank). The same thing can happen in the case of an expected appreciation — following a surplus in the balance of payments — and foreign capital inflows. In the case of sterilization, the money supply does not increase because the central bank sells domestic assets for an amount equivalent to the increase in net foreign assets.

the assumption that there is no differential risk of default or of possible changes in financial market rules and the exchange rate regimes.[10] Perfect bond substitutability implies that the agents—behaving according to rational expectations—will allocate their portfolio shares indifferently between domestic and foreign bonds with the same expected rate of return.

Finally, it is assumed that purchasing power parity (PPP) holds. PPP relies, in turn, on the assumption that prices are perfectly flexible, and therefore any change in the nominal exchange rate will not be reflected in the real exchange rate. Perfect flexibility of prices and, in particular, of the price of labor ensures that output will be at its full-employment level.

In a system of a fixed exchange rate, the assumptions in the model can be summarized as follows:

$$i = i^*$$ (2)

$$p = p^*$$ (3)

$$y = \bar{y}$$ (4)

where i (i^*) refers to domestic (world) nominal interest rate, p (p^*) to domestic (world) price level, and y ($\bar{y}$) to domestic (full-employment) output.

Given that the money supply equals the sum of international reserves (R) and domestic credit (DC),[11] equilibrium in the money market requires that

$$R = M_d - DC$$ (5)

Thus,

$$\Delta R = \Delta M_d (p, Y, i) - \Delta DC$$ (6)

An increase in the demand for money raises international reserves, whereas an increase in domestic credit by the central bank reduces international reserves.

Therefore, in a fixed exchange rate system, balance of payments disequilibria can be adjusted through a reduction of domestic credit to a level consistent with the evolution of money demand.

---

[10]Nor is it assumed that the agents are risk-neutral.

[11]It is assumed that there is no banking system.

In a flexible exchange rate system, the uncovered interest parity, $i - i^*$, is equal to the expected depreciation of domestic currency:

$$i - i^* = E\left(\frac{\Delta e}{e}\right) \tag{7}$$

where e is the nominal exchange rate, defined as units of domestic currency in terms of foreign currency.

The depreciation expectation is formed rationally and corresponds to the expected inflation differential if PPP holds:

$$E\left(\frac{\Delta e}{e}\right) = E\left(\frac{\Delta p}{p}\right) - E\left(\frac{\Delta p^*}{p^*}\right) \tag{8}$$

For the monetary approach to be able to explain the determination of the balance of payments or the exchange rate in its original formulation, all the above assumptions should hold, together with a stable demand for money function. However, available empirical evidence has shown that all these assumptions generally do not hold. Moreover, the relationship between the exchange rate and the various components of the balance of payments, in particular the current account, cannot be easily explained by the monetary approach. Within the narrow version of the monetary approach one can explain that relationship only through price shocks (such as the two oil shocks of 1973 and 1979, which raised the world demand for dollars) or through announcement effects of unexpected outturns in the trade balance.[12]

Therefore, a new generation of models has been originated — still in the tradition of asset-demand models of the balance of payments, but with some of the original assumptions of the monetary approach relaxed. These so-called portfolio-balance models are able to offer explanations of the current account/exchange rate relationship by taking into consideration the capital account and thus the real (wealth) effects of current account imbalances. The counterpart of current account surpluses consists of a shift of wealth from foreigners to residents. The increase in wealth for

---

[12]The "sticky-price" version of the monetary approach (Dornbusch (1976 b)) can also explain the current account/exchange rate relationship. When the one-good representation of international trade is relaxed, and the existence of imperfect information and contracts is taken into account, prices do not adjust instantaneously following a monetary expansion. Therefore, in the short run, sticky prices cause liquidity effects as a consequence of monetary expansion. The subsequent fall in the interest rate will cause an "overshooting" of the depreciation of the exchange rate.

residents raises money demand and also the demand for domestic bonds if these are not perfect substitutes for foreign bonds. Preferences for domestic bonds can derive from special tax treatment of government bonds as well as from political risk attached to the foreign bonds.

The portfolio-balance models allow for a more complex view of the adjustment mechanism. First, they take into account the fact that the asset market reacts more quickly than the goods market, thus generating risks of overshooting and cumulative destabilizing effects. Second, they take into account the existence of nontraded goods and securities — that is, imperfect goods and financial markets.[13] The latter implies, in turn, that any change in financial policy affects not only the balance of payments but also prices and the domestic interest rate. Under these circumstances, fiscal expansion, by affecting domestic interest rates, can lead to the financial crowding out of private firms. This mechanism was not an option in the original version of the monetary approach applied to small, open economies.

Because the monetary approach focuses on "the direct connection between the money market and the balance of payments, rather than working through the implied changes in the goods or financial assets markets,"[14] it can provide simple and comprehensive indicators for the economic stance. However, it offers few instruments for devising and monitoring adjustment policies for intermediate targets, which in the short run often move in a direction that is opposite to the final result. Therefore, a so-called fiscal approach has been proposed to provide theoretical underpinning for the use of fiscal targets in Fund adjustment programs.[15]

2. Fiscal Approach

In contrast with the absorption approach, the fiscal approach, which was developed by the Cambridge Economic Policy Group (CEPG) in the mid-1970s, focuses on public sector saving as the only relevant determinant of the current account of the balance of payments. In common with the monetary approach, the fiscal approach extends the balance of payments theories of the 1960s to consider stock demand for assets as well as

---

[13]See Dornbusch (1976 b).

[14]Blejer and Frenkel (1987), p. 497.

[15]See International Monetary Fund (1987), Kelly (1982), and Milne (1977). The absorption approach has also been seen as the theoretical basis of Fund-supported programs. However, this approach only takes account of the role the public sector plays in policy implementation.

expenditure decisions. The fiscal approach lumps the private expenditure for consumption and investment together

$$E = (1 - \alpha) \, Y_t^P + \alpha \, Y_{t-1}^P \tag{9}$$

where nominal private expenditure E, at time t, is a stable proportion of nominal disposable income at t and is lagged one year, Y_t^P and Y_{t-1}^P. From their econometric work on the U.K. economic model, Cripps, Fetherston, and Godley (1976) found that the coefficients of disposable income summed to almost unity; they thus decided to disregard any multiplier/accelerator mechanism in favor of a pure stock adjustment model; the private sector holds a given asset portfolio, determines expenditure in order to maintain it at the desired level,[16] and adjusts its expenditure quickly to changes in income. The stock adjustment can be modeled as follows:

$$W_t^* = \beta \, Y_t^P \tag{10}$$

where W_t^* is the desired wealth of time t and Y_t^P is private disposable income in the same period. The actual increases in wealth are

$$\Delta W_t = \gamma (W_t^* - W_{t-1}) \tag{11}$$

Since the wealth increase is equal to the period saving, this equation can also be written as

$$S_t = \gamma \, (W_t^* - W_{t-1}) \tag{12}$$

or

$$S_t = \gamma \beta (Y_t^P - W_{t-1}) \tag{13}$$

The demand for the net stock of financial assets is assumed to be a "small and stable" proportion of the disposable income of the private sector.[17] Interest rates are fixed and investment demand is totally interest

---

[16]An objection that has been raised to the CEPG interpretation of this statistical evidence is that the equation is an approximation of the national accounts identity. Chrystal (1979), using the CEPG data, found that the coefficient of the current income was equal to 0.92, which is not significantly different from unity, and that the R^2 of the estimated equation was equal to 0.999. The different results of the CEPG estimates depended on an a priori restriction of the current income parameter, which cannot be considered a genuine correction for the simultaneous-equation bias.

[17]See Cripps and Godley (1976).

inelastic. Hence, the fiscal approach (which ignores net income and transfers from abroad) models the current account of the balance of payments,
$X - Z$, as determined by the fiscal balance, $T - G$, and private balance,
$S - I$, as follows:

$$X - Z = (S - I) + (T - G) \tag{14}$$

Under certain conditions, the fiscal and monetary approaches can be
considered mirror images of each other. In their simplest version — with
only one financial asset and private expenditure depending solely on asset
stock disequilibrium — the monetary approach concentrates on the official
settlement accounts and lumps everything else into "items above the
line." The fiscal approach concentrates on the current account and lumps
everything else into "items below the line."[18]

The flow equilibrium conditions for the commodity and money markets
can be written:

	Foreign Sector	Government Sector	Private Sector	Equation
Fiscal approach	$(X - Z) =$	$(T - G)$	$+ (S - I)$	(15)
Monetary approach	$\Delta R \quad =$	$- \Delta DC$	$+ \quad \Delta M^d$	(16)

With capital movements equal to zero, the sum of each column equals
zero, showing the perfect similarity of the theoretical form of the fiscal
and monetary approaches.

However, the fiscal and the monetary approaches are rooted in substantially different views about the working of the labor market and price and
output flexibility. Whereas most versions of the monetary approach assume continuous full employment, the fiscal approach considers output
and employment to be flexible. Therefore, a fiscal expansion raises output, which is *not* assumed to be at its full-employment level, and, thus,
also raises tax revenue. The fiscal deficit will be less than the initial fiscal
expansion. In addition, there will be no crowding out of the private sector
because of the assumption of perfect, open financial markets, which implies $i = i^*$, and also because of a marginal private propensity to spend
that is assumed to be unity for both consumption and investment.

Accordingly, the policy recommendations of the two approaches for
achieving equilibrium of the external balance are far apart. The key rec-

---

[18]See McCallum and Vines (1981).

ommendation of the New Cambridge school for the U.K. economy was that import restrictions be introduced to offset the government expenditure that should continue to play a role in supporting domestic demand. According to the monetary approach, the burden of adjustment should fall on domestic credit creation and on the government deficit, which is considered the main cause of increases in domestic credit.

The differences in the policy recommendations depend on the sensitivity of exports to changes in domestic prices and of prices to changes in demand. In the monetary approach, the parameter that measures the price sensitivity of exports tends toward plus infinity because of the assumption of a small, open economy for which PPP holds and the demand for exports is infinite. In the fiscal approach, this parameter has a positive, but finite value. In the monetary approach, the parameter that measures the price effect of changes in demand in the price equation is equal to plus infinity because the labor supply curve is vertical; in the fiscal approach, the same parameter is equal to zero, because any change in demand will change the output—not at the full employment level—rather than the prices. The sensitivity of prices to changes in the exchange rate is assumed equal to unity by both approaches because money illusion is excluded. However, the fiscal approach allows for lags in real wage resistance (that is, the exchange rate elasticity of prices is less than unity in the short run). In its formulation of the fiscal approach, the CEPG proposed import quotas or an increase in import tariffs to offset the effects of government expenditure. The CEPG's argument was that increasing tariffs would have the same result as an autonomous reduction in the import propensity of the U.K. economy.[19]

Despite these unorthodox policy recommendations, which depend on the assumption of a (stationary) quasi-steady state in which private saving equals zero and interest rates are fixed, Milne (1977) and Kelly (1982) extended the model from the industrial country framework so that it could be applied to analyses of Fund-supported stabilization programs in developing countries. The fiscal approach to the determination of the balance of payments is based upon the national accounts identity, which states that the current account of the balance of payments is equal to the government balance and the private sector balance between investment and saving (equation (14)). However, Milne's estimates of equation (14), also quoted by

---

[19]It was shown by Blinder (1978) that the CEPG comparative static experiment with an "import quota" was not really an "import quota" effect, but an autonomous downward shift in the import function: ". . . By plugging up some of the 'linkage' from the circular flow, this change naturally raises national income. Further, since prices are independent from demand, this demand stimulus does not move the price level."

Kelly,[20] differ little from estimations of the national accounts identity; given the current account identity and treating the private balance as a constant, the parameter of the public balance is bound to be not significantly different from unity.

3. An Alternative Fiscal Approach Model

A model that can explain changes in the current account of the balance of payments can be built within the fiscal approach framework, once the behavioral content of private and public saving and investment is specified and once the criticisms of the rather simple behavioral relationship between income and private expenditure of the private sector that characterize the fiscal approach are taken into account. The direct effect of government spending and of different kinds of taxes on aggregate demand, and therefore on the current account, should not be overlooked, nor should the effect on private consumption of increases in debt, in the monetization of debt (inflation tax), and in taxes. The full exogeneity of the private sector in the determination of the current account stated by the fiscal approach can be relaxed without having to substitute the full exogeneity of the public sector, which is only necessary in a neutral framework à la Barro.

Barro's neutrality hypothesis (Barro (1974)) states that government expenditure has the same impact on the intertemporal allocation of national consumption whether it is financed by taxes or by debt, because, in order to fulfill the intertemporal budget constraint, agents discount the value of the present government debt by the equivalent future tax liabilities necessary to service the debt.[21] The assumptions necessary for this hypothesis to hold are the absence of distortionary taxes (that is, only lump-sum taxes are allowed), perfect capital markets, and agents with an infinite life span (or perfect intergenerational chains). The infinite horizons of the

---

[20]Kelly (1982) showed that equation (14) could be equally expressed by financial identities, once capital flows are taken into account:

$$CA = \Delta DC_p - \Delta M_s - L_{pg} + K_p + \Delta NDC_g + K_g + L_p$$

$$CA - K_p - K_g = \Delta DC_p - \Delta M_s + \Delta NDC_g = -\Delta R$$

where DC_p is domestic credit to the private sector, NDC_g is net domestic credit to the government, M_s is the money supply, L_{pg} denotes the funds loaned to government by the private sector, $K_{p(g)}$ is the capital flow to the private (government) sector, and R is foreign official reserves. For a more complete description of national account and financial identities, see Appendix II.

[21]For an exhaustive treatment of the implication of relaxing some of these assumptions, see Leiderman and Blejer (1988).

agents make the intertemporal budget constraint of individuals equal to that of the government; with perfect financial markets, this equality results in the same discount rate for the individual and the government. In this framework, expenditure-financing policy has no consequences on the current account of the balance of payments, because every fiscal expansion is offset by an equal response by the private sector. It has been demonstrated that once taxes other than lump-sum taxes are introduced in the Barro model (Barro (1978)), or allowances are made for borrowing constraints (Tobin and Buiter (1976)) or for myopia, or finite horizons for the agents are introduced (Blanchard (1985)), the neutrality hypothesis does not hold.

In order to obtain real effects from current and anticipated financing policy, one or more of the equivalence assumptions must be relaxed. The model considered here has three sectors: households, firms, and government.

The private saving function is based on the Blanchard-Yaari model[22] which allows for finite horizons of the agents and thus maintains the distinction between individual and government discount rates. In this model, an agent faces a probability of death, ω, which is constant throughout the agent's life. The existence of insurance companies allows a transfer of wealth from those who die; thus, total financial wealth, W, accumulates at the rate r, the interest rate, and individual — financial and human — wealth accumulates at the rate $r + \omega$.

The aggregate consumption function is a linear function of aggregate financial and human wealth:

$$C = (\omega + \theta)(H + W) \tag{17}$$

where ω is the constant probability of death and θ is the discount factor (pure time preference rate). Accumulation of human wealth is given by

$$\dot{H} = (r + \omega)H - Y \tag{18}$$

where Y is non-interest income; financial wealth is given by

$$\dot{W} = rW + Y - C \tag{19}$$

If the government and foreign sectors are introduced, and government spending is financed either by lump-sum taxes, T, or by debt, D, the consumption function becomes

---

[22]See Blanchard (1985) and Yaari (1965).

$$C = (\omega + \theta) \left(\frac{Y - T}{r + \omega} + D + F \right) \tag{20}$$

where government debt and net foreign assets have been substituted for nonhuman wealth.[23] The dynamic foreign budget constraint is

$$\dot{F} = rF + Y - C - G \tag{21}$$

which amounts to net income from foreign assets and total saving of the economy. The government dynamic budget constraint is

$$\dot{D} = rD + G - T \tag{22}$$

$\dot{D}$ is equal to zero because D, G, and T are assumed to be constant. Only at time t_0 do D and T increase permanently.

In the steady state, a change in foreign assets is a decreasing function of government debt as well as of consumption

$$\frac{dF}{dD} = - \frac{1}{(\omega - \theta - r)} \frac{1}{(r + \omega)} (\omega + \theta) \omega \tag{23}$$

$$= - \frac{(\omega + \theta) \omega}{\omega + \theta - r} \frac{1}{r + \omega} \gtreqless -1 \text{ because } r \gtreqless \theta \tag{24}$$

When $r = \theta$, the change in foreign assets will exactly offset the change in debt—that is, $F = -D$.

When agents have infinite horizons ($\omega = 0$), foreign assets are independent of changes in D; in other words, the debt-neutrality condition holds.

This result is quite different from that predicted by Barro's neutrality hypothesis, according to which a zero increase in consumption is to be

---

[23]If we take the parameters estimated by Hayashi (1982) and quoted by Blanchard (1985), ($\omega = 0.10$; $r = 0.03$; $\theta = -0.03$), we obtain

$$\frac{\partial C}{\partial T} = (0.10 - 0.03) \frac{1}{0.03 + 0.10} \simeq 0.5$$

$$\frac{\partial C}{\partial D} = (\omega + \theta) = 0.07$$

The effect of an increase in taxes on consumption is an increase equal to half the initial stimulus; an equal increase in debt will bring about an increase in consumption equal to one tenth of the original impulse.

expected in the case of a debt increase, corresponding to an increase in private saving equal to $-D$, with no effect on foreign assets in an open economy framework. Indeed, with $\omega = 0$ — that is, an infinite life span — individuals have the same budget constraint — same horizon and same interest rate — as government, and they are thus indifferent to the timing of taxes.

In a two-period framework, households maximize a two-period utility function subject to an intertemporal budget constraint.[24]

$$Max \left[U(C_1) + \frac{U(C_2)}{(1 + \delta + \omega)} \right] \tag{25}$$

where

$$U(C) = C^{1-\sigma} \tag{26}$$

$$U'(C) = C^{-\sigma} \tag{27}$$

As usual, the first-order condition for intertemporal utility maximization requires that the marginal rate of substitution between consumption in two consecutive periods equal the reciprocal of the market discount rate to the private sector

$$\frac{U'(C_1)}{U'(C_2)} = \left(\frac{1 + r}{1 + \delta + \omega} \right) \tag{28}$$

$$\left(\frac{C_1^{-\sigma}}{C_2^{-\sigma}} \right) = \left(\frac{1 + r}{1 + \delta + \omega} \right) \tag{29}$$

$$\left(\frac{C_1}{C_2} \right)^{-\sigma} = \left(\frac{C_2}{C_1} \right)^{\sigma} = \left(\frac{1 + r}{1 + \delta + \omega} \right) \tag{30}$$

$$\left(\frac{C_2}{C_1} \right) = \left(\frac{1 + r}{1 + \delta + \omega} \right)^{\frac{1}{\sigma}} \tag{31}$$

---

[24]A discussion of the importance of the assumptions regarding the utility function for the current account can be found in Svensson and Razin (1983).

Whether consumption will rise over time depends on the ratio between the real interest rate, on the one hand, and the sum of the discount rate and the probability of death, on the other hand.

Human and nonhuman wealth must be equal to the discounted value of household consumption.

$$C_1 + \frac{C_2}{1 + r + \omega} = H + W \tag{32}$$

where human wealth, H, is equal to the discounted value of labor income minus taxes.

$$H = Y_1 - T_1 + \frac{Y_2 - T_2}{1 + r + \omega} \tag{33}$$

The hypothesis of utility maximization implies that, at any age, consumers allocate resources according to their life resources — that is, the present value of their labor income and the stock of wealth in their possession.[25]

Private savings are equal to private disposable income less private consumption:

$$S_p = Y_1 - T_1 - C_1 \tag{34}$$

Thus, from equation (31) and equation (32), the two-period private saving function will be

$$S_p = Y_1 - T_1 - \left[\frac{1}{1 + \left(\frac{1 + r}{1 + \delta + \omega}\right)^{\frac{1}{\sigma}} \left(\frac{1}{1 + r + \omega}\right)} \right] \cdot$$

$$(H + W) \tag{35}$$

Changes in the interest rate on financial assets will change the intertemporal allocation of resources because of the intertemporal substitution effect as well as the wealth effect.

---

[25]This proposition is common to the life-cycle hypothesis developed by Modigliani, as well as the permanent-income hypothesis developed by Friedman.

The investment function is a stock-adjustment function: firms make investments in order to achieve the optimal, desired capital stock, K^*; net investment will then be used to partially adjust the actual to the desired capital stock:

$$\text{net } I_t = (1 - \lambda)(K_t^* - K_{t-1}) \qquad t = 1, 2 \tag{36}$$

where λ is the adjustment coefficient between zero and one.

Government expenditure is given and taxes are set in order to comply with the government budget constraint

$$G_1 + \frac{G_2}{1 + r} = T_1 + \frac{T_2}{1 + r} \tag{37}$$

where the implicit initial stock of bonds is assumed to be zero. Government saving is defined as

$$S^G = T_1 - G_1 \tag{38}$$

The private-saving equation (35), the investment equation (36), and the government-saving equation (38) constitute the three building blocks for the following current account equation:[26]

$$S_{p_1} + S_{g_1} - I_1 = CA_1 \tag{39}$$

The macroeconomic equilibrium is achieved when private and public savings minus total domestic investment equal the current account.

In this framework, the role played by intertemporal substitution effects suggests that fiscal policy can modify the current account balance indirectly through its effects on investment and saving behavior. Therefore, a cut in the budget deficit through an increase in taxes can cause an improvement or a deterioration in the current account according to the substitution effect. A cut in public investment expenditure will have the same uncertain effect, once the assumption of fixed output is relaxed. The following section tries to estimate empirically the model discussed here, specifying the above equations in order to take into account historical and institutional characteristics of the countries examined. Moreover, the hypothesis of the direct effect of government expenditure, revenue, and deficits on the current account will be tested.

---

[26]From the various constraints, one obtains $CA_2 = - CA_1$.

III. Empirical Model

1. Specification and Estimates

An empirical approximation of the equations described above is estimated for ten South American countries, using annual data for the period 1973-83.[27] The period chosen includes the two oil shocks, the increase in world interest rates, and the emergence of the debt crisis in developing countries. Pooled time-series and cross-sectional data have been used to estimate the model, owing to the limited availability of data. In order to avoid the problem of heteroskedasticity often connected with pooled time series, all variables are deflated by a measure of size; most of the variables used in the regressions are scaled to gross domestic product (GDP) at market prices, and some variables are scaled to total population. In order to take into account the different institutional characteristics, ten country dummies replace the constant in the estimates. The sources of the data are the United Nations' National Accounts, World Bank's *World Debt Tables*, and the Fund's *International Financial Statistics* yearbook and *Government Finance Statistics Yearbook*. In order to ensure that public revenue and expenditure, and private investment and saving, are consistent with the current account of the balance of payments, the United Nations' National Accounts are also used as the source of fiscal data whenever possible. An attempt has been made to construct a coherent set of information and classification rules, which is especially important when working with cross-country data.[28]

The model estimated in this section is a five-equation system of government current expenditure, government current revenue, total investment, private saving, and the current account of the balance of payments. The equations have been estimated with ordinary least squares because the model is recursive. The notation used is listed below:

$$CA = \text{current account balance of the balance of payments}$$
$$CE = \text{government current expenditure}$$
$$CR = \text{government current revenue}$$
$$GCF = \text{government capital formation}$$
$$GDPPC = \text{GDP per capita}$$
$$I = \text{total investment}$$

---

[27]The countries in the sample are Argentina, Bolivia, Brazil, Chile, Colombia, Ecuador, Paraguay, Peru, Uruguay, and Venezuela.

[28]For instance, a lagged relation between the government surplus/deficit and the current account can be derived from a different classification of the accounts—that is, using accrual versus cash-basis recording.

INF = inflation rate
$INFTAX$ = inflation tax computed on the government's outstanding domestic debt at the end of the year
$RFIR$ = real foreign interest rate
$RGDPG$ = real GDP growth
RIR = real domestic interest rate
S^G = government saving = $CR - CE$
S^P = private saving
XZ = exports plus imports (i.e., trade component of total output)

A bar over a variable denotes its ratio to GDP, and the suffix $t - 1$ denotes a one-year lag. According to the definition of a recursive model, the structural equations can be ordered in the following way:

$$\overline{CE} = f_1(GDPPC, RFIR, RIR, \overline{CE_{t-1}}, INF) \tag{40}$$

$$\overline{CR} = f_2(GDPPC, XZ, \overline{CR_{t-1}}) \tag{41}$$

$$\overline{I} = f_3(RGDPG, \overline{GCF}, \overline{I_{t-1}}) \tag{42}$$

$$\overline{S^P} = f_4(RGDPG, \overline{CR}, \overline{S^G}, \overline{S^P_{t-1}}, INFTAX) \tag{43}$$

$$\overline{CA} \equiv (\overline{CR} - \overline{CE}) + (\overline{S^P} - \overline{I}) \tag{44}$$

The first three equations consist only of exogenous variables on the right-hand side. The fourth equation includes two previously estimated endogenous variables, and all the previous equations enter into the fifth equation—the current account equation. In this recursive system the error terms are assumed to be independent. Thus, each equation has been estimated with ordinary least squares without incurring a simultaneous bias. (See Table 1.)

a. Expenditure Equation

The structural equation of current government expenditure depends, on the one hand, on the population structure, the size of the outstanding government debt—domestic and foreign—the interest rate on government debt, and the inflation rate; and, on the other hand, on cyclical elements such as unemployment benefits. The higher the ratio of people over 65 years of age to the total population, the higher will be health expenditures and current transfers for pensions; the higher the proportion of the population aged 0-14 years—and a high proportion is typical of developing countries—the higher will be education expenditure.

Table 1. Summary of Specifications and Estimates for the Model[1]

	Current Expenditure ($\overline{CE}$)					Equation (40)	
	GDPPC	RFIR	RIR	$\overline{CE_{t-1}}$	INF	$\bar{R}^2$	SEE
(a)[2]	0.05 (2.60)	0.02 (1.25)	0.06 (1.12)	0.36 (2.10)	0.02 (2.70)	0.92	0.02

	Current Revenue ($\overline{CR}$)				Equation (41)	
	GDPPC	XZ	$\overline{CR_{t-1}}$	INF	$\bar{R}^2$	SEE
(a)[2]	0.09 (3.76)	0.15 (2.09)	0.22 (1.90)		0.90	0.02
(b)	0.09 (3.74)	0.15 (2.15)	0.20 (1.76)	−0.003 (−0.81)	0.90	0.02

	Total Investment ($\overline{I}$)				Equation (42)	
	RGDPG	$\overline{I_{t-1}}$	GCF	RIR	$\bar{R}^2$	SEE
(a)	0.04 (1.31)	0.56 (5.87)			0.80	0.04
(b)[2]	0.04 (1.41)	0.55 (6.63)	1.26 (4.59)		0.85	0.03
(c)	0.04 (1.31)	0.61 (6.13)		−0.05 (−1.61)	0.81	0.03

	Private Saving ($\overline{S}^P$)							Equation (43)	
	RIR	$\overline{CR}$	RGDPG	$\overline{S^P_{t-1}}$	INFTAX	$\overline{S}^G$	$\overline{I}^P$	$\bar{R}^2$	SEE
(a)[2]		−0.67 (3.15)	0.15 (3.90)	0.19 (2.06)	−1.34 (3.65)	0.16 (0.82)		0.76	0.03
(b)		−0.51 (−3.90)	0.17 (5.11)	0.24 (2.79)	−1.38 (−3.98)		0.28 (2.82)	0.78	0.03
(c)	−0.04 (−1.44)	−0.47 (−3.30)	0.16 (4.69)	0.19 (2.22)	−1.24 (−3.40)			0.76	0.03

[1]The figures in parentheses below the coefficients are *t*-statistics.
[2]Equations chosen for derivation of the reduced form for the current account of the balance of payments on page 195.

From the estimates, the coefficient of the GDP per capita variable shows that current expenditure is not countercyclical, possibly because expenditures are very inelastic, as is evidenced by the positive and significant coefficient of the lagged dependent variable. Both the domestic and foreign interest rate coefficients are positive, but only the first one is significant at the 1 percent level of significance. Inflation increases current expenditure, even if with a very small impact and only at the 10 percent level of significance. Neither of the population variables—the percentage of the population over 65 years old and that below 14 years old—had coefficients significantly different from zero; therefore, equations including these variables are not shown.

b. Current-Revenue Equation

The current-revenue equation is based on previous studies of taxable capacity,[29] which estimate the ratio of taxes to GDP by regressing it on economic variables that proxy the base to which the tax rates are applied ("tax handles"). A theoretical shortcoming of these tax-handle models (which were designed to overcome basic shortcomings of the simple "tax-ratio" approach that previously prevailed) is that they implicitly assume that revenue determination is the first step in determining the fiscal balance. In other words, the tax-revenue equation is estimated as the first equation of a recursive simultaneous-equation model[30] on the basis of which expenditure, and then the deficit, are decided. If this implicit assumption is removed, expenditure and outstanding debt can enter as explanatory variables in the determination of tax revenue, and taxes are determined in order to comply with the government budget constraint. Moreover, the "tax-smoothing principle" proposed by Barro (1978) can be taken into account; according to this principle, smoothing tax revenues over time minimizes collection costs and any excess burden of taxation. To test this hypothesis, some approximation of the present value of future public expenditure should be introduced into the equation.

The results reported in Table 1 are more favorable to the tax-handle approach than to the tax-smoothing principle: the coefficients of GDP per capita and the trade component of total output are positive and significant at the 1 percent level; this trade component, XZ, was remarkably stable throughout different estimates, confirming the relevance for developing

---

[29]See Tait, Grätz, and Eichengreen (1979).
[30]See Tabellini (1985).

countries of taxes based on international trade.[31] The coefficient of lagged tax revenue, a proxy for historical administrative capacity, is significant at the 2.5 percent level.

In equation (41b), the inflation coefficient showed a consistently negative sign that can be interpreted as a further confirmation of the "Tanzi effect" of high inflation on revenue collection.[32] However, the coefficient was not significantly different from zero. The tax-smoothing principle was tested, adding public expenditure, domestic debt (lagged one year) and foreign debt (lagged one year) to the explanatory variables. None of these variables proved to be significant, and the lagged foreign debt appeared with the wrong (negative) sign.

c. Investment Equation

The investment equation (36) lies within the framework of stock-adjustment models. As has been shown by Blejer and Khan (1984), the market imperfections in the developing countries — such as the lack of developed financial markets, institutional constraints in the labor and foreign exchange markets, and the large share of public investment in total investment — make it difficult to apply other optimizing investment theories in the estimation of investment in these countries. These general problems, which are due to the necessary assumptions of the neoclassical models of investment, are compounded by scarcity of data; no data exist on capital stocks or the user cost of capital.

The behavior of agents aiming to achieve an optimal capital stock can be modeled with the accelerator hypothesis; according to this hypothesis, given a constant capital-output ratio and full utilization of capital equipment, a proportional change in capital stock corresponds to any change in output.

$$\frac{K_t}{Y_t} = \alpha; K_t = \alpha \Delta Y_t \tag{45}$$

The actual capital stock becomes a function of past levels of desired capital, which depend on past levels of output O:

$$\text{net } I_t = (1 - \lambda)(\alpha O_t - K_{t-1}) \tag{46}$$

---

[31]Substituting GDP per capita for domestic demand (GDP less exports) and adding the relevant exports separately, as suggested by Tait, Grätz, and Eichengreen (1979), worsens the regression fit; the same effect results from substituting the foreign trade component of GDP with imports, as suggested by Tabellini (1985).

[32]Tanzi (1978).

Following the standard procedure in order to obtain gross investment as a function of past net investment and depreciation δ,[33] the ratio of investment to GDP was estimated, giving the equation the following form:

$$\frac{I_t}{Y_t} = (1 - \lambda) \frac{\alpha Y_t - (1 - \delta) \alpha Y_{t-1}}{Y_t} + \lambda \frac{I_{t-1}}{Y_t} \tag{47}$$

In the framework of the flexible accelerator, the adjustment coefficient is assumed to vary systematically with underlying economic conditions, such as the various stages of the cycle and the cost and availability of financial resources. In the estimates, the cyclical component has been approximated by GDP growth, and several financial variables were taken into account, such as current and past levels of profits and the rate of return, which play a crucial role in determining the desired level of capital stock.

The availability of financial resources plays a larger role in determining investment than their cost, because of the seriously limited financial markets in developing countries. The three main sources of finance for private investment in developing countries are retained profits, the flow of domestic credit to the private sector, and foreign loans. Accordingly, private domestic credit and private long-term foreign loans, together with two series of real interest rates, were taken into account in the estimates as variables affecting λ.[34]

Finally, government investment is included as an explanatory variable in order to test the crowding-out hypothesis against the hypothesis of complementarity of public and private investment. The insertion of this variable is crucial, because it represents the only direct effect of fiscal policy on investments. (Taxes on profits are ruled out in this case.) Moreover, government investment in developing countries is largely financed by foreign loans and grants, which brings the availability of foreign capital into the picture.

The results of the equations estimated reject the crowding-out of private investment by government investment; the coefficient of government capital expenditure is larger than 1, at the 1 percent level of significance, and thus has a multiplicative effect on private investment. The stock-adjustment model confirms its explanatory power, with the coeffi-

---

[33]See Wallis (1979), p. 83.

[34]According to Blejer and Khan (1985), investment in developing countries is positively influenced by the availability of domestic credit. An interesting consequence of their model of financial repression is that a rise in the interest rate will stimulate investment.

cient of the one-year-lagged investment remaining consistently above 0.5 at the 1 percent level of significance. The real GDP growth coefficient is significant and shows the expected positive sign.

Domestic costs of borrowing are very difficult to measure because of administered interest rates and selective credit policies; two series of interest rates have been used in the estimates—a real rate on deposits, *RIR*, and an actual rate of interest on foreign debt, *RFIR*, to approximate the world interest rate (actual $i + \dot{e} - \dot{p}$). However, introducing *RIR* and *RFIR* will not substantially change the results, and both show insignificant t-tests (-1.61 and 1.17, respectively). It is worth noticing that whereas the real deposit rate has the expected negative sign, the real foreign interest rate has a positive sign. Even more disappointing are the effects of financial variables representing the quantity of financial resources made available for investment finance.[35] This is due to the lack of data on short-term loans, which usually go to the private sector. Still, credit availability influences total investment through government investment, because public investment in developing countries largely corresponds to the sum of foreign grants and loans.

d. Saving Equation

The saving equations estimated here draw on equation (35). A number of additional variables have been included in an attempt to capture life-cycle aspects of the saving decisions. The specification also reflects elements of a partial adjustment process, so as to take into account the presence of habit formation in savings behavior.

If the probability of death, ω, is zero, the present value of future taxes should equal the market value of government debt. In this case, any increase in debt should be offset by an equivalent increase in wealth. A serious problem facing anyone trying to test the above propositions for developing countries is the absence of reliable series for household financial wealth. In fact, the only available proxy for household wealth is government debt. Thus, the proposition that government bonds are not net wealth cannot be tested, except through the indirect effect on private savings. However, the same relationship should hold—in the case of an infinite life span—between fiscal deficits and private savings: the coefficient of the deficit in the private-saving equation should be positive and equal to 1.

---

[35]Private foreign long-term debt, *PLTD*, and private domestic credit, *PDC*, exhibit coefficients not significantly different from zero and not statistically significant. Moreover, private domestic credit shows a negative sign.

This hypothesis does not appear to be supported by the estimates, which yield 0.16 for the fiscal deficit coefficient; an increase in expenditure financed by taxes will, therefore, increase the propensity to save, compared with a debt-financed deficit. The latter effectively discourages saving because the government offers better terms of trade between current and future consumption than do the financial markets. Hence, the deficit coefficient should be positive, because agents still expect future taxes to increase, but less than 1, depending, among other things, on the age structure of the population.

The coefficient of the ratio of taxes to GDP, which measures the influence on private savings of disposable income, has the expected negative sign.[36] Even more important, the coefficient of the tax variable in the saving equation shows that an increase of 1 percent in taxes will reduce savings by 0.67 percent: it is interesting to note that this coefficient, derived from actual data, lies between the parameters proposed by Barro (1974) and Blanchard (1985) of 1 and ½, respectively. Barro deduces his parameter directly from his theoretical model, whereas Blanchard's is derived from a separate study by Hayashi (1982). This result rejects Barro's neutrality hypothesis, leaving room for fiscal policy to affect the current account through its effects on private saving.

A test was also included for money illusion by agents. Using equation (43c) in Table 1, it was found that the coefficient of capital losses on debt caused by the inflation rate more than offset the coefficient of nominal interest payments; if agents have target levels of wealth, one would expect the two coefficients to have opposite signs and similar magnitudes. Moreover, nominal interest payments are already included in disposable income and current government savings, so that the coefficient should be close to zero. However, the uncertainty deriving from high inflation also justifies a negative effect on savings, partly explaining capital flight. The inflation tax calculated on the government debt therefore becomes an important explanatory variable. Additional testing was felt to be advisable, however, since half of the countries for which the domestic debt series was available suffered from hyperinflation, implying a considerable degree of indexation. Accordingly, an inflation tax measured on the stock of money was included as a variable; however, the resulting coefficient

---

[36]From the definition of disposable income, $Y_d = GDP - CR$. Taking the ratios to GDP, one obtains $\dfrac{Y_d}{GDP} = -\dfrac{CR}{GDP} + 1$. GDP was used instead of gross national product (GNP), since it was more readily available for a large number of countries.

proved to be insignificant. This result may be explained by the phenomenon of currency substitution and reduction in money balances that occurs in high-inflation countries, where imperfect indexation of government bonds can give rise to substantial capital losses.

Equation (43a) was chosen for several reasons. The positive coefficient on government saving accorded well with the implications of the life-cycle hypothesis and the estimates showed it to be closer to zero than to 1, as recently suggested by Modigliani, Jappelli, and Pagano (1985). The t-test showed that the coefficient of government current spending, which was tried in order to test for the substitutability of private sector consumption and government spending, was not significant. Real GDP growth turns out to have a positive and highly significant coefficient that agrees well with the predictions of the life-cycle hypothesis, which states that the wealth-income ratio is a decreasing function of the growth rate and that "between countries with identical individual behavior, the aggregate saving rate will be higher the higher the long-run growth rate of the economy" (Modigliani (1986), p. 300). Finally, the lagged dependent variable shows the expected positive sign and carries some explanatory power, tending to confirm the presence of past habit formation in saving behavior.[37]

The unsatisfactory results of the population and financial variables should be noted. The ratio of population over 65 years old did not show a significant coefficient, nor did the real rate on deposits and total—domestic and foreign—government debt.

e. Current Account Equation

The current account balance is therefore determined by means of the national accounts identity, $CA = (CR - CE) + (S^P - I)$. Substituting the estimated values of the equations discussed above[38] yields

$$\overline{CA} = 0.04\ GDPPC + 0.15\ \overline{XZ} + 0.22\ \overline{CR_{t-1}} - 0.02\ RFIR$$

$$- 0.06\ RIR - 0.36\ \overline{CE_{t-1}} - 0.02\ INF - 0.67\ \overline{CR}$$

$$- 1.34\ INFTAX + 0.16\ \overline{S^G} + 0.11\ RGDPG + 0.19\ \overline{S^P_{t-1}}$$

$$- 1.26\ \overline{I^g} - 0.55\ \overline{I_{t-1}} \tag{48}$$

---

[37]Brown (1952).

[38]For the reasons stated in the above discussion of the estimates, equations (40a) and (41b) have been chosen for current expenditure and current revenue, respectively; equation (42b) for investment; and equation (43a) for saving.

Two important determinants of the short-run movements of the current account turn out to be the inflation tax and government capital expenditure, with the former affecting private saving negatively, and the latter exerting a multiplicative effect on investment. Public saving, calculated as current revenue less current expenditure, shows an indirect positive effect of 0.16. These results support the view that capital expenditure and the way in which the deficit is financed, rather than the balance of current government spending, influence the current account of the balance of payments.

Among the financial variables determining the current account, any increase in real domestic and foreign interest rates appears to worsen the current account, through their effect on current government expenditure. In the short term also, the availability of financial resources from abroad worsens the current account, raising investment through government capital expenditure.

The estimates presented here confirm the role of imperfections in capital markets in the determination of investments in developing countries and the low elasticity of current revenue to GDP growth shown by previous studies.

Finally, the lagged variables for saving, current revenue, and current expenditure illustrate the important role played by history and the institutional and administrative framework (though the structure of the population did not influence the results as expected).

IV. Concluding Remarks

The empirical results show that fiscal choices relating to the composition of public expenditure and the structure of taxation have crucial consequences for the current account of the balance of payments. In particular, the inflation tax appears to have a large negative impact on private savings and, hence, on the current account. This effect could well explain the capital flight experienced in Latin American countries, which combine an unsustainable fiscal stance with large foreign and domestic official debt.[39]

One may note that the failure of debt neutrality, shown by the results of the empirical estimates, creates a critical role for fiscal policy, since a change in the taxation-borrowing mix (for given government expenditure) appears to have a major influence on the current account through its ef-

---

[39]See Ize and Ortiz (1989).

fect on savings. However, the absence of debt neutrality does not appear
to imply any significant financial crowding out of private investment,
since investment seems to be largely independent of foreign and domestic
real interest rates, as is private saving. However, interest rates do contribute to the decrease of public saving through their effect on current
government expenditure.

Government capital expenditure has a crowding-in effect on private investment (providing an additional increase of 1.26 in total investment for
every unit increase of public capital formation), but, since it also increases
absorption, it will tend to worsen the current account, other things being
equal. However, this would tend to be offset by the rise in profits, which,
by increasing private savings, would improve the current account. Therefore, if projects show adequate returns, the initial negative position of the
current account will be sustainable.

It would be interesting to see whether the results presented here for
Latin American countries were true for other geographical areas. In any
case, further research might include a study of the effect of terms of trade
changes by distinguishing between tradable and nontradable goods in the
model.

APPENDICES

I. VARIABLES

AD = country dummy for Argentina
BD = country dummy for Bolivia
BRD = country dummy for Brazil
CD = country dummy for Chile
CE = government current expenditure
COD = country dummy for Colombia
CR = government current revenue
e = nominal exchange rate
ED = country dummy for Ecuador
FG = government foreign grants
FIR = interest rate on government foreign debt
GCF = government capital expenditure
GDD = government domestic debt
GDP = gross domestic product
$GDPPC$ = GDP per capita
GFD = government foreign debt

$GFDX$ = government foreign debt in domestic currency

H = human wealth

i = nominal interest rate

I = total investment

INF = inflation rate

$INFTAX$ = government domestic debt adjusted for inflation according to the inflation adjustment factor in noncontinuous time, $\dot{p}/(1 + \dot{p})$

IP = interest payment for government domestic debt

$Ip\,(g)$ = private (government) investment

$IPTOT$ = total interest payments for government foreign and domestic debt

K = capital stock

$M_{d(s)}$ = money demand (supply)

$(N)DC$ = (net) domestic credit

p = price level

$P14$ = percent of population over 14 years of age

$P65$ = percent of population over 65 years of age

PD = country dummy for Paraguay

PDC = domestic credit to the private sector

PED = country dummy for Peru

$PLTD$ = private long-term foreign debt in domestic currency

POR = percent of population between zero and 14 years of age

$RFIR$ = real interest rate on foreign government debt

$RGDPG$ = real GDP growth

RIR = real interest rate on deposits

S^{G} = government saving (current revenue less current expenditure)

S^{P} = private saving

UD = country dummy for Uruguay

W = nonhuman wealth

X = exports

XZ = ratio of foreign trade to GDP—that is, (imports + exports)/GDP

Y_{d} = disposable income

Z = imports

ω = probability of death

II. Coordinating the National Account and Financial Identities of the Balance of Payments

It is worthwhile to express the national account and financial identities for the balance of payments in the more complex framework of the Fund's accounts. The accounting framework used by the Fund mirrors a highly complex financial structure: the scope of the integrated system of financial, external, and government accounts is not limited to efficient monitoring of stabilization programs; it can also provide a framework that guarantees the internal consistency of any economic adjustment package.

Let us consider three sectors: the government, the monetary system (central bank, financial institutions, and banks), and the private sector. The following notation will be used:

$$A = \text{government deposits}$$
$$B = \text{government domestic debt}$$
$$B^* = B^{*H} + B^{*m} + B^{*f} = \text{government foreign debt}$$
$$B^f \, (B^{*f}) = \text{government domestic (foreign) debt held by foreigners}$$
$$B^{II} \, (B^{*II}) = \text{government domestic (foreign) debt held by nonbank residents}$$
$$B^m \, (B^{*m}) = \text{government domestic (foreign) debt held by the monetary sector}$$
$$C_N = \text{consumption of nontradables}$$
$$C^P = \text{private consumption}$$
$$C_T = \text{consumption of tradables}$$
$$f^* = \text{foreign assets}$$
$$G_N = \text{government expenditure on nontradables}$$
$$G_T = \text{government expenditure on tradables}$$
$$i = \text{interest rate on government debt}$$
$$i^* = \text{interest rate on foreign government debt}$$
$$\hat{i} = \text{interest rate on foreign assets}$$
$$i^A = \text{interest rate on government deposits}$$
$$I^P = \text{private investment}$$
$$L = \text{loans by the bank system}$$
$$P_T = \text{price of tradables}$$
$$R = \text{international reserves}$$
$$T = T^H + T^m + eT^{*f} = \text{transfers to government}$$
$$T^f = \text{transfers from abroad (foreign aid)}$$
$$T^H = \text{taxes from nonbank residents}$$
$$T^m = \text{taxes from the monetary sector}$$

Y_N = output on nontradables

Y_T = output on tradables

π = relative price of nontradables over the price of tradables — that is, the inverse of the real exchange rate

$\rho\,(\rho^*)$ = interest rate on private domestic (foreign) loans

The budget constraints can be written as follows:

Government Sector

$$G_T + \pi G_N + \frac{iB}{P_T} + \frac{i^*B^*e}{P_T} \equiv \frac{\Delta B}{P_T} + \frac{e\Delta B^*}{P_T} + \frac{\Delta A}{P_T} + \frac{i^A A}{P_T}$$

$$+ \frac{T^H}{P_T} + \frac{T^m}{P_T} + \frac{eT^{*f}}{P_T}$$

Real government expenditure on tradable and nontradable goods and services, (G_T, G_N), and on interest payments on domestic and foreign bonds, (iB, i^*B^*) should be equal to the sum of domestic and foreign bonds issued; changes in government deposits, ΔA; and interest payments on them, i^*A; and tax revenues from the household, monetary, and foreign sectors, $(T^H, T^m, \text{and } T^{*f})$—all in real terms.

Monetary Sector

$$\frac{e\Delta R}{P_T} + \frac{\Delta B^m}{P_T} + \frac{e\Delta B^{*m}}{P_T} + \frac{\Delta L}{P_T} - \frac{\Delta A}{P_T} \equiv \frac{iB^m}{P_T} + \frac{i^*eB^{*m}}{P_T}$$

$$+ \frac{\rho L}{P_T} + \frac{\rho^*Re}{P_T} - \frac{T^m}{P_T} + \frac{\Delta M}{P_T} - \frac{i^A A}{P_T}$$

According to the budget constraint of the monetary sector, the domestic counterpart of changes in international reserves, $e\Delta R$, plus any changes in government domestic and foreign debt held by the monetary sector $(\Delta B^m$ and $e\Delta B^{*m}$, respectively), plus the increase in loans to the private sector, ΔL, minus changes in government deposits, ΔA, should be equal to the changes in money supply and operating income — interest payments on government domestic and foreign debt $(iB^m$ and ieB^{*m}, respectively), on private loans ρL, and on international reserves (ρ^*Re), minus the interest payments on government deposits, $i^A A$, and taxes paid to government, T^m.

Private Sector

$$C_T + \pi C_N + I + \frac{\Delta M}{P_T} + \frac{\Delta B^H}{P_T} + \frac{e\Delta B^{*H}}{P_T} + \frac{e\Delta f^*}{P_T} \equiv$$

$$\frac{\Delta L}{P_T} + Y_T + \pi Y_N - \frac{T^H}{P_T} + \frac{iB^H}{P_T} + \frac{i^* B^{*H} e}{P_T} + \frac{\hat{i} e f^*}{P_t} - \frac{\rho L}{P_T}$$

The right-hand side of the equation states that the resources available to households and firms consist of disposable income originating in the tradable and nontradable sectors, plus capital income from government bonds and foreign assets, plus the flow of credit net of interest payments. The left-hand side of the equation indicates the uses of these resources, which consist of consumption of tradables and nontradables, investment, and changes in money, government bonds, and foreign asset holdings.

Consolidating the three sectors gives

$$G_T + \pi G_N + C_T + \pi C_N + I - \left(Y_T + \pi Y_N + \frac{eT^{*f}}{P_T} \right) + \frac{iB^f}{P_T}$$

$$+ \frac{i^* eB^*}{P_T} - \frac{\hat{i} e f^*}{P_T} - \frac{\rho^* eR}{P_T} \equiv - \frac{e\Delta R}{P_T} + \frac{\Delta B^f}{P_T} + \frac{e\Delta B^{*f}}{P_T} - \frac{e\Delta f^*}{P_T}$$

where the difference between income and total absorption of the economy equals the changes in international reserves, foreign assets, and government bonds. If bonds are not taken into account, what remains is the typical presentation of the absorption view of payments imbalances. For developing countries, the following additional assumptions should be made: no domestic government debt is held by foreigners ($B^f \equiv 0$); no foreign government debt is held by the monetary system ($B^{*m} \equiv 0$); and there are rudimentary domestic financial markets ($B^H \equiv 0$, $B^{*H} \equiv 0$). Simplifying the notation yields

$$Y \equiv Y_T + \pi Y_N$$

$$G \equiv G_T + \pi G_N$$

$$C \equiv C_T + \pi C_N$$

The monetary system is therefore reduced to

$$\frac{e\Delta R}{P_T} + \frac{e\Delta(B^m - A)}{P_T} + \frac{\Delta L}{P_T} \equiv \frac{\Delta M}{P_T}$$

the government sector is equal to

$$G - T^H - \frac{eT^{*f}}{P_T} + \frac{ei^*B^{*f}}{P_T} - \frac{\rho L}{P_T} - \frac{\rho^* eR}{P_T} \equiv \frac{\Delta(B^m - A)}{P_T} + \frac{e\Delta B^{*f}}{P_T}$$

and the private sector is equal to

$$C + I - \left(Y - \frac{T}{P_T} + \frac{\hat{i}f^*e}{P_T} - \frac{\rho L}{P_T}\right) \equiv -\frac{\Delta M}{P_T} - \frac{e\Delta f^*}{P_T} + \frac{\Delta L}{P_T}$$

Consolidating the three sectors now yields

$$G + C + I - \left(Y - \frac{i^*eB^{*f}}{P_T} + \frac{\rho^* eR}{P_T} + \frac{\hat{i}ef^*}{P_T} + \frac{eT^{*f}}{P_T}\right) \equiv$$

$$-\frac{e\Delta R}{P_T} + \frac{e\Delta B^{*f}}{P_T} - \frac{e\Delta f^*}{P_T}$$

where total domestic absorption and net income from abroad are equal to changes in international reserves. If, in addition, private agents cannot borrow or lend abroad (because of restrictions designed to avoid capital flight) ($\Delta f^* \equiv 0$), and if the government is experiencing credit rationing from abroad ($\Delta B^{*f} \leq 0$), then total absorption and property income from abroad will be equal to changes in international reserves in the monetary approach. Therefore, balance of payments changes can be explained with a single use of the demand-for-money function.

A sufficiently wide accounting framework, starting from the current account of the balance of payments identity, on which the fiscal approach developed in Cambridge in the 1970s was founded, can therefore provide the base for the absorption model and, with further elaboration, for the monetary approach to the balance of payments.

BIBLIOGRAPHY

Allen, Polly R., and Peter B. Kenen, *Asset Markets, Exchange Rates, and Economic Integration: A Synthesis* (New York: Cambridge University Press, 1980).

Argy, Victor, and Michael G. Porter, "The Forward Exchange Market and the Effects of Domestic and External Disturbances Under Alternative Exchange Rate Systems," *Staff Papers*, International Monetary Fund (Washington), Vol. 19 (November 1972), pp. 503-28.

Barro, Robert J., "Are Government Bonds Net Wealth?" *Journal of Political Economy* (Chicago), Vol. 82 (November-December 1974), pp. 1095-117.

_____, "A Stochastic Equilibrium Model of an Open Economy under Flexible Exchange Rates," *Quarterly Journal of Economics* (New York), Vol. 92 (February 1978), pp. 149-64.

Beveridge, W. A., and Margaret R. Kelly, "On the Determination of Public Debt," *Journal of Political Economy* (Chicago), Vol. 87 (October 1979), pp. 940-71.

_____, "Fiscal Content of Financial Programs Supported by Stand-by Arrangements in the Upper Credit Tranches, 1969-78," *Staff Papers*, International Monetary Fund (Washington), Vol. 27 (June 1980), pp. 205-49.

Bilson, John F.O. (1978 a), "The Monetary Approach to the Exchange Rate: Some Evidence," *Staff Papers*, International Monetary Fund (Washington), Vol. 25 (March 1978), pp. 48-75.

_____ (1978 b), "Rational Expectations and the Exchange Rate," Chap. 5 in *The Economics of Exchange Rates*, ed. by Jacob A. Frenkel and Harry G. Johnson (Reading, Massachusetts: Addison-Wesley, 1978).

Blanchard, Olivier J., "Debt, Deficits, and Finite Horizons," *Journal of Political Economy* (Chicago), Vol. 93 (April 1985), pp. 223-47.

Blejer, Mario I., and Jacob A. Frenkel, "Monetary Approach to the Balance of Payments," in *The New Palgrave: A Dictionary of Economics*, Vol. 3, ed. by John Eatwell, Murray Milgate, and Peter Newman (London and Basingstoke: Macmillan, 1987), pp. 497-99.

Blejer, Mario I., and Mohsin S. Khan, "Government Policy and Private Investment in Developing Countries," *Staff Papers*, International Monetary Fund (Washington), Vol. 31 (June 1984), pp. 379-403.

Blinder, Alan S., "What's 'New' and What's 'Keynesian' in the 'New Cambridge' Keynesianism?" in *Public Policies in Open Economies*, ed. by Karl Brunner and Allan H. Meltzer, Carnegie-Rochester Conference Series on Public Policy, Vol. 9 (Amsterdam: North-Holland, 1978), pp. 67-85.

Boughton, James. M., *The Monetary Approach to Exchange Rates: What Now Remains?* Essays in International Finance, No. 171 (Princeton, New Jersey: International Finance Section, Department of Economics, Princeton University, 1988).

Bovenberg, A. Lans, "The Effect of Investment Incentives on Real Interest Rates, Real Exchange Rates, and Trade Flows" (unpublished, International Monetary Fund, November 1986).

_____, "Indirect Taxation in Developing Countries: A General Equilibrium Approach," *Staff Papers*, International Monetary Fund (Washington), Vol. 34 (June 1987), pp. 333-73.

Brown, T. M., "Habit Persistence and Lags in Consumer Behaviour," *Econometrica* (Chicago), Vol. 20 (July 1952), pp. 355-71.

Buiter, Willem, *Structural and Stabilization Aspects of Fiscal and Financial Policy in the Dependent Economy*, NBER Working Paper No. 2023 (Cambridge, Massachusetts: National Bureau of Economic Research, 1986).

Chrystal, K. Alec, *Controversies in British Macroeconomics* (Oxford, England: Philip Allan, 1979).

Cripps, T. Francis, Martin Fetherston, and Wynne A. H. Godley, "What Is Left of 'New Cambridge'?" *Economic Policy Review* (Cambridge, England), Vol. 2 (March 1976), pp. 46-49.

Cripps, T. Francis, and Wynne A. H. Godley, "A Formal Analysis of the Cambridge Policy Group Model," *Economica* (London), Vol. 43 (November 1976), pp. 335-48.

Dooley, Michael P., and Peter Isard, *The Portfolio-Balance Model of Exchange Rates*, International Finance Discussion Papers, No. 141 (Washington: Board of Governors of the Federal Reserve System, May 1979).

Dornbusch, Rudiger (1976 a), "The Theory of Flexible Exchange Rate Regimes and Macroeconomic Policy," *Scandinavian Journal of Economics* (Stockholm), Vol. 78 (No. 2, 1976), pp. 255-75.

_____ (1976 b), "Expectations and Exchange Rate Dynamics," *Journal of Political Economy* (Chicago), Vol. 84 (December 1976), pp. 1161-76.

_____ , "Exchange Rate Economics: Where Do We Stand?" in *Brookings Papers on Economic Activity: 1* (1980), The Brookings Institution (Washington), pp. 143-85.

_____ , and Stanley Fischer, "Exchange Rates and the Current Account," *American Economic Review* (Nashville, Tennessee), Vol. 70 (December 1980), pp. 960-71.

Frankel, Jeffrey A., "On the Mark: A Theory of Floating Exchange Rates Based on Real Interest Differentials," *American Economic Review* (Nashville, Tennessee), Vol. 69 (September 1979), pp. 610-22.

_____ , "A Test of Substitutability in the Foreign Exchange Market," *Southern Economic Journal* (Chapel Hill, North Carolina), Vol. 49 (October 1982), pp. 406-16.

Frenkel, Jacob A., "A Monetary Approach to the Exchange Rate: Doctrinal Aspects and Empirical Evidence," *Scandinavian Journal of Economics* (Stockholm), Vol. 78 (No. 2, 1976), pp. 200-24.

_____ , "The Forward Exchange Rate, Expectations, and the Demand for Money: The German Hyperinflation," *American Economic Review* (Nashville, Tennessee), Vol. 67 (September 1977), pp. 653-70.

_____ , "Exchange Rates, Prices, and Money: Lessons from the 1920's," *American Economic Review, Papers and Proceedings of the Ninety-Second Annual Meeting of the American Economic Association* (Nashville, Tennessee), Vol. 70 (May 1980), pp. 235-42.

_____ , and Harry G. Johnson, "The Monetary Approach to the Balance of Payments," Chap. 1 in *The Monetary Approach to the Balance of Payments*, ed. by Jacob A. Frenkel and Harry G. Johnson (London: Allen & Unwin, 1976).

Frenkel, Jacob A., and Richard Levich, "Transaction Costs and Interest Arbitrage: Tranquil versus Turbulent Periods," *Journal of Political Economy* (Chicago), Vol. 85 (December 1977), pp. 1209-26.

Frenkel, Jacob A., and Assaf Razin, "Fiscal Policies in the World Economy," *Journal of Political Economy* (Chicago), Vol. 94, Part 1 (June 1986), pp. 564-94.

Fry, Maxwell J., "Terms-of-Trade Dynamics in Asia: An Analysis of National Saving and Domestic Investment Responses to Terms-of-Trade Changes in 14 Asian LDCs," *Journal of International Money and Finance* (Guilford, England), Vol. 5 (March 1986), pp. 57-73.

Godley, Wynne, and Francis Cripps, *Macroeconomics* (Oxford, England: Oxford University Press, 1983).

Haque, Nadeem U., "Fiscal Policy and Private Sector Saving Behavior: Tests of Ricardian Equivalence in Some Developing Economies" (unpublished, International Monetary Fund, July 31, 1987).

Hayashi, Fumio, "The Permanent Income Hypothesis: Estimate and Testing by Instrumental Variables," *Journal of Political Economy* (Chicago), Vol. 90 (October 1982), pp. 895-916.

International Monetary Fund, *Theoretical Aspects of the Design of Fund-Supported Adjustment Programs: A Study by the Research Department of the International Monetary Fund,* IMF Occasional Papers, No. 55 (Washington, 1987).

Isard, Peter, "How Far Can We Push the 'Law of One Price'?" *American Economic Review* (Nashville, Tennessee), Vol. 67 (December 1977), pp. 942-48.

_____, *Factors Determining Exchange Rates: The Roles of Relative Price Levels, Balances of Payments, Interest Rates and Risk,* International Finance Discussion Papers, No. 171 (Washington: Board of Governors of the Federal Reserve System, December 1980).

Ize, Alain, and Guillermo Ortiz, "Fiscal Rigidities, Public Debt, and Capital Flight," Chap. 3 in this volume.

Johnson, Harry G., *Further Essays in Monetary Economics* (Cambridge, Massachusetts: Harvard University Press, 1975).

Kelly, Margaret R., "Fiscal Adjustment and Fund-Supported Programs, 1971-80," *Staff Papers,* International Monetary Fund (Washington), Vol. 29 (December 1982), pp. 561-602.

Kouri, Pentti J.K., "The Exchange Rate and the Balance of Payments in the Short Run and in the Long Run: A Monetary Approach," *Scandinavian Journal of Economics* (Stockholm), Vol. 78 (No. 2, 1976), pp. 280-304.

_____, and Jorge Braga Macedo, "Exchange Rates and the International Adjustment Process," *Brookings Papers on Economic Activity: 1* (1978), The Brookings Institution (Washington), pp. 111-50.

Krugman, Paul R., "Purchasing Power Parity and Exchange Rates: Another Look at the Evidence," *Journal of International Economics* (Amsterdam), Vol. 8 (August 1978), pp. 397-407.

_____, *Consumption Preferences, Asset Demands, and Distribution Effects in International Financial Markets,* NBER Working Paper No. 651 (Cambridge, Massachusetts: National Bureau of Economic Research, March 1981).

Leiderman, Leonardo, and Mario I. Blejer, "Modeling and Testing Ricardian Equivalence," *Staff Papers,* International Monetary Fund (Washington), Vol. 35 (March 1988), pp. 1-35.

Levich, Richard, "On the Efficiency of Markets for Foreign Exchange," in *International Economic Policy,* ed. by Rudiger Dornbusch and Jacob A. Frenkel (Baltimore: Johns Hopkins University Press, 1979), pp. 246-69.

McCallum, John, and David Vines, "Cambridge and Chicago on the Balance of Payments," *Economic Journal* (Cambridge, England), Vol. 91 (June 1981), pp. 439-53.

McKinnon, Ronald, "Floating Exchange Rates, 1973-74: The Emperor's New Clothes," in *Institutional Arrangements and the Inflation Problem*, ed. by Karl Brunner and Allan H. Meltzer, Carnegie-Rochester Conference Series on Public Policy, Vol. 3 (Amsterdam: North-Holland, 1976), pp. 79-114.

Masson, Paul R., and Malcolm Knight, "International Transmission of Fiscal Policies in Major Industrial Countries," *Staff Papers*, International Monetary Fund (Washington), Vol. 33 (September 1986), pp. 387-438.

Mathieson, Donald J., "The Impact of Monetary and Fiscal Policy Under Flexible Exchange Rates and Alternative Expectations Structures," *Staff Papers*, International Monetary Fund (Washington), Vol. 24 (November 1977), pp. 535-68.

Milne, Elizabeth, "The Fiscal Approach to the Balance of Payments," *Economic Notes* (Siena), Monte dei Paschi di Siena, Vol. 6 (No. 1, 1977), pp. 89-107.

Modigliani, Franco, "Life Cycle, Individual Thrift, and the Wealth of Nations," *American Economic Review* (Nashville, Tennessee), Vol. 76 (June 1986), pp. 297-313.

―――, and Albert K. Ando, "Tests of the Life Cycle Hypothesis of Savings: Comments and Suggestions," *Bulletin of the Oxford University Institute of Statistics* (Oxford, England), Vol. 19 (May 1957), pp. 99-124.

Modigliani, Franco, T. Jappelli, and M. Pagano, "The Impact of Fiscal Policy and Inflation on National Saving: The Italian Case," *Quarterly Review*, Banca Nazionale del Lavoro (Rome), No. 153 (June 1985), pp. 91-126.

Mundell, Robert A., "Capital Mobility and Stabilization Policy Under Fixed and Flexible Exchange Rates," *Canadian Journal of Economics and Political Science* (Toronto), Vol. 29 (November 1963), pp. 475-85.

Mussa, Michael, "The Exchange Rate, the Balance of Payments and Monetary and Fiscal Policy under a Regime of Controlled Floating," *Scandinavian Journal of Economics* (Stockholm), Vol. 78 (No. 2, 1976), pp. 229-48.

Niehans, Jürg, "Some Doubts about the Efficacy of Monetary Policy under Flexible Exchange Rates," *Journal of International Economics* (Amsterdam), Vol. 5 (August 1975), pp. 275-81.

Obstfeld, Maurice, *Portfolio Balance, Monetary Policy, and the Dollar-Deutsche Mark Exchange Rate*, Discussion Paper 62 (New York: Columbia University, Department of Economics, March 1980).

―――, "Can We Sterilize? Theory and Evidence," *American Economic Review, Papers and Proceedings of the Ninety-Fourth Annual Meeting of the American Economic Association* (Nashville, Tennessee), Vol. 72 (May 1982), pp. 45-50.

―――, "Exchange Rates, Inflation and the Sterilization Problem, Germany, 1975-1981," *European Economic Review* (Netherlands), Vol. 21 (March/April 1983), pp. 161-89.

Sachs, Jeffrey, "The Current Account in the Macroeconomic Adjustment in the 1970s," *Brookings Papers on Economic Activity: 1* (1981), The Brookings Institution (Washington), pp. 201-68.

―――, "The Current Account in the Macroeconomic Adjustment Process," *Scandinavian Journal of Economics* (Stockholm), Vol. 84 (No. 2, 1982), pp. 147-59.

_____, and Charles Wyplosz, *Real Exchange Rate Effects of Fiscal Policy*, NBER Working Paper No. 1255 (Cambridge, Massachusetts: National Bureau of Economic Research, April 1984).

Svensson, Lars E.O., and Assaf Razin, "The Terms of Trade and the Current Account: The Harberger-Laursen-Metzler Effect," *Journal of Political Economy* (Chicago), Vol. 91 (February 1983), pp. 97-125.

Tabellini, Guido, "International Tax Comparisons Reconsidered" (unpublished, International Monetary Fund, May 30, 1985).

Tait, Alan A., Wilfrid L.M. Grätz, and Barry J. Eichengreen, "International Comparisons of Taxation for Selected Developing Countries, 1972-76," *Staff Papers*, International Monetary Fund (Washington), Vol. 26 (March 1979), pp. 123-56.

Tanzi, Vito, "Inflation, Real Tax Revenue, and the Case for Inflationary Finance: Theory with an Application to Argentina," *Staff Papers*, International Monetary Fund (Washington), Vol. 26 (September 1978), pp. 417-58.

_____, Mario I. Blejer, and Mario O. Teijeiro, "Inflation and the Measurement of Fiscal Deficits," *Staff Papers*, International Monetary Fund (Washington), Vol. 34 (December 1987), pp. 711-38.

Tobin, James, and Willem Buiter, "Long-Run Effects of Fiscal and Monetary Policy on Aggregate Demand," Chap. 4 in *Monetarism*, ed. by Jerome L. Stein, Studies in Monetary Economics, Vol. 1 (Amsterdam: North-Holland, 1976).

van Wijnbergen, Sweder, "Interdependence Revisited: A Developing Countries Perspective on Macroeconomic Management and Trade Policy in the Industrial World," *Economic Policy: A European Forum* (Cambridge, England), Vol. 1 (November 1985), pp. 81-137.

Vines, David A., "Economic Policy for an Open Economy: Resolution of the New School's Elegant Paradoxes," *Australian Economic Papers* (Adelaide), Vol. 15 (December 1976), pp. 207-29.

Wallis, Kenneth F., *Topics in Applied Econometrica* (Oxford, England: Basil Blackwell, 1979).

Wood, Adrian, *A Theory of Profits* (Cambridge, England: Cambridge University Press, 1975).

Yaari, Menachem E., "Uncertain Lifetime, Life Insurance, and the Theory of the Consumer," *Review of Economic Studies* (Edinburgh), Vol. 32 (April 1965), pp. 137-50.

9

Lags in Tax Collection and the Case for Inflationary Finance: Theory with Simulations

Vito Tanzi[*]

I. Introduction

It has often been argued that many developing countries, in their pursuit of growth through capital accumulation, may have no choice but to run fiscal deficits in order to finance their development expenditures. The reasons given are the following: (a) that their tax bases are inadequate to allow a high tax burden; (b) that even when adequate tax bases are available, the countries' tax administrations are too inefficient to take advantage of them; or (c) that, in any case, the political realities are such that high tax burdens are not possible.[1] In the absence of developed capital markets or external borrowing, these fiscal deficits are often financed wholly or partly by central banks (i.e., through money creation). This printing of money brings about increases in the general price level and thus reduces the real value of the monetary unit. This reduction can

*This paper is a modified version of my article, "Inflation, Real Tax Revenue, and the Case for Inflationary Finance: Theory with an Application to Argentina," which appeared in the September 1978 issue of International Monetary Fund *Staff Papers*. In the preparation of this paper, I have benefited from the assistance of various people. Particular thanks must go to Ke-young Chu, Andrew Feltenstein, and Mohsin S. Khan. Ke-young Chu provided very helpful suggestions concerning revisions I made to the paper in developing its current version. I would also like to thank Hernán Puentes and Dante Simone. Mrs. Chris Wu provided very competent research assistance.

[1]These arguments have often been made in connection with Latin American countries. They form one of the key elements of the structuralist view of inflation. A good review of the theoretical case for inflationary finance to sustain development expenditure is contained in Aghevli (1977), pp. 1295-1307.

be seen, as Friedman and Bailey showed many years ago, as a kind of tax on those who are holding money.[2]

If the real growth of the economy is zero (or is ignored) and if a steady rate of inflation π has established itself so that desired real balances are equal to actual real balances, the rate of inflation is equivalent to the rate of change of the money supply and is also equivalent to the tax rate. The tax base, on the other hand, is equivalent to the real cash balances held, (M/P). Therefore, the inflation tax revenue R^π is

$$R^\pi = \pi \left(\frac{M}{P} \right) \tag{1}$$

If the economy is growing at a rate of growth g, some additional real balances will be demanded to meet that growth.[3] If the income elasticity of the demand for money is assumed to be unity, then equation (1) becomes

$$R^\pi = (\pi + g) \left(\frac{M}{P} \right) \tag{2}$$

In this paper, the real growth of the economy will be ignored, as I shall be dealing with essentially short-run situations, so that equation (1) will continue to indicate the revenue from the inflation tax.

The case for or against inflationary finance has traditionally been argued on the basis of the welfare costs of this means of financing public expenditure as compared with alternative means. Those who have opposed deficit financing have followed Bailey's contention that the ratio of welfare cost to government revenue becomes quite high at relatively low rates of inflation.[4] Thus, the revenue from the tax system soon becomes preferable to inflationary finance on the basis of a welfare criterion.[5] Aghevli, on the other hand, has argued that since additional normal tax revenue may not be available to developing countries, it may be academic to compare alternative revenue sources. In such a case, the relevant comparison should be between the total cost of inflationary finance and the benefits (in terms of additional future consumption) derived from the additional government expenditure.

---

[2]See Friedman (1942). See also Bailey (1956). More than six decades ago, Keynes was also interested in the issue of inflationary finance; see Keynes (1923), Chap. 2, pp. 37-60.

[3]See Aghevli (1977) and, especially, Friedman (1971).

[4]See Bailey (1956). The welfare cost is measured by the area under the demand curve for real balances.

[5]Bailey estimated that the total collection costs of normal tax revenues (i.e., welfare costs, compliance costs, and direct administrative costs) amounted to about 7 percent of revenue collected. This figure seems low for developing countries.

There is, however, another important element that ought to be considered when the case for or against inflationary finance is argued — namely, the effect of inflation on the existing tax system. Depending on the character of the tax system of a country, inflation may (a) lead to an increase in real tax revenue; (b) lead to a decrease in real tax revenue; or (c) leave the real value of this revenue unaffected. Most writers dealing with inflationary finance have implicitly assumed the third of these alternatives, although the second alternative has been contemplated in a few studies.[6] In this paper, the relationship between inflationary finance and the collection lag in tax revenue is explored in detail.[7] The paper will consist of four sections. Section II is purely theoretical; it will discuss the factors that are important in determining the total amount of revenue that a government is likely to get when it pursues inflationary finance. Section III applies the theory developed in Section II to a simulation exercise that uses alternative sets of realistic values for the parameters. Section IV is a concluding section.

II. Theory

1. Revenue from Inflationary Finance

As indicated above, the revenue from inflationary finance is equivalent to the product of the inflation rate π_t and the real cash balances (M/P). Given the real balances, an increase in π_t generated by the money created to finance a deficit would be accompanied by higher inflationary finance revenue. And, alternatively, given the inflationary expectations, the higher are the real balances, the higher will be the revenue from inflationary finance. However, the real cash balances are affected by inflationary expectations. The higher are the latter, the lower will be the former.

As the cost of holding money increases, individuals try to economize on real balances. They reduce their balances to the point where the last monetary unit held gives them services (utility, productivity, etc.) worth at least the anticipated opportunity cost of holding that unit, which is assumed to be equal to the expected rate of inflation.[8] This relationship is shown in Figure 1, where LL represents a demand schedule for real bal-

---

[6]The first of these studies seems to have been Olivera (1967). Another treatment can be found in Aghevli and Khan (1977) and (1978). Of interest also is Dutton (1971).

[7]For an analysis of collection lags in an inflationary situation, see Tanzi (1977). The collection lag is the time that elapses between a taxable event (i.e., earning of income, sale of a commodity) and the time when the tax payment related to that taxable event is received by the government.

[8]Positive real interest rates are ignored for the sake of convenience.

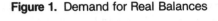

Figure 1. Demand for Real Balances

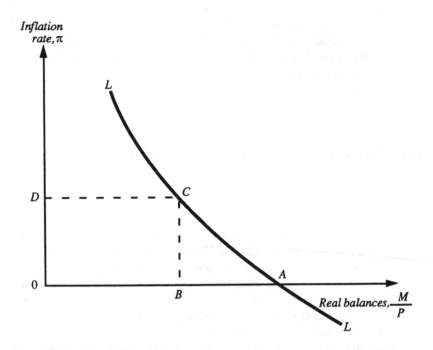

ances. When $\pi = 0$, M/P is equal to OA. At this point no money is being created to finance a deficit, the inflation tax is zero, and the real balances are higher than at any point where $\pi > 0$. As π assumes positive values, the revenue from inflation tax becomes positive.[9] For a while, the positive effect on R^π coming from higher values of π more than compensates for the negative effect coming from the fall in M/P.

At some combination of M/P and π, the product of these two variables would be maximized and the inflation tax would generate the highest revenue. This is assumed to occur at point C in Figure 1; the revenue is given by the area $OBCD$. At this point, the percentage increase in the rate of monetary expansion just equals the percentage decrease in M/P. An at-

---

[9]Throughout this theoretical discussion it is assumed that the change in the rate of inflation is owing exclusively to changes in nominal money and that changes in nominal money are brought about exclusively by the central bank's direct financing of the fiscal deficit. Of course, in the real world, money creation can come through other channels — for example, through the balance of payments.

tempt by the government to raise more revenue by increasing the money supply at a faster rate than OD would be met with failure, since the LL curve would become elastic beyond point C—at that point the elasticity of the LL curve would equal -1.

Following Cagan[10] and most empirical studies of the demand for real balances under inflationary conditions, the equation for the LL curve can be described as follows:

$$\left(\frac{M}{P}\right)^d = a\left(\frac{Y}{P}\right)e^{-b\pi} \tag{3}$$

If one deals with short-run situations, this equation can be written as

$$\left(\frac{M}{Y}\right)^d = ae^{-b\pi} \tag{4}$$

where $(M/Y)^d$ denotes the ratio of money demanded to income; a denotes the reciprocal of the velocity of money when inflationary expectations are zero—that is, it denotes the M/Y ratio when $\pi = 0$; π denotes inflationary expectations; e denotes the base for natural logarithms, and b measures the sensitivity of the demand for real balances to the anticipated rate of inflation. The absolute value of the exponent of e—that is, $|b\pi|$—is the elasticity of the demand for money E_m.

Combining equations (1) and (4); expressing the macrovariables (R and M) as ratios of income; and continuing to assume that actual price changes are equal to inflationary expectations, the equation for revenue from inflationary finance R^π can be specified as follows:

$$R^\pi = \pi ae^{-b\pi} \tag{5}$$

If the value of b is known, this equation can be used to estimate R^π for different rates of inflation reflecting different expansions of nominal money. Equation (5) is equal to zero when the rate of inflation is zero and reaches the maximum when $dR^\pi/d\pi = 0$. This occurs when the elasticity of the demand for real balances is unity—at point C in Figure 1. At that point, $|b\pi| = 1$, so that the revenue-maximizing rate of inflation is $\pi = 1/b$.[11] Since b can be estimated econometrically, the revenue-maximizing rate can be determined for particular countries.[12]

---

[10]See Cagan (1956).

[11]Ibid., pp. 80–81.

[12]The value of b has been determined for many countries. Some representative values are used in the simulation exercise in Section III.

Figure 2. Real Revenue from Inflation

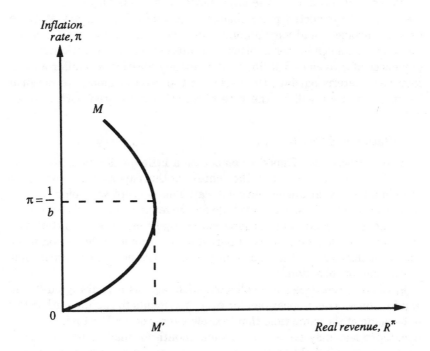

Given b, the values of R^π obtained in connection with alternative rates of inflation can easily be derived. Figure 2 shows the inflation revenue curve, OM, thus obtained. OM' is the maximum amount obtained when the rate of inflation π is equal to $1/b$.

The inflation tax could be evaluated according to standard tax analysis.[13] In other words, one could ask the following questions: Is the tax equitable, vertically and/or horizontally? Is it shifted? Is it elastic if the economy is growing? Is it neutral? What are the welfare losses associated with it? What are its effects on growth? What are its effects in (a) a closed economy, and (b) an open economy? An analysis along these lines would be interesting but it is beyond the scope of this paper. In any case, many of these questions have been dealt with *in extenso* in the relevant literature. Here I shall be interested principally in the relationship between the revenues from the inflation tax and those from normal tax sources, a relationship that has received only scant attention.

---

[13]Some evaluation along this line is contained in Shoup (1969), pp. 452-61.

One aspect of the relationship illustrated in Figure 2 that needs to be emphasized at this point is the importance of the monetary base. Even in the absence of expected price changes, the ratio of the money stock to national income would vary among countries, being quite small in some countries and much higher in others. Because of this, the inflationary consequences of a given deficit financed by money creation will differ among countries. Ceteris paribus, the higher is the ratio of money to national income, the lower will be the rate of inflation associated with a given deficit.

2. Inflation and Tax Revenue

Before proceeding, I need to elaborate a little on the meaning of the elasticity of the tax system in the context of this paper, as this concept is used in a somewhat unconventional way. This concept will refer, first, to built-in elasticity; thus, it will exclude any revenue owing to discretionary tax changes. Second, and perhaps more important, it is a concept that relates taxes collected in a given period to the income in the period when the event that created the legal ability occurred rather than to the income at the time of collection.[14]

In all countries, taxes are collected with lags, as it is always difficult, and for some taxes impossible, for exact payments to the tax authorities to be made at the same time that taxable events occur. For total tax revenue, these lags may be as short as one month for many advanced countries — where withholding at the source and advance payments are common for income taxes and where, owing to better accounting procedures, the tax liabilities related to indirect taxes can be determined more quickly — and as long as perhaps six months for developing countries. By the same token, the elasticity of total tax revenue as defined above may be less than unity, equal to unity, or more than unity. Industrialized countries are likely to have systems that have short collection lags and high elasticities (i.e., greater than one) unless inflation adjustments (i.e., indexation) introduced into the tax system have reduced the elasticity to unity. Developing countries, on the other hand, are more likely to have tax systems with lower elasticities and longer collection lags. If collection lags are characterized as short and long, we could have the following six combinations:

---

[14]For more details, see Tanzi (1977), pp. 155-56. Since real growth is ignored in this paper, the concept of elasticity is related to price changes alone and is thus unaffected by real income changes.

| | Collection Lags | |
Elasticity	Long	Short
< 1	A	B
= 1	C	D
> 1	E	F

Of these combinations, D and F would be more typical of industrialized countries — D for those with indexation of income taxes, and F for those without indexation — while A and C would be more typical of developing countries. A short lag combined with a unitary elasticity of the tax system (combination D) implies that inflation will have little effect on real tax revenue. A short lag combined with an elasticity greater than unity (combination F) implies that inflation will bring about increases in real tax revenue. A long lag and a unitary elasticity of the tax system (combination C)

Figure 3. Inflation and Real Tax Revenue

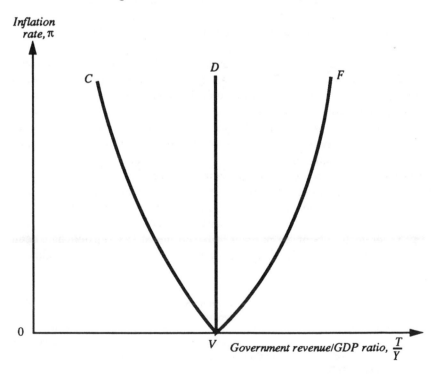

will inevitably lead to a fall in real tax revenue when prices rise.[15] And this fall will be even more significant if the long lag is combined with an inelastic tax system (combination A).

In the analysis that follows, I shall ignore combinations B and E; furthermore, since A is just an extreme version of C, I shall discuss only C. Consequently, the discussion will be limited to cases D, F, and C. These three cases are illustrated graphically in Figure 3.

The vertical axis of Figure 3 continues to measure the inflation rate. On the horizontal axis, we measure real tax revenue or, alternatively, the ratio of tax revenue to national income. Assume that, in the absence of inflation, real revenue would be OV. Assume also that the country enters an inflationary period.

If the country is characterized by combination D, its real tax revenue will hardly be affected. This situation can then be represented by line VD. If situation F prevails, real revenue would increase and would continue to increase as long as the average price $level$ (not just the rate of inflation) continues to increase. If one assumes that the rates of inflation on the vertical axis are maintained, a higher inflation rate will always be associated with a higher price level. This situation can then be represented by line VF.[16] If situation C (or A) prevails, inflation will bring about a fall in real tax revenue. This last situation is one that I wish to analyze in more detail.

At $\pi = 0$, revenue from taxes is equal to OV. As π increases, real revenue falls as shown by VC. The $percentage$ fall in tax revenue depends not only on the rate of inflation but also on the collection lag, as long as we assume that the elasticity is equal to one.[17] However, and this is the important point here, the $absolute$ size of the fall depends also on the initial ratio of taxes to national income (i.e., on the initial tax burden). The higher is the initial tax burden, the greater will be the absolute loss in tax revenue associated with a given increase in the rate of inflation.

Let us take a numerical example. If the average lag in tax collection is seven months (and we continue to assume that $E_m = 1$), an increase in the rate of inflation from 0 to 3 percent per month will reduce the real value of tax revenue by about 20 percent.[18] If the initial tax burden had been 10 percent of national income, the reduction in the tax revenue would cor-

---

[15]This is the situation that was analyzed in detail in Tanzi (1977). It must be recalled that discretionary changes are being ruled out.

[16]It should be remembered that the movement from V toward F is not reversible, since it is the $level$ of prices, rather than the $rate$ of inflation, that determines real tax revenue. The price index will continue to rise as long as $\pi > 0$.

[17]See Tanzi (1977), Table 1, p. 158.

[18]Ibid.

respond to 2 percent of national income; however, if the initial tax burden had been 30 percent, the reduction would correspond to 6 percent of national income. If, in the absence of inflation, the budget had been in balance, inflation would bring about a deficit. But this deficit would be only 2 percent of national income in the first case and 6 percent in the second case.

The impact of different lags and rates of inflation on the real value of one dollar of tax revenue can be estimated by multiplying that dollar by $1/(1 + p)^n$ where p is the *monthly* rate of inflation and n is the collection lag, expressed in months. If the elasticity of the tax system is unitary, the effect of inflation on the tax burden can be calculated by solving the following equation:

$$T^\pi = \frac{T_0}{(1 + p)^n} = \frac{T_0}{(1 + \pi)^{n/12}} \tag{6}$$

In equation (6), T_0 denotes the ratio of tax revenue to national income when the rate of inflation is zero; T^π denotes that ratio when inflation is π; and n denotes the collection lag, while p and π denote the rate of inflation on a monthly and on an annual basis, respectively.

3. Total Revenue During Inflation

In Subsection II.1., it was shown that the revenue gain from a given inflation tax is directly related to the base of this tax, which is the real stock of money. The higher is the ratio of this stock to national income M/Y, the larger, ceteris paribus, will be the revenue that can be obtained from inflationary finance. On the other hand, in Subsection II.2, it was found that the revenue losses (as percentages of national income) associated with given rates of inflation will be greater, the greater is the ratio of normal taxes to national income in the absence of inflation.

Given the collection lag, and assuming that we are dealing with situations where the elasticity of the tax system is either unitary or less than unity, if the initial M/Y is high while the initial T/Y is low, the inflation tax is more likely to make some significant contribution to total public sector revenue. On the other hand, if the initial M/Y ratio is low while the tax burden is high, the contribution that inflationary finance can make to total resources available to the government is much smaller. In this case, it is conceivable that the government might even gain from deflation, as this would be associated with increases in real tax revenue.

In any case, it should have become obvious from the above analysis that unless one assumes a tax system without lags and with unitary elasticity, one cannot isolate the revenue from inflationary finance from the inflation-induced changes in normal taxes, as has been done in the literature. In the case emphasized in this paper—line VC in Figure 3—inflationary finance will always bring about some losses in normal tax revenue.[19] One interesting question then is the following: At what rate of inflation is total revenue (i.e., inflation tax revenue *plus* normal tax revenue) maximized? This question can be answered either algebraically or graphically.

Since the revenue from deficit financing is given by

$$R^\pi = \pi \cdot ae^{-b\pi}$$

and the revenue from the tax system by

$$T^\pi = \frac{T_0}{(1 + \pi)^{n/12}}$$

total revenue $(TR)^\pi$ will be given by

$$(TR)^\pi = \pi ae^{-b\pi} + \frac{T_0}{(1 + \pi)^{n/12}} \tag{7}$$

Taking the derivative of TR^π with respect to π and setting it equal to zero would give us the value of π that maximizes total revenue.[20]

In Figure 4 the vertical axis continues to measure the rate of inflation. It should be recalled that we have assumed that expected inflation is equal to actual inflation and is equal also to the rate of change of the money supply. On the horizontal axis, the macrovariables are expressed as percentages of national income Y. As we have assumed away any change in real output, the horizontal axis also measures changes in real values.

---

[19]On the other hand, if the case typified by line VF were assumed, inflationary finance would bring about gains in normal tax revenue.

[20]From equation (7), we get

$$TR^\pi = \pi ae^{-b\pi} + T_0(1 + \pi)^{-n/12}$$

$$\frac{dTR^\pi}{d\pi} = [ae^{-b\pi} + (-ab\pi e^{-b\pi})] - \frac{n}{12} T_0 (1 + \pi)^{-(n/12)-1} = 0$$

$$\frac{dTR^\pi}{d\pi} = ae^{-b\pi} - ab\pi e^{-b\pi} - \left(\frac{n}{12}\right) \frac{T_0}{(1 + \pi)^{(12+n)/12}} = 0$$

Figure 4. Inflation, Tax Revenue, and Inflationary Finance

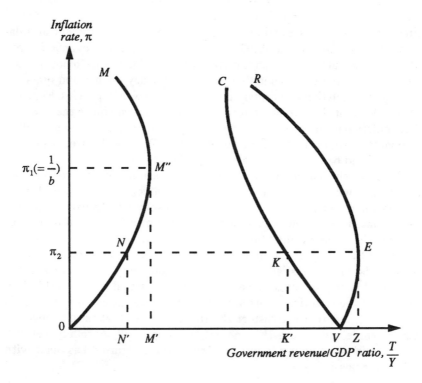

Curve OM measures the revenue from the inflation tax. This curve is the same as curve OM in Figure 2. Point O in Figure 4 indicates that, at zero inflation, the revenue from the inflation tax is also zero. As the rate of inflation increases, the inflation tax will generate more and more revenue. At point M'', the revenue from the inflation tax is maximized and is equal to OM'. The corresponding rate of inflation is π_1 ($=1/b$).

Line VC corresponds to line VC in Figure 3. This line shows the behavior of normal tax revenue in relation to various rates of inflation. The higher the inflation rate, the lower will be the ratio of tax revenue to national income. Ignoring the possibility of negative rates of inflation, normal tax revenue is maximized at zero inflation (at point V).

Curves OM and VC can be added horizontally to get total (i.e., normal tax *plus* inflation tax) revenue in relation to inflation. This total revenue curve is VR. Total government revenues would be maximized at a rate of inflation of π_2, where the curve VR reaches its easternmost point.[21] This revenue would then be equal to OZ; inflationary finance would contribute ON' $(= K'Z)$; and normal tax revenue would contribute $N'Z$ $(= OK')$. Since revenue from normal taxes has fallen by $K'V$ as a result of inflation, the *net* contribution of inflationary finance to total revenue is only VZ, which is much lower than the gross contribution ON'. Obviously, concentrating on the gross contribution of inflationary finance and ignoring the effect of inflation on normal taxes can lead to wrong policies. Figure 4 shows also that the rate of inflation, π_1, that would maximize the revenue from inflationary finance could very well bring about a large enough fall in normal tax revenue to make the government end up with lower resources than it would have had in the absence of inflation.

Figure 4 thus indicates that a partial-equilibrium approach to inflationary finance will often give results that are not correct. The role of inflationary finance in generating net additional resources to governments can be evaluated only within a general-equilibrium framework that takes into account the effect of inflation on the tax system of a country.[22] The response of the tax system to inflation varies from country to country, since it depends on the elasticity and the collection lag of the particular tax system. It is only in particular circumstances, typified by line VD in Figure 2, that the traditional partial analysis will give the correct answer. In most cases, inflation will distort the tax system so that normal revenue may increase or decrease, thus magnifying or (partially or totally) neutralizing the increase owing to inflationary finance. Figure 4 has dealt with this latter possibility.

III. A SIMULATION EXERCISE

In the previous section, it was shown that the total revenue that the government of a country can obtain from its existing tax system and from inflationary finance is related to the rate of inflation. It was also shown that, given the rate of inflation and assuming that the elasticity of the tax system is unity, the structural and/or institutional factors that determine total revenue are the following: T_0, the ratio of total tax revenue to na-

---

[21]The issue of whether this rate would be dynamically stable is ignored here.

[22]By the same token, the welfare cost of inflationary finance cannot be limited to measurement of the area under the demand-for-money function, as suggested by Bailey, but must take into account the distortions introduced into the tax system itself by inflation. These distortions may be as significant as the traditional welfare cost.

tional income at a zero inflation rate; n, the average collection lag for the tax system; a, the reciprocal of the velocity of money—or the ratio of money to income—at a zero inflation rate; and b, the sensitivity of the demand for money with respect to the rate of inflation.

To get a quantitative idea of how these variables may interact in different countries, I will take alternative, but realistic, estimates for each of them and provide solutions to the basic equations developed in Section I; this is done in this section. In the simulation exercise, I shall consider four alternative values for T_0—namely, 0.10, 0.20, 0.30, and 0.40. These values cover most countries, with the exception of a few very poor ones—such as Nepal, Afghanistan, Bangladesh—and some very wealthy ones—such as Denmark, the Netherlands, Norway, and Sweden. For the collection lag, expressed in months, I shall use four alternative values—2, 4, 6, and 8. These four values are likely to cover the situations of most countries.

For the ratios of narrow money ($M1$) to income a, I shall take three alternative values—0.10, 0.20, and 0.30—that are typical of many countries. For the sensitivity b of the demand for money with respect to inflation, one can rely on published studies in which this parameter has been estimated for many countries that have gone through periods of significant inflation.[23] In most of these studies, b has ranged from around 0.5 to around 3.0. Following Aghevli,[24] I shall alternatively consider values of 0.5, 1.0, 2.0, and 3.0.

The impact of inflation on the ratio of taxes to income (assuming unitary elasticity of the tax system) is obtained by solving equation (6) for assumed values of T_0 and n. Table 1 in the Appendix gives the results obtained in connection with annual rates of inflation ranging from 5 percent to 500 percent. The table is largely self-explanatory: the absolute revenue loss associated with a given rate of inflation increases with the size of the lag and with the size of the initial tax burden. Given the size of the lag, the higher is the initial ratio of taxes to income, the greater will be the revenue loss; and, given the initial tax burden, the longer is the lag, the greater will be the absolute fall in revenue. And, of course, given the initial tax burden and the lag, the higher is the rate of inflation, the greater will be the revenue loss.

The revenue from inflationary finance is obtained by solving equation (5) in connection with the alternative values of a, the initial ratio of money to income, and b, the sensitivity of the demand for money to inflation. Table 2 in the Appendix gives the results. This table is also self-

---

[23]See, inter alia, Cagan (1956), Campbell (1970), Diz (1970), Vogel (1974), and Aghevli and Khan (1977).

[24]Ibid.

explanatory. For each value of b, the maximum revenue from inflationary finance is obtained when the rate of inflation is equal to $1/b$. It will be recalled that at that point the absolute value of the elasticity of the demand for real balances with respect to the rate of inflation—which is equal to $|\pi b|$—is one. Given the value of b, the greater is the initial value of a, the greater will be the potential revenue from inflationary finance.

Combining the results in Tables 1 and 2 in the Appendix, one could obtain the answer to the basic question of the net effect of inflationary finance on total governmental revenue. However, a more direct and complete picture can be derived by directly solving equation (7) in connection with alternative values for a, b, T_0, and n for annual rates of inflation ranging from 5 percent to 500 percent. Some of these results are given in Table 3 in the Appendix. For the calculation of these results, the assumed values for a, b, T_0, and n are as above—namely,

$$a = 0.20$$
$$b = 0.50, 1.0, 2.0, 3.0$$
$$T_0 = 0.10, 0.20, 0.30, 0.40$$
$$n = 2, 4, 6, 8$$

Figure 5 illustrates the results for $a = 0.2$, $b = 0.5$, $T_0 = 0.2$, and $n = 6$. Figure 6 illustrates the impact of alternative values of T_0 and n.[25]

In most countries, policymakers would have some idea of the values of a and T_0; and they should be able to derive a value for n.[26] Thus, if a realistic value could be assumed for b, they could use these tables to estimate the net revenue that, ceteris paribus, they would obtain from inflationary finance. These tables indicate that total revenue is maximized at rates of inflation that are lower than $1/b$. In fact, in cases where the initial tax burden is relatively high and the lag is relatively long, the government is likely to obtain maximum revenue at a zero rate of inflation, especially when the value of b is on the higher side of the range. These tables indicate that the scope for raising revenue through inflationary finance is far more limited than has been assumed in the literature.

Before leaving this section, a word of caution is necessary in connection with the use of these tables. They have been developed following a theoretical framework based on various important assumptions. These assumptions do not detract from the theoretical validity of this framework, but they must not be ignored when the tables are used to analyze actual

---

[25]Note that in contrast to the practice followed in Figures 1-4, where the rate of inflation was shown along the vertical axis, the rate of inflation is hereinafter shown along the horizontal axis.

[26]The method followed in the determination of n is described in Tanzi (1977).

Figure 5. Inflation, Tax Revenue, and Inflationary Finance

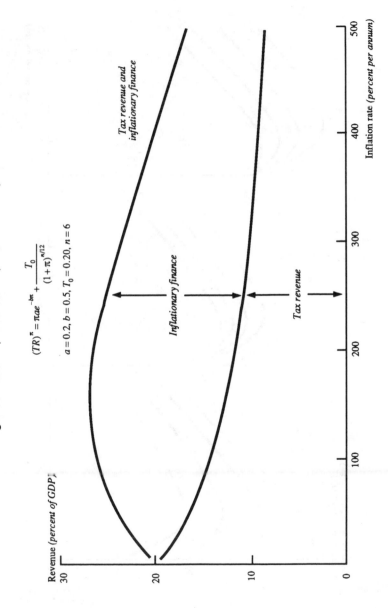

$$(TR)^\pi = \pi a e^{-b\pi} + \frac{T_0}{(1+\pi)^{n/12}}$$

$a = 0.2, b = 0.5, T_0 = 0.20, n = 6$

Revenue (percent of GDP)

Tax revenue and inflationary finance

Inflationary finance

Tax revenue

Inflation rate (percent per annum)

Figure 6. Impact of Inflation on Tax Revenue and Inflationary Finance

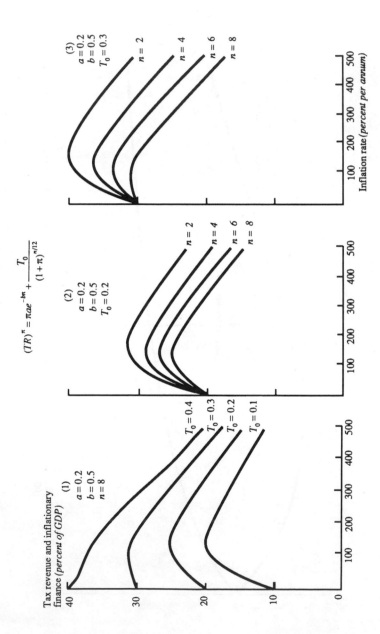

$$(TR)^\pi = \pi a e^{-b\pi} + \frac{T_0}{(1+\pi)^{n/12}}$$

Sources: Table 3 in the Appendix.

experiences. In any case, these tables should be taken to indicate orders of magnitude rather than precise results.

The most important assumptions are the following: (a) The changes in tax revenue brought about by inflation are passive, or automatic, ones and do not reflect (and, in fact, specifically ignore) discretionary changes. Obviously, if the government of a country introduces new taxes, eliminates existing ones, or modifies the collection mechanism, or, alternatively, if taxpayers increase the degree of evasion or noncompliance, the actual performance of the tax system can be substantially different from the simulated performance. (b) Private banks do not share in the creation of money — that is, the money multiplier is assumed to be one; therefore, the total increase in nominal money accrues to the government as revenue. If private banks share in the process of money creation — that is, if the money multiplier is greater than one — the actual revenue from inflationary finance associated with a given rate of inflation will be lower than the simulated one. The higher the money multiplier, the greater this difference will be.

(c) The money supply changes only as a consequence of the financing of the deficit rather than for other reasons (such as accumulation of foreign reserves, extension of credit to the private sector). In reality, if the money supply is changing because of other factors, actual revenue from inflationary finance will differ from simulated revenue. (d) Inflationary expectations are identical to actual price changes; consequently, there is a direct and immediate correspondence between actual price changes and changes in the nominal stock of money. If inflationary expectations adjust with lags to actual price changes, actual revenue from inflationary finance for particular years would also differ from simulated revenue. (e) Only direct central bank financing of the deficit is assumed to bring about inflation through money creation. There is, however, the possibility that while the government may be financing a deficit through borrowing from the private sector by selling bonds, the central bank may, in turn, be creating money through open market operations. In such a case, the central bank financing of the deficit would be indirect, but would still lead to money creation and inflation.

IV. Summary and Conclusions

The extent to which lags in the collection of taxes can limit the role of deficit financing or can play a direct role in the inflationary process has not been appreciated. With the exception of the few studies cited in footnote 6, there is no literature on this subject. The role of lags in this process depends on several factors that, at the cost of being somewhat repetitive, are worth emphasizing.

The first factor is, of course, the price elasticity of the tax system. The lower is that elasticity, the greater will be the impact of the collection lag. To simplify the issues, in the previous analysis an elasticity of approximately unity has been assumed. This is probably a realistic assumption for many developing countries.[27] The second factor is the ratio of tax revenue to national income (i.e., the tax burden). The existence of lags will bring about a given percentage fall in total tax revenue during inflation. This percentage fall will translate into a larger or smaller absolute fall, depending on the original tax burden. The third factor is the ratio of the money supply to national income. Ceteris paribus, the larger is that ratio, the lower will be the inflationary impact of a fall in revenue (or an increase in public expenditure) financed by printing money. The fourth factor, which is closely connected with the previous one, is the elasticity of the demand for real balances with respect to expected inflation. A high elasticity will bring about a substantial fall in the stock of real money, so that, a posteriori, the inflationary impact of a given deficit is likely to be greater than anticipated.

The model that has been developed provides, of course, a stylized version of what would happen in a given country that is pursuing inflationary finance. The model is inevitably based on several important assumptions that may or may not hold for particular countries. For example, to the extent that a developed capital market allows the government to finance its fiscal deficit through borrowing from the private sector, and to the extent that this borrowing "crowds out" some private expenditure, the inflationary implications of this action will be less serious than central bank financing of the deficit. Equally significant is the fact that the fiscal deficit and the subsequent money creation may lead to losses in foreign reserves, which could neutralize some of the effects of the fiscal deficit on money creation.

The major conclusion that can be derived from the foregoing analysis is that, on the basis of realistic assumptions supported by empirical evidence, the existence of lags in tax collection implies that a government's gains from the pursuit of inflationary finance are likely to be lower than has commonly been assumed. If the lags are long and the initial tax burden is high, the loss in revenue may be substantial and may neutralize any gain coming from central bank financing of the deficit. This is an argument against inflationary finance that is quite different from the tradi-

---

[27]The validity of this assumption is supported by the empirical results obtained for Brazil, Colombia, the Dominican Republic, and Thailand in Aghevli and Khan (1978).

tional one based exclusively on welfare-cost considerations of alternative sources of revenue. Even the most favorable case toward inflationary finance—in which all revenues are invested in productive investments projects[28]—appears to be considerably weakened by this analysis, as the *net* addition to government's total revenue may, under plausible conditions, be zero or even negative.

Finally, this paper has shown that the literature on inflationary finance has dealt with just one special case, namely, the one in which inflation leaves real tax revenue unchanged—line *VD* in Figure 3. In most cases, however, inflation brings about changes in real tax revenue. These changes are positive for some countries and negative for others. In any case, these changes have to be taken into account in a truly general theory of inflationary finance. The foregoing analysis could be generalized to incorporate situations where the price elasticity of the tax system is different from one and where there is real growth in the economy.

---

[28]See Aghevli (1977).

Appendix

Table 1. Inflation and Revenue from Tax System[1]

(Ratios of total tax revenue to gross domestic product)

π	$T_0 = 0.1$				$T_0 = 0.2$				$T_0 = 0.3$				$T_0 = 0.4$			
	$n=2$	$n=4$	$n=6$	$n=8$	$n=2$	$n=4$	$n=6$	$n=8$	$n=2$	$n=4$	$n=6$	$n=8$	$n=2$	$n=4$	$n=6$	$n=8$
0.050	0.099	0.098	0.098	0.097	0.198	0.197	0.195	0.194	0.298	0.295	0.293	0.290	0.397	0.394	0.390	0.387
0.100	0.098	0.097	0.095	0.094	0.197	0.194	0.191	0.188	0.295	0.291	0.286	0.282	0.394	0.387	0.381	0.375
0.150	0.098	0.095	0.093	0.091	0.195	0.191	0.187	0.182	0.293	0.286	0.280	0.273	0.391	0.382	0.373	0.364
0.200	0.097	0.094	0.091	0.089	0.194	0.188	0.183	0.177	0.291	0.282	0.274	0.266	0.388	0.376	0.365	0.354
0.250	0.096	0.093	0.089	0.086	0.193	0.186	0.179	0.172	0.289	0.278	0.268	0.259	0.385	0.371	0.358	0.345
0.300	0.096	0.092	0.088	0.084	0.191	0.183	0.175	0.168	0.287	0.275	0.263	0.252	0.383	0.367	0.351	0.336
0.350	0.095	0.090	0.086	0.082	0.190	0.181	0.172	0.164	0.285	0.271	0.258	0.246	0.380	0.362	0.344	0.327
0.400	0.095	0.089	0.085	0.080	0.189	0.179	0.169	0.160	0.284	0.268	0.254	0.240	0.378	0.358	0.338	0.320
0.450	0.094	0.088	0.083	0.078	0.188	0.177	0.166	0.156	0.282	0.265	0.249	0.234	0.376	0.353	0.332	0.312
0.500	0.093	0.087	0.082	0.076	0.187	0.175	0.163	0.153	0.280	0.262	0.245	0.229	0.374	0.349	0.327	0.305

0.600	0.092	0.085	0.079	0.073	0.185	0.171	0.158	0.146	0.277	0.256	0.237	0.219	0.370	0.342	0.316	0.292
0.700	0.092	0.084	0.077	0.070	0.183	0.168	0.153	0.140	0.275	0.251	0.230	0.211	0.366	0.335	0.307	0.281
0.800	0.091	0.082	0.075	0.068	0.181	0.164	0.149	0.135	0.272	0.247	0.224	0.203	0.363	0.329	0.298	0.270
0.900	0.090	0.081	0.073	0.065	0.180	0.161	0.145	0.130	0.270	0.242	0.218	0.196	0.359	0.323	0.290	0.261
1.000	0.089	0.079	0.071	0.063	0.178	0.159	0.141	0.126	0.267	0.238	0.212	0.189	0.356	0.317	0.283	0.252
1.200	0.088	0.077	0.067	0.059	0.175	0.154	0.135	0.118	0.263	0.231	0.202	0.177	0.351	0.308	0.270	0.236
1.400	0.086	0.075	0.065	0.056	0.173	0.149	0.129	0.112	0.259	0.224	0.194	0.167	0.346	0.299	0.258	0.223
1.600	0.085	0.073	0.062	0.053	0.171	0.145	0.124	0.106	0.256	0.218	0.186	0.159	0.341	0.291	0.248	0.212
1.800	0.084	0.071	0.060	0.050	0.168	0.142	0.120	0.101	0.253	0.213	0.179	0.151	0.337	0.284	0.239	0.201
2.000	0.083	0.069	0.058	0.048	0.167	0.139	0.115	0.096	0.250	0.208	0.173	0.144	0.333	0.277	0.231	0.192
2.500	0.081	0.066	0.053	0.043	0.162	0.132	0.107	0.087	0.243	0.198	0.160	0.130	0.325	0.263	0.214	0.174
3.000	0.079	0.063	0.050	0.040	0.159	0.126	0.100	0.079	0.238	0.189	0.150	0.119	0.317	0.252	0.200	0.159
3.500	0.078	0.061	0.047	0.037	0.156	0.121	0.094	0.073	0.233	0.182	0.141	0.110	0.311	0.242	0.189	0.147
4.000	0.076	0.058	0.045	0.034	0.153	0.117	0.089	0.068	0.229	0.175	0.134	0.103	0.306	0.234	0.179	0.137
4.500	0.075	0.057	0.043	0.032	0.151	0.113	0.085	0.064	0.226	0.170	0.128	0.096	0.301	0.227	0.171	0.128
5.000	0.074	0.055	0.041	0.030	0.148	0.110	0.082	0.061	0.223	0.165	0.122	0.091	0.297	0.220	0.163	0.121

The inflation rate is denoted by π, the ratio of total tax revenue to gross domestic product at a zero inflation rate by T_0, and the average collection lag for the tax system by n.

Table 2. Revenue from Inflationary Finance[1]

(Ratios to gross domestic product)

π	a = 0.10				a = 0.20				a = 0.30			
	b = 0.5	b = 1.0	b = 2.0	b = 3.0	b = 0.5	b = 1.0	b = 2.0	b = 3.0	b = 0.5	b = 1.0	b = 2.0	b = 3.0
0.5000	0.0049	0.0048	0.0045	0.0043	0.0098	0.0095	0.0090	0.0086	0.0146	0.0143	0.0136	0.0129
0.1000	0.0095	0.0090	0.0082	0.0074	0.0190	0.0181	0.0164	0.0148	0.0285	0.0271	0.0246	0.0222
0.1500	0.0139	0.0129	0.0111	0.0096	0.0278	0.0258	0.0222	0.0191	0.0417	0.0387	0.0333	0.0287
0.2000	0.0181	0.0164	0.0134	0.0110	0.0362	0.0327	0.0268	0.0220	0.0543	0.0491	0.0402	0.0329
0.2500	0.0221	0.0195	0.0152	0.0118	0.0441	0.0389	0.0303	0.0236	0.0662	0.0584	0.0455	0.0354
0.3000	0.0258	0.0222	0.0165	0.0122	0.0516	0.0444	0.0329	0.0244	0.0775	0.0667	0.0494	0.0366
0.3500	0.0294	0.0247	0.0174	0.0122	0.0588	0.0493	0.0348	0.0245	0.0881	0.0740	0.0521	0.0367
0.4000	0.0327	0.0268	0.0180	0.0120	0.0655	0.0536	0.0359	0.0241	0.0982	0.0804	0.0539	0.0361
0.4500	0.0359	0.0287	0.0183	0.0117	0.0719	0.0574	0.0366	0.0233	0.1078	0.0861	0.0549	0.0350
0.5000	0.0389	0.0303	0.0184	0.0112	0.0779	0.0607	0.0368	0.0223	0.1168	0.0910	0.0552	0.0335

0.6000	0.0444	0.0329	0.0181	0.0099	0.0889	0.0659	0.0361	0.0198	0.1333	0.0988	0.0542	0.0298
0.7000	0.0493	0.0348	0.0173	0.0086	0.0987	0.0695	0.0345	0.0171	0.1480	0.1043	0.0518	0.0257
0.8000	0.0536	0.0359	0.0162	0.0073	0.1073	0.0719	0.0323	0.0145	0.1609	0.1078	0.0485	0.0218
0.9000	0.0574	0.0366	0.0149	0.0060	0.1148	0.0732	0.0298	0.0121	0.1722	0.1098	0.0446	0.0181
1.0000	0.0607	0.0368	0.0135	0.0050	0.1213	0.0736	0.0271	0.0100	0.1820	0.1104	0.0406	0.0149
1.2000	0.0659	0.0361	0.0109	0.0033	0.1317	0.0723	0.0218	0.0066	0.1976	0.1084	0.0327	0.0098
1.4000	0.0695	0.0345	0.0085	0.0021	0.1390	0.0690	0.0170	0.0042	0.2086	0.1036	0.0255	0.0063
1.6000	0.0719	0.0323	0.0065	0.0013	0.1438	0.0646	0.0130	0.0026	0.2157	0.0969	0.0196	0.0040
1.8000	0.0732	0.0298	0.0049	0.0008	0.1464	0.0595	0.0098	0.0016	0.2195	0.0893	0.0148	0.0024
2.0000	0.0736	0.0271	0.0037	0.0005	0.1472	0.0541	0.0073	0.0010	0.2207	0.0812	0.0110	0.0015
2.5000	0.0716	0.0205	0.0017	0.0001	0.1433	0.0410	0.0034	0.0003	0.2149	0.0616	0.0051	0.0004
3.0000	0.0069	0.0149	0.0007	0.0000	0.1339	0.0299	0.0015	0.0001	0.2008	0.0448	0.0022	0.0001
3.5000	0.0608	0.0106	0.0003	0.0000	0.1216	0.0211	0.0006	0.0000	0.1825	0.0317	0.0010	0.0000
4.0000	0.0541	0.0073	0.0001	0.0000	0.1083	0.0147	0.0003	0.0000	0.1624	0.0220	0.0004	0.0000
4.5000	0.0474	0.0050	0.0001	0.0000	0.0949	0.0100	0.0001	0.0000	0.1423	0.0150	0.0002	0.0000
5.0000	0.0410	0.0034	0.0000	0.0000	0.0821	0.0067	0.0000	0.0000	0.1231	0.0101	0.0001	0.0000

[1] The inflation rate is denoted by π, the sensitivity of the demand for money with respect to the rate of inflation by b, and the ratio of money to income at a zero inflation rate by a.

Table 3. Revenues from Taxes and Inflationary Finance[1]

(Ratios to gross domestic product)

$a = 0.20; \quad b = 0.50$

π	$T_0 = 0.1$				$T_0 = 0.2$				$T_0 = 0.3$				$T_0 = 0.4$			
	$n=2$	$n=4$	$n=6$	$n=8$	$n=2$	$n=4$	$n=6$	$n=8$	$n=2$	$n=4$	$n=6$	$n=8$	$n=2$	$n=4$	$n=6$	$n=8$
0.050	0.109	0.108	0.107	0.107	0.208	0.207	0.205	0.203	0.307	0.305	0.303	0.300	0.407	0.403	0.400	0.397
0.100	0.117	0.116	0.114	0.113	0.216	0.213	0.210	0.207	0.314	0.310	0.305	0.301	0.413	0.407	0.400	0.394
0.150	0.126	0.123	0.121	0.119	0.223	0.219	0.214	0.210	0.321	0.314	0.308	0.301	0.419	0.410	0.401	0.392
0.200	0.133	0.130	0.127	0.125	0.230	0.224	0.219	0.213	0.327	0.319	0.310	0.302	0.424	0.413	0.401	0.390
0.250	0.140	0.137	0.134	0.130	0.237	0.230	0.223	0.216	0.333	0.323	0.312	0.303	0.430	0.415	0.402	0.389
0.300	0.147	0.143	0.139	0.136	0.243	0.235	0.227	0.220	0.339	0.327	0.315	0.304	0.435	0.418	0.402	0.387
0.350	0.154	0.149	0.145	0.141	0.249	0.240	0.231	0.222	0.344	0.330	0.317	0.304	0.439	0.421	0.403	0.386
0.400	0.160	0.155	0.150	0.145	0.255	0.244	0.235	0.225	0.349	0.334	0.319	0.305	0.444	0.423	0.404	0.385
0.450	0.166	0.160	0.155	0.150	0.260	0.249	0.238	0.228	0.354	0.337	0.321	0.306	0.448	0.425	0.404	0.384
0.500	0.171	0.165	0.160	0.154	0.265	0.253	0.241	0.231	0.358	0.340	0.323	0.307	0.452	0.427	0.404	0.383
0.600	0.181	0.174	0.168	0.162	0.274	0.260	0.247	0.235	0.366	0.345	0.326	0.308	0.459	0.431	0.405	0.381
0.700	0.190	0.182	0.175	0.169	0.282	0.266	0.252	0.239	0.373	0.350	0.329	0.309	0.465	0.434	0.405	0.379
0.800	0.198	0.189	0.182	0.175	0.289	0.272	0.256	0.242	0.379	0.354	0.331	0.310	0.470	0.436	0.405	0.378
0.900	0.205	0.196	0.187	0.180	0.294	0.276	0.260	0.245	0.384	0.357	0.332	0.310	0.474	0.438	0.405	0.376
1.000	0.210	0.201	0.192	0.184	0.299	0.280	0.263	0.247	0.389	0.359	0.333	0.310	0.478	0.439	0.404	0.373
1.200	0.219	0.209	0.199	0.191	0.307	0.285	0.267	0.250	0.395	0.362	0.334	0.309	0.482	0.439	0.401	0.368
1.400	0.225	0.214	0.204	0.195	0.312	0.288	0.268	0.251	0.398	0.363	0.333	0.306	0.485	0.438	0.397	0.362
1.600	0.229	0.217	0.206	0.197	0.314	0.289	0.268	0.250	0.400	0.362	0.330	0.302	0.485	0.435	0.392	0.355
1.800	0.231	0.217	0.206	0.197	0.315	0.288	0.266	0.247	0.399	0.359	0.326	0.297	0.483	0.430	0.385	0.348
2.000	0.230	0.216	0.205	0.195	0.314	0.286	0.263	0.243	0.397	0.355	0.320	0.291	0.480	0.424	0.378	0.339

2.500	0.317	0.357	0.407	0.468	0.273	0.304	0.341	0.387	0.230	0.250	0.275	0.306	0.187	0.197	0.209	0.224
3.000	0.293	0.334	0.386	0.451	0.253	0.284	0.323	0.372	0.213	0.234	0.260	0.293	0.174	0.184	0.197	0.213
3.500	0.268	0.310	0.364	0.433	0.232	0.263	0.303	0.355	0.195	0.216	0.243	0.277	0.158	0.169	0.182	0.199
4.000	0.245	0.287	0.342	0.414	0.211	0.242	0.284	0.338	0.177	0.198	0.225	0.261	0.142	0.153	0.167	0.185
4.500	0.223	0.265	0.321	0.396	0.191	0.223	0.265	0.321	0.159	0.180	0.208	0.245	0.127	0.137	0.152	0.170
5.000	0.203	0.245	0.302	0.379	0.173	0.205	0.247	0.305	0.143	0.164	0.192	0.230	0.112	0.123	0.137	0.156
0.050	0.397	0.400	0.403	0.406	0.300	0.302	0.305	0.307	0.203	0.205	0.206	0.208	0.106	0.107	0.108	0.109
0.100	0.393	0.399	0.406	0.412	0.300	0.304	0.309	0.313	0.206	0.209	0.212	0.215	0.112	0.113	0.115	0.117
0.150	0.390	0.399	0.408	0.417	0.299	0.306	0.312	0.319	0.208	0.212	0.217	0.221	0.117	0.119	0.121	0.124
0.200	0.387	0.398	0.409	0.421	0.298	0.307	0.315	0.324	0.210	0.215	0.221	0.227	0.121	0.124	0.127	0.130
0.250	0.384	0.397	0.410	0.424	0.297	0.307	0.317	0.328	0.211	0.218	0.225	0.232	0.125	0.128	0.132	0.135
0.300	0.380	0.395	0.411	0.427	0.296	0.308	0.319	0.332	0.212	0.220	0.228	0.236	0.128	0.132	0.136	0.140
0.350	0.377	0.394	0.411	0.430	0.295	0.308	0.321	0.335	0.213	0.221	0.230	0.240	0.131	0.135	0.140	0.144
0.400	0.373	0.392	0.411	0.432	0.293	0.307	0.322	0.337	0.213	0.223	0.232	0.243	0.134	0.138	0.143	0.148
0.450	0.370	0.390	0.411	0.433	0.292	0.307	0.322	0.339	0.214	0.223	0.234	0.245	0.135	0.140	0.146	0.151
0.500	0.366	0.387	0.410	0.435	0.290	0.306	0.323	0.341	0.213	0.224	0.235	0.248	0.137	0.142	0.148	0.154
0.600	0.358	0.382	0.408	0.436	0.285	0.303	0.322	0.343	0.212	0.224	0.237	0.251	0.139	0.145	0.151	0.158
0.700	0.350	0.376	0.405	0.436	0.280	0.300	0.321	0.344	0.210	0.223	0.237	0.253	0.140	0.146	0.153	0.161
0.800	0.342	0.370	0.401	0.435	0.275	0.295	0.319	0.344	0.207	0.221	0.236	0.253	0.139	0.146	0.154	0.163
0.900	0.334	0.363	0.396	0.433	0.269	0.291	0.315	0.343	0.204	0.218	0.235	0.253	0.138	0.146	0.154	0.163
1.000	0.326	0.356	0.391	0.430	0.263	0.286	0.312	0.341	0.200	0.215	0.232	0.252	0.137	0.144	0.153	0.163
1.200	0.309	0.342	0.380	0.423	0.250	0.275	0.303	0.335	0.191	0.207	0.226	0.248	0.131	0.140	0.149	0.160
1.400	0.292	0.327	0.368	0.415	0.236	0.263	0.293	0.328	0.181	0.198	0.218	0.242	0.125	0.134	0.144	0.155
1.600	0.276	0.313	0.356	0.406	0.223	0.251	0.283	0.320	0.170	0.189	0.210	0.235	0.117	0.127	0.137	0.150
1.800	0.261	0.299	0.343	0.396	0.211	0.239	0.272	0.312	0.160	0.179	0.201	0.228	0.110	0.119	0.130	0.144
2.000	0.246	0.285	0.331	0.387	0.198	0.227	0.262	0.304	0.150	0.170	0.193	0.221	0.102	0.112	0.123	0.137

$a = 0.20; \quad b = 1.00$

Table 3 (continued). Revenues from Taxes and Inflationary Finance[1]

(Ratios to gross domestic product)

π	$T_0 = 0.1$				$T_0 = 0.2$				$T_0 = 0.3$				$T_0 = 0.4$			
	$n=2$	$n=4$	$n=6$	$n=8$	$n=2$	$n=4$	$n=6$	$n=8$	$n=2$	$n=4$	$n=6$	$n=8$	$n=2$	$n=4$	$n=6$	$n=8$
							$a = 0.20$;	$b = 1.00$								
2.500	0.122	0.107	0.094	0.084	0.203	0.173	0.148	0.128	0.285	0.239	0.201	0.171	0.366	0.304	0.255	0.215
3.000	0.109	0.093	0.080	0.070	0.189	0.156	0.130	0.109	0.268	0.219	0.180	0.149	0.347	0.282	0.230	0.189
3.500	0.099	0.082	0.068	0.058	0.177	0.142	0.115	0.095	0.255	0.203	0.163	0.131	0.332	0.263	0.210	0.168
4.000	0.091	0.073	0.059	0.049	0.168	0.132	0.104	0.083	0.244	0.190	0.149	0.117	0.321	0.249	0.194	0.151
4.500	0.085	0.067	0.053	0.042	0.161	0.123	0.095	0.074	0.236	0.180	0.138	0.106	0.311	0.237	0.181	0.138
5.000	0.081	0.062	0.048	0.037	0.155	0.117	0.088	0.067	0.229	0.172	0.129	0.098	0.303	0.227	0.170	0.128
							$a = 0.20$;	$b = 2.00$								
0.050	0.108	0.107	0.107	0.106	0.207	0.206	0.204	0.203	0.307	0.304	0.302	0.299	0.406	0.403	0.399	0.396
0.100	0.115	0.113	0.112	0.110	0.213	0.210	0.207	0.204	0.312	0.307	0.302	0.298	0.410	0.404	0.398	0.392
0.150	0.120	0.118	0.115	0.113	0.218	0.213	0.209	0.204	0.315	0.309	0.302	0.296	0.413	0.404	0.395	0.387
0.200	0.124	0.121	0.118	0.115	0.221	0.215	0.209	0.204	0.318	0.309	0.301	0.292	0.415	0.403	0.392	0.381
0.250	0.127	0.123	0.120	0.117	0.223	0.216	0.209	0.203	0.319	0.309	0.299	0.289	0.416	0.402	0.388	0.375
0.300	0.129	0.125	0.121	0.117	0.224	0.216	0.208	0.201	0.320	0.308	0.296	0.285	0.416	0.399	0.384	0.369
0.350	0.130	0.125	0.121	0.117	0.225	0.216	0.207	0.198	0.320	0.306	0.293	0.280	0.415	0.397	0.379	0.362
0.400	0.130	0.125	0.120	0.116	0.225	0.215	0.205	0.196	0.320	0.304	0.289	0.276	0.414	0.394	0.374	0.356
0.450	0.131	0.125	0.120	0.115	0.225	0.213	0.203	0.193	0.319	0.302	0.286	0.271	0.413	0.390	0.369	0.349
0.500	0.130	0.124	0.118	0.113	0.224	0.212	0.200	0.189	0.317	0.299	0.282	0.266	0.411	0.386	0.363	0.342
0.600	0.129	0.122	0.115	0.109	0.221	0.207	0.194	0.182	0.314	0.293	0.273	0.255	0.406	0.378	0.352	0.329
0.700	0.126	0.118	0.111	0.105	0.218	0.202	0.188	0.175	0.309	0.286	0.265	0.245	0.401	0.370	0.341	0.315
0.800	0.123	0.115	0.107	0.100	0.214	0.197	0.181	0.167	0.304	0.279	0.256	0.235	0.395	0.361	0.330	0.303
0.900	0.120	0.110	0.102	0.095	0.209	0.191	0.175	0.160	0.299	0.272	0.247	0.225	0.389	0.353	0.320	0.291
1.000	0.116	0.106	0.098	0.090	0.205	0.186	0.168	0.153	0.294	0.265	0.239	0.216	0.383	0.345	0.310	0.279

1.200	0.258	0.291	0.329	0.373	0.199	0.224	0.252	0.285	0.140	0.157	0.176	0.197	0.081	0.089	0.099	0.109
1.400	0.240	0.275	0.316	0.363	0.184	0.211	0.241	0.276	0.129	0.146	0.166	0.190	0.073	0.082	0.092	0.103
1.600	0.225	0.261	0.304	0.354	0.172	0.199	0.231	0.269	0.119	0.137	0.158	0.184	0.066	0.075	0.086	0.098
1.800	0.211	0.249	0.294	0.347	0.161	0.189	0.223	0.263	0.111	0.129	0.152	0.178	0.060	0.070	0.081	0.094
2.000	0.200	0.238	0.285	0.340	0.152	0.181	0.215	0.257	0.103	0.123	0.146	0.174	0.055	0.065	0.077	0.091
2.500	0.177	0.217	0.267	0.328	0.134	0.164	0.201	0.247	0.090	0.110	0.135	0.166	0.047	0.057	0.069	0.085
3.000	0.160	0.201	0.253	0.319	0.121	0.151	0.190	0.240	0.081	0.101	0.127	0.160	0.041	0.051	0.064	0.081
3.500	0.147	0.189	0.243	0.312	0.111	0.142	0.182	0.234	0.074	0.095	0.122	0.156	0.037	0.048	0.061	0.078
4.000	0.137	0.179	0.234	0.306	0.103	0.134	0.176	0.230	0.069	0.090	0.117	0.153	0.034	0.045	0.059	0.077
4.500	0.128	0.171	0.227	0.301	0.096	0.128	0.170	0.226	0.064	0.085	0.113	0.151	0.032	0.043	0.057	0.075
5.000	0.121	0.163	0.220	0.297	0.091	0.123	0.165	0.223	0.061	0.082	0.110	0.148	0.030	0.041	0.055	0.074

$a = 0.20; \quad b = 3.00$

0.050	0.396	0.399	0.402	0.405	0.299	0.301	0.304	0.306	0.202	0.204	0.205	0.207	0.105	0.106	0.107	0.108
0.100	0.390	0.396	0.402	0.409	0.296	0.301	0.305	0.310	0.203	0.206	0.209	0.212	0.109	0.100	0.112	0.113
0.150	0.384	0.392	0.401	0.410	0.292	0.299	0.305	0.312	0.201	0.206	0.210	0.215	0.110	0.112	0.115	0.117
0.200	0.376	0.387	0.398	0.410	0.288	0.296	0.304	0.313	0.199	0.205	0.210	0.216	0.111	0.113	0.116	0.119
0.250	0.368	0.381	0.395	0.409	0.282	0.292	0.302	0.313	0.196	0.203	0.209	0.216	0.110	0.113	0.116	0.120
0.300	0.360	0.375	0.391	0.407	0.276	0.288	0.299	0.312	0.192	0.200	0.208	0.216	0.108	0.112	0.116	0.120
0.350	0.352	0.369	0.386	0.405	0.270	0.283	0.296	0.310	0.188	0.197	0.205	0.215	0.106	0.111	0.115	0.120
0.400	0.344	0.362	0.382	0.402	0.264	0.278	0.292	0.308	0.184	0.193	0.203	0.213	0.104	0.109	0.113	0.119
0.450	0.336	0.356	0.377	0.399	0.258	0.272	0.288	0.305	0.179	0.189	0.200	0.211	0.101	0.106	0.112	0.117
0.500	0.328	0.349	0.372	0.396	0.251	0.267	0.284	0.303	0.175	0.186	0.197	0.209	0.099	0.104	0.110	0.116
0.600	0.312	0.336	0.362	0.390	0.239	0.257	0.276	0.297	0.166	0.178	0.191	0.205	0.093	0.099	0.105	0.112
0.700	0.298	0.324	0.352	0.383	0.228	0.247	0.269	0.292	0.158	0.171	0.185	0.200	0.087	0.094	0.101	0.109
0.800	0.285	0.313	0.343	0.377	0.217	0.238	0.261	0.287	0.150	0.164	0.179	0.196	0.082	0.089	0.097	0.105
0.900	0.273	0.302	0.335	0.372	0.208	0.230	0.254	0.282	0.142	0.157	0.174	0.192	0.077	0.085	0.093	0.102
1.000	0.262	0.293	0.327	0.366	0.199	0.222	0.248	0.277	0.136	0.151	0.169	0.188	0.073	0.081	0.089	0.099

Table 3 (concluded). Revenues from Taxes and Inflationary Finance[1]

(Ratios to gross domestic product)

π	$T_0 = 0.1$				$T_0 = 0.2$				$T_0 = 0.3$				$T_0 = 0.4$			
	$n=2$	$n=4$	$n=6$	$n=8$	$n=2$	$n=4$	$n=6$	$n=8$	$n=2$	$n=4$	$n=6$	$n=8$	$n=2$	$n=4$	$n=6$	$n=8$
							$a = 0.20;$	$b = 3.00$								
1.200	0.094	0.083	0.074	0.066	0.182	0.160	0.141	0.125	0.270	0.237	0.209	0.184	0.357	0.314	0.276	0.243
1.400	0.091	0.079	0.069	0.060	0.177	0.154	0.133	0.116	0.263	0.228	0.198	0.172	0.350	0.303	0.262	0.227
1.600	0.088	0.075	0.065	0.056	0.173	0.148	0.127	0.108	0.258	0.221	0.189	0.161	0.344	0.294	0.251	0.214
1.800	0.086	0.073	0.061	0.052	0.170	0.144	0.121	0.102	0.254	0.214	0.181	0.153	0.339	0.285	0.241	0.203
2.000	0.084	0.070	0.059	0.049	0.168	0.140	0.116	0.097	0.251	0.209	0.174	0.145	0.334	0.278	0.232	0.193
2.500	0.081	0.066	0.054	0.044	0.163	0.132	0.107	0.087	0.244	0.198	0.161	0.130	0.325	0.264	0.214	0.174
3.000	0.079	0.063	0.050	0.040	0.159	0.126	0.100	0.079	0.238	0.189	0.150	0.119	0.318	0.252	0.200	0.159
3.500	0.078	0.061	0.047	0.037	0.156	0.121	0.094	0.073	0.234	0.182	0.141	0.110	0.311	0.242	0.189	0.147
4.000	0.076	0.058	0.045	0.034	0.153	0.117	0.089	0.068	0.229	0.175	0.134	0.103	0.306	0.234	0.179	0.137
4.500	0.075	0.057	0.043	0.032	0.151	0.113	0.085	0.064	0.226	0.170	0.128	0.096	0.301	0.227	0.171	0.128
5.000	0.074	0.055	0.041	0.030	0.148	0.110	0.082	0.061	0.223	0.165	0.122	0.091	0.297	0.220	0.163	0.121

[1] The inflation rate is denoted by π, the ratio of total tax revenue to gross domestic product at a zero inflation rate by T_0, the ratio of money to income at zero inflation by a, the sensitivity of the demand for money with respect to the rate of inflation by b, and the average collection lag for the tax system by n.

BIBLIOGRAPHY

Aghevli, Bijan B., "Inflationary Finance and Economic Growth," *Journal of Political Economy* (Chicago), Vol. 85 (December 1977), pp. 1295-1307.

_____, and Mohsin S. Khan, "Inflationary Finance and the Dynamics of Inflation: Indonesia, 1951-72," *American Economic Review* (Nashville, Tennessee), Vol. 67 (June 1977), pp. 390-403.

_____, "Government Deficits and the Inflationary Process in Developing Countries," *Staff Papers*, International Monetary Fund (Washington), Vol. 25 (September 1978), pp. 383-416.

Bailey, Martin J., "The Welfare Cost of Inflationary Finance," *Journal of Political Economy* (Chicago), Vol. 64 (April 1956), pp. 93-110.

Cagan, Phillip, "The Monetary Dynamics of Hyperinflation," in *Studies in the Quantity Theory of Money*, ed. by Milton Friedman (University of Chicago Press, 1956), pp. 25-117.

Campbell, Colin D., "The Velocity of Money and the Rate of Inflation: Recent Experiences in South Korea and Brazil," in *Varieties of Monetary Experience*, ed. by David Meiselman (University of Chicago Press, 1970), pp. 341-86.

Diz, Adolfo C., "Money and Prices in Argentina, 1935-1962," in *Varieties of Monetary Experience*, ed. by David Meiselman (University of Chicago Press, 1970), pp. 71-162.

Dutton, Dean S., "A Model of Self-Generating Inflation: The Argentine Case," *Journal of Money, Credit and Banking* (Columbus, Ohio), Vol. 3 (May 1971), pp. 245-62.

Friedman, Milton, "Discussion of the Inflationary Gap," *American Economic Review* (Nashville, Tennessee), Vol. 32 (June 1942), pp. 308-14. This was republished in Friedman's *Essays in Positive Economics* (University of Chicago Press, 1953), pp. 251-62.

_____, "Government Revenue from Inflation," *Journal of Political Economy* (Chicago), Vol. 79 (July-August 1971), pp. 846-56.

Keynes, John Maynard, *A Tract on Monetary Reform* (London: Macmillan, 1923).

Olivera, Julio H.G., "Money, Prices and Fiscal Lags: A Note on the Dynamics of Inflation," Banca Nazionale del Lavoro, *Quarterly Review* (Rome), Vol. 20 (September 1967), pp. 258-67.

Shoup, Carl S., *Public Finance* (Chicago: Aldine, 1969).

Tanzi, Vito, "Inflation, Lags in Collection, and the Real Value of Tax Revenue," *Staff Papers*, International Monetary Fund (Washington), Vol. 24 (March 1977), pp. 154-67.

Vogel, R.C., "The Dynamics of Inflation in Latin America, 1950-1969," *American Economic Review* (Nashville,Tennessee), Vol. 64 (March 1974), pp. 102-14.

10

Government Spending, the Real Interest Rate, and Liquidity-Constrained Consumers' Behavior in Developing Countries

Nicola Rossi*

I. INTRODUCTION

The importance of the mobilization of domestic savings in developing countries can hardly be understated, given the present state of international capital markets. Unfortunately, however, the understanding of the actual determinants of domestic savings in developing countries is still scanty. A number of empirical investigations (mainly reproducing the literature relating to developed economies) have been carried out in recent years, but the paucity of reliable data has made it difficult to test the underlying hypotheses and obtain results that warrant a reasonable degree of confidence.

The purpose of the present paper is to provide additional — and, it is to be hoped, more conclusive — empirical evidence on this topic. In order to allow a comparison with the most recent work on the subject, I shall estimate Euler equations for the representative consumer's stochastic dynamic optimization problem. However, in contrast to much of the previous literature, the theoretical framework for the present paper is based on the consideration that some of the basic assumptions on which saving functions for developing countries have been estimated may not be en-

*This paper was first published in the March 1988 issue of International Monetary Fund *Staff Papers*. I wish to thank Mario I. Blejer, Thanos Catsambas, Riccardo Faini, Alain Ize, T. Jappelli, Jeroen Kremers, and Vito Tanzi for discussions and comments that contributed substantially to the development of this paper. I am also very grateful to Bruce Fuller for kindly providing some of the data.

tirely realistic. In particular, a significant fraction of the population in developing countries can be expected to be affected by liquidity constraints that substantially diminish consumers' ability to substitute consumption intertemporally, as is assumed by the well-known life-cycle theory. This is attributable to a number of factors, including capital market imperfections. While the gravity of capital market imperfections continues to be a matter of debate, even in countries with apparently sophisticated financial institutions and well-developed capital markets (see Hayashi (1985) for a review and also Hubbard and Judd (1986)), this phenomenon has never been explicitly accounted for in developing countries, although there are several reasons why such imperfections are likely to be exacerbated in those countries (Blejer and Cheasty (1989)). Allowance is therefore made for departing from optimal behavioral rules by the representative consuming unit described by the theory.

In the context of a theoretically plausible model of consumer behavior that allows for borrowing constraints, two major issues are addressed.

First, the long-debated issue of the real interest rate elasticity of savings is taken up again. As is well known, the effects of the rate of return on the level of savings and the rate of capital formation are of central importance to both economists and policymakers, since they bear on a number of the central questions of macroeconomics. The relevance of the interest rate elasticity of savings is further enhanced in development economics, where some of the competing views on the role of financial conditions in the economic growth process rely crucially on the degree of responsiveness of aggregate savings to changes in the rate of return.

Notwithstanding considerable research to determine the interest rate responsiveness of savings behavior in developed economies, the traditional view that changes in the rate of return are likely to have only a minor effect on the savings rate holds (Modigliani (1986), p. 304), though controversy still exists (Summers (1984)). In the case of developing countries, the lack of empirical work on the responsiveness of savings in the 1960s and early 1970s is emphasized in the surveys by Mikesell and Zinser (1973) and Snyder (1974), who describe the evidence as sketchy at best.[1]

---

[1]Leaving aside studies on the relationship between changes in interest rates in the organized money markets and the volume of saving done through financial intermediaries, both surveys report the works of Williamson (1968) and Gupta (1970). The first author examines the role of real interest rates in determining personal saving in selected Asian countries (Burma (now Myanmar), India, Japan, the Republic of Korea, the Philippines, and Taiwan Province of China) over the period 1950-64 and concludes that real rates of interest are, if anything, negatively correlated with national savings. Williamson's results, particularly as they apply to India, are disputed by Gupta, who questions his savings data as well as his choice of the real interest rate. After examining data for a longer period than Williamson used, Gupta finds, instead, that interest rates play a significant role in determining household saving behavior in India.

More recently, further attempts have been made (Fry (1978, 1980); Giovannini (1983, 1985); McDonald (1983); and Pereira Leite and Makonnen (1984)) to explore this relationship. However, they can be questioned on the basis of their limited geographical coverage; the unreliability of available data; and, in some cases, their underlying methodology. Consequently, their results cannot be used with confidence for policy analysis.

Fry (1978, 1980) estimates a (national) savings function for seven Asian countries[2] for 1962-72. He apparently finds strong support for the hypothesis of a negative real interest rate elasticity of domestic consumption. He estimates this elasticity to be about -0.2. Similar conclusions are reached by McDonald (1983) and Pereira Leite and Makonnen (1984). McDonald focuses on factors determining saving behavior in 12 Latin American countries[3] and provides evidence of a negative relationship between the real interest rate and private consumption in most of the countries examined of a magnitude roughly comparable with that found by Fry. Pereira Leite and Makonnen's study, on the other hand, concentrates on six African countries[4] and provides evidence of a limited, but positive relationship between private savings and the real interest rate.

The hypothesis of a positive and significant relationship between real interest rates and savings in developing countries is questioned by Giovannini (1983, 1985), who replicates Fry's results and shows that "the apparent empirical success of the high interest elasticity hypothesis depends in a crucial way on the presence in the sample of a few observations that have a disproportionately large influence on the estimated" response of savings to the real interest rate (1985, p. 199). In this work, Giovannini extends the analysis to 18 developing countries[5] and, bypassing many of the econometric problems with aggregate-savings equations, estimates the elasticity of intertemporal substitution in (private) consumption. Using annual data, Giovannini finds that in only 5 out of 18 countries is the

---

[2]Burma (now Myanmar), India, the Republic of Korea, Malaysia, the Philippines, Singapore, and Taiwan Province of China. The main data sources are various issues of International Bank for Reconstruction and Development, *World Tables*, and International Monetary Fund, *International Financial Statistics*.

[3]Argentina, Chile, Colombia, Costa Rica, Guatemala, Haiti, Honduras, Mexico, Panama, Paraguay, Peru, and Uruguay. The main data source is International Monetary Fund, *International Financial Statistics*, various issues.

[4]Benin, Burkina Faso, Côte d'Ivoire, Niger, Senegal, and Togo. The main data source is International Monetary Fund, *International Financial Statistics*, various issues.

[5]Argentina, Brazil, Colombia, Jamaica, and Mexico in Latin America; Burma (now Myanmar), India, Indonesia, the Republic of Korea, Malaysia, the Philippines, Singapore, Taiwan Province of China, and Thailand in Asia and the Pacific; Greece, Portugal, and Turkey in Southern Europe; and Kenya in Africa. The main data source is International Monetary Fund, *International Financial Statistics*, various issues.

intertemporal substitutability in consumption not likely to be very small,[6] therefore implying, other things being equal, that the interest rate elasticity of savings is positive.

Giovannini's work represents a considerable improvement in the knowledge of savings behavior in developing countries. However, it can hardly be considered conclusive. First, his main result relates to the difficulty of obtaining precise estimates of the relevant parameters. In 11 out of 18 cases, the coefficient of intertemporal substitution is positive, but with standard errors so large as to permit one to draw any sort of conclusion. Since Giovannini's sample period in most cases covers the 1960s, this result is not unexpected, given the very low variability of real rates in that period. Second, as far as geographical coverage is concerned, Giovannini's work does not provide evidence for those regions for which evidence is most lacking—that is, Africa and the Middle East.[7] Third, as Giovannini points out, some assumptions under which the elasticity of substitution is estimated in his 1985 work may not be realistic in developing countries. In particular, some fraction of aggregate consumption is likely to be accounted for by consumption of liquidity-constrained individuals, for which the first-order condition on which estimation is based does not hold.[8] While the existence of liquidity constraints implies a relatively small elasticity of savings[9] and can therefore explain Giovannini's results, it also implies misspecification of the estimated unrestricted first-order condition. Further investigation is called for.

Therefore, Section II provides a framework for the estimation of the degree of intertemporal substitution in consumption, in which liquidity constraints are explicitly allowed for. Section II addresses also the second major issue dealt with in this paper. It extends the representative consumer's utility function to include government spending and assesses the role of public expenditure in private consumption decisions. The importance of the response of private spending to changes in government spending stems from the observation that, if government spending is a

---

[6]Burma (now Myanmar), Greece, India, Jamaica, and Turkey.

[7]In terms of 1975 regional gross domestic product (GDP), Giovannini (1985) covers just 2 percent of sub-Saharan Africa, 43 percent of East and South Asia and the Pacific, 72 percent of Latin America, and 64 percent of Southern Europe. In contrast, Fry (1978, 1980) and McDonald (1983) cover only approximately 45 percent of both East and South Asia and the Pacific, and Latin America. Finally, Pereira Leite and Makonnen (1984) limit themselves to nearly 6 percent of sub-Saharan Africa.

[8]Giovannini (1985, p. 215) mentions that "some preliminary experiments where the presence of liquidity constraints was allowed in the model, were not very satisfactory, but yielded the same estimates of the intertemporal substitution elasticity."

[9]Indeed, over some range, liquidity-constrained individuals can be totally unresponsive to changes in real interest rates. See, however, Jackman and Sutton (1982).

substitute for private spending, then policies seeking to restrain government expenditure are likely to induce higher private consumption. However, most adjustment programs in developing countries attempt to ensure that government deficits do not absorb an unduly high share of private savings. Indeed, the creation of public surpluses (presumably through tight expenditure policies) is often seen as a way of generating loanable funds savings for use by private sector investors that avoids the problems involved in implementing more traditional policies aimed at mobilizing private savings. This approach, however, disregards the fact that direct crowding out can partly or fully counteract government efforts.[10] Indeed, for some Latin American countries, McDonald (1983) provides evidence of a sizable degree of substitution between private and public consumption. But his results rest on an inappropriate definition of disposable income and should therefore be investigated further.

As Section III makes clear, an effort is made to construct as accurate and extensive a data set as existing sources allow. In particular, the empirical analysis in Sections IV and V focuses on private savings behavior over the period 1973-83 in 49 developing countries, grouped in six sets of pooled time-series cross-section observations, each one referring to a single geographical region.

Finally, Section VI presents the main conclusions of the analysis and its policy implications.

II. THEORY

Research on consumption in the early 1980s (reviewed in Deaton (1986) and King (1985)) has been marked by the important works of Hall (1978), Grossman and Shiller (1981), and Hansen and Singleton (1982) which open the possibility of a direct estimation of the parameters of the intertemporal utility function characterizing the behavior of a representative individual without requiring explicit solutions of the consumer's dynamic-optimization problem. In addition, Hansen and Singleton (1982) have shown how one can test the overidentifying restrictions implied by the

---

[10]Notice that this discussion disregards the question of whether consumption is sensitive to choice of tax versus debt financing of current government expenditure and concentrates instead on the extent to which government spending directly substitutes for private consumer expenditure. Both are cases of direct crowding out, but their "dimensions" are different: the Ricardian-equivalence proposition is concerned with what is regarded as income and wealth by the private sector, as opposed to what is regarded as consumption by the private sector in the latter case.

hypothesis of continuous optimization of a stable, additively separable objective function.

Following this line of research, I posit that aggregate consumption can be modeled as the outcome of optimizing decisions of a representative consumption unit (household).[11] The household faces an economic environment in which future opportunities are uncertain, and it has a stationary utility function that is additively separable through time and is defined over a composite consumption good as follows:

$$V_t = E_t\left[\sum_{\tau=t}^{T} \rho^{\tau-t}(U_\tau^\gamma/\gamma)\right] \qquad (\gamma < 1) \tag{1}$$

with

$$U_\tau = (C_\tau^{1-\alpha}G_\tau^\alpha) \qquad (0 \le \alpha \le 1) \tag{2}$$

In equations (1) and (2), V_t denotes expected utility at t, E_t denotes the expectations operator conditional on information available at t, ρ denotes a constant-discount factor, C_τ denotes private consumption of goods at τ, and G_τ denotes government expenditure in period τ. The parameter γ in equation (1) controls intertemporal substitution: large and negative values of γ are characteristic of consumers who are willing to smooth consumption over time and who respond only to substantial changes in incentives. Finally, U denotes a function that is increasing and concave in a Cobb-Douglas aggregate of per capita private and public consumption.

The consumer (household) maximizes equation (1), subject to the following period-to-period budget constraint:

$$A_\tau = A_{\tau-1}R_\tau + Y_\tau - C_\tau \tag{3}$$

where A_τ denotes real assets at the end of period τ, R_τ denotes the real rate of return between periods $\tau - 1$ and τ, and Y_τ denotes real non-property income (net of taxes) in period τ. As long as the optimum path lies in the interior of the budget set, we can use simple perturbation arguments to establish certain characteristics of the optimal path. At any point along an optimal path the representative consumption unit cannot make itself better off by forgoing one unit of consumption at time t and using the proceeds to purchase any other good at any other point in time. Formally, at time t the marginal condition will be given by

---

[11]Incidentally, notice that casting the analysis in terms of a household makes the "immortality" assumption, which is required for an aggregate version of the Euler condition to hold, slightly more palatable. See, however, Deaton's (1986, p. 13) comments.

$$E_t[R_{t+1}(\partial V_t/\partial C_{t+1})/(\partial V_t/\partial C_t) - 1] = E_t[F_{t+1} - 1] = 0 \qquad (4)$$

which, apart from implicitly defining F_{t+1}, is satisfied for any freely traded risky asset (even if other assets, such as human capital, cannot be traded freely) and holds for consumers who expect with certainty to be alive in the next period, regardless of the length of horizon of their maximization problem. Notice also that condition (4) does not depend on any assumption about expectations regarding future labor income, government spending, or rates of return.

Estimation of the first-order condition for utility maximization (e.g., equation (4)) represents an alternative approach to estimating standard consumption functions. The difficulties associated with the latter are well known and mostly concern the Lucas critique: the relation between consumption, income, and interest rates depends on the wider macroeconomic context and may not be stable over time, even though preferences remain unchanged. However, the research done so far has provided only limited support for the econometric restrictions implied by the Euler equation approach. Furthermore, the assumptions usually underlying the application of the Euler equation approach are far from being generally accepted. (See Ando and Kennickell (1986), Blinder and Deaton (1985), Deaton (1986), and King (1986).)

Under rational expectations and market clearing, the first-order condition (4) holds ex post except for an error term uncorrelated with information available to the consumption unit at time t. In other words,

$$F_{t+1} = 1 + \epsilon_{t+1} \qquad (5)$$

where ϵ_{t+1} denotes the forecast error having a zero mean and a constant variance (σ^2).

In a setting characterized by intertemporal separability and constant relative risk aversion, given by equations (1) and (2), and with lowercase letters denoting natural logarithms and Δ the difference operator, equations (4) and (5) imply[12]

$$\Delta c_{t+1} = \psi_c + \psi_r E_t r_{t+1} + \psi_g E_t \Delta g_{t+1} + u_{t+1} \qquad (6)$$

where $\psi_c = \psi_c(\rho, \sigma^2, \gamma, \alpha)$; $\psi_r = \dfrac{1}{[\gamma(\alpha - 1) + 1]}$; and $\psi_g = \gamma\alpha\psi_r$.

---

[12]It is assumed that r_{t+1}, g_{t+1}, and c_{t+1} follow a joint lognormal distribution. See Hansen and Singleton (1982).

Since $\psi_r > 0$, ψ_g is greater than, equal to, or less than zero, depending on whether γ is positive, zero, or negative. In equation (6), the error term u_{t+1} reflects the impact of "news" (or "surprises") about current levels of income, interest rates, and government spending. It is therefore orthogonal to all past information.[13]

As it stands, though, equation (6) still disregards the possibility that some consumers may face constraints on the amount they borrow, or that loan rates available to them may be higher than the corresponding lending rates prevailing in the market. These situations may arise for a number of reasons, including imperfections in capital markets and tax policy. For example, the tax system can generate divergencies between after-tax rates on borrowing and lending. Alternatively, large transaction costs, the possibility of bankruptcy, and/or asymmetric information about creditworthiness in the hands of lenders and borrowers can result in lenders denying loans to potential borrowers with particular characteristics.

Suppose, then, that the liquidity constraint takes the form of a restriction on the total net stock of traded assets, as follows:

$$-A_t \leq \phi_t + \phi y_t \qquad (\forall t) \tag{7}$$

where a negative value of A_t indicates net indebtedness in period t. The additional condition $A_T \leq 0$ provides the necessary endpoint constraint. Equation (7) is expressed in terms of the net position in order to allow the use of illiquid assets as collateral. According to the equation, potential lenders make the size of the loan conditional upon non-property income. Notice that the lending rule is time dependent, since the intercept ϕ_t is allowed to respond to changes in government legislation and macroeconomic conditions in general.

Expressing liquidity constraints in the form of equation (7), that is, exogenous stock constraints, is important because such borrowing restrictions can be exploited by stabilization policy (Hubbard and Judd (1986)). Of course, other alternatives are conceivable. For example, Hayashi (1985) discusses the case of imperfect information in the loan market and shows that it is not necessarily exploitable for stabilization purposes. (See also King (1986).)

Under the additional constraints given by equation (7), it can be shown (as in Muellbauer (1983, 1986 a) and Zeldes (1985)) that equation (6) has to

---

[13]Notice that formulation (6) does not allow transitory elements of consumption owing to imperfect execution of plans, which would introduce a first-order moving-average component into the error term. This assumption is not as strong as it seems at the aggregate level, since transitory elements should be uncorrelated between individuals and should therefore average out.

be augmented by adding a term $[\psi_r \mu_t]$ where μ_t is an increasing function of the shadow price associated at t with credit rationing or, in other words, is the marginal increase in expected lifetime utility derived from a unit relaxation of the credit constraint in period t. Since agents are constrained from borrowing more, but not from saving more, μ_t is zero when the constraint is not binding and positive when it is binding.

In principle, μ_t could be derived by solving the whole intertemporal programming problem. However, a sufficiently general solution is hardly likely to be operational. As an alternative, Muellbauer (1986 a, p. 10) therefore suggests that, "if consumers are most likely to want to borrow and hence, other things being equal, to encounter credit restrictions when future income prospects look bright compared with current circumstances," then, in the aggregate, μ_t is likely to depend positively on terms like $E_t(z_{t+1} - c_t)$ where $Z_t = A_{t-1}(R_t - 1) + Y_t$—that is, real disposable income.[14] In other words, consumers whose liquidity is constrained at t may not expect it to be constrained at $t + 1$ and may therefore be forced to let their consumption path follow their income path more closely. Equation (6) would therefore be rewritten as

$$\Delta c_{t+1} = \psi_0 + \psi_r E_t r_{t+1} + \psi_g E_t \Delta g_{t+1} + \psi_\mu E_t(z_{t+1} - c_t)$$

$$+ u_{t+1} \tag{8}$$

which can be interpreted as an approximation to the Euler equation for consumption that incorporates credit constraints. Abstracting from real interest rate and government spending effects, as ψ_μ tends to one in equation (8), consumption developments increasingly mimic income developments. Notice that, for $\psi_g = \psi_\mu = 0$, equation (8) reduces instead to Hall's (1981) original formulation, which was estimated by Giovannini (1985).[15]

III. The Data Set

A thorough empirical analysis of private saving behavior in developing countries raises several difficult statistical problems, which stem mostly

---

[14]Non-property income would certainly be a more appropriate variable, since credit-rationed consumers are likely to show only a minimal level of assets. Disposable income is, however, preferred in the light of the information available. See, however, Appendix I.

[15]Interestingly, equation (8) bears a close resemblance to the empirically successful consumption function attributable to Davidson and others (1978).

from the inadequacies in the data and their lack of comparability. A reasonable number of observations on aggregate time-series data is available, on a consistent basis, for only a few developing countries. In the great majority of cases, less than 20 annual observations are available.[16] In such a situation, pooling cross-section and time-series data for a number of countries seems to be the most sensible procedure, provided that sufficient allowance is made for obvious institutional and cultural differences among countries.

Following this line of research, the empirical analysis of the present paper is based on six sets of pooled time-series, cross-section data, with each one referring to what, it is to be hoped, is a homogeneous geographical region.[17] The first set includes 12 countries in sub-Saharan Africa. To give a different order of magnitude, this sample covers 40 percent of the 1975 gross domestic product (GDP) of the whole region, as defined in the World Bank's *World Tables*. The second set includes five countries in North Africa and the Middle East that accounted for 61 percent of the whole region's 1975 GDP. The third set covers nine countries in East and South Asia and the Pacific, or 46 percent of that region's 1975 GDP. The fourth and fifth sets cover eight countries in Central America (including the Caribbean) and nine in South America, respectively, with coverage in terms of 1975 regional GDP of 76.2 percent and 83.1 percent, respectively.[18] Finally, the sixth set of data includes six Southern European countries, accounting for 77 percent of the 1975 regional GDP. The sample as a whole contains 11 low-income, and 38 middle-income, countries. Low-income countries are, therefore, somewhat underrepresented.[19] Appendix I provides a detailed description of the data set.

It is important to recall that appropriate measurement is particularly difficult for real interest rates, where the problem of choosing a particular

---

[16]For example, McDonald's (1983) and Giovannini's (1985) regressions rarely present more than 15 degrees of freedom.

[17]Stratifying country observations on a geographical basis is just one of the many possibilities, although it seems to be the most obvious one if preference parameters are, to some extent, influenced by institutional and cultural differences. Alternative criteria include, among others, size, economic performance, and per capita income. The last one is indirectly taken into account in what follows.

[18]In addition to the countries listed in Table 8 of Appendix I, the South American sample originally also included Argentina. As it turned out, however, the Argentine subsample, ranging from 1973 to 1980, was dominated by two large outliers in 1974 and 1976. Given the small size of the subsample, it was therefore decided to omit the country altogether.

[19]Reference is made here to the developing countries eligible to use the International Development Association's (IDA's) resources. On the basis of that classification, low-income countries are approximately two fifths of the 142 developing countries.

interest rate series from series that may be available is coupled with the question of appropriately deflating nominal interest rates (Khatkhate (1985)). In this respect, the approach described in the previous section turns out to be particularly useful, because the relationship represented by equation (6) should hold for all real rates of return on freely traded assets.

In order to provide an indication of the robustness of the results, two alternative measures of the nominal rate are used. On the one hand, domestic interest rates on time deposits of commercial banks, which constitute a relatively large segment of the financial system in developing countries, are considered.[20] On the other, implicitly making reference to the small, open economy model, the nominal interest rate is derived as the relevant foreign interest rate adjusted for expected changes in the exchange rate. The latter alternative implies that the relevant real interest rate depends on the rate of change of the real price of home goods (Dornbusch (1983)). Of course, it may be argued that the small, open economy stereotype is inappropriate for most developing countries that are characterized by pervasive foreign exchange and trade controls. However, it has been suggested (by Tanzi and Blejer (1982)) that, even in countries with severe restrictions on capital movements and other exchange controls, it is unlikely that economic agents will be prevented from illicitly substituting foreign currency and foreign financial assets for domestic currency and domestic financial assets if incentives to do that are sufficiently strong.[21]

IV. Estimation

For estimation purposes, let us rewrite the theoretical model described in Section II as follows:

$$\Delta c^i_{t+1} = \psi^i_c + \psi_r E_t r^i_{t+1} + \psi_g E_t \Delta g^i_{t+1} + \psi_{\mu,\ell} E_t(z^j_{t+1} - c^j_t)$$

$$+ \psi_{\mu,m} E_t(z^k_{t+1} - c^k_t) + \zeta_z[z^i_{t+1} - E_t(z^i_{t+1})]$$

$$+ \zeta_g[g^i_{t+1} - E_t(g^i_{t+1})] + \zeta_r[r^i_{t+1} - E_t(r_{t+1})] + \bar{v}_{t+1} + v^i_{t+1}$$

$$(\forall j\epsilon\ell, \forall k\epsilon m) \qquad\qquad\qquad\qquad (9)$$

---

[20]Nevertheless, in a few cases, it proved necessary to use discount rates. See Appendix I for details.

[21]It should be recognized that in most developing countries, the capital market is small and usually confined to one central city, and wealth is held in the form of consumer durables, such as jewelry and livestock. In such cases, rates of return on financial instruments are likely to be largely irrelevant.

where the suffix i identifies the ith country in each of the geographical areas referred to in the previous section. In other words, the constant term in equation (9), being a function of the variance of the forecast error, is allowed to differ among countries because, for example, countries with a higher share of their gross domestic product originating in agriculture are likely to face higher uncertainty. In addition, the coefficient of the proxy for borrowing constraints, ψ_μ, is allowed to take different values in low-income countries (i.e., those countries identified by the superscript j and belonging to the subset identified by the suffix "ℓ") and in middle-income countries (i.e., identified by the superscript k and belonging to the subset "m"). Low-income countries are taken to be the countries currently eligible for use of International Development Association (IDA) resources. Of course, according to the interpretation of ψ_μ used in this paper, one would expect $\psi_{\mu,\ell} > \psi_{\mu,m}$.[22] Finally, the original error term in equation (6)—that is, u_{t+1}—is now linearly decomposed into three innovation terms referring to z, g, and r, respectively, as well as two random components that have zero means but are not necessarily homoskedastic, because the variance of different countries' forecast errors may differ and this difference could be only partially incorporated into the innovation terms. The first component is country specific and is uncorrelated across countries (v_{t+1}^i), while the second one is an area-wide component, which equally affects all countries in a particular geographical area ($\bar{v}_{t+1}$).[23] The obvious example of the latter type of component would be one indicating the effect of the recent drought in sub-Saharan Africa, provided the drought's effects were not already incorporated in the income "news."

Notice that the variable r_t^i is alternatively defined as $[q_t^i - \Delta p_t^i]$ where q_t denotes the domestic nominal interest rate and p^i denotes the (logarithm of the) consumer price level, or as $[q_t^* + \Delta e_t^i - \Delta p_t^i]$ where, apart from p_t^i, q_t^* denotes the representative nominal interest rate paid on foreign-currency assets, and e_t denotes the (logarithm of the) exchange rate, defined as units of domestic currency per unit of foreign currency.

Disregarding, for the time being, the expected (or unexpected) nature of the variables on the right-hand side of equation (9), the appropriate estimator for the kind of setting described by equation (9) is given by what is known, if we can regard each country as a group, as the *between-within*

---

[22]It may be argued that since the intensity of borrowing constraints varies across countries, so can the parameters of the underlying representation of preferences vary. On the basis of the available evidence (Zeldes (1985)), this does not appear to be the case.

[23]Countries are not randomly selected, and therefore the area-wide shock cannot be analyzed in an "error-component" kind of model. Besides, the available evidence suggests that the fixed-effects estimator is robust with respect to various forms of dynamic misspecification. See Baltagi and Griffin (1984).

groups, fixed-effects estimator. As Mundlak (1978) shows, this estimator amounts to applying ordinary least squares to equation (9) expressed in terms of "transformed" variables — that is,

$$\Delta \bar{c}_{t+1}^i = \psi_r E_t \bar{r}_{t+1}^i + \psi_g E_t \Delta \bar{g}_{t+1}^i + \psi_{\mu,\ell} E_t (\bar{z}_{t+1}^j - \bar{c}_t^j)$$

$$+ \psi_{\mu,m} E_t (\bar{z}_{t+1}^k - \bar{c}_t^k) + \zeta_z [\bar{z}_{t+1}^i - E(\bar{z}_{t+1}^i)]$$

$$+ \zeta_g [\bar{g}_{t+1}^i - E_t (\bar{g}_{t+1}^i)] + \zeta_r [\bar{r}_{t+1}^i - E_t (\bar{r}_{t+1}^i)] + \bar{v}_{t+1}^i$$

$$(\forall j \epsilon \ell, \, \forall k \epsilon m) \tag{10}$$

where the transformation takes the following form:

$$\bar{x}_t^i = x_t^i - (1/T) \sum_j x_j^i - (1/N) \sum_k x_t^k + (1/NT) \sum_j \sum_k x_j^k$$

$$(j = 1 \dots T; \, k = 1 \dots N) \tag{11}$$

for a generic variable x_t, and where T and N denote the number of time periods and the number of countries, respectively. In other words, the transformed variable is the original variable *minus* the country and time means *plus* the total mean. Notice that the transformation eliminates the constant term and the area-wide error term. In general, the transformation would eliminate all variables not simultaneously indexed on i and t. Therefore, if the nominal interest rate is given by the adjusted foreign interest rate, the term $E_t \bar{r}_{t+1}^i$ reduces to $E_t [\Delta(e_{t+1}^i - p_{t+1}^i)]$.

Reverting to the modeling of expected and unexpected (or "surprise") variables, in equation (10) use is made of the well-known two-step procedure involving the estimation of an auxiliary set of equations describing the variables about which expectations are formed and then substituting the estimated residuals and predicted values as appropriate in the relevant structural equation.[24] A vector autoregression (VAR) is estimated for the transformed variables $\bar{z}$, $\bar{g}$, and $\bar{r}$; the right-hand-side variables of the VAR include lagged consumption, lagged disposable income, lagged government spending, lagged nominal interest rate (or lagged devaluation), two lags of the price level, and a time trend.[25] In general, the VAR equations for $\bar{z}$ and $\bar{g}$ fit the transformed data quite well, while, as one would

---

[24]Besides being simpler computationally, the two-step procedure (like other limited-information methods) reduces the contamination of the estimated coefficients in the structural equation by specifying errors in the auxiliary equations.

[25]In order to identify the system given by equation (10) and the vector autoregression, the strong assumption of zero covariance between v_{t+1} and the "surprises" in

expect (Hall (1981)), the real interest rate $\bar{r}$ appears to be more difficult to predict. (See Appendix II.) Disposable income and government spending are strongly autoregressive; in addition, they help to predict each other, while increased inflation signals a future slowdown in the rate of growth.

Once anticipated and unanticipated series are available, equation (10) can be estimated by ordinary least squares. However, as shown by Pagan (1984), the two-step procedure does not yield correct estimates of all the standard errors. In particular, while the standard errors of the coefficients of the "surprise" variables are correct, standard errors for the remaining coefficients have to be obtained using a two-stage least-squares regression that omits the surprise terms and uses the VAR as the first stage.

V. Empirical Results

Tables 1-6 report the estimates of the coefficients of equation (10) for the six geographical regions described in Section III. Before examining the tables in detail, it is worth emphasizing their main implications. First, the omission of liquidity constraints appears to consistently and seriously bias downward the estimates of the intertemporal elasticity of substitution. Second, where liquidity constraints are substantial (as in regions where the use of IDA resources is common), intertemporal substitution is weak and very large changes in incentives are necessary to induce postponement of consumption. Third, as expected, low-income countries suffer most from liquidity constraints and therefore react strongly to expected income changes, although there is no clear-cut pattern in the way different countries react to unexpected income shocks. In short, the picture that emerges from the evidence is a highly coherent one in which differences in behavioral responses appear to be linked more to the stage of development of different areas or countries than to unexplained shifts in preferences.

In Tables 1-6, the columns labeled (ii) and (iv) report the coefficient estimates for the two measures of the real interest rate and the six subsamples, respectively, their heteroskedasticity-consistent (White (1980)) standard errors (derived as above), as well as some diagnostic statistics, such

---

disposable income, government spending, and the real interest rate is necessary. Furthermore, it should be noticed that the system given by equation (10) and the vector autoregression is observationally equivalent to the system given by equation (10) without "surprises," but with simultaneity affecting z, g, and r. Therefore, the interpretation used in the present paper relies on the author's choice.

Table 1. Sub-Saharan Africa: Parameter Estimates and Test Statistics[1]

	$r^i = q^i - \Delta p^i$		$r^i = q^* - \Delta(e^i/p^i)$	
	(i)	(ii)	(iii)	(iv)
ψ_r	0.06 (0.38)	0.33 (0.43)	−0.04 (0.16)	—[2]
ψ_g	—	−0.32 (0.21)	—	−0.25 (0.21)
$\psi_{\mu,m}$	—	0.22 (0.08)	—	0.23 (0.08)
$\psi_{\mu,\ell}$	—	0.72 (0.19)	—	0.70 (0.19)
ζ_z	—	0.41 (0.07)	—	0.42 (0.07)
ζ_g	—	0.06 (0.08)	—	0.02 (0.08)
ζ_r	—	0.04 (0.10)	—	−0.01 (0.07)
γ	−16.27 (112.89)	−3.25 (5.73)	—	—
$\gamma(1-\alpha)$	—	−2.24 (4.48)	—	—
α	—	0.31 (0.22)	—	0.20 (0.13)
$\alpha/(1-\alpha)$	—	0.45 (0.46)	—	0.25 (0.21)
$\hat{\sigma}$	0.07	0.05	0.07	0.05
R^2	0.51	0.72	0.51	0.72
D-W	1.74	1.81	1.75	1.82
Chow	0.59[3]	0.76[4]	0.60[3]	0.71[5]
n. ob.	104	104	104	104

Note: D-W denotes the Durbin-Watson statistic; Chow denotes the Chow test; and n. ob. denotes the number of observations.

[1]The regressions also include a dummy variable for Swaziland taking a value of 1 in 1973, and of −1 in 1974. This accounts for two large outliers but does not affect the remaining coefficients. Its coefficient takes a value of −0.51 (0.03) in the equations of columns (i) and (iii), and −0.47 (0.02) in the equations of columns (ii) and (iv).

[2](Incorrectly signed and insignificant) coefficient set to zero.

[3]Distributed as $F(20,82)$.

[4]Distributed as $F(20,76)$.

[5]Distributed as $F(20,77)$.

as the Durbin-Watson statistic for fixed-effects models given in Bhargava and others (1982), and a Chow stability test across the 1981-83 period.[26] This period coincides with the downward trend of oil prices (in U.S. dollars) and, therefore, also with substantial (and, in recent times, unprecedented) shifts of real income from oil exporting to oil importing countries. In addition, the same period witnesses the emergence of the debt crisis. Stability tests are expected to detect possible structural breaks related to these events. To allow for comparison with previous work, columns (i) and (iii) in Tables 1-6 report the results derived by following Giovannini (1985) and estimating Hall's (1981) original formulation (corresponding to equation (10) with $\psi_g = \psi_{\mu,\ell} = \psi_{\mu,m} = \zeta_z = \zeta_g = \zeta_r = 0$).

Tables 1-6 also report the estimates of the implied behavioral parameters, as well as some interesting functions of the same parameters, along

[26]Estimation and hypothesis testing were carried out by means of the PC version of the Time Series Processor (TSP) (Version 4.01).

Table 2. Middle East and North Africa: Parameter Estimates
and Test Statistics

| | $r^i = q^i - \Delta p^i$ | | $r^i = q^* - \Delta(e^{i}/p^i)$ | |
	(i)	(ii)	(iii)	(iv)
ψ_r	0.99 (0.77)	0.98 (0.68)	0.23 (0.44)	1.17 (0.51)
ψ_g	—	—[1]	—	—[1]
$\psi_{\mu,m}$	—	0.22 (0.09)	—	0.41 (0.14)
$\psi_{\mu,\ell}$	—	—	—	—
ζ_z	—	0.38 (0.14)	—	0.39 (0.11)
ζ_g	—	0.09 (0.14)	—	0.08 (0.14)
ζ_r	—	0.02 (0.42)	—	−0.12 (0.19)
γ	−0.01 (0.79)	−0.02 (0.71)	−3.38 (8.41)	0.15 (0.37)
$\gamma(1 - \alpha)$	—	—	—	—
α	—	—	—	—
$\alpha/(1 - \alpha)$	—	—	—	—
$\hat{\sigma}$	0.07	0.06	0.07	0.05
R^2	0.06	0.39	0.01	0.47
D-W	1.77	1.86	1.78	1.68
Chow	0.43[2]	0.54[3]	0.30[2]	0.33[3]
n. ob.	44	44	44	44

Note: D-W denotes the Durbin-Watson statistic; Chow denotes the Chow test; and n. ob.
denotes the number of observations.

[1](Incorrectly signed and insignificant) coefficient set to zero.
[2]Distributed as $F(10,33)$.
[3]Distributed as $F(10,29)$.

with their standard errors derived by linearizing the underlying nonlinear functions.[27] In particular, the tables show estimates of the parameters γ and α. In the restricted model, the former parameter controls the intertemporal elasticity of substitution in consumption, which is given, instead, by $\gamma(1 - \alpha)$ in the full model (equation (10)). The latter parameter defines the weight of government spending in the Cobb-Douglas consumption index (equation (2)) and, if nondistortionary taxes are available and perfect transformation in production is assumed, it also defines the optimal provision of public goods as a percentage of private ones (i.e., $\alpha/(1 - \alpha)$).

In general, the full model constitutes a substantial improvement over its restricted version. The available diagnostic does not suggest misspecification, and, in particular, the hypothesis of parameter constancy across the 1981-83 period cannot be rejected except in South America.

Contrary to Giovannini's (1985) findings, there is quite clear-cut evidence of a positive relationship between the rate of growth of per capita

[27]These standard errors should be interpreted with some care, considering the poor approximation usually provided by the linearization. See Krinsky and Robb (1986).

Table 3. East and South Asia and Pacific: Parameter Estimates and Test Statistics

| | $r^i = q^i - \Delta p^i$ | | $r^i = q^* - \Delta(e^i/p^i)$ | |
	(i)	(ii)	(iii)	(iv)
ψ_r	0.07 (0.17)	0.18 (0.18)	−0.04 (0.10)	0.09 (0.11)
ψ_g	—	−0.03 (0.10)	—	—[1]
$\psi_{\mu,m}$	—	0.17 (0.14)	—	0.23 (0.16)
$\psi_{\mu,\ell}$	—	0.79 (0.39)	—	0.65 (0.33)
ζ_z	—	0.58 (0.04)	—	0.63 (0.05)
ζ_g	—	−0.05 (0.04)	—	−0.04 (0.05)
ζ_r	—	0.12 (0.08)	—	−0.01 (0.02)
γ	−12.79 (31.78)	−4.74 (5.82)	—	−10.23 (13.74)
$\gamma(1 - \alpha)$	—	−5.40 (5.73)	—	—
α	—	0.03 (0.12)	—	—
$\alpha/(1 - \alpha)$	—	0.04 (0.13)	—	—
$\hat{\sigma}$	0.03	0.02	0.03	0.02
R^2	0.01	0.65	0.01	0.63
D-W	2.11	2.33	2.14	2.16
Chow	0.60[2]	0.73[3]	0.62[2]	0.67[4]
n. ob.	84	84	84	84

Note: D-W denotes the Durbin-Watson statistic; Chow denotes the Chow test; and n. ob. denotes the number of observations.

[1](Incorrectly signed and insignificant) coefficient set to zero.

[2]Distributed as $F(21,62)$.

[3]Distributed as $F(21,56)$.

[4]Distributed as $F(21,57)$.

consumption and the expected real interest rate. Furthermore, in three regions out of six (Middle East and North Africa, Southern Europe, and Central America), the coefficient ψ_r also turns out to be positive and significantly different from zero, although this result depends on the definition of the real interest rate. It may be argued that assets denominated in foreign currency are unlikely to be a significant item in private portfolios in sub-Saharan Africa, while indications are that the reverse is true in the Middle East and North Africa and in Southern Europe.[28] In general, however, the restricted model estimated by Giovannini (1985) tends to bias downward the estimate of ψ_r.

Notwithstanding these results, ψ_r still remains quite small and the intertemporal elasticity of substitution therefore tends to take on negative values that are larger, in absolute terms, than those observed in devel-

---

[28]The apparent negative and strong relationship between consumption growth and the expected real interest rate (defined in terms of the world interest rate) in South America should not be taken too seriously in the light of the quite poor performance of the underlying VAR equations in that case.

Table 4. Southern Europe: Parameter Estimates and Test Statistics[1]

	$r^i = q^i - \Delta p^i$		$r^i = q^* - \Delta(e^{i}/p^i)$	
	(i)	(ii)	(iii)	(iv)
ψ_r	0.08 (0.08)	—[2]	0.05 (0.06)	0.17 (0.05)
ψ_g	—	—[2]	—	—[2]
$\psi_{\mu,m}$	—	0.39 (0.09)	—	0.49 (0.14)
$\psi_{\mu,\ell}$	—	—	—	—
ς_z	—	0.61 (0.11)	—	0.58 (0.10)
ς_g	—	−0.18 (0.10)	—	−0.17 (0.11)
ς_r	—	−0.04 (0.05)	—	−0.09 (0.05)
γ	−11.66 (13.24)	—	−18.44 (21.74)	−4.98 (2.15)
$\gamma(1 - \alpha)$	—	—	—	—
α	—	—	—	—
$\alpha/(1 - \alpha)$	—	—	—	—
$\hat{\sigma}$	0.04	0.03	0.04	0.03
R^2	0.30	0.71	0.30	0.77
D-W	1.60	1.58	1.61	1.84
Chow	0.46[3]	0.54[4]	0.35[3]	0.53[5]
n. ob.	56	56	56	56

Note: D-W denotes the Durbin-Watson statistic; Chow denotes the Chow test; and n. ob. denotes the number of observations.

[1]The regressions also include two dummy variables taking a value of 1 in 1974 for both Cyprus and Portugal. They do not affect the remaining coefficients and their coefficients take the following values: −0.19 (0.01), −0.10 (0.02), −0.20 (0.01), −0.08 (0.02) for the first dummy variable in the equations of columns (i) through (iv), respectively; 0.09 (0.01), 0.07 (0.01), 0.09 (0.01), 0.05 (0.01) for the second dummy variable in the equations of columns (i) through (iv), respectively.

[2](Incorrectly signed and insignificant) coefficient set to zero.

[3]Distributed as $F(14,39)$.

[4]Distributed as $F(14,36)$.

[5]Distributed as $F(14,35)$.

oped economies.[29] In addition, with the exceptions of the Middle East and North Africa, and Central America and the Caribbean, the estimates of γ do not tend to differ widely across regions, and they indicate a reduced response by the consumers to changes in incentives. It is important to stress that, if the sample excluded 1982 and 1983, South America, too, would show a positive ψ_r coefficient that was significantly different from zero.[30] As is apparent from the results of the Chow test, however, the relationship weakens considerably in the early 1980s. Therefore, although the extent of the misspecification of the restricted model is apparent and

[29]Using U.S. data, Hansen and Singleton (1982) find values of the intertemporal elasticity of substitution of between plus and minus unity. Summers (1984) presents various estimates of γ ranging from −18.0 to 0.4, while Bean (1986) estimates it to be about −1.5.

[30]Equal to 0.09 (0.04) and implying that γ is equal to −10.4 (6.1).

Table 5. Central America and Caribbean: Parameter Estimates and Test Statistics

	$r^i = q^i - \Delta p^i$		$r^i = q^* - \Delta(e^i/p^i)$	
	(i)	(ii)	(iii)	(iv)
ψ_r	0.37 (0.16)	0.35 (0.17)	−0.05 (0.19)	—[1]
ψ_g	—	—[1]	—	—[1]
$\psi_{\mu,m}$	—	0.22 (0.21)	—	0.34 (0.19)
$\psi_{\mu,\ell}$	—	—	—	—
ζ_z	—	0.45 (0.10)	—	0.49 (0.10)
ζ_g	—	0.02 (0.06)	—	0.03 (0.06)
ζ_r	—	0.19 (0.07)	—	−0.13 (0.03)
γ	−1.86 (1.32)	−1.86 (1.39)	—	—
$\gamma(1-\alpha)$	—	—	—	—
α	—	—	—	—
$\alpha/(1-\alpha)$	—	—	—	—
$\hat{\sigma}$	0.05	0.04	0.05	0.04
R^2	0.08	0.44	0.01	0.39
D-W	1.28	1.46	1.13	1.49
Chow	1.29[2]	1.19[3]	1.54[2]	1.12[4]
n. ob.	74	74	74	74

Note: D-W denotes the Durbin-Watson statistic; Chow denotes the Chow test; and n. ob. denotes the number of observations.

[1](Incorrectly signed and insignificant) coefficient set to zero.

[2]Distributed as $F(18,55)$.

[3]Distributed as $F(18,50)$.

[4]Distributed as $F(18,51)$.

substantial, the main thrust of Giovannini's work remains largely unaffected.

Government spending never appears to play a substantial role in the regressions. No definite pattern of substitution emerges from the estimates. On the contrary, private consumption is mostly insensitive to the expected path of government spending, with the exception of sub-Saharan Africa where, for what it is worth, the implied estimate of the optimal provision of public goods (as a percentage of private consumption) exceeds the average government spending/private consumption ratio over the 1973-83 period (i.e., 0.27).

Most of the improvement with respect to the restricted formulation shown in columns (i) and (iii) is therefore clearly attributable to the liquidity-constraint proxies and to the impact of "news" on disposable income. The "surprise" variables explain a substantial amount (from 10 percent to nearly 35 percent)[31] of the variance of the error in the regressions

---

[31]Between 10 percent and 15 percent in sub-Saharan Africa, and North Africa and the Middle East; nearly 20 percent in Latin America; and about 30 percent in both Southern Europe and East and South Asia and the Pacific.

Table 6. South America: Parameter Estimates and Test Statistics

	$r^i = q^i - \Delta p^i$		$r^i = q^* - \Delta(e^i/p^i)$	
	(i)	(ii)	(iii)	(iv)
ψ_r	0.09 (0.07)	0.01 (0.05)	-0.31 (0.15)	—[1]
ψ_g	—	—[2]	—	—
$\psi_{\mu,m}$	—	0.65 (0.12)	—	0.71 (0.10)
$\psi_{\mu,\ell}$	—	—	—	—
ζ_z	—	0.48 (0.09)	—	0.48 (0.09)
ζ_g	—	0.02 (0.05)	—	-0.04 (0.05)
ζ_r	—	0.01 (0.04)	—	-0.05 (0.04)
γ	-9.83 (8.11)	-154.52 (1,153.8)	—	—
$\gamma(1-\alpha)$	—	—	—	—
α	—	—	—	—
$\alpha/(1-\alpha)$	—	—	—	—
$\hat{\sigma}$	0.05	0.04	0.05	0.03
R^2	0.06	0.57	0.06	0.60
D-W	1.66	1.51	1.47	1.64
Chow	1.20[3]	2.24[4]	1.18[3]	2.57[5]
n. ob.	88	88	88	88

Note: D-W denotes the Durbin-Watson statistic; Chow denotes the Chow test; and n. ob. denotes the number of observations.

[1](Incorrectly signed and insignificant) coefficient set to zero.

[2]Incorrectly signed coefficient (-0.40 with standard error equal to 0.10) set to zero.

[3]Distributed as $F(25,62)$.

[4]Distributed as $F(25,58)$.

[5]Distributed as $F(25,59)$.

reported in columns (ii) and (iv) in Tables 1-6, as the rational-expectations approach to the consumption function suggests. Statistically, the innovation in income is the most important such variable.

However, it cannot be safely said that only unexpected changes in income cause consumption to change, as modern versions of the permanent-income hypothesis suggest. The coefficients of the liquidity constraint proxies ($\psi_{\mu,\ell}$ and $\psi_{\mu,m}$) are always positive, of substantial magnitude, and significantly different from zero.[32] In addition, $\psi_{\mu,\ell}$ turns out to be always greater and significantly different from $\psi_{\mu,m}$, and both coefficients are roughly of the same order of magnitude across regions.[33] Interestingly, as one would expect, the relationship between the rate of growth of consumption and the expected real interest rate shows up more clearly and strongly where the proxy for liquidity constraints plays a minor role.

---

[32]Comparable estimates of ψ_μ for developed economies are available for only the U.S. economy: Muellbauer (1986 b) estimates it to be about 0.1.

[33]The exception is South America, where the coefficient of the liquidity-constraint proxy for the low-income country (Bolivia) turns out to be negative and to possess a large standard error. In addition, $\psi_{\mu,m}$ tends to take on higher values than it does in other regions.

Table 7. Six Regions: Real Interest Rate Elasticities of Consumption[1]

| | $r^i = q^i - \Delta p^i$ | | $r^i = q^* - \Delta(e^i/p^i)$ | |
	(i)	(ii)	(iii)	(iv)
Sub-Saharan Africa	-0.06	-0.25	—	—
Middle East and North Africa	-1.05	-1.04	-0.24	-1.25
East and South Asia and the Pacific	-0.08	-0.18	—	-0.09
Southern Europe	—	—	-0.05	-0.18
Central America and the Caribbean	-0.37	-0.37	—	—
South America	-0.10	-0.01	—	—

[1]Elasticities are computed assuming that $\rho = 1 + r = 1.03$ and assuming, for simplicity, that $\alpha = 0$. Changes in these assumptions imply only marginal changes in the elasticities.

In order to clarify further these issues, Table 7 focuses on the effects of changes in interest rates on consumption. To characterize fully the consumer's response to random shocks, a closed-form solution to the stochastic control problem described in Section II would be needed. Since such solutions remain intractable, this paper follows Mankiw and others (1985) and concentrates on the effects of interest rate changes in a deterministic environment. The elasticities reported in Table 7 illustrate the changes in consumption at t in response to temporary changes in the real interest rate, from t to $t + 1$. These are short-run elasticities, in the sense that the effect of such changes after $t + 1$ is ignored.[34]

Figures in Table 7 describe the percentage change in consumption following a 1 percent change in the variable $(1 + r)$. Hence, if the real rate of interest jumps from, say, 3 to 4 percent in sub-Saharan Africa, the corresponding reduction in consumption as implied by model (10) is about 1/4 of 1 percent.

Table 7 conveys the same message as Tables 1-6, although in a different form. In particular, the relationship between the degree of responsiveness of consumption to changes in the real interest rate and the magnitude of liquidity constraints (as described by the coefficients $\psi_{\mu,\ell}$ and $\psi_{\mu,m}$) is, if anything, emphasized.

Assuming that $\psi_\mu = 0$ yields the Euler equation satisfied under market clearing, or, in other words, assuming that $\{\psi_\mu[E_t(z_{t+1}) - c_t]\}$ can provide an estimate of the Lagrange multiplier associated with transferring resources between tomorrow and today,[35] the pervasiveness of liquidity con-

---

[34]Changes in the subsequent period are, however, mediated through changes in future wealth. Hence, for consumers with long horizons, this is likely to be a valid approximation.

[35]Of course, one expects $\{\psi_\mu[E_t(z_{t+1}) - c_t]\} \geq 0$, at least on the average across time periods and countries. In a world with borrowing constraints, as opposed to one without, consumption can be expected to grow faster, but never slower.

straint can be seen easily by computing the (lower) rate of growth of consumption that would have taken place in the absence of such constraints.[36] It turns out that sub-Saharan Africa, North Africa and the Middle East, and South America, which witnessed average growth rates of per capita consumption of about 0.6 percent, 4.8 percent, and 1.7 percent, respectively, in 1973-83, would actually have experienced much lower rates of growth (about -0.4 percent, 3.2 percent, and 0.9 percent, respectively). In contrast, East and South Asia and the Pacific, and Southern Europe, whose per capita consumption levels grew by 3.2 percent and 2.4 percent, respectively, over the same period, would have had annual growth rates approximately 0.3 percent lower. The only region that actually experienced, on average, negative values of the $[E_t(z_{t+1}) - c_t]$ variable over that period — Central America and the Caribbean — is the only region to show an estimate of ψ_μ that is not significantly different from zero.

VI. POLICY IMPLICATIONS

Analyses based on intercountry data are subject to several well-known caveats, and the results obtained should be viewed with caution. This is even truer when, as in the present case, data problems are known to be substantial. Nonetheless, the results of the present study appear to be robust in most respects. They provide a coherent picture of private saving behavior in developing countries, offer reasons for the existing behavioral differences among geographical regions, and suggest a number of important policy implications.

With respect to the issue of the real interest rate elasticity of savings, the available evidence indicates that in all regions considered, the expected growth of consumption does change with changes in the real interest rate. In addition, in regions such as the Middle East and North Africa, Southern Europe, and Central America and the Caribbean, the response of consumption growth to the expected real interest rate is also significantly different from zero. However, if the magnitude of the estimated parameters is to be taken seriously, the effective mobilization of domestic savings through changes in saving incentives is likely to require changes in the real interest rates, which, given the existing constraints, may prove infeasible, especially in low-income developing countries. In such a case, a

---

[36]All the computations that follow are based on the estimates reported in column (ii) of Tables 1-6. Calculations made on the basis of the estimates of column (iv) do not change the picture.

viable alternative is the one considered by Blejer and Cheasty (1989)—that is, the generation of budgetary surpluses. As long as these are derived by expenditure restraints, they are not likely to crowd in additional private expenditure and thereby be counteracted by private agents' behavior.

More far reaching, however, are the implications of the existence of pervasive liquidity constraints for fiscal policy design and implementation. The small size of current resources, compared with lifetime resources, and consumers' limited ability to borrow against future income clearly affect the way they look at issues such as the efficacy of temporary tax cuts and the effects of government budget deficits on aggregate demand. In Tobin's (1980, p. 57) words, liquidity-constrained consumers are not "indifferent to the opportunity to defer tax payments. Even if they themselves must pay the taxes later, they will increase their consumption now. In effect, the government lends to them at its borrowing rate of interest, an option not otherwise available in the credit market." Fiscal policy ineffectiveness arguments are therefore affected if a substantial number of consumers are liquidity constrained,[37] although, in assessing the effects of debt-financed tax cuts, the distribution of tax changes across consumers has to be considered. Of course, the reduced responsiveness of saving to changes in the real interest rate further emphasizes the role of traditional stabilization policies.

The same arguments that, under borrowing constraints, can lead to countercyclical policies *on efficiency grounds* also impinge on a number of issues in tax policy evaluation and tax reform. If liquidity constraints are present, traditional arguments in favor of wage and consumption taxation or proportional taxation and against capital taxation and progressive income taxation lose some of their appeal. For example, Hubbard and Judd (1986, p. 27) show that "a switch from progressive to proportional income taxation would speed up tax collection, raising tax rates on low-income consumers and reducing their consumption substantially when liquidity constraints are important." In other words, tax exemptions, as well as other forms of social insurance, would not only obey considerations of equity but would also be grounded in efficiency considerations.

Similarly, the usual conclusion suggesting that substantial efficiency costs are likely to characterize capital income taxation, as opposed to labor income taxation, is likely to be reversed to some extent when liquidity constraints are introduced. Again, this is because capital income taxation

---

[37]Actually, the simulation study by Hubbard and Judd (1986, pp. 33-43) clearly points out that, in the discussion on the Ricardian-equivalence proposition, borrowing constraints are likely to be substantially more important than the absence of intergenerational wealth redistribution (i.e., finite horizons).

effectively delays the collection of tax payments over an individual's life cycle.

It should be stressed that tax policies designed to lessen the burden of borrowing constraints may induce substantial welfare gains if the public does not substitute easily between present and future consumption. If, as appears to be the case in developing countries, people prefer even consumption paths and show low elasticities of intertemporal substitution, the welfare cost of borrowing constraints is likely to be exacerbated. In this respect, the results of this paper underline the role of financial reforms in developing countries.

In recent years, a substantial amount of work has been carried out in developed economies on the effects of liquidity constraints on consumers' behavior. Given the importance of considering capital market imperfections as pre-existing distortions in normative and positive economic analyses, it is surprising that liquidity constraints have received so little attention in the analysis of saving behavior in developing countries, where they seem to be a simple matter of common-sense observation.

APPENDICES

I. THE DATA

The data set for the present study has been constructed by assembling information from all available international sources: United Nations, *National Accounts Statistics;* International Monetary Fund, *International Financial Statistics* Yearbook and *Government Finance Statistics Yearbook;* and International Bank for Reconstruction and Development, *World Tables*; as well as national sources as needed.

As is well known, because of the unreliability and internal inconsistency of data and the varying methodology in different countries, data in the present sample may be subject to a wide margin of error. In addition, in assembling different sources of information, attention should be paid to conceptual differences and their implications. These remarks apply, in particular, to the construction of the variable Z_t (i.e., the per capita private disposable income, in constant prices), to the estimation of the real interest rate, and to the definition of G_t.

Per capita private final consumption expenditure, in constant prices (index: 1980 = 1), is denoted by C_t. Sources: United Nations, *National Accounts Statistics: Main Aggregates and Detailed Tables, 1983* (New York, 1986), Tables 1.1 and 1.2, for consumption data; various issues of International Bank for Reconstruction and Development, Economic Analysis and

Projections Department, *Social Indicators of Development*, for population data.

Per capita government final consumption expenditure, in constant prices (index: 1980 = 1), is denoted by G_t. Sources: same as for C_t above. According to the definitions in the United Nations' *National Accounts Statistics*, this item comprises compensation of employees and other purchases of goods and services. This study therefore disregards capital expenditure and, what is more important, neglects the long-debated question of the correct definition of current, as opposed to capital, expenditure.

Per capita private disposable income, in constant prices (index: 1980 = 1), is denoted by Z_t. Defined as gross national product (GNP), *minus* consumption of fixed capital (CFC, when available), *plus* net transfers from abroad (NTA, when available), *minus* tax revenue (TR), *plus* subsidies and current transfers (SCT, when available), deflated by private final consumption implicit price index. Table 8 reports the availability of these data for the 49 countries in the sample. Sources: United Nations, *National Accounts Statistics: Main Aggregates and Detailed Tables, 1983* (New York, 1986), Table 1.12 for gross national products, consumption of fixed capital, and net current transfers from abroad; United Nations, *National Accounts Statistics: Main Aggregates and Detailed Tables, 1983* (New York, 1986), Table 1.4 and/or International Monetary Fund, *Government Finance Statistics Yearbook* (Washington, 1985), Summary Table and Table C for tax revenue and subsidies and current transfers; and International Bank for Reconstruction and Development, Economic Analysis and Projections Department, *Social Indicators of Development*, for population data. Notice that, while national disposable income (i.e., gross national product *minus* consumption of fixed capital *plus* net current transfers from the rest of the world) is often reported in the United Nations' *National Accounts Statistics*, the same is seldom true for the general government current receipts and disbursements, and, in particular, for the current tax revenue and for subsidies and current transfers. Therefore, in such cases, use was made of International Monetary Fund, *Government Finance Statistics Yearbook*, thereby combining transactions recorded on a payments basis and flows measured and classified by their characteristics at the time of transaction (as in the *Government Finance Statistics Yearbook*), with transactions recorded on an accrual basis and flows measured and classified by future use or purpose (as in the United Nations' *National Accounts Statistics*).

The real interest rate is denoted by r_t. It is defined as $(1 + r^i) = (1 + q^i)/(1 + \Delta p^i)$ or, alternatively, as $(1 + r^i) = (1 + q^*)[(1 + \Delta e^i)/(1 + \Delta p^i)]$. Table 8 reports the definitions of the domestic nominal interest rate and of the inflation rate adopted for each country. Sources (apart from national sources): United Nations, *National Accounts Statistics: Main Aggregates*

Table 8. Six Regions: Availability and Sources of Input Data

Country	Private Disposable Income					Real Rate of Interest	
	GNP	CFC	NTA	TR	SCT	NR	IR

Sub-Saharan Africa

Country	GNP	CFC	NTA	TR	SCT	NR	IR
Botswana	nas	nas	nas	nas	nas	br, ifs	pcd, nas
Burundi	nas	n.a.	n.a.	gfs	n.a.	dr, ifs	pcd, nas
Cameroon	nas	nas	nas	nas	nas	br, ifs	pcd, nas
Ethiopia	wt	n.a.	n.a.	gfs	gfs	tr, ifs	pcd, nas
Ghana	nas	nas	nas	gfs	gfs	br, ifs	pcd, nas
Kenya	nas	n.a.	nas	gfs	gfs	dr, ifs	pcd, nas
Liberia	nas	n.a.	n.a.	gfs	gfs	dr, ifs	pcd, nas
Malawi	nas	n.a.	n.a.	nas	gfs	br, ifs	pci, ifs
South Africa	nas	nas	nas	nas	nas	tr, ifs	pcd, nas
Swaziland	nas	n.a.	nas	gfs	gfs	dr, ifs	pcd, nas
Zambia	nas	nas	nas	gfs	gfs	dr, ifs	pci, ifs
Zimbabwe	nas	n.a.	nas	nas	nas	dr, ifs	pcd, nas

North Africa and Middle East

Country	GNP	CFC	NTA	TR	SCT	NR	IR
Iran	nas	nas	nas	nas	nas	br, ifs	pcd, nas
Jordan	nas	nas	nas	gfs	gfs	br, ifs	pci, ifs
Morocco	nas	n.a.	nas	gfs	gfs	br, ifs	pci, ifs
Syria	nas	n.a.	n.a.	gfs	n.a.	br, ifs	pcd, nas
Tunisia	nas	nas	nas	nas	nas	br, ifs	pcd, nas

East and South Asia and Pacific

Country	GNP	CFC	NTA	TR	SCT	NR	IR
Fiji	nas	n.a.	nas	gfs	gfs	br, ifs	pcd, nas
India	nas	nas	nas	nas	nas	dr, dk	pcd, nas
Indonesia	nas	nas	n.a.	gfs	gfs	dr, ifs	pcd, nas
Korea, Republic of	nas	nas	nas	nas	nas	dr, ifs	pcd, nas
Malaysia	nas	n.a.	n.a.	gfs	gfs	dr, ifs	pcd, nas
Pakistan	nas	nas	n.a.	gfs	gfs	dr, dk	pcd, nas
Philippines	nas	nas	nas	nas	nas	dr, dk	pcd, nas
Sri Lanka	nas	nas	nas	nas	nas	dr, ifs	pcd, nas
Thailand	nas	nas	nas	nas	nas	dr, ifs	pcd, nas

Southern Europe

Country	GNP	CFC	NTA	TR	SCT	NR	IR
Cyprus	nas	nas	nas	gfs	gfs	dr, ifs	pcd, nas
Greece	nas	nas	nas	nas	nas	dr, ifs	pcd, nas
Israel	nas	nas	nas	nas	nas	dr, ns	pcd, nas
Malta	nas	nas	nas	nas	nas	dr, ifs	pcd, nas
Portugal	nas	nas	nas	nas	nas	dr, ifs	pcd, nas
Turkey	nas	nas	nas	gfs	gfs	dr, ifs	pcd, nas

Table 8 *(concluded).* Six Regions: Availability and
Sources of Input Data

Country	Private Disposable Income					Real Rate of Interest	
	GNP	CFC	NTA	TR	SCT	NR	IR
Central America and Caribbean							
Costa Rica	nas	nas	nas	nas	nas	dr, ifs	pcd, nas
Dominican Republic	nas	nas	nas	gfs	gfs	dr, dk	pcd, nas
El Salvador	nas	nas	nas	gfs	gfs	dr, dk	pcd, nas
Guatemala	nas	n.a.	nas	gfs	gfs	dr, dk	pcd, nas
Honduras	nas	nas	nas	nas	nas	dr, ifs	pcd, nas
Jamaica	nas	nas	nas	nas	nas	dr, ifs	pci, ifs
Mexico	nas	nas	nas	gfs	gfs	dr, ifs	pcd, nas
Panama	nas	nas	nas	nas	nas	dr, ifs	pcd, nas
South America							
Bolivia	nas	n.a.	nas	gfs	gfs	dr, dk	pcd, nas
Brazil	nas	nas	n.a.	nas	nas	tr, ifs	pcd, nas
Chile	nas	nas	nas	gfs	gfs	dr, ifs	pcd, nas
Colombia	nas	n.a.	nas	nas	nas	dr, ifs	pcd, nas
Ecuador	nas	nas	nas	nas	nas	dr, ifs	pcd, nas
Paraguay	nas	nas	n.a.	nas	nas	dr, dk	pcd, nas
Peru	nas	nas	nas	nas	nas	dr, dk	pcd, nas
Uruguay	nas	nas	nas	gfs	gfs	dr, dk	pcd, nas
Venezuela	nas	nas	nas	gfs	gfs	dr, dk	pci, ifs

Notes:

CFC: Consumption of fixed capital.

GNP: Gross national product.

IR: Interest rate deflator.

NR: Nominal rate of interest.

NTA: Net transfers from abroad.

SCT: Subsidies and current transfers.

TR: Tax revenue.

br: Bank rate and discount rate.

dk: Khatkhate (1985).

dr: Deposit rate.

gfs: International Monetary Fund, *Government Finance Statistics Yearbook* (Washington, 1985).

ifs: International Monetary Fund, *International Financial Statistics* (Washington, 1985), various issues.

n.a.: Not available.

nas: United Nations, *National Accounts Statistics: Main Aggregates and Detailed Tables, 1983* (New York, 1986).

ns: National sources.

pcd: Implicit price index of final private consumption.

pci: Consumer price index.

tr: Treasury bill rate.

wt: International Bank for Reconstruction and Development, *World Tables: The Third Edition*, Volume I: Economic Data (Baltimore: Johns Hopkins University Press, 1981).

and Detailed Tables, 1983 (New York, 1986), Tables 1.1 and 1.2 (for the private final consumption deflator); and International Monetary Fund, *International Financial Statistics* Yearbook (Washington, 1985) for interest rates, exchange rates, and the consumer price index.

For each country in the six subsamples, Table 9 reports the time period considered, the average and the standard deviations of the ratio to GNP of gross private savings as derived by subtracting private final consumption from the measure of disposable income mentioned above, as well as the average and the standard deviations of the ratio to GNP of gross private savings as derived by adding the current account surplus to gross capital formation and subtracting government gross savings. The comparison of the two average ratios is a useful check on the quality of the approximation embodied in our definition of private disposable income. As is apparent from the table, in most cases the two averages are quite close to each other. However, substantial discrepancies arise in a few cases, such as South Africa, Iran, Jamaica, Greece, and Israel. Tracing the reasons for these discrepancies is, of course, far from easy. However, the discrepancies are likely to be due partly to the fact that our approximation to the concept of disposable income disregards interest payments on the public debt and, therefore, in some cases, substantially underestimates income.[38] Unfortunately, there are very few countries for which statistics are available that allow one to isolate the volume of interest payments on domestic public debt paid to the private sector. In addition, in cases such as South Africa, the difference partially derives also from a sizable statistical discrepancy that allows the reconciliation of the national accounting aggregates.

As Table 9 shows, the sample is characterized by a substantial variability across time and across countries, with the latter variability seen both between and within regional subsets.

II. VAR ESTIMATION

This appendix reports in detail the VAR equations estimated for the six geographical regions and the two alternative definitions of the real rate of return. In all tables (Tables 10-21), the symbols are the same ones used in the text of this paper.

---

[38]This implies, however, that the variable Z_t is nearer to the concept of net nonproperty income required by the theory of Section II.

Table 9. Six Regions: Coverage and Main Characteristics of Data

| | | Private Savings/GNP Ratios | |
	Period	Estimated mean (S.E.)	Residual mean (S.E.)
		Sub-Saharan Africa	
Botswana	1973–81	0.111 (0.086)	0.068 (0.071)
Burundi*	1973–81	0.038 (0.037)	. . . . . .
Cameroon	1973–81	0.069 (0.043)	0.112 (0.041)
Ethiopia*	1973–81	0.094 (0.036)	0.100 (0.029)
Ghana*	1973–81	0.081 (0.020)	0.129 (0.032)
Kenya*	1973–82	0.206 (0.034)	0.163 (0.033)
Liberia*	1973–82	0.316 (0.045)	0.291 (0.071)
Malawi*	1973–83	0.171 (0.071)	0.122 (0.075)
South Africa	1973–83	0.114 (0.032)	0.262 (0.036)
Swaziland	1973–82	0.227 (0.140)	0.127 (0.127)
Zambia*	1973–82	0.116 (0.076)	0.203 (0.072)
Zimbabwe	1973–82	0.235 (0.023)	0.213 (0.020)
		North Africa and Middle East	
Iran	1973–79	0.462 (0.072)	0.233 (0.078)
Jordan	1973–83	0.496 (0.093)	0.466 (0.096)
Morocco	1973–83	0.207 (0.030)	0.147 (0.031)
Syria	1973–81	0.220 (0.035)	0.229 (0.081)
Tunisia	1973–83	0.082 (0.037)	0.137 (0.022)
		East and South Asia and Pacific	
Fiji	1973–82	0.185 (0.048)	0.161 (0.053)
India*	1973–83	0.134 (0.016)	0.201 (0.016)
Indonesia	1973–83	0.091 (0.024)	0.106 (0.026)
Korea, Republic of	1973–83	0.133 (0.027)	0.190 (0.024)
Malaysia	1973–81	0.288 (0.023)	0.238 (0.024)
Pakistan*	1973–82	0.085 (0.013)	0.110 (0.014)
Philippines	1973–82	0.122 (0.012)	0.207 (0.015)
Sri Lanka*	1973–82	0.112 (0.029)	0.127 (0.031)
Thailand	1973–83	0.140 (0.023)	0.194 (0.016)
		Southern Europe	
Cyprus	1973–83	0.180 (0.024)	0.250 (0.023)
Greece	1973–83	0.095 (0.036)	0.249 (0.030)
Israel	1973–83	0.065 (0.049)	0.361 (0.051)
Malta	1973–83	0.250 (0.051)	0.171 (0.041)
Portugal	1973–81	0.189 (0.051)	0.234 (0.063)
Turkey	1973–81	0.119 (0.023)	0.136 (0.036)

Table 9 *(concluded)*. Six Regions: Coverage and
Main Characteristics of Data

| | | Private Savings/GNP Ratios | |
	Period	Estimated mean (S.E.)	Residual mean (S.E.)
		Central America and Caribbean	
Costa Rica	1973–83	0.055 (0.028)	0.119 (0.031)
Dominican Republic	1973–81	0.076 (0.036)	0.141 (0.020)
El Salvador	1973–82	0.140 (0.024)	0.164 (0.026)
Guatemala	1973–83	0.139 (0.027)	0.123 (0.028)
Honduras	1973–83	0.059 (0.048)	0.096 (0.033)
Jamaica	1973–82	0.015 (0.046)	0.146 (0.036)
Mexico	1973–83	0.188 (0.024)	0.218 (0.041)
Panama	1973–80	0.201 (0.017)	0.219 (0.041)
		South America	
Bolivia*	1973–83	0.172 (0.070)	0.115 (0.071)
Brazil	1973–82	0.144 (0.035)	0.184 (0.021)
Chile	1973–83	0.035 (0.049)	0.079 (0.035)
Colombia	1973–83	0.178 (0.016)	0.157 (0.011)
Ecuador	1973–83	0.110 (0.038)	0.154 (0.030)
Paraguay	1973–83	0.108 (0.032)	0.185 (0.016)
Peru	1973–83	0.068 (0.023)	0.042 (0.064)
Uruguay	1973–83	0.104 (0.035)	0.118 (0.027)
Venezuela	1973–82	0.215 (0.051)	0.204 (0.041)

Notes: An asterisk (*) indicates that a country is designated as eligible to borrow from the International Development Association. S.E. denotes standard error.

Table 10. Sub-Saharan Africa: VAR Estimation

| | Dependent Variable | | |
	Δz_t	Δg_t	r_t
z_{t-1}	− 0.52 (0.15)	0.11 (0.09)	0.07 (0.07)
g_{t-1}	− 0.12 (0.09)	− 0.34 (0.07)	− 0.06 (0.06)
g_{t-1}	0.19 (0.10)	0.00 (0.00)	− 0.03 (0.03)
q_{t-1}	− 0.30 (0.55)	0.07 (0.66)	0.87 (0.38)
Δp_{t-1}	− 0.17 (0.14)	− 0.18 (0.15)	0.11 (0.15)
p_{t-1}	0.06 (0.05)	0.02 (0.05)	− 0.09 (0.07)
d	− 0.06 (0.06)	− 0.04 (0.03)	0.01 (0.02)
t	− 0.02 (0.02)	0.004 (0.02)	− 0.02 (0.01)
D-W	1.76	1.91	1.86
R	0.22	0.23	0.08
$\hat{\sigma}$	0.09	0.08	0.07
n. ob.	104	104	104
$\sigma(x)$	0.096	0.084	0.066
$\sigma(\hat{x})$	0.045	0.040	0.019
$\sigma(x - \hat{x})$	0.085	0.073	0.063

Notes: D-W denotes the Durbin-Watson statistic, n. ob. the number of observations. The variable d takes values of 1 in 1974 and of − 1 in 1975 for Swaziland. Figures in parentheses are White's (1980) standard errors.

Table 11. Sub-Saharan Africa: VAR Estimation

	Dependent Variables		
	Δz_t	Δg_t	$\Delta(e - p)_t$
z_{t-1}	−0.52 (0.15)	0.11 (0.09)	0.06 (0.12)
g_{t-1}	−0.11 (0.09)	−0.34 (0.06)	−0.07 (0.09)
c_{t-1}	0.20 (0.10)	−0.09 (0.07)	0.02 (0.09)
Δe_{t-1}	0.09 (0.10)	0.04 (0.08)	0.39 (0.19)
Δp_{t-1}	−0.14 (0.14)	−0.18 (0.15)	0.61 (0.28)
p_{t-1}	0.03 (0.05)	0.03 (0.05)	−0.16 (0.11)
d	−0.06 (0.06)	−0.05 (0.03)	−0.06 (0.06)
t	−0.02 (0.02)	−0.003 (0.02)	−0.04 (0.02)
D-W	1.73	1.91	1.89
R	0.23	0.23	0.18
$\hat{\sigma}$	0.09	0.08	0.10
n. ob.	104	104	104
$\sigma(x)$	0.096	0.084	0.106
$\sigma(\hat{x})$	0.046	0.040	0.045
$\sigma(x - \hat{x})$	0.084	0.073	0.096

Notes: D-W denotes the Durbin-Watson statistic, n. ob. the number of observations. The variable d takes values of 1 in 1974 and of −1 in 1975 for Swaziland. Figures in parentheses are White's (1980) standard errors.

Table 12. Middle East and North Africa: VAR Estimation

	Dependent Variable		
	Δz_t	Δg_t	r_t
z_{t-1}	0.02 (0.12)	0.20 (0.12)	0.04 (0.03)
g_{t-1}	−0.27 (0.17)	−0.61 (0.13)	−0.09 (0.03)
c_{t-1}	−0.58 (0.30)	−0.59 (0.33)	−0.18 (0.07)
q_{t-1}	3.40 (3.73)	1.08 (3.22)	3.45 (0.64)
Δp_{t-1}	−0.20 (0.41)	−0.42 (0.49)	−0.31 (0.10)
p_{t-1}	0.06 (0.21)	−0.54 (0.26)	0.23 (0.05)
t	0.02 (0.04)	−0.08 (0.04)	−0.01 (0.01)
D-W	2.08	1.65	2.35
R	0.26	0.42	0.44
$\hat{\sigma}$	0.09	0.09	0.02
n. ob.	44	44	44
$\sigma(x)$	0.092	0.106	0.028
$\sigma(\hat{x})$	0.047	0.068	0.018
$\sigma(x - \hat{x})$	0.080	0.081	0.021

Notes: D-W denotes the Durbin-Watson statistic, n. ob. the number of observations. Figures in parentheses are White's (1980) standard errors.

Table 13. Middle East and North Africa: VAR Estimation

	Dependent Variable		
	Δz_t	Δg_t	$\Delta(e_t - p_t)$
z_{t-1}	−0.01 (0.10)	0.15 (0.12)	−0.14 (0.06)
g_{t-1}	−0.26 (0.17)	−0.59 (0.13)	−0.08 (0.07)
c_{t-1}	−0.52 (0.27)	−0.53 (0.34)	0.04 (0.13)
Δe_{t-1}	0.07 (0.39)	−0.37 (0.43)	−0.31 (0.17)
Δp_{t-1}	−0.14 (0.45)	−0.22 (0.62)	0.004 (0.21)
p_{t-1}	−0.15 (0.19)	−0.58 (0.21)	0.01 (0.11)
t	0.03 (0.04)	0.09 (0.04)	0.03 (0.02)
D-W	1.97	1.62	2.17
R	0.24	0.42	0.37
$\hat{\sigma}$	0.09	0.09	0.04
n. ob.	44	44	44
$\sigma(x)$	0.092	0.106	0.047
$\sigma(\hat{x})$	0.045	0.069	0.028
$\sigma(x - \hat{x})$	0.080	0.080	0.037

Notes: D-W denotes the Durbin-Watson statistic, n. ob. the number of observations. Figures in parentheses are White's (1980) standard errors.

Table 14. East and South Asia and Pacific: VAR Estimation

	Dependent Variable		
	Δz_t	Δg_t	r_t
z_{t-1}	−0.56 (0.14)	0.28 (0.18)	−0.15 (0.11)
g_{t-1}	0.04 (0.06)	−0.45 (0.08)	−0.05 (0.05)
c_{t-1}	0.35 (0.15)	0.12 (0.18)	0.04 (0.11)
q_{t-1}	0.02 (0.27)	−0.69 (0.35)	0.67 (0.19)
Δp_{t-1}	0.13 (0.09)	−0.02 (0.14)	−0.08 (0.10)
p_{t-1}	−0.004 (0.04)	−0.17 (0.05)	0.14 (0.04)
t	0.01 (0.02)	0.03 (0.02)	−0.001 (0.01)
D-W	1.78	1.62	1.95
R	0.19	0.33	0.31
$\hat{\sigma}$	0.04	0.05	0.03
n. ob.	84	84	84
$\sigma(x)$	0.045	0.059	0.037
$\sigma(\hat{x})$	0.020	0.034	0.021
$\sigma(x - \hat{x})$	0.040	0.048	0.031

Notes: D-W denotes the Durbin-Watson statistic, n. ob. the number of observations. Figures in parentheses are White's (1980) standard errors.

Table 15. East and South Asia and Pacific: VAR Estimation

	Dependent Variable		
	Δz_t	Δg_t	$\Delta(e_t - p_t)$
z_{t-1}	-0.55 (0.14)	0.27 (0.17)	-0.25 (0.29)
g_{t-1}	0.02 (0.06)	-0.38 (0.06)	0.02 (0.15)
c_{t-1}	0.36 (0.14)	0.12 (0.17)	0.04 (0.23)
Δe_{t-1}	0.10 (0.06)	0.05 (0.04)	-0.19 (0.09)
Δp_{t-1}	0.13 (0.08)	-0.09 (0.16)	-0.11 (0.17)
p_{t-1}	-0.01 (0.04)	-0.14 (0.05)	0.25 (0.07)
t	0.01 (0.02)	0.02 (0.01)	0.001 (0.003)
D-W	1.82	1.74	1.92
R	0.22	0.30	0.13
$\hat{\sigma}$	0.04	0.05	0.08
n. ob.	84	84	84
$\sigma(x)$	0.045	0.059	0.085
$\sigma(\hat{x})$	0.021	0.032	0.030
$\sigma(x - \hat{x})$	0.040	0.049	0.079

Notes: D-W denotes the Durbin-Watson statistic, n. ob. the number of observations. Figures in parentheses are White's (1980) standard errors.

Table 16. Southern Europe: VAR Estimation

	Dependent Variable		
	Δz_t	Δg_t	r_t
z_{t-1}	-0.24 (0.13)	0.31 (0.12)	0.09 (0.16)
g_{t-1}	-0.24 (0.12)	-0.38 (0.11)	0.32 (0.20)
c_{t-1}	-0.16 (0.16)	-0.44 (0.16)	-0.10 (0.23)
q_{t-1}	0.50 (0.29)	-0.001 (0.25)	0.27 (0.68)
Δp_{t-1}	-0.15 (0.14)	0.07 (0.11)	-0.57 (0.25)
p_{t-1}	-0.05 (0.04)	-0.05 (0.03)	0.10 (0.07)
d_1	-0.10 (0.03)	0.07 (0.03)	-0.09 (0.03)
d_2	0.04 (0.02)	0.02 (0.02)	-0.03 (0.03)
t	0.02 (0.02)	0.02 (0.02)	0.02 (0.03)
D-W	1.72	2.06	1.49
R	0.45	0.29	0.32
$\hat{\sigma}$	0.05	0.05	0.08
n. ob.	56	56	56
$\sigma(x)$	0.063	0.053	0.093
$\sigma(\hat{x})$	0.043	0.029	0.052
$\sigma(x - \hat{x})$	0.047	0.045	0.077

Notes: D-W denotes the Durbin-Watson statistic, n. ob. the number of observations. The variables d_1 and d_2 take values of 1 in 1974 for both Cyprus and Portugal. Figures in parentheses are White's (1980) standard errors.

Table 17. Southern Europe: VAR Estimation

	Dependent Variable		
	Δz_t	Δg_t	$\Delta(e_t - p_t)$
z_{t-1}	-0.20 (0.12)	0.27 (0.10)	-0.65 (0.25)
g_{t-1}	-0.24 (0.12)	-0.30 (0.09)	-0.29 (0.19)
c_{t-1}	-0.23 (0.16)	-0.32 (0.16)	0.25 (0.28)
Δe_{t-1}	-0.03 (0.07)	0.20 (0.05)	-0.54 (0.16)
Δp_{t-1}	-0.19 (0.15)	-0.09 (0.11)	0.30 (0.24)
p_{t-1}	-0.01 (0.03)	-0.05 (0.02)	0.04 (0.05)
d_1	-0.09 (0.03)	0.06 (0.03)	0.03 (0.04)
d_2	0.02 (0.02)	0.03 (0.02)	0.01 (0.03)
t	0.02 (0.02)	0.01 (0.02)	0.06 (0.03)
D-W	1.80	2.19	2.05
R	0.43	0.44	0.46
$\hat{\sigma}$	0.05	0.04	0.09
n. ob.	56	56	56
$\sigma(x)$	0.063	0.053	0.114
$\sigma(\hat{x})$	0.042	0.035	0.077
$\sigma(x - \hat{x})$	0.048	0.039	0.083

Notes: D-W denotes the Durbin-Watson statistic, n. ob. the number of observations. The variables d_1 and d_2 take values of 1 in 1974 for both Cyprus and Portugal. Figures in parentheses are White's (1980) standard errors.

Table 18. Central America and Caribbean: VAR Estimation

	Dependent Variable		
	Δz_t	Δg_t	r_t
z_{t-1}	-0.85 (0.14)	0.08 (0.22)	-0.49 (0.23)
g_{t-1}	0.17 (0.07)	-0.38 (0.19)	0.14 (0.08)
c_{t-1}	0.84 (0.14)	0.48 (0.18)	0.55 (0.20)
q_{t-1}	-0.18 (0.21)	-0.30 (0.20)	-0.12 (0.28)
Δp_{t-1}	-0.22 (0.10)	-0.14 (0.12)	-0.48 (0.14)
p_{t-1}	0.16 (0.05)	0.05 (0.07)	0.17 (0.06)
t	-0.03 (0.01)	0.001 (0.02)	-0.01 (0.01)
D-W	1.33	1.15	1.70
R	0.40	0.22	0.25
$\hat{\sigma}$	0.05	0.08	0.06
n. ob.	74	74	74
$\sigma(x)$	0.064	0.082	0.072
$\sigma(\hat{x})$	0.041	0.038	0.036
$\sigma(x - \hat{x})$	0.050	0.072	0.062

Notes: D-W denotes the Durbin-Watson statistic, n. ob. the number of observations. Figures in parentheses are White's (1980) standard errors.

Table 19. Central America and Caribbean: VAR Estimation

	Dependent Variable		
	Δz_t	Δg_t	$\Delta(e_t - p_t)$
z_{t-1}	− 0.81 (0.13)	0.10 (0.21)	0.48 (0.32)
g_{t-1}	0.17 (0.07)	− 0.38 (0.19)	0.07 (0.10)
c_{t-1}	0.78 (0.15)	0.44 (0.18)	− 0.40 (0.29)
Δe_{t-1}	− 0.12 (0.05)	− 0.06 (0.05)	0.9 (0.14)
Δp_{t-1}	− 0.03 (0.12)	− 0.03 (0.17)	− 0.11 (0.22)
p_{t-1}	0.13 (0.05)	0.002 (0.07)	0.07 (0.11)
t	− 0.03 (0.01)	0.001 (0.02)	0.01 (0.02)
D-W	0.124	1.14	1.99
R	0.43	0.21	0.08
$\hat{\sigma}$	0.05	0.08	0.10
n. ob.	74	74	74
$\sigma(x)$	0.064	0.082	0.104
$\sigma(\hat{x})$	0.042	0.038	0.030
$\sigma(x - \hat{x})$	0.049	0.072	0.099

Notes: D-W denotes the Durbin-Watson statistic, n. ob. the number of observations. Figures in parentheses are White's (1980) standard errors.

Table 20. South America: VAR Estimation

	Dependent Variable		
	Δz_t	Δg_t	r_t
z_{t-1}	− 0.90 (0.20)	− 0.13 (0.24)	2.13 (0.77)
g_{t-1}	0.23 (0.07)	− 0.37 (0.13)	0.05 (0.21)
c_{t-1}	0.65 (0.20)	0.28 (0.24)	− 1.53 (0.71)
q_{t-1}	0.01 (0.03)	− 0.02 (0.03)	0.53 (0.12)
Δp_{t-1}	− 0.10 (0.05)	0.02 (0.05)	− 0.20 (0.21)
p_{t-1}	0.03 (0.01)	0.01 (0.02)	0.05 (0.04)
t	− 0.04 (0.03)	− 0.02 (0.04)	− 0.05 (0.07)
D-W	1.84	1.42	1.66
R	0.42	0.20	0.45
$\hat{\sigma}$	0.06	0.08	0.16
n. ob.	88	88	88
$\sigma(x)$	0.070	0.085	0.204
$\sigma(\hat{x})$	0.045	0.038	0.137
$\sigma(x - \hat{x})$	0.053	0.076	0.151

Notes: D-W denotes the Durbin-Watson statistic, n. ob. the number of observations. Figures in parentheses are White's (1980) standard errors.

Table 21. South America: VAR Estimation

	Dependent Variable		
	Δz_t	Δg_t	$\Delta(e_t - p_t)$
z_{t-1}	− 0.87 (0.20)	0.05 (0.21)	0.42 (0.33)
g_{t-1}	0.21 (0.08)	− 0.41 (0.12)	0.06 (0.14)
c_{t-1}	0.63 (0.20)	0.25 (0.22)	− 0.36 (0.33)
Δe_{t-1}	− 0.14 (0.08)	− 0.23 (0.09)	0.22 (0.14)
Δp_{t-1}	0.05 (0.08)	0.22 (0.10)	− 0.32 (0.14)
p_{t-1}	0.02 (0.02)	− 0.01 (0.02)	− 0.02 (0.02)
t	− 0.04 (0.03)	− 0.01 (0.04)	0.03 (0.04)
D-W	1.82	1.54	1.90
R	0.45	0.25	0.18
$\hat{\sigma}$	0.05	0.08	0.10
n. ob.	88	88	88
$\sigma(x)$	0.070	0.085	0.103
$\sigma(\hat{x})$	0.047	0.042	0.043
$\sigma(x - \hat{x})$	0.052	0.074	0.093

Notes: D-W denotes the Durbin-Watson statistic, n. ob. the number of observations. Figures in parentheses are White's (1980) standard errors.

REFERENCES

Ando, A., and A. Kennickell, "How Much (or Little) Life Cycle Is There in Micro Data? The Cases of U.S. and Japan," in *Macroeconomics and Finance: Essays in Honor of Franco Modigliani*, ed. by R. Dornbusch, S. Fischer, and J. Bossons (Cambridge, Massachusetts: MIT Press, 1986).

Baltagi, Badi H., and James M. Griffin, "Short and Long Run Effects in Pooled Models," *International Economic Review* (Osaka), Vol. 25 (October 1984), pp. 631-45.

Bean, Charles R., "The Estimation of 'Surprise' Models and the 'Surprise' Consumption Function," *Review of Economic Studies* (Edinburgh), Vol. 53 (August 1986), pp. 497-516.

Bhargava, A., and others, "Serial Correlation and the Fixed Effects Model," *Review of Economic Studies* (Edinburgh), Vol. 49 (October 1982), pp. 533-49.

Blejer, Mario I., and Adrienne Cheasty, "Fiscal Policy and the Mobilization of Savings for Growth," Chap. 2 in this volume.

Blinder, Alan S., and Angus S. Deaton, "The Time Series Consumption Function Revisited," *Brookings Papers on Economic Activity: 2* (1985), The Brookings Institution (Washington), pp. 465-511.

Davidson, James E.H., and others, "Econometric Modelling of the Aggregate Time-Series Relationship between Consumers' Expenditure and Income in the United Kingdom," *Economic Journal* (Cambridge, England), Vol. 88 (December 1978), pp. 661-92.

Deaton, Angus S., *Life-Cycle Models of Consumption: Is the Evidence Consistent with the Theory?*, Working Paper No. 1910 (Cambridge, Massachusetts: National Bureau of Economic Research, 1986).

Dornbusch, Rudiger, "Real Interest Rates, Home Goods, and Optimal External Borrowing," *Journal of Political Economy* (Chicago), Vol. 91 (February 1983), pp. 141-53.

Fry, Maxwell J., "Money and Capital or Financial Deepening in Economic Development?" *Journal of Money, Credit and Banking* (Columbus, Ohio), Vol. 4 (November 1978), pp. 464-75.

———, "Saving, Investment, Growth and the Cost of Financial Repression," *World Development* (Oxford, England), Vol. 8 (April 1980), pp. 317-27.

Giovannini, Alberto, "The Interest Elasticity of Savings in Developing Countries: The Existing Evidence," *World Development* (Oxford, England), Vol. 11 (July 1983), pp. 601-607.

———, "Saving and the Real Interest Rate in LDCs," *Journal of Development Economics* (Amsterdam), Vol. 18 (August 1985), pp. 197-217.

Grossman, Sanford J., and Robert J. Shiller, "The Determinants of the Variability of Stock Market Prices," *American Economic Review: Papers and Proceedings of the Ninety-Third Annual Meeting of the American Economic Association* (Nashville, Tennessee), Vol. 71 (May 1981), pp. 222-27.

Gupta, K. L., "Personal Saving in Developing Nations: Further Evidence," *Economic Record* (Burwood, Victoria, Australia), Vol. 46 (June 1970), pp. 243-49.

Hall, Robert E., "Stochastic Implications of the Life Cycle-Permanent Income Hypothesis," *Journal of Political Economy* (Chicago), Vol. 86 (December 1978), pp. 971-87.

———, *Intertemporal Substitution in Consumption*, Working Paper No. 720 (Cambridge, Massachussets: National Bureau of Economic Research, 1981).

Hansen, Lars P., and Kenneth J. Singleton, "Generalized Instrumental Variables Estimation of Nonlinear Rational Expectations Models," *Econometrica* (Bristol, England), Vol. 50 (September 1982), pp. 1269-86.

Hayashi, Fumio, *Tests for Liquidity Constraints: A Critical Survey*, Working Paper No. 1720 (Cambridge, Massachusetts: National Bureau of Economic Research, 1985).

Hubbard, R. Glenn, and Kenneth L. Judd, "Liquidity Constraints, Fiscal Policy, and Consumption," *Brookings Papers on Economic Activity: 1* (1986), The Brookings Institution (Washington), pp. 1-59.

Jackman, Richard, and John Sutton, "Imperfect Capital Markets and the Monetarist Black Box: Liquidity Constraints, Inflation and the Asymmetric Effects of Interest Rate Policy," *Economic Journal* (Cambridge, England), Vol. 92 (March 1982), pp. 108-28.

Khatkhate, Deena R., "Assessing the Level and Impact of Interest Rates in Less Developed Countries" (unpublished, International Monetary Fund, 1985).

King, Mervyn A., "The Economics of Saving: A Survey of Recent Contributions," in *Frontiers of Economics*, ed. by Kenneth J. Arrow and Seppo Honkapohja (Oxford, England and New York: Basil Blackwell, 1985), pp. 227-94.

———, "Capital Market 'Imperfections' and the Consumption Function," *Scandinavian Journal of Economics* (Oxford, England), Vol. 88 (No. 1, 1986), pp. 59-80.

Krinsky, Itzhak, and A. Leslie Robb, "On Approximating the Statistical Properties of Elasticities," *Review of Economics and Statistics* (Cambridge, Massachusetts), Vol. 68 (November 1986), pp. 715-19.

McDonald, Donogh C., "The Determinants of Saving Behavior in Latin America" (unpublished, International Monetary Fund, 1983).

Mankiw, N. Gregory, and others, "Intertemporal Substitution in Macroeconomics," *Quarterly Journal of Economics* (Cambridge, Massachusetts), Vol. 100 (February 1985), pp. 225-51.

Mikesell, Raymond F., and James E. Zinser, "The Nature of the Savings Function in Developing Countries: A Survey of the Theoretical and Empirical Literature," *Journal of Economic Literature* (Nashville, Tennessee), Vol. 11 (March 1973), pp. 1-26.

Modigliani, Franco, "Life Cycle, Individual Thrift, and the Wealth of Nations," *American Economic Review* (Nashville, Tennessee), Vol. 76 (June 1986), pp. 297-313.

Muellbauer, John, "Surprises in the Consumption Function," *Economic Journal* (Cambridge, England), Vol. 93, Supplement (March 1983), pp. 34-50.

———(1986 a), "Notes on Uncertainty, Liquidity Constraints and Aggregation in the Consumption Function" (unpublished: Oxford, England: Nuffield College, 1986).

———(1986 b), *Habits, Rationality and Myopia in the Life-Cycle Consumption Function*, Discussion Paper No. 112 (London: Center for Economic Policy Research, June 1986).

Mundlak, Yair, "On the Pooling of Time Series and Cross Section Data," *Econometrica* (Evanston, Illinois), Vol. 46 (January 1978), pp. 69-85.

Pagan, Adrian, "Econometric Issues in the Analysis of Regressions with Generated Regressors," *International Economic Review* (Osaka), Vol. 25 (February 1984), pp. 221-47.

Pereira Leite, Sergio, and Dawit Makonnen, "Saving and Interest Rates in the BCEAO Countries: An Empirical Analysis" (unpublished, International Monetary Fund, 1984).

Snyder, Donald W., "Econometric Studies of Household Saving Behaviour in Developing Countries: A Survey," *Journal of Development Studies* (London), Vol. 2 (January 1974), pp. 139-53.

Summers, Lawrence H., "The After-Tax Rate of Return Affects Private Savings," *American Economic Review: Papers and Proceedings of the Ninety-Sixth Annual Meeting of the American Economic Association* (Nashville, Tennessee), Vol. 74 (May 1984), pp. 249-53.

Tanzi, Vito, and Mario I. Blejer, "Inflation, Interest Rate Policy, and Currency Substitution in Developing Economies: A Discussion of Some Major Issues," *World Development* (Oxford, England), Vol. 10 (September 1982), pp. 781-89.

Tobin, James, *Asset Accumulation and Economic Activity: Reflections on Contemporary Macroeconomic Theory* (Oxford, England: Basil Blackwell, 1980).

White, Halbert, "A Heteroskedasticity-Consistent Covariance Matrix Estimator and a Direct Test for Heteroskedasticity," *Econometrica* (Bristol, England), Vol. 48 (May 1980), pp. 817-38.

Williamson, J. G., "Personal Saving in Developing Nations: An Inter-temporal Cross-Section from Asia," *Economic Record* (Burwood, Victoria, Australia), Vol. 44 (June 1968), pp. 194-210.

Zeldes, S., "Consumption and Liquidity Constraints: An Empirical Investigation," Working Paper No. 24-85 (unpublished, Philadelphia: University of Pennsylvania, Rodney L. White Center for Financial Research, 1985).

11

Fiscal Dimensions of Trade Policy

Ziba Farhadian-Lorie and Menachem Katz

I. Introduction

The recent pattern of trade liberalization in developing countries and the renewed protectionist sentiment in industrial countries have revived interest in trade policy. Earlier trade reform failures in some Latin American countries still loom over the new liberalization drive. These failures have been attributed in great part to large budget deficits and policy inconsistencies that rendered the reforms unsustainable.[1] The present paper focuses on the fiscal dimensions of trade policy. Its main purpose is to assemble empirical findings on the use of trade taxes and to review the fiscal aspects of trade policy as they relate both to efficiency and to macroeconomic stabilization.[2]

Trade policy generally describes the set of instruments employed to regulate a country's international trade. This set of instruments consists of trade taxes and subsidies, import and export quotas, and other nontariff barriers. The focus of this discussion is trade taxes, which serve several objectives. First, they raise revenue for the government; second, they provide an instrument for correcting market distortions; third, they provide protection for local industry and employment; and, finally, they act as an instrument of macroeconomic stabilization. The use of trade taxes for each of these objectives inevitably gives rise to by-products: in particular, trade taxes for revenue will have protective effects, and trade taxes for macroeconomic stabilization will have fiscal effects.

The literature on optimal taxation and on trade and development has demonstrated that a reliance on trade taxes could create adverse effects

---

[1]A recent paper by Corden (1987) reviews the main analytical issues of protection and liberalization.

[2]See International Monetary Fund (1986), pp. 19-20 for a discussion of the income distribution aspects of taxes on international trade.

for the efficiency of production and for the pattern of economic development. Developing countries have nevertheless relied on trade taxes in varying degrees to perform different functions. This reliance has also been noted in the context of Fund-supported programs.[3] During 1980-84, over one third of Fund-supported adjustment programs employed general or selected increases in customs duties and import duty surcharges, although a similar number of programs have included tariff reforms (reductions). More recently, trade liberalization has become a frequently used policy instrument in Fund-supported programs. Given the importance of trade taxes in developing countries, an abrupt reduction in their use without compensatory measures could create budgetary imbalances and have destabilizing macroeconomic effects. Consequently, the need to weigh short-term stabilization objectives against long-term production efficiency has posed a dilemma for policymakers and for the Fund in designing programs.[4]

Section II of this paper presents an overview of the use of trade taxes by country groups at different levels of economic development during 1973-84 and analyzes the possible reasons for differences in their reliance on trade taxes. This section also explores channels of effects between different macroeconomic variables that may lead to higher or lower taxation of trade. Section III reviews the implications for efficiency of the use of trade taxes for revenue and protection, and as an instrument for correcting market distortions. It also discusses the tariff structure when trade taxes are used as a "second-best" revenue instrument in the presence of collection costs. Section IV assembles the major conclusions of the literature on the macroeconomic effects of trade taxes under fixed and flexible exchange rates. Finally, Section V summarizes the major points raised in the paper and outlines the possible implications for policy.

II. The Use and Determinants of Reliance on Trade Taxes

This section presents an overview of the actual use of trade taxes by all the countries reporting to the Fund. The aim is to determine observable patterns of increase or decrease in the importance of trade taxes for different groups of countries. The data set on trade taxes includes import and export duties, profits of import and export monopolies, exchange

---

[3]International Monetary Fund (1986 and 1987).
[4]See Tanzi (1987 c).

profits and exchange taxes, and certain other taxes on international trade and transactions, such as taxes exclusively on travel or insurance abroad.[5] Nontariff barriers are not included in this study, mostly owing to a lack of information on their use in developing countries. Also, import duties on petroleum and related products are not separated from other import duties because of a lack of accurate data on this category of trade taxes.

1. Statistical Overview of the Worldwide Use of Trade Taxes

Table 1 and Chart 1 present an overview of the recent evolution in the use and relative importance of taxes on international trade and transactions for different groups of countries. A number of basic observations can be made from the table and the chart.

The most important determinant of reliance on trade taxes seems to be the degree of economic development (Chart 1, upper panel). Since 1972, industrial countries have shown a pattern similar to the world average by following a consistent policy of low reliance on taxes on international trade as a source of government revenue. Developing countries, however,

---

[5]This definition coincides with the standard definition of taxes on international trade in the Fund's *A Manual on Government Finance Statistics* (Washington, 1986).

Table 1. Taxes on International Trade and Transactions, Selected Years, 1973–84[1]

(As percentage of total central government revenue)

	1973	1975	1977	1980	1982	1984	Average 1972–84
World	5.8	4.8	5.1	5.1	4.8	4.4	5.0
Industrial countries	1.9	1.8	1.8	1.5	1.3	1.4	1.7
Developing countries	18.0	14.1	15.6	16.1	15.5	14.0	15.3
Oil exporting countries	11.9	7.8	8.8	10.6	9.5	12.5	9.9
Non-oil developing countries	19.3	15.5	17.2	17.4	16.9	14.6	16.6
Regional classification of developing countries							
Africa	20.8	20.7	21.8	22.0	21.7	. . .	21.3[2]
Asia	21.1	19.5	18.8	20.1	19.2	20.1	19.9[3]
Europe	12.0	11.8	19.2	13.0	10.8	14.5	13.5
Middle East	12.7	8.5	10.3	9.5	8.0	9.4	9.6
Western Hemisphere	18.5	10.8	11.9	14.4	14.5	8.3	12.5

Sources: International Monetary Fund, *Government Finance Statistics Yearbook*, various issues; *International Financial Statistics: Supplement on Government Statistics* (1986).
[1]The number of countries in each economic or regional group increases with time as more countries report data to the Fund.
[2]1972–82.
[3]1973–84.

Chart 1. Share of Trade Taxes in Central Government Revenue, 1972–84

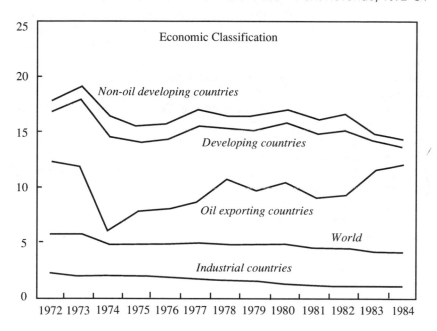

Economic Classification

Non-oil developing countries

Developing countries

Oil exporting countries

World

Industrial countries

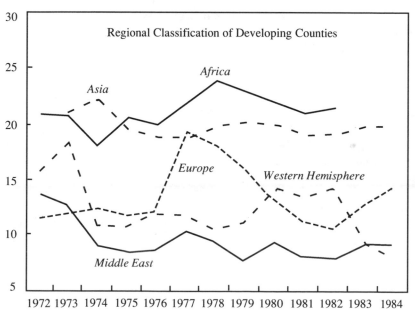

Regional Classification of Developing Counties

Africa

Asia

Europe

Western Hemisphere

Middle East

have followed a fluctuating pattern, with levels consistently above those for industrial countries. Within developing countries, the non-oil group, on the one hand, reduced its ratio of trade taxes to central government revenue during the entire period of 1973-84, with minor interruptions in this pattern during 1977, 1980, and 1982. The oil exporting countries, on the other hand, sharply increased their reliance on trade taxes after 1974, owing mostly to increases in trade taxes on petroleum.

Among developing countries, African and Asian countries consistently showed a higher degree of reliance on trade taxes than other groups, averaging 21 percent and 19 percent, respectively, during 1972-84. Ratios of trade taxation to government revenue of as much as 24 percent for African countries in 1978 and 22 percent for Asian countries in 1974 were observed. The developing countries in the Western Hemisphere followed a pattern of low trade taxes during 1974-78, averaging 11-12 percent of government revenue and reflecting mostly administrative restrictions on trade. After 1978 these countries showed signs of increased reliance on trade taxes, as their share rose to 14.5-16 percent of government revenue, owing mostly to the adoption of graduated trade liberalization programs that called for replacing nontariff barriers with trade taxes as a first phase. This increase was followed by an actual reduction to 8 percent after 1982. The developing countries of Europe reduced their reliance on trade taxes during 1978-82 to 11 percent of total government revenue, following a long period characterized by a sharply fluctuating pattern that ended in 1977. These countries seem to have chosen a more tax-protected trade policy since 1982.

2. Major Determinants of Revenue Importance of Trade Taxes

Some of the factors that affect governments' decisions to employ trade taxes, notwithstanding the distortions they create, are identified below.

Trade taxes have historically been a major source of government revenue during the early stages of economic development because they are easier to collect than domestic income or consumption taxes when the tax administration is rudimentary and tax handles are limited. A higher reliance on international trade taxes is therefore to be expected among countries with lower per capita incomes and/or lower ratios of total tax revenue (TX) to gross domestic product (GDP) because of an unsophisticated domestic tax administration. Corden (1974) mentions several channels of effects that explain the declining importance of trade taxes as sources of revenue in developed countries compared with developing countries. Among these channels are (1) a shift in the tax pattern toward nontrade taxes because collection costs of trade taxes decline less rapidly than those of other taxes; and (2) with improving productivity and competitiveness in import-substitution industries, the capacity to produce import-competing manufactured goods in response to a given level of tariff protection increases. As a result, a given structure of tariff rates has increasingly protective effects on industry, and its production-distorting cost increases.

The literature on tax efforts in developing countries also mentions the openness of the economy and the average height of the tariff structure — as long as it does not become prohibitive to trade — as being important determinants of their import taxation (Chelliah (1971) and Chelliah, Baas, and Kelly (1975)). If, according to Kuznets's suggested hypothesis, countries become less dependent on foreign trade as they become more economically developed (Corden (1974)), then the openness of the economy would be positively related to the revenue importance of trade taxes, owing to a hypothesized negative relation between openness and economic development, on the one hand, and between economic development and trade taxes, on the other. A simple version of this hypothesis was tested by Tanzi (1987 b), who found a positive and significant coefficient for the ratio of total imports to GDP as one of the determinants of the ratio of import duties to GDP.

In an attempt to determine more accurately the channels of effect among variables, we separate the estimation of the determinants of import taxes from those affecting export taxes, even though a number of variables may affect both.

a. Import Taxes

The revenue importance of import taxes is estimated here as a function of (1) the average tariff rate, shown as ID/IMP;[6] (2) the openness of the economy, which can best be represented as a ratio of imports plus exports to gross national product (GNP), rather than of total imports to GNP, to take account of the possibility that a country may adopt an export-oriented strategy; (3) a measure of sophistication of the tax system, which, again, can better be identified as the ratio of domestically collected taxes to GNP than as the ratio of total tax revenue to GNP, to take account of the fact that trade taxes do not require a very sophisticated tax administration; and (4) the level of economic development as represented by per capita income. Table 2 presents some relevant statistics on these variables for a sample of developing countries.

In addition to the four variables mentioned above, the estimation includes variables arising from the following hypothesized relations.

---

[6]ID = import duties
TX = total tax revenue
IMP = total imports

Table 2. Major Determinants of Revenue Importance of Import Duties

(Averages: 1978–84)[1]

	Import Duties Total Tax Revenue	Import Duties Total Imports	Trade GNP	Domestic Taxes GNP	Income per Capita (U.S. dollars)
Oman	5.1	1.9	85.1	11.4	6,090.2
Singapore	9.0	0.9	321.9	16.5	5,464.4
Israel	4.8	5.3	69.9	46.2	5,329.8
Venezuela	7.9	9.2	47.0	20.4	3,669.8
Barbados	17.7	7.7	85.2	21.1	3,496.7
Argentina	8.2	16.3	15.3	11.5	3,372.7
Cyprus	25.3	8.0	82.7	13.5	3,083.6
Iran, Islamic Republic of	27.4	18.1	29.5	5.9	2,945.6
Yugoslavia	37.2	13.8	39.6	5.6	2,518.4
Mexico	5.5	9.4	18.5	11.8	2,288.9
Portugal	5.4	4.2	56.6	27.3	2,155.5
Brazil	3.0	6.8	15.9	16.7	1,938.0
Korea, Republic of	17.6	8.3	63.0	13.1	1,773.3
Fiji	30.6	13.6	70.6	13.1	1,716.6
Costa Rica	9.8	4.9	65.0	13.4	1,531.6
Ghana	16.5	16.8	12.7	3.1	1,482.3
Paraguay	16.2	12.3	19.9	7.4	1,475.5
Dominican Republic	29.9	16.4	32.4	6.6	1,294.1
Colombia	14.9	11.4	22.9	7.9	1,274.0
Turkey	10.2	16.5	23.2	15.6	1,233.8

Tunisia	33.6	21.6	64.1	16.6	1,189.4
Mauritius	38.7	15.0	82.0	8.3	1,156.3
Jordan	58.0	13.7	96.0	7.8	1,069.2
Swaziland	64.2	18.9	148.9	8.4	906.1
Nicaragua	15.9	9.3	52.3	15.1	882.1
Botswana	51.7	17.6	139.8	13.5	875.8
El Salvador	10.8	4.8	50.1	7.7	804.6
Morocco	21.7	17.7	41.1	16.5	722.3
Thailand	21.7	11.1	43.8	9.7	712.0
Philippines	25.9	12.6	36.7	7.7	674.5
Guyana	7.1	4.0	116.6	30.8	582.9
Zambia	7.8	5.8	58.8	19.5	579.5
Yemen Arab Republic	68.2	23.2	62.2	6.6	444.3
Kenya	23.7	16.1	47.0	14.5	359.7
Sri Lanka	21.1	10.3	65.9	10.1	289.9
Tanzania	10.5	8.2	29.3	13.9	278.1
Zaïre	21.7	33.2	33.0	11.6	200.8
Malawi	24.2	13.8	51.6	12.5	185.1
Burkina Faso	41.3	20.2	35.4	7.4	165.0
Burma[2]	26.1	34.6	15.7	7.1	164.6
Nepal	34.1	14.5	21.7	4.4	140.9

Sources: International Monetary Fund, *Government Finance Statistics Yearbook* and *International Finance Statistics*, various issues.

[1] Countries are ranked according to nominal level of per capita income. Figures in the first four columns are percentages.

[2] Now Myanmar.

(1) Macroeconomic imbalances have often been mentioned as a reason for resorting to trade protectionism. It is possible that a country with an increasing trade deficit may try to restrict imports as an alternative to exchange rate adjustment, irrespective of the source of the trade imbalances. It is also possible that an increasing fiscal deficit may give the government an incentive to obtain more revenue through increased import duties if the revenue from that source is considered preferable to inflation taxation. We will therefore test these two possibilities by including fiscal deficit and trade deficit in the list of explanatory variables.

(2) The relationship between the inflation rate and a protectionist trade policy may not be observable through simple statistical correlation methods. A high or accelerating inflation rate in a country can be considered a sign of the need for adjustment in supply or demand, or both, in the economy. But in many developing countries, trade protectionism was tried as an alternative to, or in conjunction with, real exchange rate adjustment or other measures designed to alter the existing configuration of aggregate demand versus aggregate supply. When the cause of high inflation remains untreated, the country's stand on trade policy and the revenue importance of trade taxes can be affected in several ways. For example, to the extent that inflation—in the absence of autonomous adjustments to the structure of tax rates—increases the inflation tax revenue from domestic sources, it may create a negative relationship between the rate of inflation and the ratio of import duties to total tax revenue. Such influence from inflation cannot be expected to last in the medium term because of the limited impact of inflation on revenue raising. Countries with increasing inflation rates may also choose to control demand for imports by increasing taxes on imports or imposing quantitative restrictions on them, thereby creating a positive channel of effect between the inflation rate and import taxes. As a result, even though economic theory provides ample evidence of the importance of inflation in determining a country's trade taxes, the sign of this correlation may be ambiguous.

For notational simplicity, let

Y = ID/TX
X_1 = ID/IMP
X_2 = total trade (imports plus exports)/GDP
X_3 = domestic tax revenue (total tax revenue minus trade tax)/GDP
X_4 = fiscal deficit/GDP (+ = deficit; − = surplus)
X_5 = inflation rate
X_6 = real effective exchange rate index
X_7 = per capita income (in nominal U.S. dollar terms)
X_8 = trade balance/GDP (+ = deficit; − = surplus)

We estimate an ordinary-least-squares (OLS) regression between Y and X_2 to X_8, where all the variables, with the exceptions of X_4, X_5, and X_8, are defined in log terms. The variable X_1 is excluded from the regression because of its obvious correlation with the dependent variable. The results of the general form are reported in Table 3 (regression (1)). Estimation using several different combinations of variables was also performed to check for multicollinearity between independent variables.

A common aspect observed from the regressions in Table 3 is that all variables show the expected sign and most are highly significant: openness of the economy (X_2) and trade deficit (X_8) show positive and significant coefficients, whereas the rest show negative coefficients, with the fiscal deficit (X_4) being the only consistently insignificant variable.

In regression (1), the relative importance of domestic tax revenue in relation to GDP (X_3) is worth noting, as indicated by the high beta coefficient (-0.61). As mentioned above, and as discussed in Section III below, trade taxes and particularly import duties are an important source of revenue when the tax administration is still rudimentary and it is difficult to raise domestic taxes. Thus, the negative coefficient (-0.85) points to the inverse relationship between import taxes and domestic taxes. Per capita income (X_7) was also highly significant and relatively important $(\beta = -0.22)$, confirming the suggestion that the lower the level of per capita income, the greater the reliance on import taxes. The trade balance (X_8) and the degree of openness (X_2) of the economy were also found to be significant, with relatively high beta coefficients. This may indicate that import duties have been an important instrument in reducing trade deficits. Inflation (X_5) and the index of real effective exchange rates (X_6) were found to be statistically significant, but with relatively low beta coefficients. It is worth pointing out that the sign of the inflation coefficient is negative, which may suggest that when inflation is high, and with it the inflation tax rate, import taxes become less important. A possible channel of effect in an economy with a rising inflation rate is the overvalued exchange rate, which leads to a fall in the value of imports (Edwards (1987 b)).

The only variable with an insignificant coefficient in regression (1) was the fiscal deficit in relation to GDP (X_4). This may suggest that governments resort to taxes on imports as a source of revenue, but not necessarily as a means of reducing fiscal deficits. It should be noted, however, that when the real effective exchange rate is left out of the regression (regression (4)), the fiscal deficit becomes significant but its beta coefficient remains low, indicating its relatively low importance. Multicollinearity between a number of independent variables may exist. For example, collinearity exists between domestic tax revenue (X_3) and per capita in-

Table 3. Statistical Estimation of Major Determinants of Import Taxes: Regression Results[1]

Regression	Constant	$\ln(X_2)$	$\ln(X_3)$	X_4	X_5	$\ln(X_6)$	$\ln(X_7)$	X_8	$R^{2\,2}$	SEE[3]
(1) Coefficient	6.03	0.298	−0.85	0.004*	−0.002	−0.25*	−0.173	1.50		
t-probability	1.0	1.0	1.0	0.65	0.99	0.89	1.0	1.0	0.65	0.455
Beta[4]	—	0.28	−0.61	0.03	−0.14	−0.06	−0.22	0.29		
(2) Coefficient	6.05	0.257	−0.94	0.003*	−0.003	−0.43		1.4		
t-probability	1.0	1.0	1.0	0.48	1.0	0.99		1.0	0.62	0.478
Beta[4]	—	0.24	−0.66	0.03	−0.22	−0.11		0.27		
(3) Coefficient	7.73		−0.73	−0.002*	−0.003	−0.49	−0.15	2.25		
t-probability	1.0		1.0	0.38	1.0	0.99	0.99	1.0	0.62	0.476
Beta[4]	—		−0.52	−0.02	−0.22	−0.13	−0.19	0.43		
(4) Coefficient	5.16	0.357	−0.87	0.009	−0.06*		−0.21	1.52		
t-probability	1.0	1.0	1.0	0.94	0.30		1.0	1.0	0.64	0.462
Beta[4]	—	0.33	−0.62	0.08	−0.01		−0.27	0.29		

Notes: An asterisk (*) denotes a coefficient that is not significant at the 90 percent level.

Dependent variable: Y = import duties/total tax revenue

Independent variables: X_2 = total trade (imports plus exports)/GDP

X_3 = domestic tax revenue (total tax revenue minus trade tax)/GDP

X_4 = fiscal deficit/GDP (+ = deficit; − = surplus)

X_5 = inflation rate

X_6 = real effective exchange rate index

X_7 = per capita income (in nominal U.S. dollar terms)

X_8 = trade balance/GDP (+ = deficit; − = surplus)

[1] Pooled data for 1978–84 for 39 developing countries. The 39 countries are the same ones included in Table 2, with the exceptions of Oman and the Yemen Arab Republic, which were excluded here because of lack of complete data.

[2] Coefficient of determination.

[3] Standard error of estimate.

[4] Beta statistics are obtained by estimating an ordinary-least-squares regression using standard normalized values of the relevant variables instead of actual magnitudes. This statistic determines the change in the dependent variable, other things being equal, for a (normalized) unit change in each independent variable. As a result, beta statistics are comparable across equations, as well as within each equation.

come (X_7)—one would expect that as per capita income rises, domestic tax collection will improve. Therefore, specific importance should not be assigned to the absolute magnitude of each variable, although, as a group, they explain more than 65 percent of the variation in ID/TX. In order to reduce the possibility of multicollinearity, three other regressions were run. Regression (2) excludes per capita income (X_7), since the latter may directly affect domestic tax collection (X_3). This hypothesis is, however, not supported by the results. Regression (4) shows that inflation (X_5) and the real effective exchange rate (X_6) may be highly correlated and that exclusion of one variable weakens the impact of the other.

b. Export Taxes

Historically, export taxes have played a significant role in developing countries but have accounted for only a limited part of their total tax revenues. This is partly because only certain categories of exports—that is, primary products that have inelastic demand in international markets— can be successfully taxed by the government without substantially reducing the foreign exchange earnings of the country in the long run.[7]

Tanzi (1987 b) has noted that in many developing countries with a substantial agricultural sector, it is generally impractical to try to tax the income of that sector directly.[8] These were left little choice but to tax agricultural exports. Notwithstanding the importance of the primary product sector in a country's economy, the factor determining its reliance on export taxes is the ability of the exporters to transfer—at least part of—the tax burden to foreign consumers. If they are successful, the burden of export taxes usually does not fall entirely on the domestic consumers of the products being taxed, nor is the entire tax always paid by the exporter. As Table 4, which ranks countries from highest to lowest in terms of per capita income, shows, the relationship between the importance of the export sector in the economy—as represented by the ratio of exports to GNP—and the share of export taxes in total government revenue is rarely close. This is mostly because the tax burden cannot be transferred to the foreign consumers—unless the exporting country has monopoly power in the market. The relationship becomes particularly difficult to judge in countries that collect export taxes as advance payments on income taxation, because in these countries export taxes are not considered

---

[7]Extensive discussions on the role of export taxes appear in Tanzi (1987 a) and Sánchez-Ugarte and Modi (1986).

[8]This is mainly because agricultural production is not concentrated and the information required to tax agricultural income is normally not available.

Table 4. Export Taxes in Developing Countries

(Averages: 1978–84)

	Share of Export Taxes in			Shares in Exports in GNP
	Tax Revenue	Exports	GNP	
Oman	. . .	. . .	. . .	53.4
Singapore	. . .	. . .	. . .	141.6
Israel	. . .	. . .	. . .	24.6
Venezuela	. . .	. . .	. . .	27.2
Barbados	0.1	0.1	0.0	26.2
Argentina	4.3	5.9	0.5	8.5
Cyprus	. . .	. . .	. . .	25.5
Iran, Islamic Republic of	. . .	. . .	. . .	15.9
Yugoslavia	. . .	. . .	. . .	15.9
Mexico	13.6	21.6	2.0	10.2
Portugal	. . .	. . .	. . .	19.2
Brazil	2.1	4.3	0.4	8.2
Korea, Republic of	. . .	. . .	. . .	29.0
Fiji	1.4	1.0	0.3	25.2
Costa Rica	12.9	7.8	2.3	30.5
Ghana	25.3	21.4	1.7	6.4
Paraguay	0.7	0.9	0.1	7.1
Dominican Republic	5.6	4.3	0.6	12.5
Colombia	6.3	5.9	0.6	9.9
Turkey	. . .	. . .	. . .	8.3
Tunisia	1.0	1.1	0.3	24.1
Mauritius	15.6	8.3	2.8	34.2
Jordan	. . .	. . .	. . .	17.6
Swaziland	4.9	2.4	1.3	54.9
Nicaragua	2.5	2.1	0.4	22.3
Botswana	0.3	0.1	0.1	59.1
El Salvador	23.7	11.9	2.8	23.6
Morocco	1.2	1.9	0.3	14.4
Thailand	4.0	2.8	0.5	18.3
Philippines	1.8	1.3	0.2	14.8
Guyana	0.3	0.2	0.1	54.1
Zambia	2.1	1.8	0.5	29.8
Yemen Arab Republic	0.0	0.5	0.0	0.9
Kenya	1.1	1.1	0.2	18.1
Sri Lanka	25.6	19.4	5.2	25.4
Tanzania	3.9	6.1	0.6	8.9
Zaïre	13.7	11.9	2.6	20.2
Malawi	. . .	. . .	. . .	21.5
Burkina Faso	2.5	5.6	0.3	6.7
Burma[1]	. . .	. . .	. . .	6.7
Nepal	2.6	3.6	0.2	5.0

Sources: International Monetary Fund, *Government Finance Statistics Yearbook* and *International Financial Statistics*, various issues.

[1] Now Myanmar.

a policy tool for the promotion or discouragement of exports but rather an insured prepayment on income taxes. Unlike taxation of imports, export taxation does not seem to be correlated with economic development (as may be seen in Table 4), since reliance on export taxation is basically determined by the importance of exports as a tax base, as well as the monopolistic market power of the country.

As was done for import taxes, a test was run on export taxes to determine if the above-mentioned factors—that is, the share of exports in GDP and in per capita income—or other factors— such as the share of domestic tax revenue in total GDP, the level of the real effective exchange rate index, or the height of export tariffs (as represented by the ratio of export duties to total exports)—significantly affected the revenue importance of these taxes. Table 5 shows the results of estimating the share of export duties in total tax revenue as a function of

Z_1 = export duties/total exports
Z_2 = per capita income (in nominal U.S. dollar terms)
Z_3 = total exports/GDP
Z_4 = real effective exchange rate
Z_5 = total tax revenue minus trade tax/GDP

The results reported in Table 5 confirm that export taxes are inversely related to domestic tax revenue; as with import taxes, export taxes are most attractive to countries that do not have well-developed domestic tax administrations. Regressions (1) and (2) also indicate that the level of economic development and the relative size of the export sector are impor-

Table 5. Statistical Estimation of Major Determinants of Export Taxes: Regression Results[1]

Regression[1]	Constant	Z_1	Z_2	Z_3	Z_4	Z_5	R^2	SEE
(1) Coefficient	−0.11	1.04	−0.0005	0.13	0.015	−0.24		
t-probability	0.06	1.0	0.92	1.0	0.84	0.99	0.84	3.80
Beta	—	0.88	−0.05	0.21	0.04	−0.16		
(2) Coefficient	−0.62	1.04		0.13	0.015	−0.26		
t-probability	0.346	1.0		1.0	0.84	1.0	0.833	3.81
Beta	—	0.88		0.22	0.04	−0.169		

Notes: Dependent variable: Y = export duties/total tax revenue
Independent variables: Z_1 = export duties/total exports
           Z_2 = per capita income (in nominal U.S. dollar terms)
           Z_3 = total exports/GDP
           Z_4 = real effective exchange rate
           Z_5 = total tax revenue minus trade tax/GDP

[1]Countries included in the pooling of data are Argentina, Barbados, Botswana, Brazil, Burkina Faso, Colombia, Costa Rica, the Dominican Republic, El Salvador, Fiji, Ghana, Guyana, Kenya, Mauritius, Mexico, Morocco, Nepal, Nicaragua, Paraguay, the Philippines, Sri Lanka, Swaziland, Tanzania, Thailand, Tunisia, Zaïre, and Zambia.

tant determinants of export taxes. The beta statistics for the regressions show that the average effective export duty rate (Z_1) has the highest share in defining variations in the dependent variable. One explanation for this effect is that countries apply taxes on exports when export sectors are sizable in comparison with the total economy.

The basic results obtained from statistical observations and estimations confirm the importance of trade taxes as a source of revenue for low-income developing countries. Despite the ongoing concern in the literature about inefficiencies resulting from trade taxes, import taxes are used in these countries as a major source of revenue when other sources of tax revenue are not sufficiently well developed. Moreover, the regression results suggest that import taxes are also used to reduce trade deficits. For export taxes, the ability to impose these taxes when a country has the monopoly power in its export market determines the extent of their use. Considerations of economic efficiency are given secondary importance by policymakers in both cases.

III. Trade Taxes and Economic Efficiency

1. Introduction

This section assembles some of the major conclusions of public finance and trade theory pertaining to the efficiency of trade taxes. It reviews the efficiency of trade taxes for revenue, protection of local industry and employment, and correction of market distortions, and it focuses on the optimal structure of trade taxes when collection cost considerations are included.

Few studies on public finance and optimal taxation theory deal explicitly with open economies and trade taxes. Those studies that allow for international trade generally extend the major principles of optimal taxation to include trade taxes. Accordingly, a tax on international trade creates both consumption and production distortions and would not be part of an optimal tax package, except for collection cost considerations. Optimally, trade taxes should be harmonized with domestic consumption taxes and levied at the same rate as domestic taxes: that is, trade is taxed in the same way as domestic commodities, whereby, in order to promote the efficiency of production, inputs and intermediate goods are exempted. However, little attention has been paid to collection costs, particularly in economies where income and domestic consumption are not easily taxable. In such cases, imported inputs and intermediate goods could be considered together with imports of final consumption goods, which would be taxed in accordance with the Ramsey rule in order to minimize the deadweight loss.

Trade theory deals with trade taxes in the context of their impact on the efficient allocation of resources across countries. Within the framework of the standard Heckscher-Ohlin trade model, and under the assumptions of non-increasing returns to scale and perfect competition, trade taxes disrupt the free flow of goods among countries. When the assumption of perfect competition is relaxed, and monopoly, monopsony, or other market power is introduced at the international level, trade taxes can be justified on the grounds of the "optimal tariff argument" from the perspective of the individual country. In the presence of domestic distortions, however, trade taxes are generally viewed as inefficient instruments in the hierarchy of corrective policies. In this vein, assistance to domestic industry, and particularly to infant industry, is generally better provided by production subsidies than by protective tariffs.

2. Trade Taxes for Revenue and Protection

a. Efficiency

Non-lump-sum taxes levied for revenue purposes when lump-sum taxes are not available also introduce distortions, and the question posed by optimal taxation theory is how to raise a given amount of revenue with minimum distortion of the system. Diamond and Mirrlees (1971 a and b) demonstrate that, with the introduction of non-lump-sum taxes in a closed economy, production efficiency is still desirable, although full Pareto efficiency is not achieved. A production plan is efficient if any other feasible production plan provides a smaller net supply of at least one commodity. The model derives the conditions for production efficiency and optimal commodity taxes. The relationship between consumer prices and the slope of the production frontier defines the optimal tax structure as: "... for all commodities the ratio of marginal tax revenue from an increase in the tax on that commodity to the quantity of the commodity is a constant" (Diamond and Mirrlees (1971 a), p. 16). Shadow prices are still equal to producer prices but differ from consumer prices.

Thus, finding a second-best optimal set of commodity taxes implies a violation of Pareto efficiency, because the domestic rate of substitution in consumption is different from the domestic rate of transformation in production when production efficiency is being maintained. The optimal commodity tax system includes no taxes that violate the conditions for production efficiency. When the Diamond-Mirrlees model is extended to allow the taxation of transactions between firms, the optimal tax structure includes no taxes on intermediate goods, since they would prevent production efficiency. In the absence of "abnormal" profits, taxation of intermediate goods must be reflected in changes in final goods prices. Therefore, the revenue could have been collected by taxing final goods, causing no greater change in final goods prices and avoiding production inefficiency. This point is relevant to the discussion of the tariff structure and is pursued below.

As pointed out by Dixit (1985), international trade may be regarded as just another transformation activity; the origin of a commodity should not be a taxation criterion. The Diamond-Mirrlees efficiency condition for an open economy thus implies that the marginal rates of transformation between producing and importing should be equal. Therefore, under the small, open-economy assumptions, final goods sales direct to consumers should be subject to a tariff equal to the tax on the same kind of sales made by a domestic producer, assuming that domestic and trade taxes can be harmonized.[9]

An import tariff in a small, open economy imposed as a source of revenue (or for protection) introduces distortions into the system. The inefficiency can be best assessed by juxtaposing the distortions created by such a tariff and the distortions created by a domestic tax — say, an excise tax — where the two alternative taxes are designed to raise the same amount of revenue from an importable commodity that is both produced domestically and imported. Unlike an excise tax, which is a tax on consumption, a tariff is both a tax on consumption and a subsidy (negative tax) on production. In addition to the consumption distortions created by both taxes, the tariff also creates a production distortion and, as a byproduct, involves distribution effects in favor of domestic import-competing producers (Corden (1974)).

The combined production and consumption distortions as well as the income distribution effect are all present in import duties levied on luxury goods. A tax on luxury imports designed to discourage an undesirable demonstration effect tends to give rise to a domestically protected import-substitution industry, thus permitting the marginal rate of transformation of domestic resources into the importable good in question to exceed the marginal rate of transformation through foreign trade (Johnson (1965)). A more effective way of dealing with the equity factor would be to levy an excise tax on luxury goods that would not create production distortions and would apply equally to domestic uses and to imports (Tanzi (1987 b)).

Although optimal taxation theory has demonstrated that under certain assumptions trade taxes should not be part of an optimal tax package in a

---

[9]Tanzi (1987 b) has pointed out the practical difficulty of coordinating domestic indirect taxes with import duties in developing countries.

small, open economy, Section II above has shown that they have been an important source of revenue in developing countries. For the low-income countries, the taxing of income or even domestic consumption has proved more difficult and costly than the taxing of international trade. The latter normally requires only a small administration stationed at the port of entry, and, unless tax rates are so high as to encourage smuggling, is relatively easy to enforce.

b. The Role of Collection Costs in Determining Trade Taxes

Evidence shows that collection costs have been an overwhelming consideration in the recourse by developing countries to trade taxes as an important source of revenue. Collection costs, however, have been largely ignored in the literature on optimal taxation and trade policy (Corden (1974), Mansfield (1987)). Unlike transportation costs in trade theory, which introduce changes at the margin but leave the standard conclusions intact, the inclusion of collection costs can, in principle, change the structure of an optimal tax package. The issue of collection costs is discussed in trade theory by Corden (1974) and in optimal taxation theory in the context of closed economies by Yitzhaki (1979).

Collection costs consist of the direct labor costs needed to administer and ensure compliance, and the resource costs incurred by taxpayers in their efforts to minimize tax payments. Corden (1974) has shown that, with differential collection costs between an excise tax and a tariff in favor of the latter, it is possible to include trade taxes in an optimal tax package. The composition of such a package would depend on how collection costs are introduced.

In the literature on optimal taxation, Yitzhaki (1979) constructs a model in which collection costs are introduced explicitly. In his closed-economy model, the number of taxable commodities is a decision variable; the marginal cost of administration is defined as the additional outlay needed to raise an additional dollar in tax revenue. Collection costs for each commodity are assumed to be constant. The social cost of taxation is the sum of collection costs and the deadweight loss, and the objective is to minimize the social cost, subject to a given level of revenue. In the optimal solution, the marginal collection cost and the marginal excess burden are equal. If this model were extended to an open economy, and if collection costs on trade taxes were considerably lower than on domestic commodity taxes, it is conceivable that trade taxes would replace some domestic commodity taxes, although the deadweight loss of the former might be higher. However, international trade and trade taxes have not been formally introduced into such a model.

Collection cost considerations notwithstanding, the argument in favor of trade taxes as part of an optimal tax system cannot be carried very far. The distortions created by trade taxes in both production and consumption generally exceed the distortions created by other taxes. Moreover, the differential in collection costs between trade taxes and domestic taxes can be considerable only in low-income countries with rudimentary tax administrations. As discussed in Section II above, as countries develop, the tax base widens and the reliance on trade taxes for revenue diminishes (Corden (1974) and Tanzi (1987 a)).

The introduction of trade taxes for revenue purposes as a "third-best" policy is considered by Dixit (1985). However, the reasons for ruling out commodity taxes—collection costs—are not endogenized. Rather, the requirement is imposed that government expenditure must be financed using trade taxes alone. As a result, domestic producer prices no longer equal international producer prices, and the equality of the domestic and foreign rates of transformation in production no longer holds.

c. The Optimal Structure of Trade Taxes

Once tariffs are introduced, either as part of a second-best, or as a third-best, policy, two questions arise regarding the tariff structure that minimizes distortions: first, whether the tariff should include inputs and intermediate goods; and second, whether the tariff structure should be based on the Ramsey rule, be uniform, or aim at providing uniform effective protection.

Diamond and Mirrlees (1971 a) have shown that for production efficiency, intermediate goods should not be taxed either in a closed economy or in the context of international trade. Taxing inputs or intermediate goods prevents efficiency in production. Under the small-economy assumption, intermediate goods should not be subject to a tariff, but imported final consumer goods should be subject to the same tax as domestically produced goods. In another extension of optimal taxation to open economies, Dasgupta and Stiglitz (1974) have shown that even if the only taxes that can be levied are trade taxes, the price of an intermediate good should not differ from the international price. If, however, imports are used both as inputs and as final consumption goods, and if it is impossible to treat the same goods differently, then these goods should be taxed.

Corden (1974) has demonstrated that through the introduction of collection cost considerations, tariffs could be part of an optimal tax package. In such a case, an optimal revenue tariff structure is likely to include tariffs on inputs. A tariff on inputs alone will avoid consumption distortions but will introduce production distortions: first, the distortions created by the protection provided for the domestic production of the input; and second, the cost of negative protection imposed on the final good. However, if for a given revenue requirement taxes are to be levied on international trade, some optimum mix of the two tariffs—a tariff on a final good and a tariff on its input—is likely. This way, the protection to producers would be mitigated by the negative protection imposed by the tariff on the input. However, at the same time, a new production distortion would be created by the protection provided for domestic production of the input.

A discussion on the tariff structure that minimizes distortions would generally start with the Ramsey rule. The original optimal commodity tax structure was developed by Ramsey in the context of a purely competitive system with no foreign trade in a partial equilibrium setting. In order to minimize the distortion created by the tax—the excess burden or deadweight loss—the tax rate should be levied in inverse proportion to the demand elasticity. The more inelastic the demand for a commodity, the more highly taxed it should be. An extension of the Ramsey rule to a general equilibrium framework is presented in Stern (1984). Under the generalized Ramsey rule, the proportional reduction in the compensated demand owing to the imposition of the set of taxes should be the same for all goods. Consequently, the principle of differential taxation should be directed at those goods that cannot be varied by consumers. Only if all goods are equally complementary with leisure (and leisure is not taxed) will the Ramsey rule imply uniform tax rates for all goods.

A straightforward extension of the Ramsey rule to an open economy suggests that, to the extent that tariffs are part of a tax package, the tariff structure should consist of differential rates that are harmonized with domestic commodity taxes. A synthesis of domestic optimal taxation with optimal tariff appears in Boadway, Maital, and Prachowny (1973). The tariff in their model plays a dual role. First, it exploits monopoly-monopsony power and, second, it generates revenue that would otherwise have been generated through (non-lump-sum) distortionary domestic taxes.

Against the Ramsey rule of differential tax rates are arguments in favor of uniformity of proportionate rates. A general discussion of uniformity versus selectivity in tax structures appears in Stern (1987). Stern assembles three groups of arguments in favor of uniform tax rates: theoretical, administrative, and rent seeking. First, the theoretical arguments for optimality of uniform indirect taxes would hold under special restrictive assumptions. Second, uniform tax rates are simpler to organize and collect than selective taxes with differential rates. Third, non-uniform taxes tend to give rise to lobbying by interest groups for special tax treatment. Another argument in favor of uniformity is the lack of information available to determine selective tax rates for individual commodities. Although these arguments were developed for general tax structures, they are also relevant for trade taxes. In the same paper, Stern demonstrates that there are some grounds for uniformity but only within broad groups of goods. Uniformity for the system as a whole is neither feasible nor optimal. He notes that if tariffs exist because taxation of final goods and income is more costly, there is still no presumption in favor of uniformity.[10]

A uniform nominal tariff on both inputs and output implies uniform effective protection when there are many importable inputs but no exportable or nontraded inputs. Theoretical justification for uniformity of both nominal and effective protection is discussed by Corden (1974). If the elasticity of supply of exportables and the domestic demand for exportables were zero, and there were zero substitution between leisure and work, then tariffs would not distort the production or consumption pattern relative to exportables or leisure. The only possible distortion would be in the pattern of production and consumption of importables. Under such conditions, the optimal tariff structure would imply a uniform tariff rate. If exportables were not used as inputs in the production of importables, then a uniform nominal tariff would also be a uniform effective tariff. If, however, substitution is allowed relative to exportables and leisure, the optimal tariff structure should not be uniform and should be based on the Ramsey rule of minimizing deadweight loss: taxes on low-elasticity goods should be higher than on high-elasticity goods. Another qualification to the uniformity of nominal tariffs and effective protection is the case of domestically produced inputs that are close substitutes for exports. In this instance, uniformity of nominal tariffs would not lead to a uniform and identical effective protection.

Following the requirement of optimal taxation theory that in order to promote production efficiency, inputs should not be taxed, the exclusion of inputs from a tariff structure implies that even low nominal tariffs on final goods provide relatively high effective protection.

A detailed discussion on effective protection appears in Corden (1966), and further extensions and generalizations are included in Michaely (1977). Finally, a discussion on the limitations of the theory of effective protection appears in Dixit (1985), which suggests that trade policy is implemented by setting nominal tariffs; therefore, it might be better to conduct the entire analysis in these terms.

3. Trade Taxes and Market Distortions

The existence of market distortions or failures in the form of externalities or monopolies, or other distortions caused by institutions or policy led to the development of the "optimal tariff argument" and the theory of domestic distortions, including the infant industry argument. Landmark

---

[10]On this issue, see also De Wulf (1980).

studies on developments in this area are those by Corden (1957), Johnson (1965), and Bhagwati (1971). Extensive reviews of the literature appear in Bhagwati and Srinivasan (1983) and Corden (1984). A new analysis of trade under a variety of different market structures is developed by Helpman and Krugman (1985). The authors note, however, that the problem of modeling trade policy under these market structures remains unresolved. This point should be stressed, because the conclusions of the literature have been based largely on specific assumptions about market structures.

The principle of the second-best approach to distortions or divergences between prices and marginal costs is that distortions should be dealt with as close as possible to their source— Pigovian policies. The main objective is to restore Pareto efficiency, equating the domestic rate of substitution in consumption with both the domestic and the foreign rates of transformation in production. Trade taxes are discussed in this context as possible corrective instruments. One extension of this approach is the optimal tariff argument, by which countries with large market shares can restrict their trade to exploit their potential market power. Under such conditions, countries can impose import duties or export taxes. In the standard two-good model, the optimal export tax is the inverse of the elasticity of the foreign demand for exports in terms of imports.[11] A recent examination of the use of the optimal export tax by exporters of primary commodities found that in most of the primary producing countries the actual level of export taxation is higher than the level that can be considered country-optimal (Sánchez-Ugarte and Modi (1986)).

Most other types of distortion discussed in the literature are domestic. When the distortions are domestic, no interference in international trade is called for, except when the distortions arise in trade itself. An effective method of dealing with distortions is to list a hierarchy of corrective policy according to the side effects; the second-best policy on this list is one that does not create new distortions as by-products. Accordingly, a production subsidy should be used to deal with distortions in production, and a consumption tax, with distortions in consumption; distortions in the factor market should be dealt with by a tax or a subsidy on the factor of production. An argument often used in favor of a protective tariff is that it can alleviate unemployment problems in the domestic industry. If the domestic distortion is in the labor market— wage rigidity that causes unemployment—a second-best policy would be a uniform subsidy on employment; a third-best policy, a subsidy to output; and, lower in the ranking, a mix of a tariff and an export subsidy, or a tariff alone. If the sector

---

[11]See Corden (1984), pp. 82-86.

for importables in the home country is labor-intensive, a tariff will increase employment and output. However, excessive capital and labor will be drawn into the protected industry and will create new distortions (Corden (1957) and Johnson (1965)).

One of the most widely used arguments for a protective tariff is the infant industry argument. Infant industry assistance has been viewed in much of the literature as a corrective policy for some market imperfections (Johnson (1965), Corden (1984), and Krueger (1984)). To the extent that the distortion or imperfection is in the labor market, an employment subsidy should be granted (Baldwin (1969) and Johnson (1970)). Alternatively, if the market distortion is in the underdeveloped capital market, a credit subsidy would be granted. Protective tariffs have generally ranked only fourth or fifth best.

Thus, to the extent that market distortions occur in areas not directly related to trade, the use of trade taxes as Pigovian policies is viewed as inefficient. It is also worth noting that when encouragement for domestic production is desirable, as for infant industries, policy would generally call for a production or input subsidy rather than the tariff protection. This is true even though a tariff can also generate revenue, whereas a subsidy puts a burden on the budget. A subsidy is more efficient and creates fewer distortions, and revenue needs should be satisfied according to optimal taxation principles in the least distortive manner (Tanzi (1987 b) and Dixit (1985)).

IV. Trade Taxes and Macroeconomic Stabilization

Trade taxes have been widely used as a policy instrument both to reduce budget deficits and to correct external imbalances. Unlike other fiscal measures that affect the external balance indirectly through the saving-investment mechanism, trade taxes affect the external balance directly through changes in relative prices and indirectly through changes in government and private saving and investment. This section briefly reviews the macroeconomic effects of trade taxes under fixed and flexible exchange rates.

With few exceptions (Tower (1973) and Dornbusch (1987)), the literature on the macroeconomics of trade policy has not dealt with the fiscal aspects of trade policy. The traditional literature, the Laursen-Metzler-Mundell approach, has focused on the terms of trade effects while assuming away their fiscal dimensions. Accordingly, a restrictive trade policy in the form of an import tariff whose proceeds are redistributed to the public would improve the external current account and increase output under a fixed exchange rate and, hence, have a contractionary effect on output and cause an appreciation of the exchange rate.

Recent studies on the macroeconomic effects of trade policy have employed intertemporal optimization frameworks while again assuming away their fiscal dimensions. In models of exportables and importables (Razin and Svensson (1983) and van Wijnbergen (1987)), temporary import tariffs tend to improve the external current account, whereas the result of permanent tariffs is ambiguous. When nontradables are added to the models (Edwards (1987 a and b) and Ostry (1987)), it is generally impossible to determine a priori how a tariff would affect the current account.

The analysis on the macroeconomic effects of trade policy with fiscal policy draws on Mundell (1961), Tower (1973), Dornbusch (1980 and 1987), and Razin and Svensson (1983). Most contributions in this area have shied away from dealing with the impact of trade taxes for revenue, assuming that the proceeds from the tax are redistributed and that the initial tax is zero to avoid any welfare effects. Indeed, this issue has not yet been fully studied. Notwithstanding the welfare effects, Tower (1973) and Dornbusch (1987) study the macroeconomic consequences of imposing a uniform ad valorem tariff on imports for revenue purposes.

The imposition of a nonprohibitive tariff increases government revenue by the tariff rate times the value of imports — the tax base — and the proceeds are used to reduce the budget deficit and thus increase government saving. The tariff will have an income effect equal to the increase in the revenue generated by the tariff, and a substitution effect (away from importables) caused by the change in relative prices. These two effects lead to a reduction in the demand for imports and, under a fixed exchange rate regime, to an improvement in the external trade and current account. In fact, if the import-demand elasticity is unity and in the absence of a relative price effect on saving — zero Laursen-Metzler effect — the improvement in the trade account (and current account) will be equal to the increase in government revenue (which is equal to the increase in government saving). The effect of a tariff on output will be expansionary if the import-demand elasticity is greater than unity (assuming a zero Laursen-Metzler effect). Under such conditions, the substitution effect that shifts demand from imported to domestic goods will outweigh the negative income effect caused by the tariff, and an expansion in output will take place. The introduction of the Laursen-Metzler effect will not qualitatively change the direction of the effect of the tariff on either the external trade account or the output under a fixed exchange rate regime, nor is it likely to have direct fiscal effects.

Under a flexible exchange rate regime, income and substitution effects caused by the import tariff will cause an incipient external surplus that will be equilibrated by an appreciation of the exchange rate. This, together with a possibly contractionary Laursen-Metzler effect, will cause output to fall.

In the large-country case, the extent to which the rest of the world would have to pay for the imposition of the tariff would depend on the relative strength of the income and substitution effects. A relatively strong income effect would tend to leave world prices unchanged but reduce demand, whereas a strong substitution effect would cause an improvement in the terms of trade for which the rest of the world would have to pay. The exact nature of the final outcome would obviously depend on the financial and trade policies of the rest of the world.

V. Summary and Implications for Policy

This paper has reviewed the fiscal dimensions of a major instrument of trade policy—taxes on international trade. Trade taxes are used for government revenue, for protection, for income redistribution, and for stabilization. First, the study has shown that developing countries rely heavily on trade taxes. Although in industrial countries trade taxes constitute less than 2 percent of central government revenue, in non-oil developing countries they amount to some 16 percent. African and Asian countries generate over one fifth of central government revenue from trade taxes; in developing countries in the Western Hemisphere, the proportion is one eighth. An examination of the factors contributing to countries' reliance on trade taxes indicates that countries with low per capita incomes tend to rely more heavily on trade taxes, reflecting a narrow domestic tax base and a rudimentary tax administration. Other important factors are the trade deficit and the real effective exchange rate.

Trade taxes create distortions in both production and consumption and would generally not be part of an optimal tax package. The origin or destination of commodities should not be a taxation criterion. Optimally, tariffs should be harmonized with domestic taxes, and, for production efficiency, inputs and intermediate goods should not be taxed. Only to the extent that domestic taxes are not available would trade taxes be considered. In such cases, imported inputs and intermediate goods could be considered together with imports of final consumer goods, which would be taxed at differential rates to minimize the welfare loss. However, the exemption of imported inputs or intermediate goods could provide a relatively high rate of effective protection to local industry even if nominal tariff rates on final goods were low.

Within the standard Heckscher-Ohlin trade model and under perfect competition both domestically and internationally, trade taxes disrupt the free flow of goods among countries and create a welfare loss. When the assumption of perfect competition is relaxed, and monopoly, monopsony, or other market power is introduced at the international level, trade taxes could exploit this market power, using the optimal tariff argument. Internationally, however, this would lead to a reduction in world trade and welfare.

Trade taxes are generally viewed, in the hierarchy of corrective policies, as inefficient instruments for correcting domestic distortions. Assistance to domestic industry, particularly infant industries, is generally better provided by means of subsidies to labor or capital. This is true even though a tariff can also generate revenue, whereas a subsidy incurs an additional burden on the budget. According to optimal taxation principles, revenue needs should be satisfied in the least distortive manner, and a direct subsidy is most efficient and creates less distortion.

Given the distortions created by trade taxes, their effectiveness as an instrument for correcting macroeconomic imbalances merits consideration. Under a fixed exchange rate, a restrictive trade policy — the imposition of a tariff on imports — can be effective in improving the external current account and output, whereas under a flexible exchange rate, a restrictive trade policy will have a contractionary effect on output and cause an appreciation of the exchange rate.

Unlike other fiscal policy measures that affect the external balance indirectly through the saving-investment mechanism, trade taxes affect the external balance directly through their effect on relative prices, and indirectly through changes in government saving.

Recent studies employing intertemporal optimization frameworks have demonstrated that temporary tariffs whose proceeds are redistributed to the public under some conditions improve the external current account for the time being, whereas the impact of permanent tariffs is ambiguous. When nontradables are added to the model, possible substitution between present and future and between tradables and nontradables makes it impossible to determine a priori how a tariff affects the current account.

Although trade taxes may be appealing as an instrument of trade and fiscal policies, the distortions that they create for resource allocation and the welfare loss involved puts them at a disadvantage compared with other fiscal and exchange rate policies. Thus, in the effective assignment of policy instruments to achieve economic objectives, trade taxes would generally be excluded. Countries with fiscal and external imbalances should aim at correcting them by applying the most effective and least distortive policies. If the fiscal imbalance is to be reduced by increasing revenue, this revenue should be raised in such a way as to minimize distortions, and trade taxes therefore would normally not be part of such a revenue measure. To correct external imbalances, the use of the least distortive and most effective instruments would again exclude trade taxes. Although a temporary tariff is likely to improve the external current account if it is unexpected and although it may also raise revenue, trade taxes should be resisted even in the short term, since temporary measures tend to become permanent.

Another important implication for policy that is not discussed in this paper but requires further attention is the sequencing of trade liberalization and fiscal adjustment. Considering the heavy reliance of developing countries on trade taxes, a trade liberalization to reduce this reliance would first require a tax reform to replace trade taxes with domestic taxes. Failure to do this would cause large fiscal deficits and could make the trade reform unsustainable.

REFERENCES

Anjaria, Shailendra J., Naheed Kirmani, and Arne B. Petersen, *Trade Policy Issues and Developments*, Occasional Papers, No. 38 (Washington: International Monetary Fund, 1985).

Atkinson, A. B., and Joseph E. Stiglitz, *Lectures on Public Economics* (New York: McGraw-Hill, 1980).

Baldwin, Robert E., "The Case Against Infant Industry Tariff Protection," *Journal of Political Economy* (Chicago), Vol. 77 (May/June 1969), pp. 295-305.

Beenstock, Michael, and Peter Warburton, "Long-Term Trends in Economic Openness in the United Kingdom and the United States," *Oxford Economic Papers* (Oxford, England), Vol. 35 (March 1983), pp. 130-42.

Bhagwati, Jagdish N., "The Generalized Theory of Distortions and Welfare," Chap. 4 in *Trade, Balance of Payments and Growth: Papers in International Economics in Honor of Charles P. Kindleberger*, ed. by Jagdish N. Bhagwati and others (Amsterdam: North-Holland, 1971).

_____, and T. N. Srinivasan, "Trade Policy and Development," Chap. 2 in *International Economic Policy: Theory and Evidence*, ed. by Rudiger Dornbusch and Jacob A. Frenkel (Baltimore and London: Johns Hopkins University Press, 1979).

_____, *Lectures on International Trade* (Cambridge, Massachusetts: MIT Press, 1983).

Boadway, Robin W., Shlomo Maital, and Martin F. J. Prachowny, "Optimal Tariffs, Optimal Taxes, and Public Goods," *Journal of Public Economics* (Amsterdam), Vol. 2 (November 1973), pp. 391-403.

Bovenberg, A. Lans, "Indirect Taxation in Developing Countries: A General Equilibrium Approach," *Staff Papers*, International Monetary Fund (Washington), Vol. 34 (June 1987), pp. 333-73.

Boyer, Russell S., "Commercial Policy under Alternative Exchange Rate Regimes," *Canadian Journal of Economics* (Toronto), Vol. 2 (May 1977), pp. 218-32.

Bruno, Michael, "Market Distortions and Gradual Reform," *Review of Economic Studies* (Edinburgh), Vol. 39 (July 1972), pp. 373-83.

Caves, Richard E., and Ronald W. Jones, *World Trade and Payments: An Introduction* (Boston: Little, Brown, 2nd ed., 1977).

Chan, Kenneth Shun-yuen, "The Employment Effects of Tariffs under a Free Exchange Rate Regime: A Monetary Approach," *Journal of International Economics* (Amsterdam), Vol. 8 (August 1978), pp. 415-23.

Chelliah, Raja J., "Trends in Taxation in Developing Countries," *Staff Papers*, International Monetary Fund (Washington), Vol. 18 (July 1971), pp. 254-331.

———, Hessel J. Baas, and Margaret R. Kelly, "Tax Ratios and Tax Effort in Developing Countries, 1969-71," *Staff Papers*, International Monetary Fund (Washington), Vol. 22 (March 1975), pp. 187-205.

Cline, William R., ed., *Trade Policy in the 1980s* (Washington: Institute for International Economics, 1983).

Corden, W. Max, "Tariffs, Subsidies and the Terms of Trade," *Economica* (London), Vol. 24 (1957), pp. 235-42.

———, "The Structure of a Tariff System and the Effective Protective Rate," *Journal of Political Economy* (Chicago), Vol. 74 (1966), pp. 221-37.

———, *The Theory of Protection* (Oxford, England: Clarendon Press, 1971).

———, *Trade Policy and Economic Welfare* (Oxford, England: Clarendon Press, 1974).

———, "The Normative Theory of International Trade," Chap. 2 in *Handbook of International Economics*, ed. by Ronald W. Jones and Peter B. Kenen, Vol. 1 (Amsterdam: North-Holland, 1984).

———, *Protection and Liberalization: A Review of Analytical Issues*, Occasional Paper No. 54 (Washington: International Monetary Fund, 1987).

Dasgupta, Partho S., and Joseph E. Stiglitz, "Benefit-Cost Analysis and Trade Policies," *Journal of Political Economy* (Chicago), Vol. 82 (January-February 1974), pp. 1-33.

De Wulf, Luc, "Public Finance Aspects of the Use of Customs Duties in Less Developed Countries" (unpublished, International Monetary Fund, September 23, 1977).

———, "Taxation of Imports in LDCs: Suggestions for Reform," *Journal of World Trade Law* (Twickenham-Middlesex, England), Vol. 14 (July-August 1980), pp. 346-51.

Diamond, Peter A., and James A. Mirrlees (1971 a), "Optimal Taxation and Public Production, I: Production Efficiency," *American Economic Review* (Nashville, Tennessee), Vol. 61 (March 1971), pp. 8-27.

———(1971 b), "Optimal Taxation and Public Production, II: Tax Rules," *American Economic Review* (Nashville, Tennessee), Vol. 61 (June 1971), pp. 261-78.

Dixit, Avinash, "Tax Policy in Open Economies," Chap. 6 in *Handbook of Public Economics*, Vol. 1, ed. by Alan J. Auerbach and Martin Feldstein (Amsterdam: North-Holland, 1985).

Dornbusch, Rudiger, "Tariffs and Nontraded Goods," *Journal of International Economics* (Amsterdam), Vol. 4 (May 1974), pp. 177-85.

———, *Open Economy Macroeconomics* (New York: Basic Books, 1980).

———, "External Balance Correction: Depreciation or Correction?" *Brookings Papers on Economic Activity: 1* (1987), The Brookings Institution (Washington), pp. 249-69.

Edwards, Sebastian (1987 a), "The Liberalization of the Current Capital Accounts and the Real Exchange Rate," NBER Working Paper No. 2162 (Cambridge, Massachusetts: National Bureau of Economic Research, February 1987).

——— (1987 b), "Tariffs, Terms of Trade, and the Real Exchange Rate in an Intertemporal Optimizing Model of the Current Account," NBER Working Paper No. 2175 (Cambridge, Massachusetts: National Bureau of Economic Research, March 1987).

Eichengreen, Barry J., "A Dynamic Model of Tariffs and Employment under Flexible Exchange Rates," *Journal of International Economics* (Amsterdam), Vol. 11 (August 1981), pp. 341-59.

Goode, Richard, George E. Lent, and P. D. Ojha, "Role of Export Taxes in Developing Countries," *Staff Papers*, International Monetary Fund (Washington), Vol. 13 (November 1966), pp. 453-501.

Greenaway, David, *Trade Policy and the New Protectionism* (New York: St. Martin's Press, 1983).

Helpman, Elhanan, and Paul R. Krugman, *Market Structure and Foreign Trade: Increasing Returns, Imperfect Competition, and the International Economy* (Cambridge, Massachusetts: MIT Press, 1985).

International Monetary Fund, *Fund-Supported Programs, Fiscal Policy, and Income Distribution: A Study by the Fiscal Affairs Department of the International Monetary Fund*, Occasional Papers, No. 46 (Washington: International Monetary Fund, 1986).

———, *Annual Report on Exchange Arrangements and Exchange Restrictions, 1987* (Washington: International Monetary Fund, 1987).

Johnson, Harry G., "Optimal Trade Interventions in the Presence of Domestic Distortions," in *Trade, Growth, and the Balance of Payments: Essays in Honor of Gottfried Haberler*, ed. by Richard E. Caves, Harry G. Johnson, and Peter B. Kenen (Amsterdam: North-Holland; Chicago: Rand McNally, 1965), pp. 3-34.

———, "A New View of the Infant Industry Argument," in *Studies in International Economics: Monash Conference Papers*, ed. by I. A. McDougall and R. H. Snape (Amsterdam: North-Holland, 1970), pp. 59-76.

Keesing, Donald B., *Trade Policy for Developing Countries: A Background Study for World Development Report, 1979*, World Bank Staff Working Papers, No. 353 (Washington: International Bank for Reconstruction and Development, August 1979).

Khan, Mohsin S., and Roberto Zahler, "Trade and Financial Liberalization Given External Shocks and Inconsistent Domestic Policies," *Staff Papers*, International Monetary Fund (Washington), Vol. 32 (March 1985), pp. 22-55.

Krueger, Anne O., "Trade Policies in Developing Countries," Chap. 11 in *Handbook of International Economics*, Vol. 1, ed. by Ronald W. Jones and Peter B. Kenen (Amsterdam: North-Holland, 1984).

Laker, John F., "Fiscal Proxies for Devaluation: A General Review" (unpublished, International Monetary Fund, October 21, 1980).

Laursen, Svend, and Lloyd A. Metzler, "Flexible Exchange Rates and the Theory of Employment," *Review of Economics and Statistics* (Cambridge, Massachusetts), Vol. 32 (November 1950), pp. 281-99.

Mansfield, Charles Y., "Tax Administration in Developing Countries: An Economic Perspective" (unpublished, International Monetary Fund, 1987).

Michaely, Michael, *Theory of Commercial Policy: Trade and Protection* (Oxford, England: Philip Allan, 1977).

Mundell, Robert A., "Flexible Exchange Rates and Employment Policy," *Canadian Journal of Economics and Political Science* (Toronto), Vol. 27 (November 1961), pp. 509-17.

——, *International Economics* (New York: Macmillan, 1968).

Mussa, Michael, "A Monetary Approach to Balance of Payments Analysis," *Journal of Money, Credit and Banking* (Columbus, Ohio), Vol. 26 (August 1974), pp. 333-51.

Obstfeld, Maurice, "Aggregate Spending and the Terms of Trade: Is There a Laursen-Metzler Effect?" *Quarterly Journal of Economics* (Cambridge, Massachusetts), Vol. 97 (May 1982), pp. 251-70.

Ostry, Jonathan, "The Balance of Trade, the Terms of Trade and the Real Exchange Rate: An Intertemporal Optimizing Framework" (unpublished, University of Chicago, August 14, 1987).

Razin, Assaf, and Lars E. O. Svensson, "Trade Taxes and the Current Account," *Economics Letters* (Amsterdam), Vol. 13 (No. 1, 1983), pp. 55-57.

Sánchez-Ugarte, F., and Jitendra R. Modi, "Are Export Duties Optimal in Developing Countries? Some Supply-Side Considerations" (unpublished, International Monetary Fund, June 16, 1986).

Stern, Nicolas H., "Optimum Taxation and Tax Policy," *Staff Papers*, International Monetary Fund (Washington), Vol. 31 (June 1984), pp. 339-78.

——, "Uniformity Versus Selectivity in Tax Structure: Lessons from Theory and Policy," paper presented at the World Bank Conference on Political Economy: Theory and Policy Implications, held June 17-19, 1987 in Washington (London: Development Economics Research Program, Suntory-Toyota International Center for Economics and Related Disciplines, July 1987).

Svensson, Lars E. O., and Assaf Razin, "The Terms of Trade and the Current Account: The Harberger-Laursen-Metzler Effect," *Journal of Political Economy* (Chicago), Vol. 91 (February 1983), pp. 97-125.

Tanzi, Vito, "Import Taxes and Economic Development," *Economia Internazionale* (Genoa), Vol. 31 (August-November 1978), pp. 252-69.

——(1987 a), "Tax System and Policy Objectives in Developing Countries: General Principles and Diagnostic Test," *Tax Administration Review* (Panama), No. 3 (January 1987), pp. 23-34.

——(1987 b), "Quantitative Characteristics of the Tax Systems of Developing Countries," Chap. 8 in *The Theory of Taxation for Developing Countries*, ed. by David Newbery and Nicholas Stern (New York: Oxford University Press, 1987).

_____ (1987 c), "Fiscal Policy, Growth, and the Design of Stabilization Programs," in *External Debt, Savings, and Growth in Latin America: Papers presented at a seminar sponsored by the International Monetary Fund and the Instituto Torcuato di Tella, held in Buenos Aires on October 13-16, 1986*, ed. by Ana María Martirena-Mantel (Washington: International Monetary Fund, 1987), pp. 121-41.

Tower, Edward, "Commercial Policy under Fixed and Flexible Exchange Rates," *Quarterly Journal of Economics* (Cambridge, Massachusetts), Vol. 87 (August 1973), pp. 436-56.

van Wijnbergen, Sweder, "Tariffs, Employment, and the Current Account: Real Wage Resistance and the Macroeconomics of Protectionism," NBER Working Paper No. 2261 (Cambridge, Massachusetts: National Bureau of Economic Research, May 1987).

Yitzhaki, Shlomo, "A Note on Optimal Taxation and Administrative Costs," *American Economic Review* (Nashville, Tennessee), Vol. 69 (June 1979), pp. 475-80.

Part V

Fiscal Policy Issues
in Selected Countries

12

Effects of a Budget Deficit on the Current Account Balance: The Case of the Philippines

Ahsan H. Mansur

I. Introduction

The purpose of this paper is to provide an empirical study of the economy of the Philippines during the period 1970-82, with an emphasis on external developments. Since the early 1970s, the Philippines has experienced external imbalances and very low levels of external reserves, caused by both adverse external developments and expansionary domestic demand. The expansionary role of the Government in recent years is believed to have contributed to the increase in domestic demand, and, as in many other countries, the authorities tried to reduce the external deficit through policies aimed at reducing the fiscal imbalance. Notwithstanding frequent attempts to restrain government expenditure and increase tax revenue, the national government's overall budgetary position appears to have remained expansionary, and the shift in the composition of government expenditure in favor of development expenditure with a higher import content has tended to exert more pressure on the balance of payments. In the light of these considerations, this paper examines the effects of the overall budget deficit and the composition of its financing on the current account balance of the balance of payments.[1]

The relationship between fiscal deficits and the current account balance has been variously examined in the literature; for example, Milne

---

[1]Throughout this paper, current account balance (deficit) refers to the current account balance (deficit) of the balance of payments, unless stated otherwise.

309

(1976), Tahari (1978), and Kelly (1982) tested the relationship between the fiscal balance and current account balance using ad hoc single-equation specifications.[2] These studies test the relationship in an ad hoc fashion that does not necessarily imply causality; such tests rely on the assumption that changes in the budget deficit are autonomous, when in reality they are generally endogenous.

Different ways of financing the budget deficit are also expected to affect the trade balance in different ways; the same degree of fiscal imbalance will have different effects on the trade balance depending on how the deficit is financed—from external sources, or the domestic banking and nonbanking system, or from a combination of sources. Simple testing, short of a complete specification of the structural model, cannot capture these interactions between budget balance, price level, domestic aggregate demand, and the current (or trade) account balance. However, before attempting to establish a quantitative relationship through a structural model, one should determine whether recent developments indicate that the budget deficit and its financing can account for a large part of the current account imbalance. In this analysis of the Philippine economy, recent fiscal, monetary, and balance of payments developments are examined to determine if fiscal policy was, indeed, expansionary and whether any causal relationship running from the overall budget deficit to the current account balance can be established. Based on positive indications from the preliminary observations, a small macroeconomic model is specified to simulate the impacts of alternative fiscal policies on the current account balance and derive their quantitative effects.

The structural model evaluates the effects of fiscal policy changes on the current account balance through changes in aggregate demand and the rate of domestic credit expansion originating in fiscal operations. In addition to specifying the transmission mechanism from expansionary fiscal policy to developments in the external trade account, this study focused on the structure of the real economy—that is, private sector absorption, income, or output determination. Fiscal expansion contributes to the increase in real output through increases in the components of aggregate demand, which affects domestic private sector absorption and, consequently, the demand for imports. The model used in this paper considers

---

[2]Milne (1976) used time-series data to estimate the equation $TB_t = \alpha + \beta(G_t - T_t)$ where the trade balance (TB) is regressed on the budget deficit; Kelly (1982) regressed the changes in the current account on the change in the overall budget deficit using cross-sectional data for a number of Fund program countries. Using a modified version of this type of testing, Tahari (1978) found a statistically significant relationship for some countries, including the Philippines, whereas for many other countries the result was negative.

the real and monetary sectors simultaneously and determines the price level endogenously.

In the following analysis of the effects of the budget deficit on the current account, two major scenarios are considered, based on differences in the sources of financing of the budget deficit. In the first, the deficit is financed by external borrowing or by banking system credit, with credit to the private sector restrained, so that total credit from the banking system remains unchanged. In the second, the deficit is financed by an equivalent net increase in credit from the banking system. The effects of alternative financing methods on the domestic price level, output, and revenue are also analyzed. Special attention is paid to macroeconomic developments in recent years (especially during 1980-82) through the use of counter-factual simulations in which the budget deficit, measured as a percentage of gross national product (GNP), is held fixed at a desirable level.

The plan of the paper is as follows. Section II presents some preliminary observations on the nature of the fiscal policy pursued during the period under analysis and on the causal relationship between the overall government budget deficit and the current account balance. Section III outlines the structure of the model. The estimated model, along with some of its empirical characteristics, is discussed in Section IV. Section V reports on a variety of simulation exercises based on the model; concluding remarks are presented in Section VI.

II. RELATIONSHIP BETWEEN CURRENT ACCOUNT BALANCE AND BUDGET DEFICIT: SOME PRELIMINARY OBSERVATIONS

In this section, movements in the overall government budget deficit and the current account balance over the period 1970-82 are examined; the simultaneous movements between the current account balance and the capital account balance and changes in the net claims of the banking system on the Government are also examined (Chart 1).[3] A casual comparison of the movements of the various variables seems to support the contention that the Philippines' current account balance has been significantly influenced by movements in the overall budget deficit, particularly during 1980-82.

The observed relationship between budget deficits and the current account balance may be examined more closely by subjecting them to more formal tests of causality and by determining the nature (expansionary or contractionary) of budgetary policy.

---

[3]For an overview of recent fiscal, monetary, and balance of payments developments, see Appendix I.

Chart 1. Philippines: Balance of Payments and
Fiscal Developments, 1970–82

(In billions of Philippine pesos)

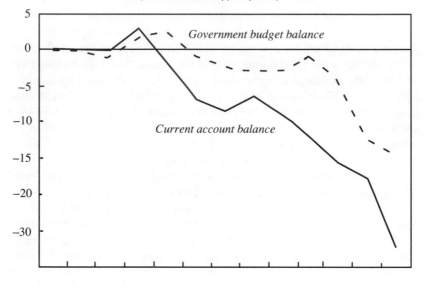

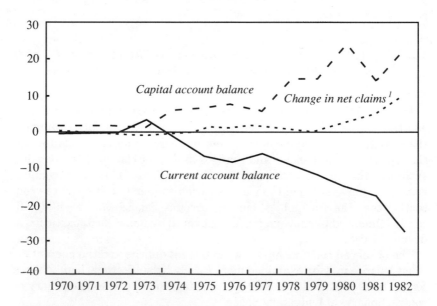

Source: International Monetary Fund, *International Financial Statistics,* various issues.
    [1]Changes in net claims in the central government owing to borrowing from the domestic banking system to finance a part of the overall budget deficit.

Comparison of the actual and cyclically adjusted (or neutral) fiscal balance indicates that in 7 out of 12 observations, the actual deficit was greater than the corresponding cyclically neutral balance, indicating an expansionary fiscal stance (Table 1 and Appendix II). When viewed in the context of stabilization, fiscal policy is found to be out of tune with the cyclical developments in the economy. In 7 out of 12 observations (in which trend GNP was used as the estimate for potential GNP for the Philippines), it was found that fiscal policy was not countercyclical.[4] In five instances when actual output was higher than the trend, the fiscal stance was expansionary or neutral after allowing for cyclical adjustments; in two instances, fiscal policy was contractionary when actual GNP was lower than the trend level.[5]

In several years, the net impulse from changes in revenue was expansionary, indicating a slower growth in revenue relative to actual GNP. In 1972 and 1975, however, when major revenue measures were undertaken as part of stabilization measures to contain the widening budget deficit, the revenue impulse was contractionary. In the years following the large increases, revenue increased at a slower rate relative to GNP, imparting expansionary impulses to the economy.

Total expenditure was more restrained in the second half of the period (1976-82); impulses owing to capital expenditure tended to be highly expansionary but were partly offset by contractionary impulses exerted through restraint in recurrent expenditure. Based on the summary measures discussed above, the stance of fiscal policy at the national government level was broadly neutral during 1970-80 and became sharply expansionary during 1980-82; this deterioration occurred despite efforts to increase revenue and contain expenditure. The shift in the composition of expenditure impulse in favor of capital expenditure, which is believed to be more import-intensive, also had adverse implications for the current account balance.

---

[4]Estimates of trends in GNP have been used as proxies for GNP, since official estimates of potential gross domestic product (GDP) are not available for the Philippines. An alternative measure of potential GNP based on the "linked peak" method was used by Riha (1975). Conceptually, trend GNP represents output levels that are attainable; and from a fiscal point of view, government expenditure should be tied to a level of economic activity that is attainable, rather than to some hypothetical full employment or potential level of output that may not be attainable in the medium term.

[5]Using an alternative approach based on Hansen and Snyder (1969) and Snyder (1970), Riha (1975) noted that in many instances during 1947-73 the estimated budget impact was destabilizing for the Philippines. Riha concluded that in periods when budget changes favorably influenced stabilization, much of the stabilization could be ascribed to fortuitous events rather than to cognizant policy.

Table 1. Philippines: Fiscal Developments Measured in Terms of Fiscal Stance and Impulses, 1971–82

	1971	1972	1973	1974	1975	1976	1977	1978	1979	1980	1981	1982
Actual GNP	49.6	55.5	71.6	99.9	114.3	132.7	152.8	177.7	221.0	265.1	330.6	336.2
Potential GNP[1]	49.3	56.4	70.7	100.2	115.3	133.8	152.5	177.1	216.3	263.2	304.1	341.4
						Billion pesos						
Revenue	4.9	7.0	9.4	11.9	16.7	17.9	19.8	23.8	29.5	34.2	35.9	38.2
Expenditure	4.5	8.1	10.4	11.7	18.2	20.6	22.7	26.2	29.7	37.8	48.1	52.6
Recurrent	(3.8)	(6.5)	(8.5)	(8.8)	(14.7)	(15.8)	(17.7)	(19.2)	(20.7)	(24.2)	(26.4)	(31.7)
Capital	(0.7)	(1.6)	(1.9)	(2.9)	(3.5)	(4.8)	(5.0)	(7.0)	(9.0)	(13.6)	(21.7)	(20.9)
Balance	0.5	−1.1	−1.0	0.2	−1.5	−2.7	−2.9	−2.4	−0.2	−3.6	−12.2	−14.4
Neutral revenue	6.6	7.4	9.6	13.4	15.3	17.8	20.5	23.8	29.6	35.5	40.7	45.0
Neutral expenditure	7.3	8.3	10.5	14.9	17.1	19.8	22.5	26.2	31.9	38.9	45.0	50.5
Recurrent	(5.3)	(6.1)	(7.7)	(10.9)	(12.5)	(14.5)	(16.5)	(19.2)	(23.4)	(28.5)	(33.0)	(37.0)
Capital	(2.0)	(2.2)	(2.8)	(4.0)	(4.6)	(5.3)	(6.0)	(7.0)	(8.5)	(10.4)	(12.0)	(13.5)
Neutral balance	−0.7	−0.9	−0.9	−1.4	−1.7	−2.0	−2.1	−2.4	−2.4	−3.4	−4.3	−5.5
Fiscal stance	−1.1	0.2	0.1	−1.6	−0.2	0.7	0.8	—	−2.2	0.2	7.9	9.9
						Percentage of GNP						
Fiscal stance	−2.1	0.3	0.2	−1.6	−0.2	0.5	0.5	—	−1.0	0.1	2.6	2.7
Fiscal impulse	...	2.5	−0.1	−1.8	1.4	0.7	—	−0.5	−1.0	1.1	2.5	0.1
Revenue impulse	...	−2.7	−0.5	1.2	−2.7	1.1	0.5	−0.4	—	0.4	1.1	0.5
Expenditure impulse	...	4.2	0.4	−3.0	4.1	−0.4	−0.5	−0.1	−1.0	0.6	1.5	−0.4
Recurrent	(...)	(3.8)	(0.5)	(−3.2)	(4.0)	(−1.0)	(−0.2)	(−0.8)	(−1.2)	(−0.4)	(−0.5)	(0.6)
Capital	(...)	(1.4)	(−0.1)	(0.2)	(0.1)	(0.6)	(−0.3)	(0.7)	(0.2)	(1.0)	(2.0)	(−1.0)

[1]Based on the simple regression of actual GNP on time.

Causality tests indicate that for both yearly and biannual data, the current account deficit of the balance of payments is correlated with the past value of the budget deficit (Appendix III). The line of causality runs from the fiscal to the balance of payments deficit, and the possibility of a reverse causality is ruled out for the Philippines on empirical grounds.

III. SPECIFICATIONS OF THE MODEL

Once the nature of the relationship between the government budget deficit and the current account balance has been determined in quantitative terms, a model can be designed that can explicitly establish the causal relationship between them. The macroeconomic model used as the basis for the simulation analysis consists of a number of behavioral equations explaining prices, output, and fiscal, monetary, and balance of payments developments. The basic model contains macroeconomic and monetary aggregates and addresses the central issue of determining the quantitative effects of the budget deficit and its alternative forms of financing on the current account balance and on the price level. Individual behavioral relationships are estimated in order to solve the whole system, and the effects of the policy changes are simulated from the solution of this system. On the fiscal side, developments in the broad components of government revenue and expenditure are considered; the effects of budgetary adjustments on the current account balance are specified so that their contribution to aggregate demand and their effects on the supply of, and the demand for, money can be observed.

1. Price Equation

Two alternative specifications for the price equation are considered. The first is based on the widely used approach to derive the price equation from the appropriately specified functional form for the demand for real money balances.[6] Demand for real money balances (broadly defined) is generally formulated as a function of the level of real income, the real balance in the previous period, and the opportunity cost of holding money. For developing economies like the Philippines, where a broad range of financial assets do not exist and the rate of interest is institutionally influenced to remain low—effectively implying a negative real rate of return—the relevant opportunity cost is the expected rate of inflation.[7] Us-

---

[6]This functional form is widely used in empirical work—for example, in Aghevli and Khan (1978), Khan and Knight (1981), and Otani and Park (1976).

[7]This assumption is valid for most of the sample period (1970-82); a process of interest rate deregulation was initiated in 1980 and was completed in 1983. Since then interest rates have been fully market determined.

ing the actual inflation rate as a proxy for the expected rate of inflation, the demand for real balances is therefore specified in log-linear form as

$$\log(M/P)_t = a_1 + b_1 \log Y_t + c_1\pi_t + d_1\log(M/P)_{t-1}; \tag{1}$$

$$b_1 > 0; \quad d_1 > 0; \quad c_1 < 0$$

where M is the stock of nominal money balances, P is the price level, Y is the level of real income, and π is the rate of inflation.

The price equation may be obtained by solving equation (1)

$$\log P_t = -a_1 - b_1 \log Y_t - c_1\pi_t + \log M_t - d_1\log(M/P)_{t-1} \tag{1'}$$

This specification, although ad hoc, can also be derived from an adaptive expectation scheme; the desired demand for real balances (M^*/P) may be expressed in logarithmic form as

$$\log(M^*/P)_t = \alpha_1 + \beta_1\log Y_t + \gamma_1\pi_1$$

Assuming that actual demand for real balances is a convex combination of the real balances of previous periods and the desired real balances of the current period,

$$\log(M/P) = \theta\log(M^*/P)_t + (1 - \theta)\log(M/P)_{t-1}$$

After substitution, this system reduces to

$$\log(M/P)_t = \theta\alpha_1 + \theta\beta_1 \log Y_t + \theta\gamma_1\pi_1 + (1 - \theta)(M/P)_{t-1}$$

which is equivalent to equation (1).

Other partial adjustment schemes for the demand-for-money function and adaptive expectation schemes for the expected rate of inflation were also examined, and none of the other variations, either independently or jointly, were found to be statistically significant in explaining the demand for real balances for the Philippines.

The alternative specification for the price equation is based on the notion that changes in the price level are due to three sources of shocks: the domestic real sector, foreign price movements relative to domestic prices, and domestic monetary developments.

$$\Delta P = P_t - P_{t-1} = a_1' + b_1'(ADD_t - Y_t^P) + c_1'(P_t^f - P_{t-1}) \tag{1''}$$

where ADD is aggregate domestic demand, Y^P is potential output, and P^f is the foreign price level. This alternate form was tested with Philippine data; except for c_1' all other coefficients were found to be statistically insignificant and the overall fit not satisfactory.[8]

2. Government Sector

Government budgetary developments are modeled explicitly to analyze the effects of fiscal policy under alternative formulations. For the purposes of simulation, a distinction has been made among three separate sources of fiscal revenues. Revenue from import duties is assumed to be a function of nominal imports; total domestic tax is specified to be a function of nominal gross domestic product (GDP); and non-tax revenue and export duties are assumed to be exogeneously determined:

$$\log TM_t = a_2 + b_2(\log IMP_t + \log PRM_t)$$

$$\log TD_t = a_3 + b_3(\log Y_t + \log P_t)$$

where TM is the tax on international trade excluding export duties, IMP is the volume of total imports, PRM is the unit value of imports, and TD is total domestic-based taxes.

This separate estimation of the major components of total taxes implicitly takes care of any potential aggregation problem that may exist when a single aggregate tax function is used. Export duties have been treated exogenously, because frequent changes in the tax rates and exemptions prevent a stable relationship between export receipts and export duties in the Philippines. Revenue from export duties has been mainly derived from export of coconut products; however, as the prices of coconut products fluctuated in the export markets, duties were adjusted to stabilize the domestic producer prices. Revenue from domestic taxes (TD) is the sum of all domestic-based taxes and is collected mainly in the form of personal and company income taxes and excise and sales taxes on goods and services. These categories of taxes are independent functions of GNP; thus, their sum may also be defined as an aggregate function of GNP without any problem of aggregation bias.[9]

---

[8]The estimated price equation in this form is

$$\Delta P = 0.04 + 0.054(ADD_t - Y_t^P) + 0.27(P_t^f - P_{t-1}) + 0.003(M_t - M_{t-1})$$
$$\quad\; (3.5) \quad\; (1.6) \qquad\qquad\quad (2.1) \qquad\qquad\qquad (1.6)$$

The t-ratios are shown in parentheses below the coefficients.

[9]The sum of the aggregate parameter vectors is equal to the estimate of the parameter vector of the aggregate equation, and the expected values from the disaggregated

(Continued on p. 318)

3. Demand for Imports

The demand for imports is specified as a function of aggregate demand, domestic prices relative to foreign prices, and a dummy variable to capture the shift in import demand that has taken place beginning in 1978. The aggregate demand variable (AD_t) used in the import demand function is defined as the sum of domestic private sector absorption, real government expenditure, and exports. In the conventional specifications, imports are generally specified as functions of income or output but are not sufficiently explicit to enable a distinction to be made between private and public sector contributions to absorption and import demand. The indirect effects of real income or output through private sector absorption will, however, be important and are captured in the proposed specification. Income or output determines private sector absorption and so plays the same role as it plays in the conventional specification of the import demand function. Moreover, a fiscal deficit generated through excessive public expenditure (financed by external borrowing or domestic credit creation), which is not directly related to GNP but is part of aggregate demand, also affects demand for imports.

$$\log IMP_t = a_5 + b_5 \log AD_t + c_5 \log(PRM_t/P_t) + d_5 D1_t;$$

$$b_5 > 0; \qquad c_5 < 0$$

$$AD_t = ABS_t^P + EXP + G_t/P_t$$

where IMP is real imports, PRM is the unit value of imports, ABS^P is private sector absorption, EXP is exports, G is government expenditure, and $D1$ is the dummy variable.

The aggregate demand variable (AD_t) has a positive effect on import demand and the price term has a negative effect. An increase in the government budget deficit through increased nominal expenditure leads to higher import demand through its effect on aggregate demand; financing the deficit through domestic credit creation increases the domestic price level to partially offset the initial expansionary thrust and its indirect effects on the demand for imports.

In an effort to establish a link between import-intensive development expenditure and import demand, real imports were regressed on real output (or aggregate demand excluding government development expendi-

---

equations also sum to those given by the aggregate equation if each kind of tax is explained by the same set of variables. For more on the problem of aggregation bias, see Theil (1954).

ture), relative price, real development expenditure, and a dummy variable. The statistical fit of real development expenditure was highly significant, but contrary to its expected sign. One possible explanation of this perverse relationship may be that the Philippines was under successive adjustment programs during most of the period covered in this study. During periods of high imports relative to exports, the Government, to reduce domestic and external imbalances, constrained current and development expenditure within certain targets, leading to a conceptually perverse, but statistically significant relationship.

4. Real Income

Reflecting the short-term nature of the model, real income is determined by the movements in aggregate demand for domestically produced goods in combination with capacity constraints. The previous peak level of output is assumed to be a proxy for the capacity output; capital accumulation, growth of the labor force, and technical progress, which are more important in the long run, are not explicitly considered. For the Philippines, however, this measure of capacity output coincides with output in the previous period. To take into account the effects of aggregate demand on output, two specifications are considered. In one form, aggregate demand for domestically produced goods (ADD) affects real output directly, so that

$$\log Y_t = a_6 + b_6 \log(ADD_t) + c_6 \log(Y_{t-1})$$

where

$$ADD_t = ABS_t^P - IMP_t + G_t/P_t$$

This specification allows for variations in real output through demand management policies, although the coefficient of $\log(ADD_t)$ is expected to be smaller than the coefficient of $\log(Y_{t-1})$.

In the second specification, real output depends on the output of the previous period and on the excess of aggregate demand over the trend level of real output (Y^*), where the trend for real output level is derived by regressing output on time

$$\log Y_t = a_6' + b_6'(\log ADD_t - \log Y^*_t) + c_6'\log(Y_{t-1})$$

and

$$Y_t^* = a_7 + b_7 t$$

This specification states that aggregate domestic demand in excess of normal output will temporarily increase real income, and any slackness in aggregate domestic demand arising from reductions in private and government demand will reduce output. The degree of responsiveness of real output to aggregate demand depends on the parameter b_6 and the size of domestic aggregate demand relative to the trend for real output.

5. Absorption Function

Private sector aggregate consumption and investment behavior are represented in terms of a single absorption function:

$$\log ABS_t^P = a_8 + b_8 \log DY_t$$

where ABS_t^P is private sector real absorption, and $DY_t = Y_t - (R_t/P_t)$ is real disposable income.

6. Fiscal Policy, Domestic Credit, and Money Supply

Government fiscal operations and the money supply are linked through the financing of budgetary deficits. In the absence of adequate nonbank sources, most of the domestic financing of the budget deficit tends to be in the form of borrowings from the domestic banking system. Changes in domestic credit (ADC_t) can take place through changes in the banking system's claims on the private sector (ACP_t) and on the government sector

$$ADC_t = (G_t - R_t - NFF_t - DNB_t) + ACP_t$$

or

$$DC_t = (G_t - R_t - NFF_t - DNB_t) + (CP_t - CP_{t-1}) + DC_{t-1}$$

where DC is total domestic credit, NFF is net foreign financing of the budget, DNB is domestic nonbank financing, and CP is credit to the private sector.

In this formulation, an expansion of the fiscal deficit not financed from external and nonbank domestic sources results in an equivalent increase in domestic credit. In economies where the financial markets are not developed, the option of nonbank domestic financing may be fairly limited.

The broad definition of the supply of money — which includes currency, demand deposits, and time deposits — is identically equal to the sum of the level of net domestic credit extended by the banking system and the net stock of international reserves (NR_t) — that is,

$$M_t = NR_t + DC_t - OTM_t$$

where OTM is the other monetary instruments not included in the definition of money in the present analysis.[10] Net international reserves should optimally be treated as endogenous to be perfectly consistent with the rest of the model. However, given the high volatility of the Philippines' net external reserves (arising from various economic and non-economic factors), a simple specification would be inappropriate. Since a detailed modeling for the determination of international reserves is beyond the scope of this paper, it is treated here as exogenous.

7. The Complete Model

The complete model has been modified slightly to capture some specific factors; dummies have been introduced in the tax functions to capture the shifts in revenue collection caused by substantive revenue measures introduced since 1975. The full structural model along with a glossary of the variables is shown in Table 2.

To elucidate the operation of the model, consider the effects of an increase in the government budget deficit, resulting from increased government expenditure and partly financed by an increased supply of central bank credit to the Government. This increase will have two direct effects: aggregate real domestic demand will increase, and so will the nominal supply of money. These direct effects will tend to increase the price level, real income, and real level of imports through different channels and feedback effects of other endogenous variables. Imports will be affected indirectly through three channels: (i) higher aggregate demand owing to an increase in real government expenditure; (ii) increased private sector absorption resulting from a higher income effect; and (iii) import prices falling relative to the general price level. The process will gradually reverse as increased import duties and taxes with domestic bases and a decreased stock of real balances reduce the budget deficit and private sector absorption; if the system is mathematically stable, imports and the current account balance will stabilize.

IV. Estimates of the Structural Model

Since the basic model given by equations (1a)-(6e) in Table 2 is simultaneous, the individual equations are estimated by the two-stage least-

---

[10]Based on the classification shown in *International Financial Statistics* (*IFS*) for the Philippines, the sum of net foreign assets and domestic credit equals the sum of money, quasi-money, bonds, and other items (net); the term OTM, which is used in this equation, is the sum of bonds and other items (net).

Table 2. Philippines: Specification of the Complete Model

1. Price Equation

$$\log P_t = \log M_t + a_1 - b_1 \log Y_t - c_1 \pi_t - d_1(\log M_{t-1}/\log P_{t-1}) \tag{1a}$$

2. Government Sector

   Tax functions:

$$\log TM_t = a_2 + b_2(\log IMP_t + \log PRM_t) \tag{2a}$$

$$\log TD_t = a_3 + b_3(\log Y_t + \log P_t) \tag{2b}$$

3. Demand for Imports

$$\log IMP_t = a_5 + b_5 \log AD_t + c_5 \log(PRM_t/P_t) + d_5 D1_t \tag{3a}$$

$$AD_t = ABS_t^p + EXP_t + G_t/P_t \tag{3b}$$

4. Real Income

$$\log Y_t = a_6 + b_6 \log ADD_t + c_6 \log Y_{t-1} \tag{4a}$$

or

$$\log Y_t = a_6'(\log ADD_t - \log Y_t^*) + c_6' \log Y_{t-1} \tag{4b}$$

where

$$Y_t^* = a_7 + b_7 t$$

$$ADD_t = AD_t - IMP_t$$

5. Private Sector Absorption

$$\log ABS_t^p = a_8 + b_8 \log[Y_t - (R_t/P_t)] \tag{5a}$$

6. Identities

$$ADD_t = ABS_t^p + EXP_t - IMP_t + G_t/P_t \tag{6a}$$

$$R_t = TM_t + TD_t + NONT_t + TEX_t \tag{6b}$$

$$DC_t = (G_t - R_t - DNB_t) + DC_{t-1} + (CP_t - CP_{t-1}) \tag{6c}$$

$$M_t = NR_t + DC_t - OMT_t \tag{6d}$$

$$TB_t = EXP_t - IMP_t \tag{6e}$$

Table 2 (concluded). Philippines: Specification of the Complete Model

Definition of Variables

Endogenous

P = price level
TM = nominal import duty
TD = nominal domestic taxes
IMP = real private sector imports
Y = real income
Y^* = normal or potential income
ABS^P = real private sector absorption
ADD = aggregate real demand for domestically produced goods
R = total revenue in nominal terms
DC = domestic credit
M = broadly defined supply of money
TB = trade balance

Exogenous

G = nominal government expenditure
PRM = import price index
t = time period
$NONT$ = non-tax revenue (nominal)
TEX = export duty (nominal)
NFF = net foreign financing (nominal)
DNB = domestic nonbank financing (nominal)
CP = credit to the private sector (nominal)
OTM = sum of bonds and other items (net)

squares method. The estimated equations are shown in Table 3, and the ratio of the coefficients to their respective standard errors are noted in the parentheses below the coefficients.

The price equation derived from the original demand-for-money function is statistically significant and has all the coefficients with the expected signs. The estimated coefficients indicate that an increase in real output and the stock of real money balances in previous periods reduces the price level, whereas increases in the rate of inflation reduce demand for real balances and raise the price level.

The equation determining taxes on international trade is statistically significant and indicates that the elasticity of import duties with respect to the value of imports is less than unity; this explains the slow growth of import duties in the Philippines as the value of imports increased over time. The statistical significance of the dummy variable (D_1) represents a shift in the import duty since 1975, when a number of new measures were adopted to increase import duty collection. The estimated buoyancy of

Table 3. Philippines: Estimates of Behavioral Equation[1]

$\log P_t = \log M_t - 0.527 - 0.231 \log Y_t + 1.025\pi_t - 0.863 \log(M/P)_{t-1}$ (1a)
              (2.08)   (2.42)   (7.13)   (10.31)

$\bar{R}^2 = 0.99$ $D\text{-}W = 2.65$ $F(3, 8) = 426.6$ $H\text{-statistic} = 1.18$

$\log(TM_t) = -1.83 + 0.87(\log IMP_t + \log PM_t) + 0.37 D1_t$ (2a)
          (−4.82)   (7.09)   (2.18)

$\bar{R}^2 = 0.99$ $D\text{-}W = 1.61$ $F(2, 9) = 66.2$

$\log(TD_t) = -2.329 + 0.947(\log Y_t + \log P_t)$ (2b)
         (−4.51)   (6.5)

$\bar{R}^2 = 0.96$ $D\text{-}W = 1.85$ $F(1, 10) = 267.9$

$\log IMP_t = -0.44 + 0.80 \log AD_t - 0.03(PRM_t/P_t) + 0.15 D2_t$ (3a)
        (−1.00)   (9.69)   (0.21)   (1.90)

$\bar{R}^2 = 0.976$ $D\text{-}W = 1.91$ $F(3, 8) = 88.41$

$\log Y_t = 0.34 + 0.29 \log ADD_t + 0.65 \log Y_{t-1}$ (4a)
       (4.44)   (3.45)   (7.25)

$\bar{R}^2 = 0.998$ $D\text{-}W = 1.88$ $F(2, 9) = 582.0$ $H\text{-statistic} = 0.19$

$\log(ABS_t) = -0.25 + 0.72 \log(Y_t - R_t) + 0.31 \log ABS_{t-1}$ (5a)
        (0.73)   (2.32)   (1.10)

$\bar{R}^2 = 0.97$ $D\text{-}W = 1.74$ $F(2, 9) = 188.7$ $H\text{-statistic} = 1.72$

[1] Figures in parentheses are the ratios of estimated coefficients to their respective standard errors; Durbin-Watson (*D-W*) statistics should not be taken at face value for the equations containing lagged endogenous variables.

taxes with domestic bases also appears to be less than unity, indicating a slackness in tax collection relative to the growth of income. These estimates also support the previous finding that expansionary fiscal impulses were being exerted on the economy through slower growth in revenue (Section II).

The specification of real output as a function of the demand for domestically produced goods and of real output in the previous period yields a better statistical fit for the Philippine data set, compared with the alternative specification containing excess domestic demand over the capacity output as an explanatory variable. Equation (4a) in Table 2 provides a better fit as a single-equation specification and also as an equation of the complete model, since the predicted values in the baseline simulations with equation (4a) are much closer to the actual values, compared with the alternative specification. Thus, in the subsequent analysis, equation (4a) is considered as the specification for real output. By allowing aggregate domestic demand to influence real output, this model allows for government real expenditure to influence real output directly. However, the elasticity of output with respect to capacity output (or the output in the previous period) is more than twice that of real output with respect to the aggregate demand for domestically produced goods and services, and thus, in the long run real output is determined mostly by the rate of growth of potential output.

The import demand function has statistically significant estimators for the coefficients of log AD and the dummy variable; the coefficient of the relative price term is not significantly different from zero, although the coefficient has the correct sign. The equation is statistically significant and the overall statistical fit is good. The estimated elasticity of imports with respect to AD is less than unity, and real government expenditure, which is a component of AD, affects the demand for imports directly.

V. SIMULATION EXERCISES

This section describes how the model simulates the impact of a change in government expenditure on the trade balance, prices, and output; the simulations consist of changing government expenditure in nominal or real terms by a certain percentage, with appropriate specifications for its financing, and tracing the impact of these changes on the rest of the model. Before conclusions can be drawn regarding the quantitative significance of fiscal adjustments, however, it must be determined how equations (1a)-(6e) in Table 2 perform as a system, compared with the observed historical data. Statistical information about the simulated values of endogenous variables indicates that all the equations perform well, both as individual behavioral relations and as a part of the complete model (Table 4). For all the equations, the means of the actuals and predicted values of the endogenous variables are very close to each other, and the standard deviations of the predicted values of endogenous variables are generally not higher than the standard deviations of the corresponding actual values. The goodness of fit of the baseline simulations, which is evident from the statistics reported in Table 4, is also reflected in Chart 2.

Starting from the baseline simulations discussed above, two general types of simulations are performed: (1) the case of a hypothetical increase in nominal government expenditure by 10 percent financed by borrowing from the domestic banking system or from external sources; (2) a simulation of what would have happened to the trade balance, prices, and output during 1978-82, if the overall budget deficit as a percentage of GNP had been at the 1978 level. The differences arising from alternative sources of financing are also considered.

1. Increase in Government Expenditure

The first type of simulation examines the sensitivity of the trade balance, output, and price level in the Philippines to arbitrary changes in the budget deficit through changes in expenditure. Consider two scenarios: government expenditure is increased by 10 percent in real and nominal terms. In the case of a real increase, the price level is assumed to be constant; in the case of a nominal increase, domestic credit will change, depending on the financing of the budget deficit. When nominal government expenditure is increased, the ultimate effect depends on the final real increase based on the endogenously determined price level. The effect of an expansionary fiscal policy on the price level depends on the financing of the increased deficit; it is most inflationary if the deficit is financed by borrowing from the domestic banking system, as the consequent increase in money supply increases the price level. The partially offsetting effect coming from the output response is also minimal in the money-financed case, because the final real increase in government expenditure is less

Table 4. Philippines: Summary Statistics for Selected Endogenous Variables, Based on the Baseline Simulation, 1970–82

Endogenous Variable	Mean Absolute Error	Post Mean Square Error	Mean[1]		Standard Deviation[1]	
			Actuals	Predicted	Actuals	Predicted
log P	0.06	0.08	. . .	. . .	. . .	. . .
log IMP	0.06	0.06	0.01	0.01	0.017	0.015
log TM	0.19	0.23	. . .	. . .	. . .	. . .
log TD	0.14	0.17	0.01	0.09	0.097	0.058
log R	0.08	0.11	0.09	0.07	0.070	0.050
log GNP	0.03	0.03	0.01	0.01	0.003	0.003
log ABS	0.03	0.03	0.01	0.01	0.010	0.003
log M	0.05	0.06	0.06	0.06	0.015	0.025

[1]Theil statistics, based on the logarithms of relative changes.

Chart 2. Philippines: Actual and Predicted Values of Selected
Variables in the Basic Simulation, 1970–82

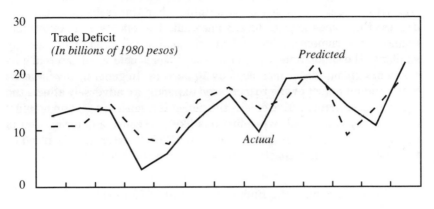

Trade Deficit
(In billions of 1980 pesos)

Predicted

Actual

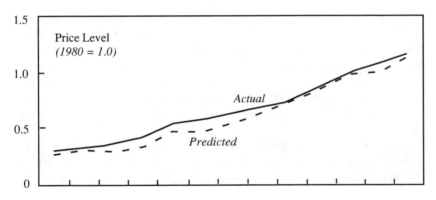

Price Level
(1980 = 1.0)

Actual

Predicted

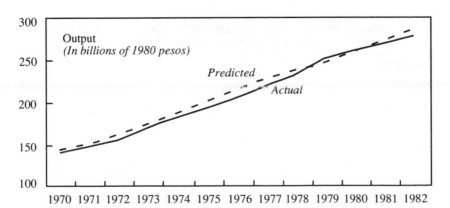

Output
(In billions of 1980 pesos)

Predicted

Actual

1970 1971 1972 1973 1974 1975 1976 1977 1978 1979 1980 1981 1982

than the initial increase. If the increased government expenditure is fully financed by external borrowing, domestic credit and the money supply will not change, and increases in output, other things being equal, will depress the domestic price level somewhat. The effects of an externally financed government budget deficit are qualitatively and quantitatively similar to the simulations where the price level is held fixed and real government expenditure is increased by 10 percent. In general, any increase in the budget deficit owing to increased expenditure adversely affects the trade balance, irrespective of how the deficit is financed; a certain nominal increase in government expenditure is likely to cause a deterioration in the trade balance in real terms when the deficit is externally financed or the price level is held constant (Tables 5 and 6 and Chart 3).

2. Effects of Keeping the Budget Deficit at 1978 Level

The budget deficit in the Philippines remained at about 1.0 percent of GNP during 1970-80, but in 1981 and 1982 it increased sharply to 4.0 percent and 4.3 percent, respectively. In light of the deterioration in the trade balance that arises when government expenditure increases relative to revenue, as pointed to in the simulations in Section V.1, it may be argued that a smaller deterioration in the trade balance could have been attained if the overall budget deficit had been held at the 1978 level as a percentage of GNP.

To examine the quantitative effects of any such adjustment in the budget deficit, government expenditure during 1979-82 is adjusted so that the measured deficit as a percent of GNP remains at the level of 1978

Table 5. Philippines: Qualitative Effects of an Increase in Central Government Expenditure

Major Endogenous Variables	Case A[1]	Case B[2]	Case C[3]
Price level	—	. . .	+
Trade deficit	+	+	+
Output	+	+	+
Revenue	+	+	+
Money supply	. . .	. . .	+

[1]Increased budget deficit owing to a 10 percent increase in government expenditure in real terms, holding the price level constant.

[2]Increased budget deficit owing to a 10 percent increase in government expenditure in nominal terms, with the deficit financed by external borrowing.

[3]Increased budget deficit resulting from a 10 percent increase in government expenditure in nominal terms, with the deficit financed by borrowing from the domestic banking system.

Table 6. Philippines: Impact of a Permanent 10 Percent Increase in Government Expenditure Under Different Forms of Financing, 1970-82[1]

	1970	1971	1972	1973	1974	1975	1976	1977	1978	1979	1980	1981	1982
Trade deficit					*Billion constant pesos*								
Original simulation	10.6	11.0	15.0	8.6	7.4	15.7	17.5	14.0	16.4	22.5	9.5	14.6	20.5
Scenario I	10.7	11.1	15.2	9.0	7.7	16.2	18.0	14.6	17.1	23.5	10.2	15.4	21.5
Scenario II	10.8	11.2	15.5	9.2	8.0	16.6	18.6	15.1	17.6	24.1	11.0	16.4	22.4
Output													
Original simulation	146.0	153.0	164.5	178.5	190.5	204.6	217.2	230.0	241.4	249.3	263.4	278.4	289.3
Scenario I	146.1	153.6	164.9	179.4	191.5	205.9	219.0	232.1	242.2	252.1	266.4	281.9	293.0
Scenario II	146.3	133.9	165.5	180.1	192.5	207.4	220.8	234.2	246.3	254.7	269.4	285.3	297.0
					1970 = 100								
Price index													
Original simulation	100.0	115.3	109.5	131.3	177.5	176.0	203.8	238.9	274.0	326.7	381.7	388.2	451.1
Scenario I	100.0	117.2	115.5	141.0	191.6	195.0	225.1	262.3	299.2	356.9	418.4	432.2	499.2
Scenario II	100.0	114.7	108.8	129.7	174.7	172.2	198.2	231.5	264.5	314.3	366.3	370.7	430.4

Source: Fund staff estimates.

[1]Original simulation refers to the basis run; Scenario I represents a 10 percent increase in government expenditure in nominal terms, financed by borrowing from the banking system; the case in which the deficit resulting from the same increase in government expenditure is financed by a net increase in the external borrowing is shown under Scenario II.

Chart 3. Philippines: Impact of a Permanent 10 Percent Increase in Government Expenditure Under Different Forms of Financing, 1970–82[1]

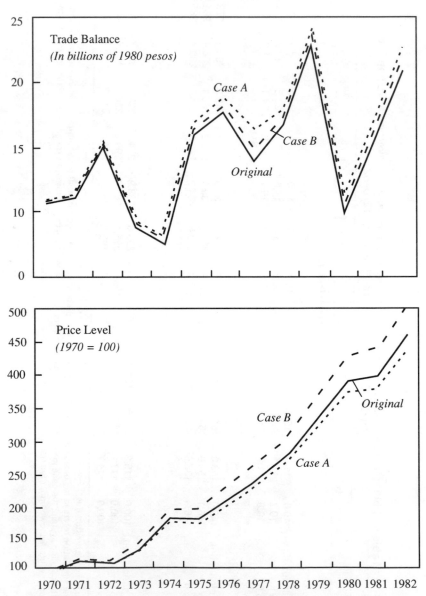

Trade Balance
(In billions of 1980 pesos)

Case A

Case B

Original

Price Level
(1970 = 100)

Case B

Original

Case A

[1]Original simulation refers to the basic run. Case A represents a 10 percent increase in government expenditure financed by external borrowing. The scenario in which the deficit is financed by a net increase in borrowing from the banking system is shown as Case B.

(in terms of actual data).[11] Qualitatively, the simulated impact of such a reduction in government expenditure is opposite to a hypothetical increase in government expenditure, as discussed earlier in this section. The hypothetical reduction would have led to a consequent reduction in the trade account deficit by about 10 percent during 1981-82, if prices remained unchanged or the financial surplus of the government were used to reduce external financing without any net effect on domestic credit; in this situation, the trade deficit in 1982 would have been 13.8 percent higher than that of 1978, compared with 25.4 percent without the adjustment (Table 7 and Chart 4). In a simulation where the reduced budget deficit in nominal terms implies a corresponding reduction in total domestic credit, the deflationary effect on the price level would have caused a smaller real reduction in government expenditure, and the consequent reduction in the trade deficit would also have been smaller. The hypothetical reduction in government expenditure would have improved the trade balance and exerted a significant deflationary effect on the price level, depending on the composition of the financing of the adjusted deficit. In any case, the simulations indicate a significant quantitative relation-

---

[11]The simulated budget deficit, however, will not necessarily remain constant as a percentage of simulated GNP, since figures for both revenue and GNP will be different from the corresponding historical data.

Table 7. Philippines: Effects on Trade Balance and Price Level Under Alternative Scenarios, 1978-82[1]

	1978	1979	1980	1981	1982
	Billion constant 1980 pesos				
Trade deficit					
Original simulation	16.4	22.5	9.5	14.6	20.6
Scenario I[2]	16.4	23.3	9.8	14.1	20.3
Scenario II[3]	16.4	23.1	9.6	13.2	18.7
	1980 = 100				
Price level					
Original simulation	71.8	85.6	100.0	101.7	118.2
Scenario I[2]	70.3	86.6	100.0	92.2	100.8
Scenario II[3]	72.0	85.6	100.0	102.2	119.6

Source: Fund staff estimates.

[1]In Scenarios I and II, government expenditure is so adjusted that during 1979-82, the measured budget deficit as a percentage of GNP remains constant at the level of 1978.

[2]The reduced budget deficit is offset by an equivalent reduction in net borrowing from the banking system.

[3]The financial saving from the reduced budget deficit is used to reduce external borrowing (net).

Chart 4. Philippines: Effects on Trade Balance and
Price Level Under Alternative Scenarios, 1970–82[1]

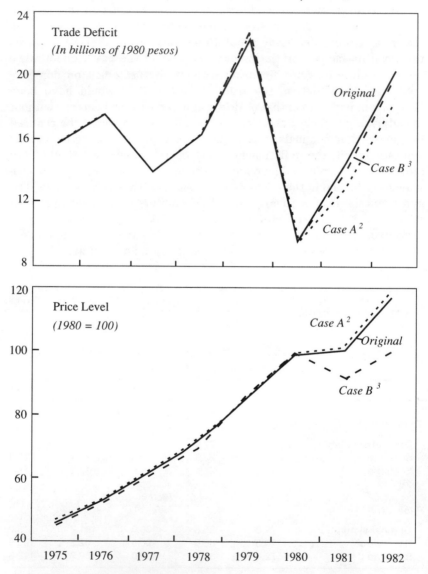

Source: Fund staff estimates.

[1]The original case represents the baseline simulation. In the other two scenarios (Case A and Case B), government expenditure is adjusted during 1979–82 so that the budget deficit measured as a percentage of GNP remains constant at the 1978 level.

[2]The reduced budget deficit is offset by a net reduction in external borrowing.

[3]The reduced budget deficit is offset by an equivalent reduction in net borrowing from the banking system.

ship between a change in real government expenditures and the balance of trade in the Philippines.

It should be noted that the sharp deterioration in the trade balance of the Philippines during 1980-82 was mainly attributable to the reduced value of exports caused by external developments. Merchandise exports remained stagnant in 1981 and declined by 12.3 percent in 1982 in U.S. dollar terms, with most of the decline attributed to lower export prices. In this paper, recent developments in exports have not been analyzed in any detail; they have been treated as being exogenously determined to avoid possible distortions arising from a simplistic or inadequate examination of the complex issues related to the determination of exports from the Philippines. The deterioration in the trade balance may be attributable to a number of external and domestic factors not covered in this study, but it can be argued that, apart from the adverse developments in exports, expansionary fiscal policy also contributed significantly to the deterioration in the trade and current accounts of the Philippines.

3. Relationship Between Simulated Real Budget Deficit and the Trade Balance

In the simulations considered above, expenditure was adjusted to certain levels and its impact on the trade balance, output, and prices was examined. In the basic model, tax revenue is endogenous to the system, depending on the nominal value of output and imports, so the overall budget balance is also endogenously determined. However, if the resultant trade balances are examined under alternative hypothetical situations, the simulations with a higher budget deficit in real terms, under all forms of financing, yield a higher deficit on the trade account in real terms (Table 8). When interpreting the results reported in Table 8, one should note that an increase in the real budget deficit over time is not necessarily reflected as a corresponding increase in the external trade deficit, because other developments not explicitly considered in the model may offset the effect of expansionary fiscal policy. If the data for any single year are observed and the impacts on the trade balance of variations in the budget deficit under different simulations are compared, a higher budget deficit (in real terms) corresponds to a higher deficit in the trade account; this is the only way the simulated budget deficit is allowed to change between the scenarios; other factors remain the same for the same year. It may be noted, however, that the effect of an expansionary fiscal policy on the trade balance is generally not as high as may be expected under the fiscal approach to the balance of payments; an increase in the budget deficit results in a less-than-equal deterioration in the trade account balance for the Philippines.

Table 8. Philippines: Comparison of Simulated Trade Deficit and Budget Deficit Under Alternative Scenarios, 1970–82

(In billions of constant 1980 pesos)

	1970	1971	1972	1973	1974	1975	1976	1977	1978	1979	1980	1981	1982
Basic Simulation													
Budget deficit	−2.2	−4.3	5.9	6.9	−1.2	5.3	6.2	4.1	5.5	3.0	6.1	12.3	11.6
Trade deficit	10.6	11.0	15.0	8.6	7.4	15.7	17.5	14.0	16.4	22.5	9.5	14.6	20.6
Scenario I[1]													
Budget deficit	0.2	−2.5	9.2	10.2	1.2	8.3	9.2	7.4	8.7	5.7	9.1	15.7	15.0
Trade deficit	10.8	11.3	15.5	9.2	8.0	16.6	18.6	15.1	17.6	24.0	11.0	16.3	22.4
Scenario II[2]													
Budget deficit	−1.0	−3.2	7.8	9.3	0.9	8.4	9.3	7.0	8.5	5.8	9.3	16.5	15.6
Trade deficit	10.7	11.1	15.2	9.0	7.7	16.2	18.0	14.6	17.1	23.5	10.2	15.4	21.5
Scenario III[3]													
Budget deficit	−2.2	−4.3	5.9	6.9	−1.2	5.3	6.2	4.1	5.5	5.2	5.9	6.9	7.4
Trade deficit	10.6	11.0	15.0	8.6	7.4	15.7	17.5	14.0	16.4	23.2	9.8	14.1	20.2
Scenario IV[4]													
Budget deficit	−2.2	−4.3	5.9	6.9	−1.2	5.3	6.2	4.1	5.5	5.5	6.0	4.6	3.6
Trade deficit	10.6	11.0	15.0	8.6	7.4	15.7	17.5	14.0	16.4	23.1	9.6	13.2	18.7

[1] A 10 percent increase in government expenditure in nominal terms, financed by borrowing from the domestic banking system.

[2] A 10 percent increase in government expenditure in nominal terms, financed by external borrowing or an equivalent reduction in the credit to the private sector.

[3] Government expenditure is so adjusted that the measured deficit during 1979–82 is constant as a percentage of GNP at the level of 1978; the reduction in the deficit is balanced through an equivalent reduction in domestic credit to the Government.

[4] Same as Scenario III, except that there is no net change in total domestic credit.

VI. Conclusions

Through empirical observations, testing, and simulations, this study has examined the responsiveness of deficits in the Philippines' trade and current accounts to changes in the central government budget deficit, with special emphasis on developments during 1980-82. Preliminary observations of the movements in the current account deficit and the budget deficit indicate a strong direct relationship between the two, which is also supported by causality tests. Fiscal policy was not necessarily counter-cyclical during 1970-80; during 1981-82, when fiscal policy assumed a countercyclical role, the fiscal stance was highly expansionary even after adjusting for cyclical variations. Based on these preliminary observations, a simple macroeconomic model was specified for the Philippines, which focused on the interactions of the government budget deficit and its associated financing with domestic absorption and imports.

Simulations based on the specified structural model indicate that an increase in the budget deficit worsens the trade balance significantly. A permanent increase in nominal government expenditure financed by borrowing from external sources causes the most deterioration in the trade balance; an equivalent increase in expenditure financed through borrowing from the domestic banking system is reflected in a sharply higher domestic price level and some deterioration in the trade deficit. The higher the inflation, the lower will be the real increase in government expenditure (given a fixed nominal increase in expenditure); the deterioration in the trade balance will be correspondingly lower in real terms. Simulations also indicate that significant reductions in the trade account deficit could be made if the overall budget deficit as a percentage of GNP were held at the level of 1978 by reducing government expenditure. If the financial savings were used to reduce net external borrowing, the trade deficit could be significantly reduced; if the savings were used to reduce the borrowing from the domestic banking system, the inflation rate could be significantly lowered and some modest improvement in the trade balance could also be achieved. Notwithstanding the strong relationship between the fiscal deficit and the trade balance, it should nevertheless be emphasized that the deterioration in the Philippines' trade and current account balances during 1981-82 was mainly attributable to adverse external developments, which reduced export receipts. The expansionary fiscal stance during 1981-82 further worsened the deteriorating balance of payments position. Fiscal adjustments in the form of a reduced overall deficit alone were probably not sufficient to reverse the developments in the current account deficit during 1981-82, but in any event, fiscal restraint was necessary to achieve a sustainable balance of payments position in the medium term.

APPENDICES

I. REVIEW OF RECENT ECONOMIC DEVELOPMENTS, 1970–82

In this appendix, budgetary, monetary, and balance of payments developments during 1970-82 are discussed in detail. This period was characterized by moderately high and stable real growth (5.8 percent a year), with successive subperiods of adverse external economic developments; to attain financial stability with a sustainable balance of payments position, the Philippine authorities undertook a number of short-term stabilization programs, which were supported by a series of stand-by arrangements with the Fund. The measures included limits on the banking system's credit to the public sector. Subceilings were introduced to limit government deficits to stated targets without recourse to unduly large external borrowing. Various revenue measures were adopted to improve the overall resource position of the public sector and to reduce recourse to domestic banks to finance the budget deficit. The overall budget deficit remained small during the 1970s, owing to these measures, but deteriorated rapidly during 1980-82.

1. Fiscal Developments

During the period 1970-80, the fiscal deficit was stable, averaging about 9.5 percent of expenditure, or 1.0 percent of GNP (Table 9). Revenue grew at a compound rate of about 25.6 percent, averaging 12.4 percent of GDP during the same period. Taxes with domestic bases increased at a relatively slower rate (22.5 percent) than taxes on international trade (32.5 percent). Thus, the share of taxes with domestic bases in total tax revenue decreased from about 78 percent in 1970 to about 62 percent in 1980; this decrease occurred despite a number of measures (e.g., increases in the sales tax, domestic excise duty, and income tax, and the introduction of a number of new tax measures) undertaken by the authorities to enhance the responsiveness of the tax system to domestic economic activity and to reduce the increasing dependence on taxes on international trade.

Expenditure (including equity contributions and net lending) increased at a compound annual rate of 23.5 percent, averaging 13.5 percent of GNP. However, current expenditure increased at a slower rate (20.5 percent) than capital expenditure (34.5 percent), and the ratio of capital expenditure to total expenditure increased from 15.2 percent in 1970 to 35.7 percent in 1980. This change in composition indicated increased development efforts in the form of infrastructure and other investment projects and efforts to contain current expenditure growth through expenditure controls on maintenance and subsidy outlays.

Table 9. Philippines: National Government Budget, Revenues and Expenditures, 1970–82

	1970	1971	1972	1973	1974	1975	1976	1977	1978	1979	1980	1981	1982
						Billion pesos							
Total tax revenue	**3.2**	**4.5**	**6.2**	**8.5**	**10.2**	**14.3**	**15.1**	**16.5**	**20.6**	**26.0**	**30.6**	**31.4**	**33.8**
Domestic-based	2.5	3.2	4.6	6.6	6.2	7.5	10.1	11.0	15.0	19.4	22.4	20.2	21.6
Income and profits	(0.9)	(1.2)	(1.0)	(2.4)	(2.8)	(3.2)	(3.7)	(4.5)	(5.1)	(6.3)	(8.3)	(7.8)	(8.3)
Goods and services	(1.4)	(1.7)	(1.7)	(1.7)	(3.0)	(3.9)	(6.2)	(6.5)	(8.7)	(11.8)	(1.2)	(11.6)	(12.2)
Other	(0.2)	(0.3)	(2.0)	(2.5)	(0.4)	(0.4)	(0.2)	(—)	(1.2)	(1.3)	(1.4)	(0.8)	(1.1)
International-trade-based	0.7	1.3	1.6	1.9	4.0	6.8	5.0	5.5	5.6	6.6	8.2	11.2	12.2
Import duties	(0.6)	(0.9)	(1.1)	(1.5)	(2.9)	(5.3)	(4.4)	(4.9)	(5.2)	(5.9)	(7.8)	(10.9)	(11.9)
Export duties	(0.1)	(0.4)	(0.5)	(0.5)	(1.1)	(1.5)	(0.6)	(0.6)	(0.4)	(0.7)	(0.4)	(0.3)	(0.3)
Non-tax revenue	**0.4**	**0.5**	**0.8**	**0.9**	**1.7**	**2.4**	**2.6**	**2.7**	**3.2**	**3.1**	**3.6**	**4.5**	**4.4**
Total revenue	**3.4**	**4.9**	**7.0**	**9.4**	**11.9**	**16.7**	**17.9**	**19.8**	**23.8**	**29.1**	**34.2**	**35.9**	**38.2**
Total revenue and grants	**3.5**	**4.9**	**7.0**	**9.5**	**12.0**	**16.8**	**18.3**	**20.0**	**24.0**	**29.3**	**34.4**	**35.9**	**38.2**
Expenditure	**4.1**	**4.4**	**8.1**	**10.4**	**11.7**	**18.2**	**20.6**	**22.7**	**26.2**	**29.7**	**37.8**	**48.1**	**52.6**
Current	3.3	3.8	6.5	8.5	8.8	14.7	15.8	17.7	19.2	20.7	24.2	26.4	31.7
Capital	0.6	0.5	1.0	1.6	1.2	2.6	2.9	2.8	4.3	4.7	8.4	12.7	9.3
Net lending	0.1	0.2	0.6	0.3	1.7	0.9	1.9	2.2	2.7	4.3	5.2	9.0	11.6
Overall balance	**−0.5**	**0.6**	**−1.1**	**−0.8**	**0.4**	**−1.4**	**−2.4**	**−2.8**	**−2.2**	**−0.4**	**−3.4**	**−12.2**	**−14.4**
Financing	**0.5**	**−0.6**	**1.1**	**0.8**	**−0.4**	**1.4**	**2.4**	**2.8**	**2.2**	**0.4**	**3.4**	**12.2**	**14.4**
Domestic	0.4	−0.6	0.7	0.6	−0.6	1.1	2.3	2.6	0.4	−2.7	1.2	6.2	11.6
Foreign	0.1	—	0.4	0.2	0.2	0.3	0.1	0.2	1.8	3.1	2.2	6.0	2.8
						Percentage of GNP							
Revenue	8.3	9.9	12.6	13.1	11.9	14.6	13.5	13.0	13.4	13.2	12.9	11.8	11.4
Expenditure	9.3	8.9	14.6	14.5	11.7	15.9	15.5	14.9	14.7	13.4	14.3	15.8	15.7
Overall balance	−1.2	1.2	−2.0	−1.1	0.4	−1.2	−1.8	−2.1	−1.2	−0.2	−1.3	−4.0	−4.3

Sources: International Monetary Fund, *Government Finance Statistics Yearbook*, various issues; and staff estimates.

The budgetary position deteriorated rapidly during 1981-82, reflecting both the operation of built-in stabilizers on the revenue side and expansionary shifts in expenditure. Growth of tax revenue averaged only 5.1 percent, and expenditure grew by about 15.8 percent. Taxes on income and profits grew slowly, owing to a squeeze in the profits of major firms engaged in the export of primary products; import duties declined as a result of a sharp fall in the growth of imports. Expenditure policies were partly influenced by the sluggish economy; although strict economy measures were imposed on current expenditure, equity contributions to the financially depressed public enterprises and accelerated implementation of the infrastructure program increased capital expenditure sharply.

Reflecting developments in the overall budget balance, bank credit to the Government increased rapidly. Net claims on the Government, which amounted to only 6.4 percent of total domestic credit at the end of 1980, increased to 14.6 percent by the end of 1982 (Table 10). During 1982, more than 36 percent of domestic credit expansion went to the Government; the corresponding share in 1980 was less than 8 percent.

2. Balance of Payments and Monetary Developments

Developments in the Philippine balance of payments have been characterized by steadily increasing trade and current account deficits. Deterioration in the trade balance during most of the period (except in 1973) was attributable to the rapid increase in imports (averaging 19.4 percent a year) relative to the growth of exports (averaging 13.8 percent a year) (Table 11). Notwithstanding increasing receipts from remittances, the deficit in the services account rose sharply during 1976-82, owing to increasing payments on freight and insurance and net investment income. Reflecting these developments in the trade and services accounts, the current account had deficits equivalent to 6.1 percent and 8.6 percent of GNP in 1981 and 1982, respectively. A steadily rising net inflow of capital tended to offset the developments in the current account balance, and the overall balance remained in surplus during most of the period.

Monetary policy was expansionary during most of the period. Total domestic credit increased at an annual average rate of about 23 percent during 1970-80; most of this rise was attributable to the nongovernment sector, since claims on the Government increased at a slower rate (12.2 percent). Government borrowing from the banking system increased sharply during 1980-82 from ₱ 6.3 billion at the end of 1980 to ₱ 22.0 billion by the end of 1982 (at an average annual rate of 87 percent); claims on the nongovernment sector increased at a rate of 17.9 percent, to ₱ 129 billion, during the same period. Money and quasi-money grew at an average annual rate of 20 percent during 1970-80 and continued to grow at about the same rate during the following two years.

Table 10. Philippines: Monetary Survey, 1970–82

(In billions of pesos)

	1970	1971	1972	1973	1974	1975	1976	1977	1978	1979	1980	1981	1982
Net foreign assets	−0.6	−0.8	0.1	4.8	6.6	2.8	0.2	—	6.7	−14.1	−20.8	−26.3	−44.7
Total domestic credit	12.8	14.3	16.5	18.6	26.1	34.3	43.5	52.3	65.0	81.4	99.1	122.1	151.0
Net claims on Government	(2.0)	(2.1)	(2.1)	(1.1)	(—)	(0.9)	(2.3)	(4.1)	(4.7)	(4.9)	(6.3)	(11.6)	(22.0)
Change in total domestic credit	1.4	1.5	2.2	2.1	7.5	8.2	9.2	8.7	12.7	16.4	17.7	23.1	28.8
Net claims on Government	(—)	(0.1)	(—)	(−1.0)	(1.1)	(0.9)	(1.4)	(1.8)	(0.6)	(0.2)	(1.4)	(5.3)	(10.4)

Source: International Monetary Fund, *International Financial Statistics*, various issues.

Table 11. Philippines: Balance of Payments, 1970–82

(In millions of U.S. dollars)

	1970	1971	1972	1973	1974	1975	1976	1977	1978	1979	1980	1981	1982
Trade balance	−26	−49	−125	275	−450	−1,196	−1,116	−838	−1,310	−1,539	−1,938	−2,223	−2,646
Exports	1,064	1,136	1,136	1,872	2,694	2,263	2,517	3,078	3,423	4,602	5,788	5,722	5,021
Imports	−1,090	−1,186	−1,261	−1,596	−3,144	−3,459	−3,633	−3,916	−4,733	−6,141	−7,726	−7,945	−7,667
Net services	141	187	158	−32	−34	−46	−257	−244	−166	−379	−542	−576	−1,196
Net transfers	119	134	188	230	277	318	268	262	314	356	434	472	474
Current account	−48	−2	5	473	−208	−923	−1,104	−820	−1,162	−1,562	−2,046	−2,327	−3,368
Capital account	241	244	281	258	853	1,094	1,197	988	2,138	2,116	3,269	2,359	4,234
Errors and omissions and other	−99	140	103	28	69	−182	−178	−214	−113	−143	−117	118	−672
SDRs	18	17	18	—	—	—	—	—	—	28	29	27	—
Overall balance	112	119	201	703	576	−11	−85	−46	863	439	1,135	177	203

Source: International Monetary Fund, *International Financial Statistics*, various issues.

This examination of the fiscal, monetary, and balance of payments developments over the period 1970-82 indicates that during most of the 1970s, the budget deficit remained low, as did the current account deficit. During 1980-82, financial stabilization programs were discontinued, the fiscal deficit and the associated domestic and external financial imbalances increased sharply, and the current account balance plunged to record deficit levels.

II. Derivation of Cyclically Neutral Fiscal Stance

Before one attributes the deteriorating balance of payments position to budgetary developments, it is desirable to establish that fiscal policy was expansionary during the period under consideration; even if the overall fiscal deficit is not expansionary, a shift in the composition of government expenditure toward higher import intensity may also cause a higher current account deficit. If none of these is true, deterioration in the current account balance may be attributable to private sector demand or to other factors.

The approach considered to determine the stance of fiscal policy involves adjusting the actual fiscal balance for cyclical effects in an effort to obtain a cyclically neutral measure of the budget balance. The summary measure used in this section was originally proposed by the German Council of Economic Experts and employed in the Fund's *World Economic Outlook* (1985).[12] The actual budget balance (B_t) may be decomposed into a cyclically neutral component (B_t^n) and the expansionary or contractionary fiscal stance (FIS_t):

$$B_t = B_t^n - FIS_t \tag{7}$$

$$= \underbrace{(t_0 Y_t^P - g_0 Y_t^P)}_{\text{normal balance}} - \underbrace{[t_0(Y_t^P - Y_t)]}_{\substack{\text{cyclical com-} \\ \text{ponent}}} - FIS_t$$

$$= (t_0 Y_t - g_0 Y_t^P) - FIS_t$$

[12]For more on this and other summary measures, see Dernburg (1975), Chand (1977), and Heller, Haas, and Mansur (1985).

where

t_0 = T_0/Y_0, base-year ratio of tax (t_0) to GNP (Y_0)
g_0 = G_0/Y_0, base-year ratio of expenditure (G_0) to GNP
Y = actual output in nominal prices
Y^P = potential output in nominal prices
T = government revenue
FIS = fiscal stance measure

The first two terms in equation (7)—normal balance and cyclical components—can be merged to define the cyclically neutral balance; the actual deficit in excess of the cyclically neutral deficit is deemed expansionary, relative to the base-year fiscal stance. To determine if the thrust of fiscal policy has been more expansionary relative to the previous year, the fiscal impulses (FI) may be examined by taking the first differences of the fiscal stance measure:

$$FI_t = FIS_t - FIS_{t-1}$$

The expansionary or contractionary nature of total budgetary expenditure and its components are also examined. Government expenditure is termed cyclically neutral if it increases proportionately with increases in nominal potential output; a more-than-proportionate increase is considered expansionary, and vice versa.

III. Causality Tests for Relationship Between Budget Deficit and Current Account Deficit of Balance of Payments

The causality test used in this paper is based on the method developed by Pierce (1977) and Pierce and Haugh (1977). In the context of this analysis, the budget deficit is viewed as causing the current account deficit if it leads the current account deficit over time; leads and lags between the two series, when both are transformed to their stationary forms, determine the direction of causality. Possible transformations include ordinary or seasonal differencing, lags, or, more generally, the power transformation of Box and Cox (1964), and certain types of detrending. The transformations remove the effect on a series of its own past values and convert it into a form in which consecutive values of the series are uncorrelated.[13]

---

[13]One might suggest that causal relationships between the budget deficit (BD) and the current account deficit (CAD) can be determined through their sample cross-correlations, or by regressing CAD on past and present values of BD and performing an F-test on the appropriate set of regression coefficients. Both these procedures (cor-

Table 12. Philippines: Cross-Correlation Coefficient Between the Budget Deficit and the Current Account Balance

	Budget Deficit	
	Previous Period $(t - 1)$	Current Period $(t - 1)$
Detrending (ordinary differencing)		
Yearly data	0.349[1]	0.460[1]
Biannual data	0.449[1]	0.188
Detrend (moving average)	0.347[1]	0.091

[1]The estimated coefficient is at least twice the value of its standard error.

The cross-correlation coefficients between the current account deficit and the budget deficit in the previous and current periods after the transformation of this data are shown in Table 12. The coefficients indicate that for both yearly and biannual data, obtained from the Fund's *International Financial Statistics*, the current account deficit of the balance of payments is correlated with the past value of the budget deficit; for annual data, the contemporaneous relationship is also statistically significant.

These significantly positive correlation coefficients indicate that, in a plausible behavioral model for the Philippines, a widening fiscal deficit caused by weak revenue performance or excessive government spending has led to a deterioration in the current account deficit; the line of causality runs from the fiscal to the balance of payments deficit.

An argument has sometimes been made for reversed causality, according to which a reduction in exports may lead to a fall in imports, which may harm government revenue and lead to a wider fiscal deficit. Examination of the data on the Philippines indicates that exports increased steadily in all years except 1975, when recession in the industrial countries caused exports to decline (Table 11). Imports, however, continued to increase, as did international-trade-based tax revenue. In fact, revenue increased sharply in 1975, owing to new revenue measures adopted as a part of the stabilization program. Thus, reverse causality running from lower exports and the consequent current account deficit to the overall fiscal deficit is not relevant for the Philippines.

---

relation and regression), however, can be misleading if autocorrelation is not appropriately taken into account; the types of autocorrelations normally found in the time series, if unattended, overestimate the significance of the tests and indicate relationships that do not exist. Consequently, it is desirable to make appropriate transformations of the time series to remove any existing autocorrelation prior to a cross-correlation analysis.

REFERENCES

Aghevli, Bijan B., and Mohsin S. Khan, "Government Deficits and the Inflationary Process in Developing Countries," *Staff Papers*, International Monetary Fund (Washington), Vol. 25 (September 1978), pp. 383-416.

Box, G.E.P., and D.R. Cox, "An Analysis of Transformations," *Journal of the Royal Statistical Society* (London), Series B, Vol. 26 (No. 2, 1964), pp. 211-43.

Chand, Sheetal K., "Summary Measures of Fiscal Influence," *Staff Papers*, International Monetary Fund (Washington), Vol. 24 (July 1977), pp. 405-49.

Dernburg, Thomas F., "Fiscal Analysis in the Federal Republic of Germany: The Cyclically Neutral Budget," *Staff Papers*, International Monetary Fund (Washington), Vol. 22 (November 1975), pp. 825-57.

Hansen, Bent, and Wayne W. Snyder, *Fiscal Policy in Seven Countries, 1955-1965: Belgium, France, Germany, Italy, Sweden, United Kingdom, United States* (Paris: Organization for Economic Cooperation and Development, 1969).

Heller, Peter S., Richard D. Haas, and Ahsan H. Mansur, "A Review of the Fiscal Impulse Measure, with Estimates of the Structural Budget Balance" (unpublished, International Monetary Fund, March 21, 1985). This was later published as *A Review of the Fiscal Impulse Measure*, IMF Occasional Papers, No. 44 (Washington: International Monetary Fund, 1986).

International Monetary Fund *World Economic Outlook: A Survey by the Staff of the International Monetary Fund* (Washington, 1985).

Kelly, Margaret R., "Fiscal Adjustment and Fund-Supported Programs, 1971-80" (unpublished, International Monetary Fund, September 28, 1982).

Khan, Mohsin S., and Malcolm D. Knight, "Stabilization Programs in Developing Countries: A Formal Framework," *Staff Papers*, International Monetary Fund (Washington), Vol. 28 (March 1981), pp. 1-53.

Milne, Elizabeth, "The Fiscal Approach to the Balance of Payments" (unpublished, International Monetary Fund, December 14, 1976).

Otani, Ichiro, and Yung Chul Park, "A Monetary Model of the Korean Economy," *Staff Papers*, International Monetary Fund (Washington), Vol. 23 (March 1976), pp. 164-99.

Pierce, David A., "Relationships—and the Lack Thereof—Between Economic Time Series, with Special Reference to Money and Interest Rates," *Journal of the American Statistical Association* (Washington), Vol. 72 (March 1977), pp. 24-26.

———, and Larry D. Haugh, "Causality in Temporal Systems: Characterizations and a Survey," *Journal of Econometrics* (Amsterdam), Vol. 5 (May 1977), pp. 265-93.

Riha, Tomás J.F., *An Evaluation of Fiscal Performance in the Philippines: 1947-73*, Discussion Paper No. 75-7 (Quezon City, Institute of Economic Development and Research, School of Economics, University of the Philippines, June 1975).

Snyder, Wayne W., "Measuring Economic Stabilization: 1955-65," *American Economic Review* (Nashville, Tennessee), Vol. 60 (December 1970), pp. 924-33.

Tahari, Amor, "Budget Deficits, Credit Creation, and the Balance of Payments: Empirical Evidence for Brazil, Philippines, Sri Lanka, Thailand, and Venezuela" (unpublished, International Monetary Fund, October 24, 1978).

Theil, Henri, *Linear Aggregation of Economic Relations* (Amsterdam: North-Holland, 1954).

13

The Inflationary Process in Israel, Fiscal Policy, and the Economic Stabilization Plan of July 1985

Eliahu S. Kreis

I. Introduction

The Israeli economy had been plagued by inflation for over 12 years (1973-85), and accelerating prices became a permanent feature. Inflation, as measured by changes in the consumer price index (at year-end), rose from less than 6 percent a year in the 1960s to about 13 percent a year from 1970 to 1972. After the October 1973 war, it accelerated to almost 30 percent in 1973 and fluctuated between 30 percent and 60 percent annually during 1974-78. Following the second oil price shock, prices rose by 111 percent in 1979 and stabilized thereafter, increasing by between 100 percent and 135 percent annually, from 1980 to the fourth quarter of 1983. The largest jump in prices occurred in the last quarter of 1983, when inflation reached over 480 percent (on an annual basis), and continued at this rate during 1984, when prices rose by 445 percent (Chart 1).

Halfhearted attempts to reduce the rate of inflation were unsuccessful, and over time, deep-rooted expectations developed that inflationary prices would persist. Although successive governments and finance ministers talked about the importance of reducing inflation, they were much more preoccupied with finding short-term political expedients and keeping unemployment rates at very low levels. As a result, the course of economic policy changed frequently during 1973-85, with the budget deficit (before grants) increasing steadily, hovering around 20 percent of gross national product (GNP) since the mid-1970s and reaching 26 percent and 29 percent of GNP in fiscal years 1981/82 and 1984/85, respectively. However, because the amount of foreign grants has also increased over time, the financing requirements have averaged about 15 percent of GNP since the early 1980s.

Chart 1.   Israel: Consumer Prices, 1981–87

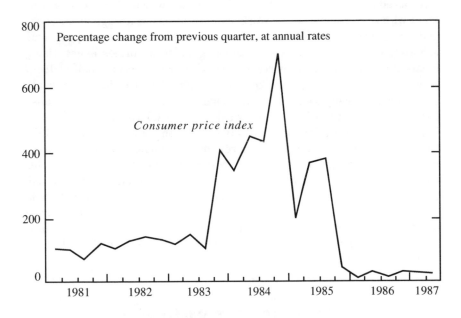

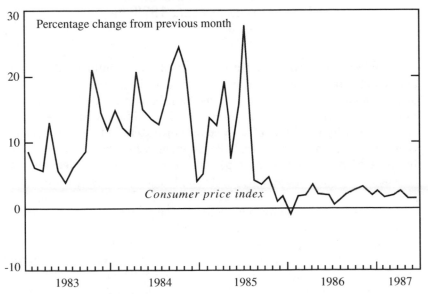

The National Unity Government, which took office in September 1984, introduced a series of disinflationary programs, which included an agreement with the employers' and workers' federations on a wage-price freeze and some cuts in budgetary expenditure. Although these programs achieved some initial success in reducing inflation, prices began rising again, averaging about 12 percent a month during the first half of 1985. Along with the rise in prices, the tax system almost collapsed, subsidy payments for basic goods and services increased, capital outflows intensified, and the balance of payments weakened considerably.

In response to the deteriorating situation, at the beginning of July 1985 the Government introduced a comprehensive economic stabilization program incorporating a wide range of fiscal, monetary, and incomes policies with the objective of dealing simultaneously with inflation and the balance of payments. Some action was also taken to liberalize foreign trade transactions. The results of the plan have been dramatic: the average monthly rate of inflation dropped from over 15 percent during the first half of 1985 to 2 percent in the last quarter of 1985, and to about 1.5 percent in 1986 and 1987 (Chart 1).

II. Characteristics and Causes of Inflation in Israel, 1973–85

The inflationary process in Israel over 1973-85 was influenced by many and complex factors, including the structure of the economy, institutional arrangements, defense considerations, high budgetary deficits, external forces, and the changes in policy measures. It would be impossible to measure or quantify the effect of each factor separately, but several explanations can be given for the overall developments. For instance, the persistence of high inflation during periods of contraction in demand and slowdowns in economic activity can be explained by the deep-seated inflationary expectations and inflation-proofing devices that developed in many areas of the economy in response to the protracted inflation. Some of these devices became institutionalized, such as the cost of living adjustment (COLA) arrangements; adjustments of tax brackets, pensions, and tax credit points; and the linkage of bonds, foreign currency clauses, and long-term savings. Furthermore, as inflation worsened, these devices improved through more frequent adjustments at higher rates. In periods of expanding demand, inflation rose in steps to new levels, as the surges in demand were automatically accommodated by a steady monetary expansion, which was quickly translated into price increases. These jumps in prices were further intensified by frequent increases in basic commodity and fuel prices and by exchange rate adjustments.

Another factor in the Israeli context is the heavy defense burden, equal to over one fourth of GNP since the October 1973 war. (During the mid-1970s, it amounted to over one third of GNP.) In addition, about one third of Israel's debt-repayment burden is defense related. Also, domestic defense spending is greatly underestimated, because it is difficult to quantify the real costs of reserve duty and the losses to the economy owing to the short-term diversion of manpower and resources to the defense effort.

1. Characteristics

Several characteristics of inflation in Israel over 1973-85 can be identified. First was its tendency to hold relatively steady for several years and then to jump to successively higher plateaus over comparatively short periods. Second was the large government deficit that affected most macroeconomic areas, particularly the monetary sector. Despite the high inflation rate, the deficit was financed mostly by the sale of linked bonds and foreign currency to the public and only fractionally by money creation. However, the Government also extended unlinked loans, the real value of which was eroded by inflation. Therefore, it is likely that the inflationary tax in Israel was negative during most of this period. A third characteristic is the lack of a direct relationship between the size of the government deficit and the rate of inflation, although it is generally recognized that the large deficit has caused the persistence of high inflation rates, either directly or indirectly. A fourth characteristic of inflation was its responsiveness to cost-demand pressures as the linkage between wage and price movements grew closer. Comprehensive indexation of financial assets resulted in inflationary shocks generally being accommodated automatically by the monetary aggregates. Fifth, given the large proportion of imported goods and products subject to price controls in the consumer price index (CPI), changes in subsidization and exchange rate policies caused sharp price changes, especially when these policy changes tended to aggravate inflation rather than reduce it. Sixth was the authorities' preoccupation with maintaining low unemployment and raising living standards, which made them reluctant to adopt appropriate anti-inflationary policies.

The inflationary process in Israel can be analyzed in terms of two sets of factors: those that exert upward pressure on the inflation rate and those that produce large changes in the inflation levels. The most important factor in the first set is the pressure on demand. The persistent large budget deficits create imbalances in the economy; in periods of flexible exchange rate policy, these imbalances protect the balance of payments but result in pressure on prices and are usually accommodated by the expansion of monetary aggregates. An additional source of excess pressure on the economy is the level of real wages, which is too high to permit full employment and a competitive external sector without also generating upward pressure on prices.

The factors responsible for the step increases in inflation are the indexation system, changes in economic policies, and internal and external shocks. Most economists now agree that the jumps characteristic of accelerating inflation in Israel are generated largely by price shocks stemming in part from external factors—including higher energy prices—but more importantly from domestic policy actions, especially changes in tax rates, the exchange rate, and the degree of subsidization of basic goods and services. Because almost all (95 percent of) financial assets are linked either to the CPI or to the exchange rate, any increase in prices, of whatever origin, is automatically accommodated by increases in liquidity and financial wealth; spending behavior is thus not constrained by real wealth effects as it would be in a non-indexed environment. The impact of wage indexation is much less important, since it is only a partial indexation and is carried out with a considerable lag. However, overall wage policy has played a crucial role in the inflationary process because of the large discretionary wage awards that have been granted—in some cases, to compensate for future inflation.

2. Causes

a. Fiscal Imbalances

The impact of inflation on the central government budget is not easy to measure, and this has occasioned much controversy in Israel in recent years. It is widely accepted that the large deficit has been primarily responsible for the persistence of high inflation, but not necessarily for the jumps from one level to higher levels. Although it is also widely accepted that only a sharp reduction in the budget deficit will produce the desired stabilization of prices, some economists disagree about whether the budget deficit's impact on inflation is direct or indirect. Essentially, the deficit is reflected in a deterioration in the current account of the balance of payments and through the accumulation of government debt, both of which lead to large devaluations and inflationary pressures. Some argue that a reduction (or elimination) of the budget deficit alone would not stabilize prices because of the inflationary inertia component that causes a downward rigidity in prices. Rather, synchronized actions in the areas of wages, credit, exchange rates, and prices are necessary to dissolve downward price rigidity and successfully combat inflationary pressure. Regardless of the methods used, it is generally agreed that a drastic reduction in the budget deficit is a precondition for a successful stabilization program.

The Central Government Budget Deficit and Its Financing. The budget deficits in Israel were very high in fiscal years 1979/80-1984/85. Although the amount of foreign grants almost doubled, and the sources of financing changed over this period, total government debt increased by one third to over 200 percent of GNP between 1979 and 1985. As a result, interest payments alone consumed about 35 percent of total revenue in 1984/85, compared with less than 20 percent in 1980/81. The large size of the deficits, reflecting the financial needs of the government, was the most important factor contributing to the development of the capital market in the country; it was the dominant influence on this market and also largely determined monetary policies. Since almost the entire domestic debt of the government was linked to the cost of living index or to a foreign currency, and since both the monetary base and unlinked financial assets made up a small portion of total financial assets, monetary aggregates accommodated themselves to the increasing rates of inflation.

Although no direct correlation between the size of the government deficit and the changes in the rates of inflation can be established, it is clear that the excess demand generated in the economy between 1973 and 1985 was manifested by inflationary pressures and balance of payments crises. Although initially the budget deficit may have been reflected in the balance of payments, the external imbalances eventually resulted in large devaluations and price shocks as a necessary means of adjustment; these, in turn, generated additional inflationary pressures—through the indexation mechanism and accommodating financial policies.

Of course, the way Israel's deficit was financed and the public's desire to save determined the degree of direct inflationary pressures. To the extent that the deficit was financed by borrowing from the private sector, it would not generate excess demand, although it would increase the domestic debt and future interest payments. Borrowing abroad would create more domestic demand but also result in a larger government external debt. The rest of the deficit would be financed by the Bank of Israel, but only partly through money creation and mostly through the sale of foreign currency to the public. During 1973-85, the Bank of Israel initially extended credit in local currency to finance the Government's domestic purchases of goods and services, but the public immediately purchased foreign exchange from the Bank, which led to lower international reserves and higher net external debt. During the years of high inflation rates, 1982/83-1984/85, a portion of the government deficit equal to slightly more than 2 percent of GNP was financed by money creation, while the equivalent of 6 percent of GDP was financed by purchases of foreign currency.

Impact of High Inflation on the Budgetary Process, Expenditure, and Expenditure Controls. The existence in Israel of very high and volatile rates of inflation for long periods has created major problems in the preparation, presentation, monitoring, and execution of the budget. During 1978/79-1982/83, attempts were made to restrict, or at least delay, the spending authority of individual ministries. One procedure limited, on a monthly or quarterly basis, the proportion of the total budgetary appropriation that could be used by the ministries. Another procedure left approximately 10 percent of the total budget as unallocated funds or reserves to be used, in part, to accommodate higher-than-planned price increases. Generally, these measures met with little success, partly because most budgets were based on price and exchange rate assumptions which invariably led to gross underestimation of actual rates of increase. Consequently, the practice of formulating a supplementary budget developed and, in the process, further weakened expenditure control procedures.

Over the fiscal years 1983/84-1985/86, the budget was prepared on the basis of prices in the first quarter of each fiscal year. However, even these constant prices were estimated a few months in advance. The expenditure figures were then adjusted quarterly according to various indices; these subsequent adjustments fully compensated for any underestimations in the previous quarter and allocated funds for the remainder of the fiscal year at a new, constant price level. These quarterly adjustments resulted not only in the validation of inflation but also made it difficult to determine the level of expenditure commitments. Indeed, entering into multiyear commitments in periods of high inflation created serious budget-management problems, since the accounting system had not been designed to handle this situation, and ad hoc steps had to be taken to monitor these commitments. Essentially, the only real control on expenditure was on cash operations through a monthly quota set by the Accountant General's Office.

Even after monthly cash quotas were established for each ministry, the high and variable rate of inflation directly contributed to expenditure overruns and a larger budget deficit. The process of raising and reducing the level of subsidies, transfers, grants, and loans helped create both open and repressed inflation. The desire to avoid a higher rate of inflation prevented or delayed the needed rise in prices of subsidized goods and services, resulting in larger expenditure and higher deficits. The higher deficit compelled the Government to cut subsidies and increase prices of public services, which, in addition to the direct impact on prices, was also reflected in higher wages and further price increases through the indexation system.

Revenue Collection. The experience gained over the period 1980/81-
1984/85 demonstrates that despite the measures taken to counterbalance
the impact of inflation, the net effect was lower revenue (although various
categories of taxes were affected differently). Only additional discretionary measures, including new taxes and rate increases, kept revenue from
falling even lower. Almost all taxes were collected with lags, which
ranged from a few days to one year. The real tax "losses" from such lags
increased with higher rates of inflation. As a result, it became very profitable for taxpayers to delay payments as long as possible, even at the risk
of having to pay high penalties. Also, the tax administration was likely to
deteriorate in periods of high and variable rates of inflation, since, under
these conditions, the accounting procedures used to prepare enterprises'
profit and loss statements make it hard to distinguish between real gains
and nominal adjustments.

The Israeli authorities introduced measures and administrative procedures to reduce the losses as much as possible and to cope with the problems of high and variable rates of inflation and tax evasion. Measures to
reduce the lag between the due date and the date payment is made included the pay-as-you-go system; deduction at the source of payment
(for example, deduction of a fixed percentage of the interest on bank deposits as income tax); and monthly payment obligations. Corporations and
individuals are assessed annual amounts based on previous years' earnings and must pay monthly advances. However, in most cases, these advances are adjusted according to the monthly rate of inflation. In other
cases, businesses must also pay a percentage of their estimated gross
sales (with estimates based on previous experience) every month. Substantial increases in tax penalties have been successful in speeding up tax
payments, particularly since both the penalties and the interest payments
are adjusted to the cost of living index and the penalties are not tax
deductible.

The acceleration of inflation during the mid-1970s posed a serious problem for taxpayers. As nominal wages rose, pushing up nominal taxable
income, taxpayers moved into higher tax brackets and their take-home
pay continued to erode. To nullify the inflationary effect, a 1975 tax reform commission recommended making upward adjustments in tax
brackets twice a year of up to 70 percent of the rise in the consumer price
index. From 1980 onward, tax brackets were adjusted upward four times
a year—by 100 percent of the rise in the CPI each time.

The increase in inflation rates also drastically eroded business profits.
As mentioned earlier, profit and loss statements of enterprises did not
reflect real developments, and attempts to exclude the inflationary component of profits were unsuccessful because of the complexity of the issues involved. Most companies kept their accounts on a historic-cost

basis—at nominal values. Tax was usually charged on the difference between recorded income and expenses. This difference included, in addition to actual profits, "inflation profits," which were mostly related to the timing of purchases and sales. To compensate for the taxes on these inflationary profits, producers increased prices faster than was necessary. Also, firms withdrew their own equity capital and replaced it with borrowed funds, which enabled them to treat the cost of credit as a tax-deductible expense. Meanwhile, they invested their own capital in government bonds, which were tax exempt.

Some tax-relief measures for business were introduced in 1980, according companies tax exemptions on nominal growth in the value of inventories up to a specified percentage of the CPI increase. Although this tax relief reduced the tax burden, it actually discriminated against firms with small or no inventories, which remained exposed to the inflationary tax. Eventually, to neutralize the adverse effects of inflation on firms' income tax, a special tax reform committee recommended, and the Knesset (Israel's legislature) approved, the Taxation Under Inflationary Conditions Law in early 1982. The adoption of this law resulted in a precipitous fall in income tax revenue from corporations and other businesses. It was estimated that these tax losses (beyond what was necessary to compensate for inflation) amounted to almost $400 million in fiscal year 1984/85, or about 2 percent of GNP. A special commission was set up in 1984 to revise this law and reduce the revenue losses to the Treasury.

Recent tax studies by the Bank of Israel indicate that the Tanzi effect on changes in tax collection amounted to 5 percent of GNP during 1983/84-1985/86. The average lag in tax collection in 1983 and 1984 was more than three weeks. With monthly inflation rates averaging 15 percent, the resulting revenue losses were about 10 percent on an annual basis. Almost the entire increase in tax collections for 1985/86 (equivalent to 6 percent of GNP) is explained by the rapid deceleration of inflation and the amendments made to the Taxation Under Inflationary Conditions Law which canceled some of the tax breaks previously extended to firms.

b. Indexation

During the 1950s and 1960s, indexation—which had been a feature of the economy before the State of Israel was established in 1948—was expanded to cover wages, contracts, financial assets, and prices. Initially, when the inflation rate was low, adjustments were made on an annual basis. But, during 1973-85, as inflation accelerated and indexation became widespread—covering mortgages, tax payments, tax brackets, social security benefits, credits, and the exchange rate—the periods of adjustment were also shortened; in 1984, adjustments were being made on a monthly basis. During most of the period from 1950 onward, the indexation arrangements were far from uniform, and there were large differences in the rates and standard of indexation, as well as in the frequency of adjustments.

It has been argued that indexation is essential if a democratic society is to function in periods of high inflation and maintain social stability. The Israeli indexation system was seen as a means of ensuring that no economic group would be impoverished. In fact, indexation enabled the public to avoid the hardships associated with inflation in other countries. However, others have argued that in the absence of indexation, no government would tolerate high inflation, and the existence of such arrangements permits the maintenance of policies that generate economic imbalances and inflation.

It should be remembered that wages and financial assets were originally indexed as a hedge against the erosion of their real values. In the absence of these adjustments in times of accelerating inflation, savings would not have been maintained and capital flight would have created conditions for even higher inflation rates. Nevertheless, it is recognized that the extensive indexation system hampered efforts to reduce inflation (even in periods of declining economic activity) and was the main cause for the transfer of price shocks to higher inflation levels.

The inflationary process in Israel appears to have operated with a ratchet effect during 1973-85. With each successive shock, inflation rose to a new level, and indexation then tended to perpetuate it at the newly established rate. This mechanism ensured that price increases were immediately passed into wages, the exchange rate, and back into prices, thus augmenting the effects of the initial shock. The indexation of financial assets meant that the growth of monetary aggregates was largely beyond the control of the monetary authorities and produced automatic liquidity expansion in line with increases in prices and adjustments of the exchange rate.

Wage Determination. The wage-determination process in Israel consisted of three components: wage indexation (cost of living adjustment (COLA)); centralized, negotiated wage adjustments; and negotiated wage adjustments at the sectoral, or enterprise, level. Wage indexation accounted for most of the wage adjustments, and changes in the frequency and degree of the adjustments, as well as an increase in the degree of indexation, reflected the acceleration of inflation since 1973. Whereas before 1973 cost of living adjustments were made annually, subsequently they were made semiannually and, from 1980 to 1983, quarterly. By 1983, the practice of granting monthly wage increases in advance of formal quarterly adjustments had become widespread, with the increase in compensation fluctuating between 70 and 90 percent, depending on the quarterly rate of inflation. (The higher the inflation, the greater was the increase in compensation.) In May 1984, the period between adjustments was reduced from three months to one month, and the increase in compensation to be paid was 80 percent when the accumulated rate of inflation reached 12 percent, and 90 percent when inflation exceeded 25 percent.

A temporary modification to this procedure was agreed to in the first package deal (November 1984), which stipulated that for three months, compensation for inflation would be limited to two thirds of the amount computed from the standard formula. In the second package deal (February 1985), the full standard formula was reinstated, but the effect on prices of the cutback in subsidies on goods and services under the 1985 stabilization plan was excluded from the cost of living index for February and March 1985. As part of the economic program announced in July 1985, the cost of living mechanism was suspended for three months, but special compensation awards were granted to offset the erosion in wages.

Cost of living allowances are supplemented by annual wage adjustments following negotiations undertaken by the Employers' Federation and the Histadrut Trade Union Federation. Until 1982, it was generally understood that these adjustments should, at a minimum, provide protection against erosion of real wages. During the 1982 round of negotiations, however, the principle of real wage maintenance was qualified, and greater emphasis was attached to the industry or economy's ability to pay. The third component of wage determination, sectoral wage negotiations, consists of specific wage agreements within sectors or enterprises and provides for some degree of differentiation in wage outcomes.

Because wage indexation does not fully compensate for the effects of inflation and is usually paid with some time lag, trends in real wages have been determined principally by discretionary wage awards. In fact, between 1977 and 1985, the COLA mechanism resulted in an erosion in real wages of as much as 14 percent annually; the real increase in wages during most of this period was generated solely by the large wage awards. Therefore, it can be contended that wage indexation has not been an important inflationary factor in recent years. It has even been argued that wage indexation in Israel may have contributed to, rather than hindered, real wage flexibility. On several occasions, the Histadrut agreed to forgo indexation temporarily. This happened most recently in July 1985, when the Histadrut, threatened by a Government emergency decree, agreed to a three-month suspension of the COLA mechanism. Such coordinated real wage reductions, it is argued, might have been harder to achieve in the absence of indexation.

Indexation of Financial Assets. Almost all financial assets in Israel are linked to the exchange rate or the consumer price index. Although indexation of liquid assets started in the mid-1950s, the proportion of indexed assets in the public's portfolio began rising in 1973, in response to the prolonged and accelerating rate of inflation, climbing to 85 percent by the end of 1984.

Medium- and long-term financial assets are almost 100 percent indexed. Because of the substantial deficits incurred by the central government since 1973, its domestic and external debts have risen to very high levels. In fact, the Government's dominance in the Israeli capital market reflects this. Indeed, a major share of financial assets held by the Israeli public is either directly or indirectly backed by the Government. Most of the funds of insurance institutions, pension plans, retirement savings plans, and other savings schemes are invested in government bonds. Foreign currency deposits and linked deposits have very high liquidity requirements (sometimes close to 100 percent) and, as such, enable the Bank of Israel to extend credit to the Government. At the end of 1985, 70 percent of the Government's internal debt was indexed to the CPI, 6 percent to the U.S. dollar, 11 percent to a combination of the domestic price and U.S. dollar indices (according to the saver's choice), and 13 percent to a basket of foreign currencies.

The Government's liabilities to the private sector are totally indexed, but there is also a large stock of unlinked private sector debt to the Government in the form of outstanding mortgage loans to households and industrial and development loans to businesses. Until 1979, these loans were not indexed and were subject to nominal interest rates well below the inflation rate; since 1979 only new loans have been indexed. However, although this practice yielded large capital gains and increased inflationary pressures in the past, its effect is diminishing because the real values of old debts are eroding rapidly, along with their impact on demand and prices.

Although some economists in Israel have claimed that the indexation mechanism guaranteed the continuation of high saving ratios, despite the high inflation, it is generally accepted that financial indexation facilitates and fuels the inflationary process. The scope of exchange rate policy has been limited by the direct and indirect linkage of large shares of total deposits to a foreign currency which, as a result of a devaluation of this currency, led to a faster rise in monetary aggregates and higher inflation. The authorities were then obliged to choose between loss of external competitiveness and increased inflation. If the exchange rate were appreciated, the attempts to return to the equilibrium level would bring about creation of excess liquidity and an increase in prices. Because of this linkage, the rate of inflation in Israel was — and remains — very sensitive to any internal or external price shocks.

III. FISCAL DEVELOPMENTS, 1979/80–1984/85[1]

Central government activities play a predominant role in economic and financial developments in Israel. The influence of the Government on economic activity is much greater than is indicated by the level of expenditure, which in recent years has accounted for over two thirds of GNP. The Government controls and directs economic activity through laws, regulations, ordinances, selective taxation, tax incentives and exonerations, and direct grants. Most of the operations of financial institutions are subject to regulations regarding source of funds and credit allocation. The capital market and new bond issues are controlled by the Government, since it must approve all domestic issues, most of which are in direct competition with its own large domestic borrowing. Also, the Government subsidizes various economic activities through direct financial transfers and low-interest credit. Finally, the central government greatly influences policies and activities in public sector enterprises.

During 1979/80-1984/85, central government expenditure and revenue averaged 68 percent and 45 percent of GNP, respectively. As a result, budget deficits (before grants) were consistently high, averaging almost one fourth of GNP during the period. However, because a substantial part (over one third) of the budget deficit was covered by foreign grants, the overall deficit (after grants) was somewhat less, averaging about 15 percent of GNP during the period (Chart 2). Foreign net loans — mostly on concessional terms — were an important source of financing over this period, although they declined from about 6 percent of GNP (over one third of total financing) in the first three years to almost nil in 1984/85 because of the switch from loans to grants in U.S. foreign aid. Concurrently, domestic borrowing rose sharply, averaging about 12 percent of GNP. However, although until 1981/82 a sizable part of this amount was mobilized through domestic bond sales, net credit by the Bank of Israel to the central government subsequently increased sharply. Excluding government indebtedness to the Bank of Israel, the overall government debt increased from about 160 percent of GNP in 1979/80 to an estimated 215 percent of GNP in 1984/85,[2] with internal debt accounting for about two thirds of the total. In the same period, interest payments rose from less than 5 percent of GNP to 15 percent of GNP.

Following the second oil price shock and rapidly accelerating prices in 1979, the Government, in fiscal year 1980/81, introduced a stabilization

---

[1]The fiscal year in Israel runs from April 1 through March 31.
[2]Average level of debt during fiscal year as proportion of GNP.

Chart 2.   Israel: Central Government Operations, 1979/80–1986/87

(As percentage of GNP)[1]

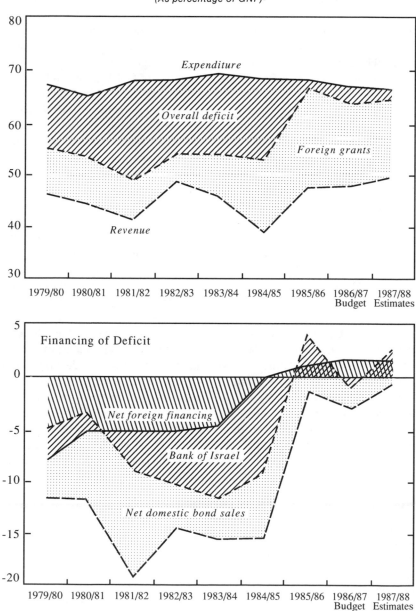

Source: Data provided by the Israeli Ministry of Finance.
[1]GNP data adjusted to fiscal-year (April–March) basis.

program which included sharp cuts in budget subsidies and other transfer payments, cuts in real wages, and an increase in taxes. But despite these efforts, the outturn continued to be expansionary; notwithstanding a reduction in total expenditure equivalent to 2 percentage points of GNP and the slowing of the rapid increase in public employment, revenue collection declined by a corresponding amount and the budget deficit (before grants) stayed, in 1980/81, somewhat above 20 percent of GNP, the same level as in the previous two years. The fiscal situation deteriorated sharply in 1981/82, when the budget deficit rose to over 26 percent of GNP, as total revenue fell further, by an amount equivalent to 3 percentage points of GNP and total expenditure increased by the same amount. The deterioration stemmed from an attempt by the Government to combat inflation through slower devaluation, a reduction in tax rates, and an increase in subsidies on basic products. Subsidies alone increased from the equivalent of $550 million in 1980/81 to $1.5 billion in 1981/82, or by 3.5 percentage points of GNP (Table 1).

The large budget deficit and the outbreak of hostilities in Lebanon prompted the Government to take strong fiscal measures, which resulted in a strong improvement of the fiscal performance in 1982/83, when the budget deficit declined by 7 percentage points, to 19 percent of GNP. The entire improvement came from revenue, and it was almost equally shared between tax and non-tax revenue. The increase in taxes was due chiefly to new tax measures introduced in midyear. Also, to counteract the expansionary influence of the larger domestic defense spending, expenditure for subsidies and transfer payments was reduced considerably. The fiscal position deteriorated again over the next two years, with the budget deficit rising sharply in 1984/85, reaching 29 percent of GNP because of a 7 percentage point fall in revenue, while expenditure declined only marginally. However, although the total expenditure ratio declined slightly, the composition shifted substantially as capital outlay fell by 3.5 percentage points of GNP and interest payments rose by a similar magnitude. Foreign grants almost doubled to 14 percent of GNP in 1984/85, compared with the annual average of the previous five years.

Notwithstanding this substantial increase in grants, the ratio of the deficit (after grants) to GNP still remained high at over 15 percent in 1984/85, similar to the ratios registered in 1982/83-1983/84. As the share of net foreign borrowing in total financing declined during the period beginning with 1980/81, domestic borrowing needs rose even more steeply than total financing, reaching over 15 percent of GNP in 1984/85.

While a sizable part of domestic financing was mobilized through the issuance of long-term bonds—principally the nonmarketables, which the National Insurance Institute (NII), pension funds, insurance companies, and commercial banks were required to purchase—net credit from the Bank of Israel to the central government rose dramatically. Starting in

Table 1. Israel: Developments in Main Budget Aggregates, 1978/79–1986/87[1]

(In percent of GNP)[2]

	1978/79	1979/80	1980/81	1981/82	1982/83	1983/84	1984/85	1985/86	Budget Proposal 1986/87	Estimate 1986/87
Total revenue	**44.7**	**46.5**	**44.3**	**41.5**	**48.7**	**45.9**	**38.8**	**47.3**	**47.8**	**49.5**
Tax revenue	38.7	39.5	35.7	35.3	38.8	37.5	34.1	39.9	40.4	44.0
Tax on incomes, profits, and capital gains	18.2	20.0	18.6	19.4	18.4	17.9	15.9	17.9	19.2	20.4
Value-added tax	8.2	7.7	6.8	7.8	8.8	9.1	7.9	10.4	10.5	11.6
Other taxes	12.3	11.8	10.3	8.1	11.6	10.5	10.3	11.6	10.7	12.0
Other	6.0	7.0	8.6	6.2	9.9	8.4	4.7	7.4	7.4	5.5
Total expenditure	**64.7**	**67.2**	**64.8**	**67.8**	**68.0**	**69.3**	**68.0**	**67.9**	**66.5**	**65.8**
Civilian	42.4	40.5	40.7	46.2	47.5	48.3	46.7	45.9	47.1	46.0
Domestic	39.4	37.9	37.5	43.2	42.2	42.7	38.9	38.5	40.3	39.5
Wages	6.3	6.2	5.8	5.8	5.4	5.1	5.1	4.6	4.5	4.5
Purchases	3.3	3.8	1.8	2.1	2.9	3.0	2.3	2.7	2.1	3.1
Transfer payments	9.7	8.3	9.7	9.8	11.3	9.9	9.2	9.2	9.4	13.1
Subsidies[3]	4.5	4.7	5.4	8.8	5.6	6.7	7.3	5.5	4.0	3.6
Interest payments	5.1	2.6	3.0	6.6	6.3	6.3	7.6	9.1	8.3	7.7
Capital and net lending	7.1	8.9	8.4	8.2	7.9	9.5	5.9	5.7	5.4	5.8
Other	3.4	3.4	3.4	1.9	2.8	2.2	1.5	1.7	6.6[4]	1.7
Abroad	3.0	2.6	3.2	3.0	5.3	5.6	7.8	7.4	6.8	6.5
Of which: Interest	(2.6)	(8.1)	(2.9)	(2.8)	(5.0)	(5.3)	(7.1)	(6.9)	(5.8)	(5.8)

Table 1 (concluded). Israel: Developments in Main Budget Aggregates, 1978/79–1986/87[1]

(In percent of GNP)[2]

	1978/79	1979/80	1980/81	1981/82	1982/83	1983/84	1984/85	1985/86	Budget Proposal 1986/87	Estimate 1986/87
Defense	22.3	26.7	24.1	21.6	20.5	21.0	21.3	22.0	19.4	19.8
Domestic	12.6	13.7	12.8	12.8	14.4	11.8	11.0	11.8	11.4	11.3
Wages	4.1	4.7	4.2	4.0	4.5	3.3	3.8	3.9	3.8	3.7
Purchases	6.7	6.8	6.4	6.8	8.0	6.5	6.0	6.7	6.6	6.8
Other[5]	1.8	2.2	2.2	2.0	1.9	2.0	1.2	1.2	1.0	0.8
Abroad	9.7	13.0	11.3	8.8	6.1	9.2	10.3	10.2	8.0	8.5
Budget balance	**– 20.0**	**– 20.4**	**– 20.5**	**– 26.3**	**– 19.3**	**– 23.4**	**– 29.2**	**– 20.6**	**– 18.7**	**– 15.0**
Foreign grants	5.9	8.9	8.9	7.3	5.0	8.0	13.9	19.3	15.7	15.7
Financing requirement	**– 14.1**	**– 11.5**	**– 11.6**	**– 19.0**	**– 14.3**	**– 15.4**	**– 15.3**	**– 1.3**	**– 3.0**	**– 0.6**
Foreign borrowing, net	9.0	8.0	4.9	5.0	5.1	4.5	0.1	– 1.1	– 1.6	– 1.5
Domestic bonds, net	5.1	6.7	8.3	10.3	3.9	3.9	6.2	5.1	4.1	3.2
Bank of Israel, net	—	– 3.2	– 1.6	3.7	5.3	7.0	9.0	– 2.7	0.5	– 1.1
Memorandum items:										
Domestic deficit	– 7.3	– 5.1	– 6.0	– 14.5	– 8.7	– 9.4	– 12.3	– 4.5	– 3.9	– 2.6
Foreign deficit (*after grants*)	– 6.8	– 6.4	– 5.6	– 4.5	– 5.6	– 6.0	– 3.0	3.2	0.9	2.0

Source: Compilation from information provided by the Israeli Ministry of Finance.
[1]Fiscal year, April 1 to March 31.
[2]GNP in fiscal years.
[3]Excludes interest subsidies.
[4]Includes unallocated expenditures.
[5]Includes transfers.

1982/83, net bond issues, especially those sold to the general public, fell rapidly as a percentage of GNP, reflecting difficulties encountered in raising funds on the domestic capital market. The weakening in the public's demand for domestic bonds also reflected its preference for financial assets denominated in foreign currencies and, until September 1984, some uncertainty about the real rate of return on government-backed savings schemes. Accordingly, greater reliance was placed on borrowing from the Bank of Israel to finance the budget deficit, and net use of the Bank of Israel's resources rose dramatically, from almost 2 percent of GNP in 1980/81 to 9 percent of GNP in 1984/85. (See Table 1.) However, despite this sharp increase, money creation was almost constant, averaging less than 2.5 percent of GNP annually between 1979/80 and 1984/85. The entire increase was funded by sales of foreign exchange to the public and a drawdown of net international reserves.

IV. DISINFLATIONARY PROGRAMS IN 1984 AND 1985, AND THE ECONOMIC STABILIZATION PLAN OF JULY 1985

1. Acceleration of Inflation

After remaining more or less stable at 120-130 percent annually between the fourth quarter of 1979 and the third quarter of 1983, inflation accelerated sharply, to 16 percent a month (490 percent annually), during the last quarter of 1983. This acceleration was accompanied by a substantial decline in real income, a weakening of domestic demand, a slowdown in economic activity, and only a moderate improvement in the balance of payments. Moreover, because of the lack of confidence in government economic policies and increasing expectations of large devaluations, the public purchased large amounts of foreign currency (equivalent to over 7 percent of gross domestic product (GDP) in the last quarter of 1983) from the Bank of Israel, and there was a massive shift into exchange rate-linked deposits. Under these circumstances, the most important task faced by the authorities was to shore up the Government's credibility and regain public confidence. Nevertheless, despite all measures taken from October 1983 to March 1984, the authorities were only able to check the acceleration of inflation and stabilize it at a monthly rate of 13 percent during the first quarter of 1984, or over 300 percent at an annual rate.

The decision to hold early elections in July 1984 and the corresponding changes in government policy again caused a loss of confidence, and public purchases of foreign exchange grew rapidly. The Government responded with a large devaluation and administrative restrictions on imports. Inflation shot up to over 500 percent at an annual rate during the second and third quarters of the year (Table 2). Similar measures were introduced again after the elections by the new National Unity Government in September, and inflation reached a record level of 24 percent in October (over 1,200 percent at an annual rate). Fears of hyperinflation prompted representatives of the Government, the labor unions, and employers' organizations to sign an agreement calling for the stabilization of prices, wages, profits, and taxes, and reduction of inflationary expectations and inflation. This agreement, known as the first "package deal," was followed by two other package deals and, finally, by the economic stabilization plan.

2. Package Deal I

Given previous experience, considerable skepticism was expressed about the potential success of a package deal that was not backed up by other necessary policy adjustments, such as cuts in government spending. However, the sense of urgency shared by all social sectors—including workers, industrialists, and political leaders—contributed to its initial success. The package deal was aimed at achieving a large and rapid drop in the inflation rate in order to calm markets while more fundamental measures were being put in place. Its principal provisions were a general price freeze and a three-month reduction in the COLA indexation to two thirds of the standard compensation for inflation. The Government agreed not to introduce new taxes or raise existing rates during the period of the freeze; and increases in rates or fees in the public sector that had already been approved were not to be implemented until the freeze ended. Prices of all imported goods and services were frozen at their levels of November 2, 1984, and payments of all import duties and taxes tied to foreign exchange were fixed at that rate. The Government also committed itself to lowering the budget deficit, partly through fiscal reforms related principally to the tax system, and to cut income tax payments by 5 percent over the three-month period commencing February 1985.

The formal agreement did not include any reference to prices of controlled goods and services, interest rates, or exchange rate adjustments, but it soon became clear after the deal went into effect that prices of subsidized goods would also be frozen, nominal interest rates lowered, and the nominal rate of depreciation of the shekel slowed; however, when the inflation rate began to abate, real interest rates rose significantly and the real effective exchange rate declined.

Because the price freeze did not become effective until November 5, 1984, and many prices were hiked in expectation, consumer prices rose strongly in early November (19.5 percent). However, from the beginning of November until the end of January 1985, prices rose at a relatively moderate 4.5 percent a month. This sharp cutback was important in calming speculation, but it was nevertheless widely recognized that the mea-

Table 2. Israel: Selected Quarterly Economic Indicators, 1982-87

(Percentage changes, unless otherwise indicated)

	1982				1983				1984				1985				1986				Preliminary 1987	
	I	II	III	IV	I	II	III	IV	I	II	III	IV	I	II	III	IV	I	II	III	IV	I	II
Prices *(quarterly on annual basis)*	109	141	158	120	118	135	137	487	311	496	536	565	222	361	247	29	7.5	29.6	12.6	30.0	19.3	16.5
GDP *(seasonally adjusted data, at 1980 prices)*	0.8	-2.2	0.7	4.4	0.6	-1.4	-0.1	0.8	-0.6	-0.8	6.0	-1.0	2.5	1.3	-2.1	-5.7	5.7	1.1	-2.2	1.2[1]	0.6[1]	...
Unemployment *(during quarter)*	5.3	5.1	4.9	4.7	4.5	4.4	4.2	5.0	5.6	5.8	5.7	6.5	5.9	6.5	7.5	6.7	7.2	7.6	6.9	6.7	5.7	5.9
Real wages *(compared with previous quarter)*	5.0	-3.0	—	1.0	15.0	-8.0	-5.6	-14.8	4.4	8.9	3.5	-8.5	4.2	-4.9	-14.6	-1.1	13.9	4.9	0.6	2.5	-3.5	6.0
Money and credit *(compared with end of previous quarter)*																						
M1	42	3	25	15	44	2	16	36	39	34	44	69	52	21	60	21	55	3	22	13	7	12
M2	55	37	7	27	33	16	13	42	71	29	53	58	64	34	112	24	18	-2	24	19	18	16
M3	28	27	24	20	26	27	35	66	51	52	60	60	44	40	25	6	7	-3	10	10	14	14
M4	22	29	22	20	3	27	29	57	47	48	58	61	41	46	25	12	14	4	10	12	12	9
M5	22	27	30	28	32	25	26	27	55	46	63	70	38	47	31	6	12	3	6	11	15	8
Credit	21	18	26	29	12	16	27	45	41	51	75	63	35	48	29	5	9	8	12	11	13	14

Table 2 *(concluded)*. Israel: Selected Quarterly Economic Indicators, 1982–87

(Percentage changes, unless otherwise indicated)

	1982				1983				1984				1985				1986				Preliminary 1987	
	I	II	III	IV	I	II	III	IV	I	II	III	IV	I	II	III	IV	I	II	III	IV	I	II
Balance of payments (*billion U.S. dollars*)																						
Trade balance	−0.2	−0.8	−1.1	−0.1	−0.6	−0.9	−1.0	−0.7	−0.6	−0.7	−0.8	−0.5	−0.6	−0.8	−0.5	−0.5	−0.4	−0.6	−0.5	−0.5	−0.8	−0.8
Balance on goods and services	−1.2	−1.3	−1.4	−0.9	−1.1	−1.3	−1.6	−1.0	−1.1	−1.1	−1.5	−1.1	−1.1	−1.1	−0.9	−0.9	−0.9	−1.0	−1.2	0.9	−1.4	...
Unrequited transfers	0.9	0.6	0.3	0.9	0.5	0.5	0.4	1.4	0.5	0.4	0.5	2.0	0.8	0.8	1.5	2.1	0.9	1.2	1.2	2.1	1.1	...
Current account	−0.2	−0.7	−1.1	−0.1	−0.6	−0.8	−1.2	0.4	−0.6	−0.7	−1.0	0.9	−0.3	−0.3	0.6	1.2	—	0.2	—	1.2	−0.3	...

Sources: Israel, Central Bureau of Statistics; and Bank of Israel.

1 Estimated.

sures were temporary and that some of the program's features were unsustainable. The fairly rapid depreciation of the shekel led to a widening gap between the prices of imported goods and the prices that had been frozen at the exchange rate level of November 1984. Also, the price freeze on subsidized items increased subsidy payments ($1.5 billion on an annual basis), imposing an unsustainable burden on the budget. These distortions and the Government's failure to implement the other economic measures it had agreed to led the parties to negotiate a second package deal, which went into effect at the beginning of February 1985.

3. Package Deals II and III

The second package deal was considerably different in character and substance from the first. It was to apply for an eight-month period, with provision for a review in July if desired by any of the three signing parties. The deal provided for controlled increase in prices, rather than a freeze, and also permitted immediate increases in prices of nonsubsidized goods averaging 5 percent, with subsequent monthly increases of between 3 and 5 percent over the period of the agreement. Furthermore, the agreement provided for substantial, immediate increases in the prices of subsidized goods; some subsidies were eliminated entirely, notably on fuel products. Provision was also made for further price increases for certain subsidized products, particularly food items, in February and March. Although these increases were not to exceed 13 percent in real terms, they were, in fact, implemented in two steps of about 25 percent each. In the calculation of wages, workers were to forgo up to 6 percent of the increase in the cost of living index caused by the elimination or reduction of subsidies in the initial stage and an additional 1.5 percent for each of the price increases on subsidized goods in February and March.[3] Workers were partly compensated for these concessions by a one-time cash payment of IS 6,575 (shekels) in February (equivalent to between 1 and 2 percent of monthly wages) and an additional IS 1,650 in both February and March. Commitments on exchange rate and interest rate policies were again omitted from the agreement, and it was understood that all tariffs, taxes, and other revenues collected by the Government would not be covered by the package deal.

The new attempt to stabilize inflationary expectations, while allowing some price flexibility, soon failed, and during February-May, inflation shot up to over 12 percent per month. Controlled price changes seemed harder for the public to grasp than a price freeze, and the former exerted a decid-

---

[3]The restriction of compensation to only two thirds of the standard formula — applicable in Package Deal I — no longer applied in Package Deal II.

edly less favorable influence on inflationary expectations. The situation was further complicated by sharp increases in the prices of subsidized goods: in February, controlled prices — that is, prices fixed directly by the Government — were raised by 25 percent, compared with 13.5 percent for the general CPI.

The return to a high inflation rate in February made it clear that the second package deal was not working and led to pressure for a return to more rigid arrangements along the lines of the first package deal. Accordingly, in March, the three signatories adopted a third package deal which included a four-month price freeze beginning April 1, 1985, with a provision for a one-step increase at the end of May. The freeze did not apply to subsidized goods and services or to indirect taxes; and some of the general provisions of the second package deal continued to apply, particularly with respect to wage compensation arrangements. The price increases permitted in the period immediately preceding the April price freeze largely accounted for the further increase in consumer prices of 12.1 percent in March. The monthly inflation rates in February and March thus approached the average inflation rate seen during the first half of 1984.

Subsidies were reduced substantially in both the second and third package deals. The cost of the subsidization prevailing in November 1984 was about $1.1 billion on an annual basis; by February 1985, after the first package deal, the cost had risen to $1.5 billion, but it subsequently fell to $900 million in June. However, these planned price adjustments and other unplanned increases pushed consumer prices beyond all projections, to 19.4 percent in April 1985, followed by further increases of 6.8 percent in May and 14.9 percent in June. (See Chart 1.)

In assessing the results of the various package deals, one must recognize that although they did not succeed in arresting price increases, they did permit a sharp change in relative prices, an erosion of real wages, stabilization of the real exchange rate, and a significant reduction in the rate of subsidies and other expenditure — all of which are necessary conditions for the successful implementation of a stabilization program. Also, the trend toward reduction of the civilian deficit of the balance of payments that had started late in 1983 continued during the first half of 1985.

4. The Economic Stabilization Plan of July 1985

The economic stabilization plan was enacted against the background of the previous package deals, which had essentially failed to attain their objective of stopping inflation. The return to monthly inflation rates exceeding 15 percent, combined with expectations that economic policy was about to change drastically and a new devaluation was to be announced soon, resulted in renewed large purchases of foreign currency (about $700 million in the second quarter of 1985). This development not only nullified the improvement in the current account but also threatened the external liquidity position of the country. Also, the premium on the black market reached a very high level (about 30 percent).

In the fiscal area, even though the original central government budget for 1985/86 (April through March) called for a cut in the budget deficit (before grants) of 7.5 percentage points of GNP, the deficit remained high during the first half of 1985, although it was lower than it had been the previous year. Monetary policy remained accommodative, and total bank credit to the private sector expanded by over 300 percent annually (or 2 percent in real terms) during the first half of 1985. Domestic demand and GDP expanded, mainly due to the recovery of private consumption. The adverse developments in all economic and financial areas, and the loss of public confidence made it clear that drastic economic measures were urgently needed—and were actually being demanded by the general public. The decision of the manufacturers' association to use its option to withdraw from the third package deal agreement prompted the Government to adopt, in early July 1985, a comprehensive emergency program for economic stabilization without first seeking the consent of the other parties.

a. Overall Purpose, Objectives, and Underlying Assumptions of the Stabilization Plan

The aim of the plan was to reduce inflation drastically and simultaneously, in order to improve the balance of payments position. As previously noted, past programs had concentrated on one of the two targets, usually to the detriment of the other. It was now assumed that the successful containment of both would lay the foundation for subsequent renewed growth and structural changes in the economy. The main objectives of the program were to reduce aggregate demand (and imports) through tight fiscal and monetary policies and to reduce inflation by establishing several synchronized nominal anchors in the areas of wages, prices, exchange rates, and credit. The plan had four main components: (1) the government budget deficit was to be cut substantially and the public work force trimmed; (2) monetary policy was to be restrained and the liquidity of linked financial assets reduced; (3) a sizable devaluation of the shekel was to be followed by a stable exchange rate against the U.S. dollar; and (4) prices were to be frozen and the COLA mechanism temporarily suspended, with immediate effect. The time span of the program was 12 months, the first 3 of which were declared an economic emergency period.

As mentioned above, because of the deep-rooted nature of inflationary expectations in Israel and the widespread institutionalization of indexation, the authorities felt that traditional measures alone were not sufficient to achieve rapid price stabilization. Restrictive monetary and fiscal policy measures were therefore supplemented by freezes of wage and price levels and of the exchange rate, in an effort to establish nominal anchors, of which the most important was the exchange rate.

Under equilibrium conditions, one monetary anchor would theoretically have sufficed to set all nominal levels. But since the Israeli economy was perceived to be in a state of disequilibrium, multiple anchors were needed. The quantity of money, the authorities felt, could not be relied on as an anchor, since it was bound to prove unstable during the disinflationary process. Bank credit could not serve as an alternative, because the Bank of Israel had only indirect control over its volume. As a result, and also because cost factors were presumed to have been an important cause of inflation in the past, the U.S. dollar exchange rate and the nominal wage were selected as the central nominal anchors. Stabilizing the U.S. dollar exchange rate was considered essential for stabilizing inflationary expectations, since this served as a widely quoted price index that was published daily, whereas the CPI was calculated only monthly and published with a two-week delay. To avoid a continued real appreciation, the exchange rate freeze against the U.S. dollar had to be conditional on a freeze of nominal wage costs (beyond an initial compensation), which justified the temporary suspension of the COLA mechanism. The price freeze, which completed the multiple anchor system, was not considered crucial to the program, but was needed to obtain the cooperation of the Histadrut, which traditionally demanded price control as a precondition for wage restraint.

b. Monetary Policy

The stabilization plan was based on restrictive fiscal policy and initial wage erosion, with the impact of the fiscal action expected to be felt only gradually. However, the success of the program rested on a sharp turnabout in inflationary expectations, and despite the price freeze, the authorities considered that only a highly restrictive monetary policy would immediately reduce domestic demand and support price stability. Therefore, the stance of monetary policy was very tight in the early phase of this plan, with some relaxation considered possible only after fiscal action had begun to take effect. It was also considered important to squeeze stocks — which were normally more responsive to credit tightening — quickly to ease the pressure on prices. Accordingly, the program called for outstanding bank credit to be cut by 10 percent in real terms in July and then kept at broadly the same level in nominal terms through October. Since almost one half of the outstanding credit was destined for exports — and there was no plan to cut this credit — the brunt of the cut fell on domestic free credit, with the corresponding implications for demand and production. Implementation of this policy was to be achieved through high real rates of interest; a lowering of nominal interest rates would be permitted only after a firm downward trend in the inflation rate had been observed and inflationary expectations reversed. This policy was reinforced by a lowering of the foreign currency lending ceiling (with ceilings applying to all foreign currency lending by the banks) aimed at discouraging capital inflows attracted by the large margin between domestic and foreign interest rates.

On the financial saving side, the policy was to encourage the use of the capital market for financing private investments and to preserve the stability of long-term saving instruments. Therefore, although the indexation of long-term financial assets was maintained, its scope was narrowed for foreign exchange-linked deposits (PATAM) by a prohibition on deposits with maturities of less than one year. Also, it was announced that the Government would gradually increase the share of tradable bonds and use more open market operations.

c. Exchange Rate and External Sector

On July 1, 1985, the shekel was devalued by 16 percent in terms of foreign currencies. (In terms of the shekel, the devaluation amounted to 19 percent; the average exchange rate of the shekel was 31 percent higher in July than in June.) The rate was fixed at IS 1,500 per U.S. dollar.[4] In conjunction with the devaluation, the authorities eliminated the requirement of a non-interest-bearing deposit of 15 percent for one year on a range of imports. The export subsidy on direct credits was eliminated by a requirement that such credits would henceforth be denominated entirely in U.S. dollars; these export credits would be charged at an interest rate equivalent to 2 percentage points above the London interbank offered rate (LIBOR). Together with the cut in the import deposit requirements, the measure was viewed as a step toward unification of the effective exchange rate. Finally, the exchange rate insurance scheme was changed from a guarantee of export profitability applicable to Europe into a commitment to pay all exporters up to 11 percent of their value added in exports.[5] This new scheme was aimed at eliminating distortions and reducing the substantial costs to the budget.

---

[4]The new sheqel (NIS), which was equal to 1,000 (old) shekels (IS), was introduced on September 4, 1985; the (old) shekel notes were allowed to circulate along with the new sheqel notes until the former were withdrawn on September 3, 1986.

[5]The original insurance scheme centered on a formula calculating the shekel appreciation vis-à-vis European currencies.

The fixing of the exchange rate at IS 1,500 per U.S. dollar was made conditional on the freezing of nominal wages and the profitability of exports. Indeed, one of the key factors in the economic plan was to maintain an acceptable level of profitability in exports. This policy implied that in the absence of changes in export subsidies, terms of trade, and relationships between foreign currencies, the trend in nominal wages would be the major factor determining the exchange rate.

d. Wages and Prices

As mentioned earlier, the stabilization plan included a three-month freeze on prices, nominal wages, and the exchange rate; this was subsequently extended for six months. Prior to the price freeze, a one-time adjustment was carried out at the beginning of July: prices of subsidized goods and services, and of other goods whose prices were traditionally fixed directly by the Government, were raised between 30 percent and 100 percent (50 percent on average); other prices were allowed to increase by up to 17 percent with special permission. These and other adjustments produced a jump of 27.5 percent in the price level in July and some spill-over into August. It was announced that starting in January 1986, the Government would gradually dismantle the price controls, starting with goods and services that only marginally influenced the CPI.

Taking into consideration the impact of the above-mentioned measures on prices and the resulting erosion of real wages owing to the temporary suspension of the COLA mechanism, the Government approved a one-time payment, equal to 14 percent of each worker's wages, to wage earners. Although the Government had obtained emergency authorization from the Knesset to enforce the COLA suspension, this proved unnecessary because the new private sector wage agreement, signed by the Histadrut and the manufacturers' association in mid-July, provided for a three-month suspension of the COLA and the 14 percent wage adjustment. This agreement, which expired on March 31, 1986, provided for a one-time, lump-sum payment equivalent to 12 percent of July's wage bill, to be paid in early September 1985. (This payment was not considered part of wages and therefore did not change the base used to determine future increases.) The agreement called for a cumulative wage supplement of 12 percent, to be paid in three installments: 4 percent in December 1985, 4 percent in January 1986, and 3.5 percent in February 1986. These wage increases were to be absorbed by the employers, who had also agreed not to increase prices. The agreement stipulated that the COLA mechanism would be reinstituted in November 1985, and that the degree of indexation would be increased; henceforth, an adjustment of 80 percent would be paid when the cumulative CPI increase reached 4 percent, or after an interval of three months, whichever came earlier.

Previously, the COLA had been paid only when the cumulative CPI increase exceeded 12 percent, or after six months.

V. THE 1985/86 AND 1986/87 BUDGETS AND FISCAL CONTENT OF THE STABILIZATION PLAN

1. The 1985/86 Budget

The 1985/86 budget was prepared in the context of continuing economic and financial difficulties and an alarming increase in the rate of inflation. Although the budget was prepared during the period of the package deals, it attempted to incorporate the objectives of the economic stabilization plan that would be announced later in the year. The two main objectives were (1) an improvement in the balance of payments; and (2) a deceleration in inflation. Both were to be achieved largely by means of a reduction in the domestic demand of the public sector and a cash injection. Prior to presenting the 1985/86 budget to the Knesset, the authorities indicated that their long-term objective was to bring about a permanent reduction in public sector domestic consumption, both civilian and defense, and in capital spending. Emphasis was placed on reducing purchases of domestic goods and services, reducing and rationalizing welfare programs and other public services, reducing the number of employees in the public sector through attrition and voluntary retirements, and curtailing grants and loans for investment projects; eligibility qualifications for granting such financial aid were also to be tightened. Expenditures on subsidies for goods and services were also to be cut sharply. A major source of concern to the authorities was the size of overall public sector debt, which had risen to extremely high levels (over 215 percent of GNP). Servicing costs of this debt (interest and principal) had been rising rapidly and were becoming the main factor behind the higher deficits.

Although the authorities were aware that stabilizing the ratio of public debt to GNP implied cutting the budget deficit by 12 percent of GNP (equivalent to about US$2.5 billion), political pressures and defense needs forced them to scale down their suggested expenditure cuts. Thus, the budget that was presented to the Knesset called for a cut in the deficit (before grants) of 7.5 percentage points of GNP, to about 21 percent of GNP, to be effected through a combination of increases in revenue and reductions in expenditure. Although the overall deficit (after grants) was still projected to exceed 9 percent of GNP, this was 5 percentage points lower than in 1984/85. (The special emergency assistance from the United States of $1.5 billion — provided over a two-year period — was not included in the budget projections.) Notwithstanding the major projected improvement in fiscal performance, net credit from the Bank of Israel was budgeted at about 8.5 percent of GNP (equivalent to about $1.9 billion) because of planned net amortization in foreign borrowing and a drop in nonbank net domestic borrowing.

Total revenue was estimated to increase by 3.5 percentage points of GNP. Tax revenue was forecast to increase by about 3 percentage points of GNP, and non-tax revenue by slightly less than 1 percentage point. This outcome was to be realized through changes in the tax laws, the temporary imposition of new taxes, increases in rates of existing taxes, and administrative actions to improve tax collection and reduce tax evasion. The new measures to increase revenue included (1) imposing a one-time tax on commercial property, such as buildings, inventories and equipment, and private cars (which was estimated to yield $250 million); (2) increasing the corporate income tax paid by canceling tax breaks previously enjoyed under the 1982 Taxation Under Inflationary Conditions Law (which was estimated to yield about $350 million); (3) making child allowances subject to income tax for families with as many as three children in the marginal tax bracket of 45 percent; (4) imposing higher rates of deposit on certain imports; (5) imposing new surcharges on those persons traveling abroad; and (6) increasing various tax rates. The full-year impact of taxes introduced the previous year was also expected to contribute to the rise in revenue. Two revenue-reducing measures were also included: a 10 percent income tax levy on taxpayers in high income tax brackets was canceled; and a 5 percent reduction in employees' income tax obligations for six months was granted. These measures were estimated to result in a 5 percent reduction in revenue from individual income taxes.

Non-tax revenue was estimated to rise, reflecting sharp increases in fees, user charges, and similar types of revenue collected directly by the ministries. Receipts from interest income and the transfer of royalties and profits of public enterprises to the central government were forecast to decline.

Total expenditure and net lending were budgeted to decline by almost 7 percent in real terms. Expenditure was to decline by slightly over 4 percentage points of GNP, to 69.5 percent, more than half of which was to come from cuts in defense-related imports. The remaining cuts were concentrated on transfer outlays and purchases of goods and services. The reduction in domestic expenditure (compared with the estimated outturn in 1984/85) was based on the decisions, announced by the Government in December 1984 and January 1985, to cut the equivalent of $1.1 billion from the 1985/86 budget.

An important target of the expenditure reductions was subsidies, which were cut by an estimated $650 million. Subsidies for oil products and electricity were completely eliminated in February 1985, and those for eggs, milk, poultry, and oil were to be reduced to a level no higher than 25 percent of the official price; for bread, water, and public transportation, subsidies would be reduced to a level no higher than 50 percent. Other cuts included about $200 million in domestic defense expenditure, but in contrast to previous years, the defense budget did not include the expected costs associated with operations in Lebanon. Curtailment of appropriations for education and health services amounted to $200 million.

Interest payments on government debt were budgeted to increase by 1 percentage point of GNP in 1985/86, mainly as a result of higher foreign payments, but transfers of funds to local authorities were to be reduced substantially. Investment incentives for industrial development were also forecast to decline by about $50 million. The real wage bill for government employees was budgeted to decline slightly, partly as a result of the elimination of some 4,000 positions in the central government during the fiscal year. The budget also proposed the elimination of more than 5,000 posts in the rest of the public sector, which was supported by the Treasury (employees of local authorities and educational and defense systems).

2. Fiscal Measures Included in the Stabilization Plan, July 1975

During the first quarter of fiscal year 1985/86 (April-June), it became clear that the budget deficit, on an annual basis, was running about $500-600 million higher than had been programmed. As a result of the reluctance of the Knesset's Finance Committee to approve laws changing some tax procedures and adjusting various fees and charges, and the Government's delays in increasing the prices of subsidized products, almost $900 million at an annual rate (compared with the budgeted $500 million) was spent on subsidies for basic products alone. Budget overruns were also registered for loans and grants for investment, transfers to the NII, and expenditure on education and health.

As was noted earlier (p. 369), one of the adverse developments that the July 1985 stabilization plan was meant to address was the rising budget deficit. The plan called for a return to the original 1985/86 budget estimates which was to be effected through the implementation of the revenue measures included in the budget and deep cuts in subsidies for basic commodities and services. Further, to compensate for shortfalls in projected revenue and overruns in expenditure, and with the objective of reducing the budget deficit even further than originally intended, the Government implemented new temporary tax measures and expenditure cuts amounting to $750 million on an annual basis (about 3 percent of GNP), or $560 million for the period July 1985-March 1986 (almost equally divided between revenue and expenditure).

The new tax measures were intended to raise revenue by $200 million, with one half of the increase intended to be temporary. Full implementation of the amended Taxation Under Inflationary Conditions Law was expected to yield about $150 million. The tax measures included a one-year, 8.3 percent surtax on income other than from wages, which was to be collected starting August 1985. The tax exemption on employee contributions to study funds (set up to finance attendance at work-related courses) was abolished, as was the exemption for subsidized meals in large enterprises. Also, the allowance for the first child in families with as many as three children was canceled, and a tax was imposed on the allowances for second and third children. Finally, the one-time tax on commercial property included in the original budget, but not yet approved, became effective on July 1, and was expected to yield about US$200 million. The value-added tax rate was reduced from 17 percent to 15 percent, and the import deposit requirement was reduced by 15 percent.

Expenditure cuts consisted mostly of further reductions in subsidies, loans, selected categories of transfer payments, and purchases of goods and services. Subsidies for basic products were reduced by over 50 percent in real terms, and subsidized loans for investment purposes were converted to direct grants equal to the implicit subsidy in each loan. The additional cuts in subsidies and transfers for basic products, investment projects, and development of export markets amounted to an estimated $250 million. The large cut in real wages also contributed significantly to the reduction in expenditure.

3. Fiscal Outturn in 1985/86

As a result of the measures implemented in July, fiscal performance improved markedly in 1985/86, compared with previous years, the original budget estimates, and the plan targets. The budget deficit before grants was cut by 9 percentage points of GNP, to 20.5 percent, almost entirely as a result of an increase of 8.5 percent of GNP in revenue and only marginal cuts in expenditure. As in the past, the Government found it more difficult to reduce direct demand through cuts in purchases of goods and services, and the burden of reducing the deficit thus fell on the tax system and subsidies. The increase in revenue reflected the positive impact of decelerating inflation on tax collections, the elimination of various tax benefits previously enjoyed by businesses, and other one-time measures introduced in the budget in midyear. Although the level of expenditure remained almost unchanged in relation to GNP, there was a change in its composition. The sharp reduction in subsidy payments and the moderate decline in wages were mostly offset by increases in interest payments and domestic defense purchases. However, real expenditure, deflated by the average CPI for 1985/86, fell substantially.[6]

As a result of the reduction in the budget deficit and the increase in foreign grants (including special emergency assistance from the United States) from 14 percent in 1984/85 to 19.3 percent in 1985/86, for the first time in many years, the overall balance (after grants) was reduced almost to equilibrium (1.3 percent of GNP). (See Table 1.) The amount of grants was more than sufficient to cover all external expenditures, including foreign amortization payments, and helped to finance part of domestic expenditure. The shift in U.S. aid from loans to grants and the special emergency assistance accounted for a $1.2 billion increase in foreign aid. Since net domestic bond sales to the private sector exceeded the financing requirements, the central government was able to make a net repayment of its debt to the Bank of Israel while reducing its external debt.

As expected, developments in expenditure and revenue (mostly revenue) differed considerably between the first quarter of the fiscal year (April-June) and the last three quarters following the introduction of the new economic plan in July.[7] The improvement in the fiscal performance, which had already started in the first quarter, intensified as the year progressed. Quarterly revenue collections were 5 percentage points of GNP higher during the period after June 1985 compared with the first quarter of the fiscal year, and over 8 percentage points of GNP higher than in the same period in the previous fiscal year. Owing to seasonal factors, average expenditure had typically been about 4 percentage points of GNP higher in the last three quarters than in the first quarter, but in 1985/86 it remained more or less constant. The overall deficit on government domestic operations was reduced from over 15 percent of GNP during the second half of 1984/85 to 3 percent of GNP in the second half of 1985/86.

4. The 1986/87 Budget and Fiscal Outturn

The 1986/87 budget was prepared within the general framework of the policies announced in the July 1985 economic stabilization plan. The budget attempted to consolidate the authorities' objectives and the measures implemented in 1985.[8] The aim was to reduce the budget deficit to a

---

[6]Owing to the high and variable rates of inflation in 1984/85 and the sharp deceleration of inflation in 1985/86, calculations in real terms and comparisons to GNP should be viewed with great caution.

[7]Since no information is available on total government operations on a quarterly basis, the data used in this section are based on information provided by the Bank of Israel for central government domestic operations.

[8]The 1986/87 budget was prepared on the basis of the original 1985/86 budget projections, taking into account the expenditure cuts announced during 1985, but adding all

(Continued on p. 378)

level at which all domestic expenditure could be financed with domestic tax and non-tax revenue and net placement of bonds. Although the proposed budget provided for some additional domestic borrowing, the authorities were concerned about the large size of government debt, the increasing share of interest payments in total expenditure and its impact on future budget deficits, and the crowding out of the private sector in the capital market. Therefore, they reaffirmed the goal of reducing the level of debt in relation to GNP.

The 1986/87 budget provided for a reduction in the deficit (before grants) by the equivalent of 3 percentage points of GNP (to 18 percent of GNP), compared with the estimated outturn for 1985/86.[9] This was to be accomplished by a large cut in expenditure, while revenue was expected to fall moderately. The financing requirement (overall deficit after grants), however, was projected to decline by only 1 percentage point, to 3 percent of GNP, and foreign grants were estimated to decline by 2.5 percentage points of GNP.[10] The projected fall in revenue was to come from non-tax revenue. Tax revenue was not projected to show much change from the previous year, because many of the tax measures introduced in July 1985 were temporary and their impact on revenue collections in 1986/87 was expected to be only partial; also, large adjustments in income tax brackets were to offset the gains from a lower rate of inflation. The level of expenditure was planned to be cut by the equivalent of almost 4 percentage points of GNP—about 2.5 percentage points from defense purchases abroad and the remainder from domestic spending—mostly in capital outlays. For the first time in many years, no provisions were made for budgeted expenditures to be adjusted to compensate for increases in prices.

Preliminary results for 1986/87 indicate a further improvement in budget performance, compared with both the approved budget and the actual outturn in 1985/86. The deficit before grants is now estimated at 15 percent of GNP, compared with the anticipated deficit of almost 19 percent, and the overall balance is now estimated to have been almost at

---

expenditure commitments approved in previous years, as well as the growth in expenditure owing to such factors as rising population and merit increases and other expenditure, such as interest payments, which are outside the control of the authorities. This level of expenditure was called the 1986/87 base budget, to which additional cuts amounting to about $550 million were applied.

[9]Since the 1986/87 budget was approved in early January 1986, the fiscal outturn for 1985/86 was estimated under changing conditions, including a rapid deceleration of inflation. In the event, the actual results in 1985/86 were much better than had been expected, and objectives for 1986/87 that were initially perceived to constitute an improvement may, in fact, have constituted a deterioration.

[10]Defense-related imports—which are based on long-term contracts and financed almost entirely by U.S. military grants—were projected to decline by the same amount.

equilibrium, compared with a projected deficit of 3 percent of GNP. Total revenue is estimated to have been 50 percent of GNP, or 2 percentage points higher than projected in the budget, and total expenditure and net lending are estimated to have been almost 66 percent of GNP, or 1 percentage point lower than projected. Although the financing requirement is estimated to have been about 0.5 percent of GNP, net placement of domestic bonds amounted to 3 percent of GNP because of the decision to make net amortization payments abroad and to reduce, for the second year in a row, outstanding credit from the Bank of Israel.

Total revenue is estimated to have increased by 8 percent in real terms, with tax revenue having risen by 12 percent and non-tax revenue having fallen by 7 percent. The strong increase in tax collection reflected the effects of decelerating inflation, the full annual impact of the elimination of various tax benefits for businesses, and the large increase in private income and consumption. Tax revenue was higher than expected in all categories, and particularly in the case of the income tax. In relation to GNP, tax revenue increased from 40 percent in 1985/86 to 44 percent in 1986/87.

Total expenditure and net lending are estimated to have been below the amount budgeted by about 2 percent, despite a supplementary budget presented to the Knesset in January 1987 authorizing the additional expenditure; the major part of this expenditure was a transfer to the NII to compensate for the 5 percent reduction in employers' payments to the NII for their employees. In relation to GNP, total expenditure is estimated to have declined by 2 percentage points, to 66 percent. With the exception of transfer payments and domestic purchases, all expenditures are estimated to have been reduced. Defense purchases abroad and interest payments were each cut by 2.5 percentage points of GNP, and subsidies by 2 percentage points. Subsidies on food products were cut by almost 60 percent in 1986/87 and fell to their lowest levels since 1980. Net lending also declined markedly because of a large increase in loan repayments, especially for housing and industry. Despite the increase in real wage rates during 1986/87, the government wage bill declined marginally in relation to GNP. However, a large part of these reductions was offset by an increase in transfer payments of 4 percentage points of GNP.

VI. Summary and Conclusions

The Israeli economy experienced large chronic budget deficits over a long period, which resulted in a huge public debt equal to over 200 percent of GNP in mid-1985. In the period 1979/80-1984/85, the budget deficit excluding grants averaged almost 25 percent of GNP; the deficit including grants averaged 15 percent. Real interest rates on the public debt increased rapidly, reaching almost 15 percent of GNP in 1984/85. After remaining stable at about 120 percent annually over the period 1979-83, inflation accelerated sharply starting in the last quarter of 1983 and rising to levels exceeding 500 percent annually during most of 1984; it then decelerated to 300 percent annually in the first half of 1985, owing to the successive package deals signed between the Government and representatives of the private sector. However, although these attempts to contain inflation were initially successful, the acceleration of inflation in mid-1985 and the worsening of the balance of payments position led the authorities to introduce a comprehensive stabilization plan in July 1985.

The achievements of the economic stabilization program up to the end of 1987 were impressive. Inflation ran at less than 20 percent annually beginning in July 1985, compared with almost 400 percent just before the introduction of the plan (Table 3). Although items amounting to about 35 percent of the CPI remained under control, there were no signs of artificial distortion in relative prices. Speculative purchases of foreign exchange stopped, and the public repatriated and sold foreign exchange to the Bank of Israel. The current account deficit shifted to a surplus; the Bank of Israel accumulated international reserves; and the net external debt of the country was reduced. The overall budget deficit (including grants) was almost eliminated. These improvements were aided by a sharp reduction in the oil import bill, an improvement in terms of trade, an apparent stabilization of the exchange rate, and the return of public confidence.

The costs of the economic and financial improvements were relatively modest. Domestic production, after falling by about 5 percent during the second half of 1985, rebounded in the first half of 1986, and in 1987 it is estimated to have grown at the highest rate seen in over a decade. In 1987, the unemployment rate, after having risen by 1.5 percentage points in early 1986, fell below the level obtaining prior to the program. (See Table 2.)

Economists in Israel have differed over the relationship between the size of the budget deficit and the rate of inflation; some have seen a direct link through pressure on prices, whereas others have argued for an indirect link through the deteriorating position of the balance of payments and the corrective devaluations. However, it is widely accepted that the large government deficit was the main factor in the persistent high inflation rates and that a sharp reduction in the deficit had to be the cornerstone of a stabilization program.

Fiscal performance, compared with the budget estimtes, improved dramatically over the period 1985/86-1986/87, exceeding the most optimis-

Table 3. Israel: Selected Annual Economic Indicators, 1968–86

(Percentage changes, unless otherwise indicated)

	1968–72	1973–78	1979	1980	1981	1982	1983	1984	1985	1986
Prices										
Average	7.1	36	78	131	117	120	146	374	305	48
During period	8.1	39	111	133	101	131	191	445	185	20
GDP at constant prices	12.0	3.6	4.7	3.5	3.8	0.5	2.5	1.7	2.8	2.2
Average exchange rates *(in relation to U.S. dollar)*	3.8	29	47	102	123	112	132	421	302	26
Gross domestic investment at constant prices	24.0	−1.8	12.0	−14.1	−5.8	13.8	12.0	−7.5	−13.6	8.1
Unemployment	—	3.3	2.9	4.8	5.1	5.0	4.5	5.9	6.7	7.1
Real wages	—	—	9.5	−3.2	10.4	−0.9	6.1	−0.4	−9.0	11.6
Public sector	—	—	15.6	−8.4	10.4	−4.8	9.4	1.3	−14.1	13.8
Business	—	—	5.9	−0.3	10.4	1.2	3.0	−1.0	−5.0	7.5
Money and credit										
Monetary base	23	25	14	107	100	103	131	454	661	32
Money supply	17	30	31	98	78	111	132	352	277	113
Total liquid assets of public	21	38	86	150	109	128	217	458	194	45
Bank credit to public	18	50	101	110	82	139	133	503	172	46
Balance of payments *(billion U.S. dollars)*										
Exports	0.9	2.6	4.7	5.8	5.9	5.6	5.5	6.2	6.6	7.6
Imports	1.8	4.5	7.9	9.0	9.4	8.8	8.8	8.8	9.0	9.6
Trade balance	−0.9	−2.2	−3.2	−3.2	−3.5	−3.2	−3.3	−2.6	−2.4	−2.0
Goods and services	−0.9	−2.5	−3.7	−3.8	−4.4	−4.8	−5.2	−4.9	−3.9	−4.0
Current account balance	−0.3	−0.9	−0.9	−0.8	−1.5	−2.2	−2.3	−1.5	1.1	1.4
(percentage of GNP)	(−5.5)	(−7.2)	(−5.0)	(−4.0)	(−6.8)	(−9.9)	(−9.3)	(−6.9)	(5.2)	(5.3)

Sources: Israel, Central Bureau of Statistics; and Bank of Israel.

tic expectations. The budget deficit (excluding grants) was cut by 12 percentage points of GNP, although almost all of the improvement during these two years came as a result of increases in revenue, and only 2 percent of GNP came from cuts in expenditure. The overall deficit (including grants) was reduced from over 15 percent of GNP in 1984/85 to slightly over ½ of 1 percent of GNP in 1985/86 and 1986/87. Financing from the Bank of Israel, after exceeding 8 percent of GNP in 1984/85, turned into net amortization equal to almost 3 percent of GNP in 1985/86 and a little over 1 percent in 1986/87. Also, net amortization of foreign debt exceeded 1 percent of GNP for these two fiscal years. The net amortizations were financed by sales of domestic bonds.

The improvement in fiscal performance, although impressive, is still temporary. Most of the gains have come from higher taxes and reductions in subsidies and some categories of transfer payments. The tax burden in Israel is one of the highest in the world. Real claims of the public sector on resources (domestic purchases of goods and services) have been reduced only moderately. The amount of internal debt scheduled to mature in the coming years is very large. A sharp reduction in taxes, for both households and corporations, will be necessary to improve the efficiency of the economy and to foster economic growth. Therefore, the more important fiscal task for the near future is to make cuts in expenditure large enough to not only reduce the budget deficit but also allow a reduction in taxes.

Chart 3. Israel: Selected Economic Data, 1970–87

(Quarterly growth rates, in percent)

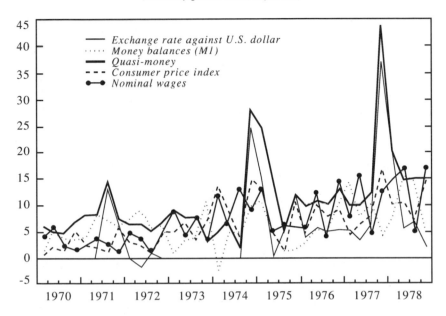

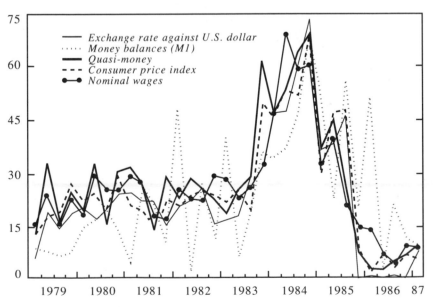

Biographical Sketches

Gloria Bartoli, an Italian, is an Economist in the Special Fiscal Studies Division of the Fund's Fiscal Affairs Department. She graduated from the University of Turin and became Assistant Professor of Economics at the University of Calabria. She worked as a consultant to several private and public institutions before joining the Fund. Ms. Bartoli has published in the areas of macroeconomic thought, microeconomic formulations of stabilization policies, credit theory, and fiscal policy.

Mario I. Blejer is Chief of the Special Fiscal Studies Division in the Fund's Fiscal Affairs Department. He received a doctorate in economics from the University of Chicago, and has taught at the Hebrew University of Jerusalem, Boston University, and New York University. He has also been a consultant to the World Bank and the Inter-American Development Bank, and has published numerous studies — in the areas of international economics, monetary theory, public finance, and macroeconomics — dealing primarily with the problems of developing countries.

Adrienne Cheasty, a citizen of Ireland, is an Economist in the Special Fiscal Studies Division of the Fund's Fiscal Affairs Department. She graduated from Trinity College (Dublin) and Yale University, and has lectured in public finance at Yale and Trinity College (Hartford, Connecticut). She has published in the areas of macroeconomic policy, social expenditures, and planned economies.

Ke-young Chu, a Korean, is Chief of the Government Expenditure Analysis Division of the Fund's Fiscal Affairs Department, and was Assistant Chief of the Department's Special Fiscal Studies Division when he began working on this book. Before joining the Fiscal Affairs Department, he was in the Research Department. He received a doctorate in economics from Columbia University. Mr. Chu has published in the areas of fiscal policy issues in developing countries and world primary commodity markets.

Ziba Farhadian-Lorie, an Iranian, is an Operations Officer in the Fund's Treasurer's Department. Before joining the Treasurer's Department, she was in the Fiscal Affairs Department. She received a doctorate in economics from George Washington University. Mrs. Farhadian-Lorie has published in the areas of monetary economics, economic development, and centrally planned economies, and has also written about the issues of population and the social cost of education in industrial countries.

Alain Ize, a Mexican, is a Senior Economist in the Special Fiscal Studies Division of the Fund's Fiscal Affairs Department. He received a doctorate in engineering economic systems from Stanford University. From 1977 to 1985 he was a Member of the Centro de Estudios Económicos of the Colegio de México, and worked simultaneously as an Advisor to the Dirección de Estudios Económicos of the Banco de México. Mr. Ize has also been a Visiting Assistant Professor in the Department of Economics of the University of California, Davis, and a Visiting Scholar at the Food Research Institute, Stanford University. He has published in the areas of macroeconomic theory and policy, financial intermediation, and international finance.

Menachem Katz, an Israeli, is a Senior Economist in the Fiscal Review Division of the Fund's Fiscal Affairs Department. He received a doctorate in economics from Columbia University and has taught at universities in the New York area. He has worked in Israel's Ministry of Finance and the Bank of Israel. Mr. Katz has published in the areas of external debt, fiscal policy, and the impact of taxation on interest rates and capital flows, and has also written about social expenditures and trade policy.

Eliahu S. Kreis, an Israeli, is an Advisor in the Fund's Western Hemisphere Department and currently is the Fund's Resident Representative in Uruguay. He was previously Resident Representative in Bolivia (1972-73) and in Chile (1975-77), and was also in the Fiscal Affairs Department. He received a doctorate in economics from the University of Oklahoma, where he also taught. Mr. Kreis has published in the areas of budgetary policies and inflation. In recent years, he has done extensive work on Israel and Argentina.

Ahsan H. Mansur, a Bangladeshi, is a Senior Economist in the Special Fiscal Studies Division of the Fund's Fiscal Affairs Department. He is a graduate of the University of Dhaka and the University of Western Ontario, and has published in the areas of applied general equilibrium, public finance, and macroeconomics.

Guillermo Ortiz, a Mexican, is Deputy Secretary of Finance and Public Credit of Mexico. He was an Executive Director of the Fund during 1986-88 and an Alternate Executive Director during 1984-86. He received a doctorate in economics from Stanford University and served as Manager of Economic Research at the Banco de México before joining the Fund. Mr. Ortiz has published in the areas of monetary and exchange rate policies, debt, and financial intermediation in Mexico and other Latin American countries.

David J. Robinson, a citizen of the United Kingdom, is an Economist in the Fund's European Department. Before joining the European Department, he was in the Fiscal Affairs Department. He is a graduate of Oxford University, where he studied mathematics and economics. Mr. Robinson subsequently joined the U.K. Treasury, where he worked on social security issues and served in Washington, D.C. as an aide to the U.K. Executive Director of the Fund.

Nicola Rossi, an Italian, is Associate Professor of Economics at the University of Venice. Previously, he was in the Fund's Fiscal Affairs Department. He received a doctorate in economics from the London School of Economics and has worked at the Banca d'Italia and taught at LUISS University (Rome). Mr. Rossi has published in the areas of the theory and measurement of consumer behavior, applied welfare analysis, and macroeconomic modeling.

Vito Tanzi, a citizen of the United States, is Director of the Fund's Fiscal Affairs Department. He received a doctorate in economics from Harvard University. A former professor of economics, he has also been a consultant to the World Bank, the United Nations, the Organization of American States, and the Stanford Research Institute. Mr. Tanzi, who has had a continuing interest in fiscal policy issues in developed and developing countries, has published widely in the areas of public finance, monetary theory, and macroeconomics. In recent years, he has written about the underground economy, fiscal deficits, the determination of interest rates, and international economic policy coordination.